Directions in Literary Criticism

Contemporary Approaches to Literature

Edited by
Stanley Weintraub and Philip Young

The Pennsylvania State University Press
University Park and London

Library of Congress Catalog Card No. 72–1066
International Standard Book Number 0–271–01116–5
Printed in the United States of America
Designed by Marilyn Shobaken

Library of Congress Cataloging in Publication Data

Weintraub, Stanley, 1929–
    Directions in literary criticism.

    1. Criticism. I. Young, Philip. 1918–   joint
author. II. Title.
PN94.W43   801'.95   72–1066
ISBN 0–271–01116–5

Contents

Preface

Where are the vogues of yesteryear? At present there do not seem to be any fashions in literary criticism—an impression that this book reinforces and helps to establish. Each individual in this gathering of critics was invited to practice his trade in whatever fashion he liked, and the results make at least one thing clear: the criticism of literature is going off in as many directions as literature itself. Criticism here is traditional and innovative, theoretical, psychological and sociological, textual and impressionistic, historical and mythic, biographical and autobiographical, sober and satiric. It takes its evidence from sources ranging all the way from bibliographic data, the facts of composition and publication, to the act of performance, the record of directorial intention and stage interpretation, and from the reaction of audiences to the response of the computer.

Even a poem can be an act of criticism, witness Pope, and even a lyric, as in the hands of Keats, can make a memorable statement about literature. Several selections in this book carry on that tradition and, in a work that is both poem and explication, Kenneth Burke extends it. Criticism in our century, it is true, has been mainly the province of scholars, and has emanated largely from the academy. So in these pages. But academic perspectives need not be narrow. In addition to poet and scholar, here we have novelist, essayist, folklorist, psychologist, and biographer. The results are eclectic because academic interests are broad.

They are also eclectic, at least in part, because every contributor to this volume has been at one time or another closely associated with Henry W. Sams, to whom the book is dedicated. His own practice of criticism, his teaching of it, his direction of doctoral dissertations in criticism—all have matched his distinguished, undoctrinaire administration of The Pennsylvania State University English Department, 1959–1971. All, that is, have been marked by his ability to detect excellence in whatever form it takes, and his effectiveness in promoting it. In a way, then, these are *his* critical approaches to literature. And so the book is not merely dedicated to him. In a very real sense it is his.

The Ocean
of Story

John Barth

The road to India is simply a long road, but it's the only way to India.
One can't expect to get through *The Thousand and One Nights* in one
night. When I worry that one of my own stories is growing overlong, I
tell myself the story of a *really* long story: *Katha Sarit Sagara*, or *The
Ocean of Streams of Story*, more or less by the 11th-century Indian poet
Somadeva.

Its title haunted me for a dozen years (as did Calderón's *La Vida Es
Sueño*) before I ever read beyond it; as an undergraduate book-filer in the
classics and Oriental-Seminary stacks of Johns Hopkins University's
Gilman Hall Library, I would push my cart daily past the ten huge sea-
green volumes of Penzer's edition (privately printed in London in 1924
and still the only English-language edition one sees) of Tawney's nineteenth-century prose translation of Somadeva's Sanskrit redaction of
King Satavahana's third-century publication of his minister Gunadhya's
Paisachi versification of the demigod Kanabhuti's retelling of the demigod Pushpadanta's version of the Great Tale first told to his consort
Parvati by the god Siva. Inevitably, semester after semester, that golden
title, *The Ocean of Story*, took my eye and fancy; but waiting on my
book-cart to be re-shelved (and read, surreptitiously, on company time)
were more navigated ways of narrative: *The Thousand and One Nights*,
The Panchatantra, the *Pent-*, *Hept-*, and *Decamerons*. One never found
allusions to *The Ocean of Story* in other literature or heard it mentioned
by one's professors and better-read friends; indeed, one never saw
Somadeva off the shelf—where I filed beside his *mare incognitum* my
resolve one day to embark upon its endless reaches. For the present there
were those famouser works to be read, more than one ever would find
time for, and from the springs of literature issued unceasingly a torrent
of new writing as well, to be breasted if possible; presently one's own
outpourings swelled the general flood; there was no time.

Until one arrived, enough years later, at the free port of understanding
that, like Magellan, one will never accomplish the whole voyage. One
will not likely *ever* get around now to Camoëns' *Lusiad*, one came to
realize, or the rest of Hardy, the end of *Eugene Onegin*, the beginning of
Jerusalem Delivered; even a second lifetime would not suffice to get

said the whole of what oneself had aspired to say. This recognition, when not traumatic, grants an extravagant liberty: the voyage being incompletable, one may take sidetrips of any length in any number, at one's pleasure! In connection, therefore, with a casual research of some years' standing through the whole corpus of frame-tale literature, I lately made at last my leisure-cruise from end to end of *The Ocean of Story*.

Was it that too long deferral of the journey staled its charm? Or that no merely actual fiction could realize the long work of my dreams upon that title? In any case, I must report that:

1. In the main, alas, the tales rehearsed by Somadeva (whose noble ambition was to tell them *all*) are less memorable than Scheherazade's, say, or Boccaccio's or Chaucer's—or less memorably recounted, in the several instances where the plots are analogous. In keeping with Somadeva's (and his precursors') conceit of an ultimate narrative ocean into which all the streams of fancy flow at last, entire Gangeses of pre-existing fiction are tapped and incorporated, such as the *Panchatantra* and the *Vetalapanchavimsati*, or *25 Tales by a Vampire*; it is principally through the numerous redactions, recensions, and meanders of these tributaries—*Siddhi-Kur, The Seven Sages, Kalilah and Dimnah, Syntipas the Philosopher, The Fables of Bidpai, Sindibad's Parables*—and later reworkings of these reworkings—Johannes de Alta Silva's *Dolopathos*, John of Capua's *Directorium Vitae Humanae*, Firenzuola's *Discorsi degli Animali*, and Doni's *Novelle*, for example— that waters from *The Ocean of Story* finally enter the mainstream of Western literature, and in most instances they gain in flavor from their circuitous journey. To put the figure more accurately, several of the springs that fed *The Ocean of Story* trickled westward also and separately, with the consequence that Somadeva's vast poem strikes one less as a source of Western narrative motifs than as a kind of anthology or compendium of such sources. Hence, in part, its persisting obscurity, except among Orientalists, despite its being, in Penzer's phrase, "for its size, the earliest collection of stories extant in the world."

2. The frame-structure, too, is less arresting or fecund than that of *The Thousand and One Nights, The Decameron*, or, for that matter, the anonymous seventeenth-century-English delight entitled *Westward for Smelts*; nothing in the circumstantial history of Prince Naravahanadatta and the Vidyaharas captures the imagination as does the image of Scheherazade yarning through the night to save her neck, or Boccaccio's twilit company beguiling themselves with fiction in despite of plagued fact. On the other hand, Somadeva's structure is considerably more complex—the most complex, I think, among the nearly 200 specimens of frame-tale literature I've thus far noted. Not only is the narrative at several points involved to the fourth degree (tales within tales within tales within tales), but at any degree, including the first or outermost, the frame may be serial and achronological—as if, for example, the pilgrimage

to Canterbury were only one among several frame-conceits in Chaucer's poem, and began outside Rochester at that, the departure from London being filled in only later; as if, moreover, his *Troilus and Criseyde* were one of several tales told by Patient Grisilde, whose tale in turn were one of several told by Chanticleer, whose tale were one of several told by the Nun's Priest, et cetera. The intrication is enormous (stout Penzer uses a schematic outline in his table of contents: the story of King Brahmadatta, for instance, is Tale 1BB in the midst of Tale 1B in the *Cont*(inuation) of Tale 1 in the *Cont*(inuation) of the *M*(ain) *I*(ntroduction) in Chapter III of Book I), but like the complexity of termite-tunnels or breast-cancer, it is more dismaying than delightful from the human point of view.

3. Just as the accounts of Hakluyt's voyagers may be more fascinating than the places they voyaged to, the Burtonesque notes and appendices (by many hands) to Penzer's edition of Somadeva—disquisitions on such heady matters as the place of collyrium in the history of cosmetic art, or the Bitch-and-Pepper motif in the literature of the world—are frequently more engaging than the texts they illuminate. Thus in the course of an indifferent sub-sub-sub-tale about the founding of the city of Pataliputra, a pokerfaced note describes two remarkable ancient customs alleged to prevail there: The first is the ancient custom of the women, annually in the rainy season, to bake cakes in the form of phalluses and offer them to any Brahman whom they judge to be (what the English field-researcher translates as) "a blockhead." The second is the equally ancient custom of the Brahmans always to refuse those cakes because they regard the first ancient custom as disgusting. One's conviction is affirmed that it would be a more splendid destiny to have cooked up Burton's version of *The Thousand and One Nights*—footnotes, Terminal Essay, and all—than to have written the original.

4. These reservations notwithstanding, *The Ocean of Story* contains at least one narrative conception of the very first rank, without real analogues that I know of in any of its contemporaries or predecessors, and more gloriously elaborate by far than any of its several analogues in later fiction: I mean the "history of the text" of the *Katha Sarit Sagara* itself, which history comprises the primary narrative frame of Book I and the *M*(ain) *I*(ntroduction) to the entire work, and happens to be among my favorite stories in the world:

One day the god Siva is so delighted at the way Parvati makes love to him that he offers her anything she wishes in reward. She asks for a story. Perching her on his lap, he tells her a short one on the subject of his own splendid exploits in a former life, including his romance with a beautiful woman whom he tactfully supposes to have been Parvati herself in one of *her* former incarnations. The goddess abruptly cuts him off: she's heard that one before; so has everybody else; what she craves is an absolutely original story that no one at all has heard and, it's implied, that no one but herself will *ever* hear, unless she chooses to repeat it. Siva comes up with the Great Tale—actually seven great tales of 100,000 couplets each. It takes a very long time to tell (if the *Odyssey*, as has been estimated, was sung in four evenings, the same minstrel at the same pace would by my reckoning need 509 evenings—a little under a year and a half—to do Siva's piece), but in this instance teller, tale, and told all happen to be immortal; Parvati sits silent and presumably entertained—until she learns that the tale's been overheard after all, by one of their house-staff! The *Gana* Pushpadanta, who has hidden invisible in the divine boudoir (as the monks in Marguerite of Navarre's *Heptameron* squat behind the shrubbery of the monastery every evening to overhear the tales Marguerite's friends exchange), repeats the Great Tale to his wife, who repeats it to Parvati, who is so incensed that she condemns not only Pushpadanta but his friend Malyavan—who'd merely pled on his behalf—to be born as mortal men: Pushpadanta will have to live on earth under the name of Vararuchi until he crosses paths in the woods with the hermit Kanabhuti (in fact the demigod Supratika, also currently doing time) and repeats to him the entire Great Tale; Malyavan will be obliged to mortality under the name Gunadhya until *he* happens to cross paths with this same Kanabhuti/Supratika, hears the Great Tale from him, and writes it down—whereupon, like the others who've been delivered of it, he'll enter heaven.

Got that?

The first of these redemptions comes to pass with comparative ease in the space of a mere four chapters properly laced with narrative digression; the second with more difficulty and corresponding interest and structural extravagance. Malyavan is reborn as Gunadhya and works his mortal way to a ministership in the court of King Satavahana, an adequate monarch in every particular except that he makes mistakes in his grammar. This failing Satavahana himself could perhaps live with, were it not that one of his favorite harem-girls is an intellectual who teases him with his solecisms; humiliated, he demands that his ministers educate him. Gunadhya volunteers to teach him Sanskrit grammar in six years flat; his rival for the King's favor, Sarvavarman, rashly declares *he'll* do the job in six months or wear Gunadhya's shoes on his head for a dozen years. Gunadhya counters that if Sarvavarman makes good his boast, he Gunadhya will renounce forever the three languages he knows: Sanskrit, Prakrit, and the vernacular dialect. Inasmuch as Sanskrit grammar could not in fact be taught in six months at that time, Gunadhya is full of confidence. But Sarvavarman, alarmed at his own impulsiveness, petitions the gods for help, and for reasons never disclosed they reveal to him a revolutionary new concise Sanskrit grammar, the Katantra, which wins him the bet and reforms subsequent education.

Reduced to silence, Gunadhya takes to the woods with a pair of his favorite students. After an unspecified wordless interval he comes across

Kanabhuti/Supratika, who has in the meanwhile been told the Great Tale by Vararuchi/Pushpadanta and is anxious to pass it along so that he too can return to heaven. But what to do about the language problem? Kanabhuti solves it by teaching Gunadhya a new tongue—Paisacha, or "goblin-language"—and reciting the Great Tale in *that*. It takes Gunadhya seven more years in the woods to throw the thing into written couplets, owing to its length, no doubt also to the Nabokovian difficulty of versifying in an adopted goblin-language, and perhaps to the nature of his medium, which happens to be his own blood. But he finally sets down the 700,000th distich, and his two faithful students rush off with the masterpiece to King Satavahana—who takes one look at it and says, presumably in perfect Sanskrit: "Away with this barbaric Paisacha!" Back to the woods it goes, where its rejected author, as a last resort, commences reading it aloud to himself. All the animals of the forest gather motionless to listen, moved to tears not only by the beauty of the composition but by the spectacle of Gunadhya's burning each page of manuscript in a hole in the rock as he finishes reading it.

Presently King Satavahana, though eating regally, falls ill of malnutrition. Medical research discloses that the cause of his malaise is a deficiency of nutritive value in the meat fetched in by the palace huntsmen, and still further investigation reveals the cause of this deficiency to be a certain mad poet out in the bush, whose narration so spellbinds the beasts of the country that they forget to ruminate. The King hurries to the forest, recognizes his minister Gunadhya, and snatches from the fire what's left of the Great Tale—alas, a mere 100,000 distichs, the other six-sevenths of the *magnum opus* having gone up in smoke. Anyhow vindicated, Gunadhya/Malyavan proceeds to heaven; the students are promoted to administrators; and Satavahana, to redeem himself, prefaces the truncated masterwork with a book called *Kathapitha*—the History of the Tale, or Story of the Story—which I've just rehearsed, and publishes the whole (in ordinary ink) under the title *Brihat Katha*, or Great Tale. Eight centuries later the Kashmirian court-poet Somadeva, to amuse another royal lady, pares down this *Brihat Katha*, including Satavahana's prefatory *Kathapitha*, to a radically terse 22,000 couplets—the mere ten folio volumes of Penzer's edition, scarcely twice the length of the *Iliad* and the *Odyssey* combined!

Whether Queen Suryavati was as pleased with this revised and abbreviated version as the goddess Parvati was with the original isn't recorded; but we may assume that in order to recite to her from memory such a short short story, Somadeva—Mr. Soma—wouldn't even have needed to make use of a certain great secret recipe for epical recall, from the chief constituent of which he takes his name. Since it may be that this pharmacological formula, rather than the narrative ones analyzed by Professors Milman Parry and Albert Lord, is the *real* key to epical composition, I offer it here from my own memory of the *Samavid-*

hana Brahmana as quoted in a footnote from the unfrequented deeps of
The Ocean of Story:

1. Fast for three nights.
2. Recite a certain incantation and then eat of the soma plant one thousand times.
3. Or bruise the soma plant in water and drink that water for a year.
4. Or ferment the soma plant and drink that liquor for a month.
5. Or drink it forever.

The Aesthetics of Traditional Narrative

Bruce A. Rosenberg

An effective way to dramatize the relation of folklorists and ethnologists to the aesthetics of the material they study is to begin with an exaggeration: the professional folklorist is often interested in the artistry of folklore when he is informally involved on his own time, but his professional stance is that of the social scientist who has little official time for such nonmeasurable phenomena as "beauty" and its formalized study, "aesthetics." Some individual exceptions may be slighted by such a statement, but in general it can be readily supported. Many folklorists, perhaps most of us, genuinely appreciate a ballad well tuned or a story well turned; but such a concern with aesthetics usually emerges during our leisure hours. Certainly, many ballad scholars are talented singers and instrumentalists in their own right, and frequently perform for their own amusement and for that of their friends. A few, such as Alan Jabbour, are members of "folk" string bands; Joe Hickerson is a fine guitarist; and my colleague Sam Bayard, who has collected fife tunes in Pennsylvania for nearly four decades, is an accomplished player himself. But Sam, like all other folklorist-performers, would never think that he was transmitting a genuine popular tradition or that his research was based upon his musicianship.

Aesthetics is the professional concern of philosophers and aestheticians; the folklorist is concerned with oral transmission, provenience, and social function. This is to be expected, since aesthetics, the study of beauty, is properly outside the academic range and scope of ethnology. However, in our private lives folklorists do talk about good folksongs and bad; we do admire talented folksingers and merely tolerate the inferior. I have myself been "accused" of being "drawn to the more successful and inventive performers,"[1] and I think now that the reason—I admit the charge—was more aesthetic than ethnological. The concern of nearly all of us, at one time or another, for the better performance and the more talented performer is an implicit admission that the aesthetic quality of the folk performance is a very real element in our professional considerations. Finally, we ought not to forget that our informants, the people who transmit the lore we study, are also interested in beauty, and that they too have their preferences for songs and for singers. Beauty is not a concept imposed upon informants by academicians, but is a genuine and living reality of the people whose art we study.

Now it would be unfair if the exaggeration with which this essay began were carried so far as to imply that no work has been done in this area; actually, much has already been written on the aesthetics of folk genres, and much of that is quite good. We think specifically of the writing of Richard Dorson, Daniel Crowley, Linda Dégh, and Francis Lee Utley.[2] We are not confronted with a vast and uncharted continent of virgin territory yearning to be explored; and we shall avoid the old canard that "this area has not been fully developed." Of course it has not been exhausted, just as no discipline within the cognizance of man has yet to be fully explored. And it is additionally the purpose of this essay to point out that the morphology of Vladimir Propp, long known to folklorists as a means of classifying folk genres, also has potential as an aid in aesthetic evaluations, and *that* is an area little explored to date.

The aesthetic criteria we shall use are those of conventional aestheticians in judging the literary arts. This implies, and this essay intends to imply, that folk art is an art that can be appreciated by the schooled, that folk narrative has many of the same aesthetic properties as the most sophisticated, and that—in other words—the difference between a German peasant's version of "The Bear's Son" and the *Grettissaga* is one of quality, and not of kind.

In fairness to traditional narrative, however, only certain aspects will be discussed. For instance, it would be ridiculous to look to the folktale for dazzling metaphors or finely-wrought rhetoric; such are the marks of careful literary creations, and simply do not exist in oral tradition. But all literature has form, and nearly all aestheticians have been concerned with this property which, as it happens, is one of the salient features of folktales. Kenneth Burke's observations on formal suspense and the information that ought to be present in art[3] are applicable to oral as well as literary genres. James Joyce, after Aquinas, discussed the relationship of the parts of literature to the whole,[4] and that discussion may be profitably turned to our evaluation of the folktale. And Santayana has brought his insights to bear on several areas which may also be used to evaluate folk narrative: symmetry of plot, the units of the manifold, types, utility, and economy.[5] Nearly all of these topics are related to the aesthetics of form.

A good starting point is a discussion of the folktale's form: does it have one, or several, as such? And is there any degree to which the teller's version of the tale can be isolated from the tale itself? Is there such an abstract entity as Tale Type 1423, "The Enchanted Pear Tree," for instance, that can be isolated and analyzed apart from the accidental teller of it, even Chaucer? *The Types of the Folk-Tale*, by A. A. Aarne (Helsinki, 1928), implies that such an abstract, autonomous entity does exist. This tale would seem to have some inherent aesthetic value, then, to be fit not only for goosegirls, bumpkins, and yokels, though perhaps improved upon (for our taste) when Chaucer retells it. To put the matter yet another way, the tale's aesthetic interest lies as well in plot as in accidental felicitous phrase. There is no doubt that aesthetic qualities are imparted by the teller and are thus implanted in his tale; we are here trying to point out the innate qualities of that tale itself.

Thousands of examples could be cited to illustrate this point. For the moment I will merely use one of my favorites, and one which happened to have caught Chaucer's attention as well: Type 706, "The Maiden without Hands." This is the story of the innocent, usually pious, but always completely selfless girl who is persecuted, often by her stepmother, and capriciously maimed by having her hands and feet cut off. A king finds her in the woods (or elsewhere) and soon marries her, but then a mother-in-law figure switches letters which appear to have the king order the maiden's burning. Again the calumniated wife is cast out, but this time the story is resolved when she is reunited with her enlightened husband, who has by now uncovered the deception of the falsified letter. In order for the narrative to proceed, the heroine must be remarkably patient and self-sacrificing, and so she is in nearly all of the collected versions. It is neither arbitrary nor accidental that Kurt Ranke places Type 706 in his section on "Bravery, Fidelity, Patience, Righteousness,"[6] or that Chaucer's maiden is named "Constance."

One would be foolish to argue that the traditional raconteur may not bring much to this—or any—story, but there is something inherent within the tale which we call "beautiful" or which we say has the potential for beauty: elements implicitly exist in a narrative's abstract (such as the Aarne-Thompson Tale Types) which suggest that an aesthetic evaluation is possible. Such an evaluation must be based upon structural features, and for an analysis of narrative tectonics morphology is ideally suited. Propp's system is a kind of deep structure for traditional narrative, the surface structure being the multiform manifestations of the tales themselves. If such narratives may be said to have aesthetic possibilities morphology would be a valuable method to assay and appraise those possibilities.

To belabor the obvious: in traditional narrative we recognize that unlike text literature, the individual performance by a specific storyteller is very important. With text literature the "performer" is in part the reader, whereas the storyteller or ballad-singer is much like an actor, though this actor is one who recreates his own materials. The contrast between oral and written performance is by no means absolute. We know, for instance, that Chaucer read his works aloud to the English court and that most of his contemporaries who knew his poetry experienced it aurally.[7] The Middle English romances, in the main heroic songs and epics of medieval Europe were primarily recited orally as well, and despite the apparent inflexible quality of print or ink upon paper, it is likely that improvisation did occur during performance. Probably the same was true of Chaucer's performances as well.

Nevertheless, despite the existence of such "transitional" texts and performances, one should not argue too strongly for the close similarity of folktale and literary tale in terms of composition, style, or structure; rather, we will only point out that the situation, as least as regards medieval manuscripts, was not entirely different from the modern. With the modern narrative prose genres of the novel and short story we have a substantially new set of aesthetic rules forced upon us by these entirely literary modes. In such fiction the skill of the writer (and of his editor) is pervasive; in traditional narrative the talent of the individual performer is at least as important, since he is not only the "author," but also assumes part of the reader's role of interpretation. Although it is commonplace to speak of the impersonality of folk performances, traditional narratives are in this respect a personal mode: they are "epical" in the jargon of James Joyce, in that the narrative is not purely personal, but equidistant from the artist and his audience. Text literature, ideally, is impersonal:

The personality of the artist . . . finally refines itself out of existence, impersonalizes itself so to speak. . . . The artist, like the God of creation, remains within or behind or beyond or above his handiwork, invisible, refined out of existence, indifferent, paring his fingernails.[8]

As has been argued, if we delete the teller and his personality, something of the tale still remains. There is an aesthetic quality inherent in traditional narrative which depends largely upon formal considerations, a proposition that is quite true of Homer's *Odyssey*, but not so cogent in Joyce's retelling of it. One of the most important of such considerations is the frustration of the audience's expectations in a way that is emotionally satisfying. At the end of the narrative, literary as well as traditional, the audience should be satisfied by the aesthetic correctness and justness of the story's outcome. It is banal but nevertheless true that the narrative establishes its own *weltanschauung*, and once having done so everything that follows should be consistent with its own premises. In this sense the movement, or thrust, or direction of the narrative may be said to be syllogistic.[9]

There is no surprise in traditional literature; when Chaucer says that he is going to tell a story about the "double woe" of Troilus, he is not giving anything away. His audience—any tradition-oriented audience—knows in advance what is to follow. That is a great deal of their motivation for listening in the first place. But that does not rule out suspense of another kind: "the suspense of certain forces gathering to produce a certain result. It is the suspense of a rubber band which we see being tautened."[10] We know that the band will be snapped—in fact we are disappointed if it is not—so that our pleasure derives not from the snapping itself but from the observation of the entire process which has developed inevitably toward an inescapable conclusion. Burke instances the brief scene in *Hamlet* when the prince three times offers the pipes to Guildenstern. Thrice does the latter refuse to play, insisting that he cannot. The episode is then brought to its inevitable end with Hamlet's speech:

Why, look you now, how unworthy a thing you make of me. You would play upon me; you would seem to know my stops; you would pluck out the heart of my mystery; you would sound me from my lowest note to the top of my compass; and there is much music, excellent voice, in this little organ, yet cannot you make it speak. 'Sblood, do you think I am easier to be played on than a pipe? Call me what instrument you will, though you can fret me, you cannot play upon me.

Polonius enters as the last note is sounded, and he is himself, merely by his appearance (because of what we know he is and because of his interruption) a call to action for the next element in the plot. A narrative well-composed will have such autonomous modules that can be isolated from the entire story and will have their own logic in terms of beginnings and ends, quite apart from the contribution that such modules will make to the thrust of the entire narrative.

Wagner withholds the completed melodic line in *Tristan und Isolde* until the exquisite consummation in the "Liebestod." He hints at this completion throughout, begins the melody many times only to deflect it before it is fully under way, but finally, only when the lovers are reunited (in death) is the entire melodic line allowed expression. We are prepared for the final aria the very first time the melody is suggested, and that early in the drama. We are also thus made aware of the inevitable end toward which all the action of the characters must tend, so that there is not any suspense which is satisfied, but rather the aesthetic correctness and logic which pleases. Chaucer uses an analogous technique in the *Man of Law's Tale;* the story could most efficiently end with Constance and her young son reunited with her long-lost husband (Alla) at the Roman banquet. But Chaucer is careful to delay his moment of pathos, and he momentarily thwarts the anticipations of the audience: first, only the son is brought to the banquet so that Alla, who has never seen him, will only vaguely sense his identity. He asks his host if he may see the child's mother, and is then reunited with his wife. But Chaucer delays the action still further: another banquet is arranged to which the emperor is invited—actually he is Constance's father—and so we are given a second, and final, and (presumably) more satisfying reconciliation scene.[11] It is a moment of great pathos, an emotion much relished by Chaucer's audience, and one frequently invoked in pious tales of the fourteenth century—and he is in no great rush to pass it by.

Thwarting or withholding the audience's emotions from some inevitable event delays the narrative somewhat, but delays can be of different sorts: traditional narrative provides us with phenomena which, if they occurred in literature, we would refer to as "forewarnings," subtle arrows which point out narrative directions. In well-written fiction, the consequences and the outcome are implicit in the style, or the event, or in the character which appears early in the story: pessimism to the point of despair and the thwarting of life principles, most extremely and dramatically, death, are all implied clearly in the opening paragraphs of *A Farewell to Arms*, for instance. Traditional narrative has its own signals which are certainly well-known by its auditors and thus clearly understood, perhaps more so than by the occasional reader of text literature. To cite just a few instances here, when the hero crosses a river or stream we can be fairly sure that he has entered an enchanted "Otherworld" and that marvels and wonders will soon befall him. He will encounter strange people and fabulous beasts, or else magic will be inflicted upon him, such as the inducement of a magic sleep or the gift of a magic ring. If he enters a wood or a forest we can expect yet another kind of experience; if he wanders upon a garden we will anticipate still further kinds of adventures. A castle in a faraway land evokes certain responses; when the hero enters it more marvels will happen, enchanted princesses will be found languishing there (or else giants), and if the hero sleeps the night there we would not be surprised if his bed careens wildly through the deserted halls. All of these events and their resultant effects can be isolated in traditional narratives.

In such art, as has just been suggested, such signals or "keys" are at least as desirable as in literature. They give the narrative momentum and direction; they lead to that satisfaction that comes from narrative events being worked out in logical and inevitable ways. The folktale abounds in them, as does the literature which derives from these tales, the romances.[12] To be effective the teller must on some psychological level sense their aesthetic appropriateness, and the auditors must know how to read the keys. When certain characters appear at certain moments in the story— such as the old man or dwarf who lives in the woods—such a character will lead or show the way to the hero's objective; when the hero has attained his goal, and is chased by the giant, or witch, or other ogre, people or animals he then meets will show him the way to rescue. Likewise, when taboos and prohibitions are levied, one is fairly certain that they will be broken or violated. For whatever reason, then, that such devices occur in traditional narratives—and the reasons are not simple— they can be isolated and usually shown to relate to their consequences.

In that these keys are crucial to structure, they are thus related importantly to suspense (and surprise), and we would do well to take heed of Kenneth Burke's distinction between information in art and in aesthetic form: the former is concerned with details about the psychology of the hero, while the latter results from a concern for the psychology of the audience.[13] Information is suited to modern fiction and the economics of the paperback; facts and data about the hero are interesting only for the first time, and suspense and surprise can be exploited from information only once. How many murder mysteries or detective stories can one read repeatedly? George Santayana has said it well: "Art is the response to the demand for entertainment, for the stimulation of our senses and imagination, and truth enters into it only as it subserves these ends."[14] We know from our experience with folktales, their tellers and listeners, that enjoyment comes from the repeated repetition of the same stories. It is not quite the same with a novel, if for no other reason than that the words are fixed, while the folktale raconteur is able to exploit the emotions which he interprets in his audience through subtle changes in language, tone, and gesture. Drama and justness of procedure are the strengths of the folktale, not information. The stories whose plots and endings are known are usually the most popular—in fact, in tradition-oriented cultures any new story may be suspect; the old ones are demanded. Clearly, a good story, however old and however often repeated, regenerates interest.

All the formal aspects of narrative which have been mentioned and which will be mentioned can be analyzed precisely by a technique known to folklorists and anthropologists since 1928, the morphology of Vladimir Propp. If properly employed, this analytical system, originally designed as a method to define the folktale and to distinguish it from other folk genres, can be a valuable instrument for aesthetic criticism. If Propp's system can be likened to a deep structure of narrative patterns, then the Aarne-Thompson indexes are a lexicon of narrative performances. The latter system is peerless in its particularity for identifying related tales and for tracing provenience; morphology was specifically formulated to illumine the relation of the parts to the whole. There is nothing inherent in the indexes that would demand that motif T 68.1 (Princess offered as prize to rescuer) precede motif H 105.1 (Dragon-tongue proof), as happens to be the case in Tale Type 300, "The Dragon Slayer"; but there is a "necessity," as Propp has shown, that demands that certain functions imply those to follow. As Axel Olrik stated in one of his "Epic Laws," folk narrative has its own logic which is, within its own world, consistent. Thus some (perceptive) peasants who are experienced in listening to folktales told within an authentic tradition may well reject folktales which seem to them to have wildly improbable endings, just as we are offended aesthetically by the theatrical device of *deus ex machina*.

The aesthetic discussion of the relation of the parts to the whole in art is a universal area for morphological examination. In obvious aesthetic concern, James Joyce is one of the most eloquent writers (following Aquinas) on *Consonantia*, as he has Stephen Dedalus explain:

. . . you pass from point to point, led by its formal lines; you apprehend it as balanced part against part within its limits; you feel the rhythm of its structure. In other words the synthesis of immediate perception is followed by the analysis of apprehension. Having first felt that it is *one* thing you feel now that it is a *thing*. You apprehend it as complex, multiple, divisible, separable, made up of its parts, the result of its parts and their sum, harmonious. That is *consonantia*.[15]

We have seen, following Kenneth Burke's lead, how the anticipations of the audience may be thwarted for an aesthetic effect in literature and how traditional narrative uses the same techniques; these delays can be easily shown in morphological analysis. For instance, when the Hero arrives at the land where the *Ziel* or *Objectiv*[16] dwells or has been taken, and the mission has been accomplished, very often he will not be allowed to return to his homeland unhindered. A monster, or giant, or demon, or witch of some kind gives chase (which, in morphological coding has been designated as Pr), causing the Hero some difficulty before he is finally safe (Rs). Or the Hero may be about to return when he decides to test his former friends by appearing in disguise (O) before identifying himself—or being identified, like Ulysses—as in function Q. Or Donors and Helpers may appear in several forms and at several times, thus delaying the inevitable.

Perhaps the most important aesthetic consideration of the folktale with which morphology can deal is the function and relationship of beginnings and endings. If we can agree with Propp that the folktale begins with either function "A" (a villainy) or function "a" (a lack or insufficiency), that it proceeds through intermediary functions to "K" (the liquidation of misfortune or lack) or "W" (wedding and accession to the throne), then we are able to see its shape clearly. For lack of a more precise term, we are able to clearly apprehend its curve[17] or balance. The ending is implicit in the opening of well-wrought narrative; Propp's morphology suggests, for instance, that the European folktale is circular, or cyclical in its thrust: first A, then K. The Hero departs from home (↑), but eventually returns (↓). An exception—and they are infrequent —is to be found in tales of banishment in which, Propp states,[18] there is no specific form of resolution: the hero may simply marry and never return. A Donor usually appears near the beginning of the hero's quest, the Helper usually after the encounter with the Villain. And the dramatic climax is usually reached at function "H" (the Hero struggles with the Villain) and "I" (victory over the Villain), or at "M" (the imposition of difficult tasks) and "N" (the completion of those tasks). After functions "I" or "N" there is a kind of falling action, and the tale moves towards its conclusion.

This circular character of the folktale, with the hero's departure followed by his return, and its cyclical character with the encounter of the Donor in multiple forms and the repetition of his request or his challenge, with the repetition of events within the tale (Olrik's *Gesetz der Widerholung*), is surprisingly consonant with contemporary literary narrative. In an interview reported in the *New York Times*, film director Arthur Penn spoke of the way in which he conceived the telling of *Little Big Man*:

We're into another way of looking at narrative now. . . . We've got to be willing to abandon a straight narrative line in terms of circular, cyclical narrative. The old style is not sufficient. We can't go in quest of just another story. The insights of psychoanalysis—Freud, Erikson—the stages of development, the repetitive characteristics of patterns of living have affected direct narrative so that seemingly disconnected events become meaningful. . . . Narrative must deal now with the significance of people laboring through cyclical problems of a changing nature.[19]

For Arthur Penn and literate authors of the Freudian tradition life is cyclical, and by extension the folktale, like *Little Big Man*, appeals to us because its cyclical or circular character is an imitation of life: the tale, in recapitulating the patterns of life, strikes an unconscious and perhaps unheard chord within the psyche of the listener. Perhaps. But recent studies in the life sciences suggest, to me at least, that other speculations are possible: I speak specifically of "Rhythmology."[20]

This is a very recent discipline concerned with the life rhythms of humans. Our lives are governed by a biological clock which we cannot manipulate or control. Despite one's diet—or lack of any nourishment—despite the absence of sunlight for extended periods, the human body runs on a twenty-four-hour clock. Body temperature fluctuates smoothly and consistently during the same period; the skin renews itself between midnight and 4 A.M. daily; and the sex-hormone output is greatest at specific times of day. These circadian cycles are superimposed over rhythms of a shorter span—ultradian cycles—and infradian rhythms, those whose duration is longer than one day. Typical of the former is the sleep cycle of 90 to 100 minutes in which we pass from light sleep (R E M, or Rapid Eye Movement) to deep and back again to light. Typical of the latter is the menstrual cycle, or the periods of irritability that most of us apparently undergo at six-week intervals.

Now Kenneth Burke has argued that rhythm in literature—the metrical quality of language—has its appeal because it is closely allied to certain bodily functions: systole and diastole, alternation of the legs in walking, inhalation and exhalation, and so forth.[21] This is speculative, of course, but Burke does offer a reasonable explanation for our fascination with the rhythms of language. Perhaps—and this also is offered as speculation—the circadian, ultradian, and infradian rhythms of life are the bases of the appeal of the cyclical character of the folktale. In some unconscious sphere of our existence, most likely biological, the thrust of the tale may be perceived as an imitation of life: briefer, more selective, more purposeful than life, but microcosmic and imitative nevertheless.

Propp's transformational grammar of narrative possibilities has made clear to us the intimate and inevitable relationship between the beginnings of tales and their conclusions: if the hero's acute lack is of a bride at the beginning of the folktale, then he will obtain one at the end;[22] when a crime sets a particular story in motion—that is, when the Hero's initial motivation is stimulated by some crime or villainy—revenge or punishment of the wicked will eventually result; or if the hero is tested for some virtue or other, he will prove himself by the time of the tale's conclusion. In fact, his demonstration of worth may be the climax, just as the attempt at revenge or the search for a bride will actually be the substance of the story.

Morphological analysis has shown this thrust of the folktale to be true with a large corpus of material, enabling us to begin to understand a great deal about the aesthetic standards of the tellers and their audiences. "Lack" always leads to its elimination and satisfaction; imbalance is corrected by subsequent balance; and chaos is supplanted by order. Such narrative patterns are essentially optimistic, despite the cruelty one often finds in the action. They argue for a sense of justice in the world, if not in reality then in expectation. The life presented by such tales is one ultimately governed by design, as was obvious to Jon Jonasson who recalled that in the Iceland of his youth the folktale was told primarily to children because of its moral value: the "bad guys" always lost. And by eliminating tragedy in any sense by which that concept would be known to us, the folktale would seem to be projective. Such a pattern is the logical outgrowth of the qualities of which we have been speaking: balance, and proportion, and economy.

Why the folktale is characteristically crisp and pithy is a matter (in part) of social function, which is not germane to this essay; extraneous characters and motivationless actions tend to be eliminated in the course of repeated transmissions. Thrift also operates in terms of what we might call efficiency: when we have function "B" (the connective incident) then we shall also have "C" (consent to counteraction). We never have function "E" (the reaction of the Hero) without "D" (the first function of the Donor). "Pr," as we have seen, cannot exist without "Rs"; "L" (the claims of the False Hero) will be inevitably followed by "Ex" (the False Hero's exposure); nor will there be "M" without "N" or "H" without "I." Characters always seem to have a dramatic function in a properly told folktale; even in a confused or an improperly told tale, the Propp system enables us to identify, immediately, any irrelevancy, as well as to establish the admirable aspects of form.

It is one thing to talk about morphological evaluations of aesthetics in the abstract, but much more useful to demonstrate how they work on the actual tale. To avoid any suspicion that the choice might be too carefully selected, we may take Propp's own example of "The Swan-Geese" tale (Propp, p. 96). The morphological formula will have to be adjusted somewhat from the form presented by Propp, owing to his (or his translator's) notorious casualness towards details. Most striking is Propp's omission of the climax of the tale, functions H and I; the trebling of the encounter with the Donor is not indicated by "3," and brackets are placed by Propp around Pr and Rs when it is obvious that only D E F should be so bracketed. The slightly revised formula for the "Swan-Geese" tale follows:

$$\gamma\,\beta\,\delta\,A\,B\,C\uparrow\ \left\{\frac{[\text{D E Neg}\qquad \text{F Neg}]^3}{\text{D E F}}\right\}\ G\,H\,I\,K\downarrow\,Pr\,[\text{D E F}]^3\,Rs$$

The necessary development of the plot is clear: from the time of the interdiction (γ), in this instance not to leave the little brother unprotected in the yard, we know that the parents will leave (β) and the interdiction will be violated (δ). As the Hero(ine) starts out to find the younger brother, Donors appear and point the way; the brother is eventually recovered and then Helpers (also coded as "D") will appear in their turn and aid in the rescue. "Epic retardation" occurs at least twice in this tale: first in the three negative replies to potential Donors, but later in the trebling of the Helper's function. A further retardation occurs in the Pr-Rs sequence itself: the *Objectiv* has been recovered at K, but although function $\downarrow$ immediately follows, the Hero(ine) and the brother do not return home safely until Rs.

The story is balanced; the climax occurs at H-I, which is much closer to the middle of the tale (as reading the story shows) than Propp's coded contraction of it indicates. Its cyclical nature is manifest in the two trebled functions, each one occurring on either side of the climax (H-I). The tale begins at "home" where the villainy is made known to the heroine, and ends there when the imbalance is eliminated. Balanced within its major components and balanced overall, the structure of the "Swan Geese" is aesthetically pleasing; the story, from this aspect, is a good one.

Valuable as is the potential of morphology for aesthetic evaluation (and I believe that it is potentially very useful for literature as well as oral narrative), no system has yet been devised to detect those minor inconsistencies to which all but the most meticulous literature is heir. Logic within the terms which the tale itself has postulated is not necessarily the same thing as an external, "objective" logic. Strange inconsistencies occur again and again in folk narratives which do not seem to upset either the tellers or their listeners. In well-known literature the quality is easy to point out. In the "Miller's Tale" the old carpenter breaks down his boarder's door to see what ails him, but moments later, when told that the matter is most private, he shuts the door behind him. That same John, we are elsewhere told, was extremely jealous of his pretty young wife, but when a suitor comes to the window he reacts indifferently. At the beginning of the "Reeve's Tale" we are told that the miller's wife "was proud," but nothing in the body of the "Tale" suggests pride. The reader is made to despise January's foolishness in the beginning of the "Merchant's Tale," to laugh contemptuously at his marriage, and then to pity him his later married life. In the *Chanson de Roland* the warrior Turgis is first killed, but then several hundred lines later we find him again fighting; when Ganelon leaves the Frankish camp it is in one location, but when he returns shortly the scene has changed. Or in *Beowulf*, when Grendel attacks the fortress, the hero allows him to eat one of his companions before he leaps into action.

When we have met with such narrative inconsistencies in Chaucer, in the *Roland*, or in *Beowulf*, we have tried desperately to rationalize them in terms of irony or of subtlety. Scholars of Old French literature who have noticed that individual scenes in medieval romance narratives are discrete—neatly bounded episodes with their own beginnings, middles, and endings—have searched for reasons in the structure of Romanesque art.[23] Jordan sought to explicate Chaucer in terms of gothic architecture, especially that of cathedrals. My own bias is for an analogy with altarpieces, particularly those which tell a story. The masons who build churches work in stone and the forces of physics; the carvers or painters of altarpieces also deal in another medium, it is true, but at least they are telling a coherent story through a sequence of scenes, each of which is discrete, modular, and an aesthetic entity in itself. One has only to look at one of the pieces by Meister Bruggemanns (several remain in northern Germany, with a particularly impressive specimen at Schleswig) to see that he carves stories in the same modular way in which medieval stories were told.

Folklorists will recognize, I trust, that inconsistencies like those enumerated occur for the sake of the drama of the individual scene. Tristram Coffin has recently said it cogently:

In our society, consistency of time, sequence, detail, and motive has become a fetish. Novelists, dramatists, movie and TV script writers have become so conscientious about these matters that almost all of them are willing to sacrifice pace to make sure no critic will accuse them of a logical inconsistency or a failure to tie up a loose end. The result is a body of self-conscious, over-disciplined expression in which the main purpose of narrative (telling a story) gets lost.[24]

What is important in oral presentation is the scene of the moment: *That* must be vivid and alive, *that* must arrest the listener's attention. As the teller begins his tale he must make the opening scene as interesting as possible; to do so he will stress certain features, diminish others, and exaggerate still others. Later on in his narrative he is still compelled to make his tale interesting and so he will use the same techniques, even though now the dramatic situation may have changed. At this point, later on in the story, exaggeration or diminution may alter the data of the narrative enough so that inconsistencies and even contradictions will occur. We may take, for example, a heroine we have already cited, the "Maiden Without Hands," recorded in Mecklenburg. When her stepmother cuts off her hands and feet she asks only that she be left in the woods to be eaten by wild animals; when her mother-in-law pretends to have her burned at the stake and then arranges her escape, she again asks only to be left at the mercy of the animals; but when her stepmother suggests that people who cut off the arms and legs of others should be cooked in oil, our long-suffering and humble maiden rushes forward and says, "but this is much too good for you" (p. 89). The king agrees and the stepmother is torn apart by four oxen.

The lack of concern for a strict consistency in narrative detail is not only the "flaw" of the folktale teller; Alfred Hitchcock has admitted much the same attitude about his movies. Such details he finds trivial and annoying; what counts is the story, and artistic means—not tricks—of committing the audience. "What I look for in planning a film," he has been recently quoted as saying, "are the opportunities for suspense and involving the audience."[25]

Was Chaucer thinking about history when he had Criseyde read the *Roman de Thebes*? Was Shakespeare thinking about geography when he gave Bohemia a coastline? These inconsistencies and anachronisms occur because of the aesthetic demands placed on the storyteller; at the same time these demands make of traditional narrative, especially the folktale, a nearly perfect dramatic form.

As Axel Olrik has noted, and the experiments of F. C. Bartlett[26] have demonstrated, the tendency in folktale transmission is for the style to acquire vividness of imagery and intensified dramatization. This happens in several ways. Salient features of characters get heightened: the old woman who asks the hero a question becomes, eventually, the ugly, mean old crone who intimidates the young boy. And the polarization, so well described by Olrik, sharpens the contrast between characters in each tableau or module; conflicts between characters may be made more intense. This is the essence of dramatic art. And the folktale, more than most other dramatic forms, is bent primarily toward the exploitation of drama, and thus can be said to be a genre of nearly "pure" dramatic form. The folktale's dramatic nature perpetuates itself, if we may give Anderson's much abused "Law of Self-Correction" a broader and universally psychological basis.

Perhaps the most significant difference, then, between written and oral narrative concerns the belief of the storyteller; usually there is belief in the historicity of the story by both teller and listener, unlike the literary author who may believe only in his narrative's metaphorical or psychological truth. The folktale teller would hardly have any justification at all to recite his stories if there was not some measure of belief.[27] Icelandic farmer Jon Noromann Jonasson has recently told me that in his country (specifically Skagafjörður in the north) folktales are told by "sagamen," who dwell at length on the truth, historicity, and moral value of the tales they tell. Jonasson himself thought that Type 706 ("The Maiden without Hands") was the sort of story usually told to children to teach them its implicit moral, but that Type 301 ("The Three Stolen Princesses") was related to him as a true anecdote (his home is where the historical Grettir, whose saga employs a version of 301, once roamed).[28] It would seem that folklore, in order to live, must be experienced live, that the recording and transcription of it deletes—"murders" in Wordsworth's famous phrase—some essential element in its transmission, and that it must be believed: to believe is to give life.

This seems also to have been Linda Dégh's findings after her intensive field work in several Hungarian villages.[29] The *Märchen*, which does not claim credibility, tends at several points to blend with the local legends, which are thought to be true. The folktale is maintained, she found, in its tradition through its dependence on living folk belief.

All of the above remarks have been made in the face of an intense and widespread prejudice on the part of literary scholars against traditional narrative, particularly the folktale. One of the most telling statements reflecting this attitude was made several years ago by the late Roger Sherman Loomis, who vigorously denied the claim that "certain of the great stories of the Matter of Britain originated in the fancies of plowmen, goosegirls, blacksmiths, midwives, or yokels of any kind."[30] Professor Loomis was in the process of recanting what he felt to be his earlier heresy: a belief that the idea of the Holy Grail had evolved from ritual to romance, and in his fervor to convert to new truths he vehemently denounced the old ones. But, as Utley has said, this is rather risky ground, and it is certain that the *Märchen* is older than most medieval romances and contributed much to the latter's form, style, and construction.[31]

Professors of literature have been persistently reluctant to see virtue in any other than printed works of famous authors, while the traditional origins of these "masterworks" are held in disdain. For instance, Fred N. Robinson once wrote of Chaucer's adaptation of Tale Type 763, "The Treasure Finders Who Murder One Another," that "his tale has sometimes been called the best short story in existence. . . . Certainly the tale was never better told than by Chaucer. In the management of the intrigue and the swift denouement it is a model of short-story method. In atmosphere and characterization it is vividly conceived, and in the dialogue not a word is wasted."[32] And Paul Olson wrote of the same author's version of Tale Type 1423, "The Enchanted Pear Tree," that "the great pear-tree scene . . . by any standards, must be one of the great comic scenes of literature."[33] The rhetoric here conceals several moot premises; clearly, the fact that the author is Chaucer has a lot to do with its extravagance. Would the praise of these critics be as warm for the same tales told by a plowman in Kansas or a goosegirl in Shropshire? If Type 763 has never been better told one would assume that the critic has heard all of the versions; and one wants to ask why the pear-tree scene becomes one of the great scenes of literature, and not of oral performances as well. This great animus against popular literature has prevented us from seeing the aesthetic qualities in traditional narratives, even when they are obviously there.

I should remark, finally, for the sake of perspective, that aesthetic implications are inherent in Propp's system, though it is by no means innately beautiful in any sense that would be understood by aestheticians. Through morphology we can clearly perceive and define the circular or cyclical aspect of the folktale and the mode by which it is emotionally fulfilling; through it we may see the balance and the economy in folk narrative, all of which are considerations in schooled literature as well. Certainly there is more to beauty than these considerations, but we cannot speak of beauty without these structural elements. As a result of Propp's system the aesthetician has a more precise method of dealing with his material than ever before. And, we should be reminded, people still tell folktales and those who listen to them still enjoy their stories, and our informants are themselves concerned with artistry and aesthetics, by whatever name.

Notes

1. Review of Bruce A. Rosenberg's *The Art of the Amercian Folk Preacher,* anon., *Virginia Kirkus Service,* April 1, 1970.
2. Examples: Richard M. Dorson, "Esthetic Form in British and American Folk Narrative," in *Medieval Literature and Folklore Studies,* eds., Jerome Mandel and Bruce A. Rosenberg (New Brunswick: Rutgers University Press, 1970), pp. 305–22; Daniel C. Crowley, *I Could Tell Old Story Good* (Berkeley: University of California Press, 1966); Linda Dégh, "Some Question of the Social Function of Story Telling," *Acta Ethnographica,* 6 (1957), 91–143; Linda Dégh, *Märchen, Erzahler und Erzahlgemeinschaft* (Berlin: Akademie-Verlag, 1962); numerous pieces by F. L. Utley, most recently, "Oral Genres as Bridge to Written Literature," *Acta Ethnographica,* 19 (1970), 389–99. Use is occasionally made of morphological techniques and their application to the structure of literary genres, for instance, William O. Hendricks, "Folklore and the Structural Analysis of Literary Texts," *Language and Style,* 3 (1970), 83–121. Isidor Levin asserts that Vladimir Propp has been interested in the aesthetics of the *byliny,* even though he has not applied his own system to its evaluation: "Vladimir Propp: An Evaluation on His Seventieth Birthday," *Journal of the Folklore Institute,* 4 (1967), 32–49. Nothing has been written on the aesthetics of Propp's system itself.
3. Kenneth Burke, *Counterstatement* (Berkeley: University of California Press, 1968), p. 124. See also the chapter "Psychology of Form."
4. James Joyce, *A Portrait of the Artist as a Young Man* (New York: The Viking Press, 1964), p. 212.
5. These subjects are from the index of George Santayana, *The Sense of Beauty* (New York: Random House, 1955).
6. Kurt Ranke, ed., *The Folktales of Germany* (Chicago: University of Chicago Press, 1966), pp. 84–89; but see Utley, "Oral Genres," p. 391: "As a Märchen, Sleeping Beauty has a happy ending; as a saints' legend, the Seven Sleepers has a religious and didactic implication; as legend, sleeping Rip Van Winkle and its German counterpart (Peter Klaus) stress the tragedy of transience."
7. See Bertrand H. Bronson, *In Search of Chaucer* (Toronto: University of Toronto Press, 1960).
8. *Portrait,* pp. 214–15.
9. *Counterstatement,* "The Psychology of Form."
10. *Counterstatement,* p. 145.
11. This is an clement which Chaucer added to his source, Nicholas Trivet, who had only one reunion.

12. "Forewarnings" in medieval romances take similar forms: Yvain about to cross the river, Parzival at the entrance of the deserted castle, or Arthur chasing the wounded white hart deep into the forest.
13. *Counterstatement*, pp. 32–33.
14. *Sense of Beauty*, p. 26.
15. *Portrait*, p. 212.
16. I have chosen the briefer German word instead of the cumbersome English translation, "the sought-after object."
17. The term is Burke's: *Counterstatement*, p. 127.
18. Vladimir Propp, *Morphology of the Folktale*, 2nd ed., trans. Laurence Scott (Austin: University of Texas Press, 1968), p. 111.
19. The *New York Times*, 21 December 1969, p. 38.
20. Jim Hampton, "Man Is Ruled By a Time Clock He Can't Regulate," *National Observer*, 28 December 1970, pp. 1 and 13.
21. *Counterstatement*, p. 140; for the observation that the folktale imitates life see Archer Taylor, "The Biographical Pattern in Traditional Narrative," *Journal of the Folklore Institute*, 1 (1964), 114–29.
22. Propp himself notes a few exceptions on p. 110 of *Morphology*.
23. See the bibliography in Helmut Hatzfeld, "Style 'Roman' dans les litteratures romanes: essai de synthese," in *Studi in onore di Italo Siciliano*, ed. Leo S. Olschki (Firenze: n.p., 1966), pp. 525–40.
24. Tristram Coffin, "Folk Logic and the Bard: Act I of *Macbeth*," in *Medieval Literature and Folklore Studies*, p. 332.
25. Quoted by Bernard Weinraub, The *New York Times* News Service, 19 June 1971.
26. F. C. Bartlett, "Some Experiments on the Reproduction of Folk Stories," in Alan Dundes, *The Study of Folklore* (Englewood Cliffs: Prentice-Hall, 1965), pp. 249 ff.
27. This has recently been reasserted by W. Edson Richmond's review of Rosenberg's *The Art of the American Folk Preacher*, in *The Georgia Review*, 24 (1970), 503–04.
28. Jonasson, a guest of Professor Michael Bell of the Pennsylvania State University, visited that campus in November 1970.
29. Linda Dégh, *Folktales and Society*, trans. Emily M. Schossberger (Bloomington: Indiana University Press, 1969), pp. 131–46. I have since spoken to Mrs. Dégh who insists that the translation of her book is misleading in that folktales are not usually held to be literally true.
30. Roger Sherman Loomis, "Arthurian Tradition and Folklore," *Folklore*, 69 (1958), 1–25.
31. Francis Lee Utley, "Oral Genres," 389–90; "Arthurian Romance and International Folktale Method," *Romance Philology*, 17 (1964), 596–607; "Folklore, Myth, and Ritual," in *Critical Approaches to Medieval Literature: Selected Papers from the English Institute*, 1958–59 (New York: Columbia University Press, 1959), pp. 83–109.
32. Fred N. Robinson, *The Works of Geoffrey Chaucer*, 2nd ed., (Boston: Houghton Mifflin, 1957), pp. 10–11.
33. Paul A. Olson, "Chaucer's Merchant and January's 'Heavene in Erthe Heere'," *English Literary History*, 27 (1961), 212.

In
Hyperborea

John Balaban

It is, Odysseus, as if you had drowned
on leaving Circe's isle, or sundered
below Charybdis: for northern gusts
bite your eyes like fish in turgid seas.
With pointed cap askew and frosting breath,
a whitened beard, you bear the well-made oar.
Among strange peoples once again, devout
of prophecy, you seek the journey's end.
Dead Teiresias promised death at sea.
Mid-winter. Small birds cry sharply, pecking out
the sun from rocks and vines. Day's lord
glooms out: a poor bloodless bantam preens
his skinny feathers by a wattled oaken door.
A pungent heat, of fodder, straw, manure,
tossed on the snow this morning, steams the air,
while barnheld horses stamp and chew. Odysseus,
plodding by, weeps for dead Penelope,
for King Telemachus, irresolute of mind.
He calls Athena, but the wily man
already knows: in snow-enshrouding lands
Athena is a stunted owl in smoke beblackened rafters.

Moral Psychology and the Study of Tragedy

Lawrence Kohlberg

"Zeus, who guided men to think, has laid it down that wisdom comes alone through suffering. . . . *Justice so moves that those only learn who suffer."* *Agamemnon.*

Whatever else is true of tragedy, it is certainly the representation of moral action in order to arouse moral emotions in the spectator. It is not surprising, then, that most moral psychologists have taken their turn in attempting to analyze tragedy. My own effort derives from 20 years of research on moral psychology, commencing as a student at the University of Chicago. It derives, also, from Henry Sams, who convinced me by example that psychologizing could really quicken and deepen one's experience of literature while remaining faithful to the nature of literary forms and who first encouraged my own fumbling efforts in that direction. The grand and foolish word "Humanities" had acquired a new meaning for me through his person. It made real to me the notion that the "humanities" imparted to a man wisdom, a humane vision, an ethical outlook which the logic-chopping and experimentation of science could never reach. So when I chose the scientific (or pseudo-scientific) path of psychology, I did my best to remember that psychology must strive for a humane vision, however weak and fumbling the actual results. If our psychology seems crude and weak in what it can say about the great human experiences, it is better to make that clear and to mark where we must go than to ignore it.

If the comments just made may be read as an apology for modern moral psychology, I still need not apologize too much. The first philosopher of tragedy told us that tragedy was a moral action to arouse moral emotions. Our definition of tragedy, he tells us, must start (a) with the *moral character* of the persons in the plot. Types of drama, he tells us, are defined by the types of moral character of the persons represented. The objects the dramatist represents are actions with agents who are necessarily either good men or bad. The difference that distinguished Tragedy and Comedy is "that the one makes its personage worse, and the other better than the men of the present day" (Aristotle *Poetics* 1448). Second, morality is not only central to the definition of the characters in tragedy, but (b) to the definition of the plot or action, which is a *moral* action. The soul of tragedy is not in its characters but in its plot, in the "change in the hero's fortunes from happiness to misery, not because of depravity but because of a great error on his part." The elements of the tragic plot, then, are Peripety, Discovery and Suffering. The plot of a tragedy is a moral action, not only in that it is action springing from moral character, but in that the action of the play starts with a moral decision by the hero in which he makes a great moral error, and this error leads to suffering through discoveries revealing this error and its meaning. Finally, (c) the aim of the tragedy, emotional catharsis in the spectator, is the arousal and release of specifically *moral emotion* (as opposed to other emotions aroused by drama). The aim of the plot, "the tragic effect," is a moral emotion, "the tragic pleasure of pity and fear."

These brief definitions of the philosopher are clarified in Elder Olson's modern restatement (pp. 37–38):

Plot is a system of actions of a determinate moral quality. Plot is always aimed at some specific effects. If we feel different emotions at the sight of the fortunes or misfortunes of characters in a play, it is because what we are seeing is in accordance with, or in opposition to, our wishes for these characters, wishes based upon *grounds of moral approval or disapproval.* But an action which incurs moral approval or disapproval must itself be possessed of a certain moral quality; thus, the foundation of emotional effectiveness in plot must clearly be moral, and plot itself is morally determinate action.*

The import of Olson's claim that the soul of tragedy is moral comes by contrasting Olson's concept that the relationship of the spectator to the hero and the events that befall him in a tragedy is specifically moral, with the notion that the relation of the spectator to the hero is one of (a) empathy or sympathy or (b) one of identification. Olson says (pp. 38–40):

Certain objections offer themselves to the view that the foundation of emotional effectiveness in plot must clearly be moral. First, why should we not simply say that our emotional reactions in drama are based upon general human sympathy? Because time and again we feel emotions which are the very opposite of those felt by the character; we do not share the calm confidence of the heroine as she moves among unsuspected danger. Well, then, can't we say we simply identify ourselves with the characters? This can mean either that we absolutely "put ourselves into the shoes" of the character, imagine ourselves as them, or it can mean that we identify our own interests with theirs. Both are false and contrary to fact. Do we in fact, in watching a play, fancy ourselves now as Claudia, now as Gertrude, now as Hamlet, now as Polonius? Or identify our aims and interests with theirs? In that case, we should view the outcome with very mixed emotions indeed. If we identify ourselves with some but not with others; on what grounds do we do so? For identification cannot itself, then, be the *principle* underlying our reactions; it requires something further to explain it. Do we, in fact, identify ourselves with anybody? Is it not rather manifestly the case that as we watch, nothing is further from our thoughts than ourselves and our self-interest?

Olson's point may be clarified by pointing to its limitations. Olson claims that the soul of any plot is moral, not only the plot of a tragedy,

---

*Excerpts from *Tragedy and the Theory of Drama* by Elder Olson are reprinted by permission of the Wayne State University Press.

and that it is incorrect to claim that the relationship of the audience to the hero in any serious literary work is one of identification. To the extent to which Olson's claim is true of any literary plot, it is true because Olson has too vague and weak a notion of the moral. Following Aristotle (and Hume), Olson defines the moral attitude as an attitude of *disinterested approval* (or disapproval). As we shall see, disinterested approval or disapproval, that is, praise or blame: (a) is not itself specifically moral; we disinterestedly approve and disapprove many actions or traits on nonmoral grounds, (b) is not the "soul" of the moral; the soul of the moral lies in the duties and rights defined by justice, and (c) drops out at the highest stages of moral judgment to which the audience is to be brought in tragedy.

As we clarify later, a tragic plot is moral because its principle is justice and injustice, the mixed justice and injustice of the hero and the mixed justice and injustice of the fate which befalls him. With regard to tragedy, Olson is correct in claiming that identification cannot be the *principle* underlying our reactions, because such a principle must tell us whom we "identify" with. This principle is the principle of justice. It is the nature of moral principles of justice to tell us whom we should identify with. The core problem of justice is the problem of distribution, "of giving each his due," of answering, "Why me?" of deciding whose claim to consider, whose perspective to take. Our conflicts as to whose role to take in a tragedy, and their emotional resolutions, are dictated by issues and principles of justice.

While the relationship of spectator to hero in tragedy centers on justice, this is not true in other forms of narrative, which are not moral actions in the same sense. In nondramatic forms a moral principle governs identifications less because the author can manipulate identification by selective presentation of interior views. The relationship of the spectator to the hero of a romance or epic is one of identification, even if this is not the relation of the audience to the hero of tragedy. The standard novel of adventure or love depends upon such an equation of reader and hero, an equation which removes the possibility of pity so central to tragedy. When we identify with the hero, we cannot pity him, for pity involves seeing him from both within and without. To identify is not to pity because we do not pity ourselves, except sentimentally. Narratives which start with identification, and end with pity, like *Love Story*, are merely sentimental. The standard novel or epic is a tale of ambition or of love, in which the hero aims higher than the average man or spectator, in which he demands more of life. The reader is expected to identify with these demands as a striving self who also desires high honor and perfect love, and to get vicarious gratification from the hero's triumphs, whatever the eventual outcome. The action of the epic moves toward kinghood and consummated love, the action of tragedy starts there. In summary, (a) the character of the hero of an epic is someone of whom we approve, but this does not make (b) the plot of an epic "morally determinate action" in anything but a trivial sense, nor does it imply (c) a specifically moral as opposed to an identificatory attitude or emotion as the aim of the work. The moral nature of tragedy is unique, and not common to all drama or narrative.

We need now to clarify the sense in which the "tragic effect" is distinctively moral as opposed to identificatory. Of this, Olson says, (pp. 152–160):

Emotions are also not peculiar to any given form, although we usually speak as if they were. Aristotle himself seems to have given some support to this notion by his remark that pity and fear are peculiar to tragedy. I do not think he means what he appears to mean; however, Aristotle or no Aristotle, the facts say otherwise. Any dramatic form can and does arouse almost every sort of emotion. Pity and fear, for instance, are aroused not merely by tragedy, but by melodrama and certain sentimental forms as well. Indeed, they can be aroused even by comedy. Thus the effect of drama must involve something more than emotion. What is that "something more"? . . .

Every emotional experience must either confirm or alter in some way our system of values; and in altering it, make it better or worse whenever it affects a moral value. This must hold true, also, of drama and the other arts, so that the effect of drama is its effect upon moral values. . . .

One kind of drama assumes the system of values of the person of ordinary morality. It proposes simply the arousing of emotions to the ultimate effect of giving pleasure, its aim is entertainment. Its effect is transitory, and its excellence consists simply in the intensity of the pleasure which it gives. That intensity is naturally dependent upon the intensity of the emotions produced; thus the serious forms of this kind tend to play upon extreme fear and other painful emotions, while the comic forms play upon the more extreme reactions of the ridiculous.

The second kind of drama goes beyond entertainment, and permits us perceptions which we should not otherwise have had; it goes beyond ordinary morality, and offers us other and better systems of values; it, in some degree, alters us as human beings. To put this in a nutshell; there is a difference between works which give us an intense experience and works which give us a significant experience.

What is this meaning, this significance? Certainly not the verbal meaning of sentences in the work. And certainly not some *moral* to be derived from the work, in the style of old-fashioned schoolteachers. The moral of *Othello* is that women should be careful how they bestow their linen, said Thomas Rymer, thinking of Desdemona's troubles with a certain handkerchief; we laugh at this, precisely because this moral—or any other—is so far removed from the significance of the play. It is not the discovery of the moral principle or precept involved, after the fashion of the moral-hunting pedagog, but the recognition that such and such a specific action *has* a certain moral quality.

I shall say, therefore, that a work possesses significance or meaning as it promotes perceptions—perceptions based on feelings—which are conducive to practical wisdom; which would, if acted upon, eventuate in such wisdom. The condition of mind which it immediately promotes is a temporary alignment of passion, emotion, and desire with right principle.

We shall agree with Olson that a significant tragedy (though not all significant drama, as he claims) must "go beyond ordinary morality and offer us other and better systems of values," that it involves the "discovery of moral principle," not "after the fashion of the moral-hunting pedagog," but in the "recognition that such and such a specific action has a certain moral quality" and that a tragic work possesses significance as it promotes perceptions based on feelings conducive to practical wisdom, and as it immediately promotes a condition of mind in which passion is aligned with right principle.

The problem, of course, is to specify what such terms as "a better system of values," "recognition of moral qualities," "feelings conducive to practical wisdom," and "right principle" mean.

Here, unfortunately, Olson falls back, as Aristotle did, on the notion that such terms are essentially defined by enlightened common sense notions of practical wisdom and of virtue and vice as habits. From the point of view of modern psychology, the outstanding quality of Aristotle's moral psychology and philosophy is not that it is inappropriate to modern culture, but that it sounds so much like modern "common sense" notions of morality. As I have elaborated elsewhere (Kohlberg, 1970), Aristotle's concept of moral character, like that of modern common sense, is that of an enlightened behaviorism, in which character is conceived of as a bag of virtues or acquired habits relevant to people in certain social roles.

The analysis of characters in tragedy which results from Aristotle's common sense behaviorism follows (Olson, pp. 81–82):

Let us take the real character first. I observe four different things about him. First, he was born with certain natural capacities. Second, as a consequence of education and the constant repetition of certain acts, he has formed habits and so has developed into a given kind of person, one of a certain moral character. Third, precisely because he is a certain kind of person, a certain bundle of habits, he will tend to act according to them. Fourth, he has a certain function or role in life; his profession or occupation in a very narrow sense, but more generally, some end which is his particular conception of what constitutes happiness.
There are four points, then, to be observed in the treatment of character: usefulness, appropriateness, likeness, and consistency. And now that I have said this, I remember that some one else said precisely the same thing.

If most of us are dissatisfied with the light which Aristotle's common sense psychology of moral character can cast on tragedy, this is not entirely true of his doctrine of catharsis. The psychological problem of tragedy is expressed by Hume as the problem as to why "there should be an unaccountable pleasure which the spectators of a well-written tragedy receive from sorrow, terror, anxiety, and other passions that are in themselves disagreeable and uneasy."

The doctrine of catharsis, of course, explains this paradox on the grounds that tragic catharsis is pleasurable because it is a release or purgation of unpleasant emotions. The doctrine of catharsis is essentially an "irrational" doctrine, release from unpleasant emotions is not a movement toward moral enlightenment or rational moral vision. The doctrine of catharsis is the doctrine that we have irrational moral emotions of pity and dread and that the tragedy purges us of these irrational moral emotions. It is not surprising, then, that the chief contribution of modern psychology to the understanding of catharsis has come from moral psychologists of the irrational, in particular Nietzsche and Freud. Freud and Nietzsche agreed fundamentally that morality was a matter of guilt, and that guilt was irrational because it arose from irrational instincts turned inward (for Freud aggression; for Nietzsche, the will to power). Both Freud and Nietzsche placed the origin of morality in a mythical past in which man turns his instinct of aggression (or will to power) inward instead of directing it against his oppressors or authorities, and with this inward turning instinct was born the sense of guilt. Nietzsche sees the full birth of morality as conscience occurring in the figure of Socrates, and sees the full development of such morality as ending Greek tragedy, which was itself a transition to the morality of conscience. Freud saw morality as born in that primal act in which the first men slew their father and paid the price of guilt as the result. In its starkest form, the Freudian analysis of tragedy is the story of Oedipus. The tragedy in drama is the formation of each man's conscience through parricidal rebellion and subsequent guilt. In this Freudian formula, the drama starts with the spectator-self divided into the impulsive hero and the authority figure he slays. The end of the play is a reunification of the divided self, of the id, and the superego. The id, the impulsive portion of the self, recognizes that it is inextricably a part of a self which also includes a moral force, the superego, a force of guilt which controls it. In submitting to this force, the force of punishment and fate, this impulsive self becomes at one with the moral self, and catharsis is achieved.

Whatever our final view of the Freudian psychology of tragedy, its contributions are clear-cut. It provides, first, a partial explanation for why certain plots are recurrent in tragedy. Those who completely doubt the Freudian interpretation need only be asked why it is that all great tragedies, Greek, Shakespearian, modern, involve the murder of another member of the family. Of all the aspects of tragic plot we could never guess from the Aristotelean analysis, this is the most astounding. We need not accept the whole Freudian doctrine to understand why our ultimate pity and terror are felt toward those who murder a member of their family, but the fact needs to be noted and dealt with. Second, the Freudian doctrine helps to explain why the primitive views of sin and punishment by fate embodied in Greek tragedy still move modern man. It tells us that even O'Neill's audience, "an intelligent audience of today, possessed of no belief in gods or supernatural retribution," had surviving in it from childhood some such beliefs or the emotions which corresponded to them. It tells us that not only do we harbor, at some level, the potentiality for the family-murdering acts of tragic heroes, but that we harbor conscience-feelings which would punish or destroy us for those acts regardless of whether such acts were a freewill choice of evil or whether they were determined so that we were not morally responsible for them.

Third, and most important, Freudianism not only helps explain, but it helps create tragedies. Among the best of modern tragedies have been those written self-consciously by Freudians intending to revivify the Greek formulae by psychoanalytic means, men like Eugene O'Neill and William Faulkner. Freudianism has served its literary purpose not merely by calling attention to recurrent universal themes of content in tragedy, but by creating a world view in which tragedy is meaningful within a scientifically oriented and morally relativistic culture. Faithful to necessities apparent in its early Athenian form, tragedy requires a crime to be committed which is both willed and unwilled; both free and foreordained, a fated act for which the actor is yet responsible. As tragic crime is foreordained but willed, so tragic punishment is both doom and self-discovery of evil. In Athenian tragedy, the fated aspects of crime and punishment were the result of cruel but moral external forces. In the modern "psychoanalytic" form of tragedy, the fated aspects of crime and punishment are the products of uncontrolled and unconscious internal forces. The crime is the fated result of immutable instinctual impulses; the inevitable doom which follows the crime is the result of unconscious and inescapable needs for punishment. Other "scientific" world views, such as the sociological determinism embodied in Dreiser's *An American Tragedy*, provide a sense of the inevitability of crime and punishment. This inevitability, however, is the product of purely external and amoral forces, and cannot be combined with the willed self-discovery and repentance characteristic of classic tragedy.

Thus the Freudian psychology is part of a Freudian world view which is itself largely tragic. It provides a context for tragedy in a scientific, rationalistic, and morally relative world.

Critics of tragedy who ignore the Freudian moral psychology do so at their peril; they run the risk of substituting moralizing about tragedies for understanding them. For instance, Olson says (pp. 237–243):

We had better recall O'Neill's purpose first: he was trying to write a modern psychological drama, with some approximation to the Greek sense of fate, so that an audience which no longer believed in gods or supernatural retribution might still have something like that sense, and be moved accordingly.

In comparison with the Greeks, however, we find a general debasement of character, motive, and action. We do not approve of Clytemnestra's crime, but we are compelled to respect her in the doing of it; we have the sense that horrible as her deed is, she thinks of it in some strange way as just and right. But it is impossible to have any respect whatsoever for Christine. True, O'Neill penetrates the moral pretexts of his characters, to reveal them as merely animal drives; but that penetration is itself a debasement. One cannot dignify human beings by regarding them as animals.

Suppose, then, that there are these debasements. What does it matter?

It matters a very great deal, so far as the seriousness of the action is concerned. O'Neill supposed that the seriousness of Greek tragedy depended upon belief in the gods, in divine intervention and retribution. He was completely mistaken. We regard as serious whatever can importantly affect our happiness or misery. It is that sense of tremendous importance which is effective, not the theology; and the proof of this is that "an intelligent audience of today, possessed of no belief in gods or supernatural retribution"—I am quoting O'Neill's description of the audience he thought he was addressing—is still profoundly moved by the Aeschylean drama.

And consequently the substitution of believed Freudian doctrines for unbelieved theology will not work. Such beliefs can have no great emotive force in themselves. They can affect us only as they relate to things which do have such force, to things which already embody the values of which I have been speaking. An animal drive or impulse, no matter how firmly we are convinced of its existence, can only affect us through our reflection on its capacity to produce goods and evils of a certain nature, magnitude, and duration.

I must conclude, therefore, that if tragedy displays an action of the utmost seriousness and significance, *Mourning Becomes Electra* is not a tragedy.

Of this we may say, first, that the basic fact cited by Olson, the fact that "an intelligent audience of today possessed of no belief in gods or supernatural retribution is still profoundly moved by the Aeschylean drama" is exactly the fact which supports O'Neill's Freudian psychology rather than refuting it. The fact that Athenian tragedy is still moving and not archaic is a fact which seems to require some form of the Freudian doctrine of the persistence in the modern unconscious of equivalents of the Greek beliefs. At least the effect of Greek tragedy is not explained by saying, with Olson, that it moves us "because it is serious." Second, we may say that Olson is wrong in claiming that O'Neill's plays do not arouse tragic emotion in many moderns, even if they fail to do so in Olson. Accordingly, it is incorrect to claim that "the substitution of believed Freudian doctrines for unbelieved theology will not work."

Nevertheless, we need to note that Olson is correct in claiming that O'Neill tragedy is not ultimate tragedy in the sense in which Greek, Shakespearian, or Russian tragedy is ultimate tragedy, and that it fails to be such because it fails to grapple with moral meaning and simply accepts, ultimately, an amoral cosmos in which human morality is merely the neurotic fate of a social animal. Only a philosophy and psychology which invests human morality with rationality and meaning, and then pits morality against a human fate of death and injustice, is one that can create an ultimate tragedy.

Such a philosophy and psychology, we call "cognitive-developmental" (Kohlberg, 1969). It was born in Hegelian German idealism, but became naturalistic and scientific in America with John Dewey, William James, and James Mark Baldwin, in Russia with Vygotsky, and in Switzerland with Piaget. Its best statement as a general philosophy and psychology of art comes in Dewey's *Art as Experience*. Unlike Freudianism, developmental psychology stresses universal mental structures or forms, structures which develop through invariant stages. These structures come into positions of conflict or contradiction with one another, and it is the conflict of these forms and their integration (rather than conflicts between hydraulic emotional forces) which is the soul of art, and of tragedy.

In the case of tragedy, the critical structures in conflict are *forms of moral thought or judgment*. In the Freudian view, the characters in drama represent the warring forces in the personality, the forces of impulse (id), conscience (superego), and of cognition or reason (ego). These forces have a certain developmental order, the id being most primitive, the superego next, the ego most mature. In contrast, the cognitive-developmental theory of personality sees all developmental stages of personality as having a moral component. There is an impulsive morality, but it is still a morality, not an "id"; there is a rational cognitive morality, but it is still a morality, not an ego. The personality is unitary; cognition and affect join in single structures rather than being divided into separate organs of impulse (id) and cognition (ego). While the personality is unitary, it progresses through stages in a sequential order. Here we draw upon our theory and findings concerning stages of moral development (Kohlberg, 1968, 1969, 1971; Kohlberg and Turiel, 1973). These stages are defined in Table 1 (see pp. 47ff.), together with quotations from dramatic characters to represent them. The stages are culturally universal.

By following a group of 50 American boys from childhood through adulthood, longitudinally, and by studying individuals of different ages in a variety of cultures (Mexico, Taiwan, Israel, Turkey), we have been able to demonstrate that moral stages are sequential and invariant, that insofar as moral change occurs it is movement from one stage to the next in a sequence.

Not only are the moral stages culturally universal, but they correspond to a progression in cultural history. Principled moral thinking appeared first in human history in the period 600–400 B.C., when universal human ideals and rational criticism of customary morality developed in Greece, Palestine, India, and China. A sequence in historical and cultural evolution generally consistent with the stages of individual development was traced by Hobhouse (1906) using ethnographic material.

Because our stages are culturally universal, they are relevant to the analysis of literature in any culture or historical era. Besides their universality, there is another property which makes them relevant to literary analysis. Our stages define moral types not only for the psychologist, but for the common consciousness. Individuals intuitively understand and recognize all moral stages below their own, though not above their own. It has been found (Rest, 1973) that individuals can correctly transpose or state moral judgments at any level up to their own, but distort higher moral levels downward. Finally, individuals show a hierarchical preference among the moral stages, most preferring the highest stage they comprehend. (See Kohlberg and Turiel, 1973.)

In summary, then, the development of morality generates moral structures which are conscious and cognitive, though they also have an emotional component. These structures are filters determining the writer's and the audience's perception of the characters and action of a drama. We retain all lower moral structures, but subordinate them to higher structures. A low comedy in which the "hero" amorally outwits his enemies depends upon the survival of a Stage 2 instrumental egoistic system of morality in each of us; a soap opera depends upon the survival in us of a Stage 3 "be nice," "be loving" moral system in which "goodness leads to happiness." More complex literature embodies these types of moral thought in characters but lets no type of moral thought triumph in a simple way. Ketto (1956) says:

While tragedy does not represent the triumph of a single higher moral point of view, there is an element of moral development, of movement to a higher stage of moral judgment, in the tragic process in which "wisdom comes alone through suffering." This is perhaps most apparent in the classic Greek tragedies. In these tragedies there is a development or "education" of the chorus itself. This is especially evident in Aeschylus' Oresteia trilogy which represents a movement from the endless cycle of blood retaliation to a morality of civic union and order. The progression represents the movement from the stage of morality of arbitrary taboo based on kinship, supported by tradition and by blood-atonement [corresponding to our Stage 1] to more universal norms of a civic order [corresponding to our Stage 4] supported by loyalty to the state and by impartial punishment in rational support of this order.

The modes of thought represented correspond rather exactly to Hobhouse's stages of moral evolution of cultures, less exactly to our parallel stages of individual development. (A comparison of the Guard in *Antigone*, a "childish" Stage 1, as quoted in Table 1, with the Oresteian chorus suggests the difference between a cultural and an individual Stage 1.) The morality of each of the choruses in the Agamemnon trilogy is a morality of Stage 1 orientation or blood-atonement. The chorus of the *Agamemnon* says, "The truth stands ever beside God's throne eternal, he who has wrought shall pay; that is law."

The chorus of the Libation Bearers says: "For the word of hatred spoken, let hate be a word fulfilled. The spirit of Right cries out aloud and extracts atonement due: blood stroke for the stroke of blood shall be paid."

The ultimate embodiment of blood atonement is the chorus of the Eumenides who say: "You must give back for blood from the living man red blood of your body."

Associated with the morality orientation of blood-atonement is a Stage 1 conception of moral rules as particular taboos linked to blood kinship. The Furies explain that Clytemnestra's murder of Agamemnon was not as evil as Orestes' murder of his mother because "the man she killed was not of blood congenital."

A third characteristic of the Stage 1 morality of the Oresteian chorus is the belief in a morality based on fear. The Eumenides (*Agamemnon*) say:

Here is overthrow of all the young laws, if the claim of this matricide shall stand good, his crime be sustained.
Should this be, every man will find a way to act at his own caprice; there are times when fear is good.
Should the city, should the man rear a heart that nowhere goes in fear, how shall such a one anymore respect the right?

The conclusion of the trilogy, of course, is acceptance of a "new morality" of civic order by the chorus of the Eumenides:

Let not the dry dust that drinks the black blood of citizens through passion for revenge and for bloodshed be given our state to prey upon. Let them render grace for grace. Let love be their common will; let them hate with single heart. Much wrong in the world thereby is healed.

This new morality is, of course, the Stage 4 civic morality which decries blood-atonement for the sake of the state and for civic unity. It is important to recognize that the core moral concern in Aeschylean tragedy, and indeed in all tragedy, is justice.

As Neitzsche tells us (1871, p. 228):

The most wonderful thing is the Aeschylean yearning for *justice*. The double personality of the Aeschylean Prometheus might be expressed in the abstract formula: "Whatever exists is alike just and unjust, and in both cases equally justified."

While in one sense justice is synonomous with morality, in another sense it represents a specific issue defining moral stages. In addition to the issues of Justice (Punitive Justice, Positive Commutative Justice or Reciprocity, and Distributive Justice) issues such as Law, Life, Property, Authority, Conscience, define our moral stages. We characterized the Eumenides as being Stage 1 on Law (Arbitrary Taboo) and conscience (Fear of Punishment) as well as on Punitive Justice (Talion). The central issue in the Oresteia, however, is the Justice issue.

It is important to note the centrality of justice because "the wisdom learned through suffering" in tragedy is not the wisdom of a generally higher stage of morality but a new attitude toward justice.

If the Orestes does, in a sense, represent a movement to, or a triumph of, a higher morality over a lower morality, this is not generally the case in Greek tragedy. The tragedies of Sophocles represent a tragic hero whose moral error is still an expression of, or connected with the hero's Stage 4 conventional civic morality. The Stage 4 civic morality which terminates the Oresteia is the source of strain and tragedy in Sophocles. The Oedipus cycle commences with Oedipus endeavoring to search out, to curse and to punish the murderer of Laius, and doing this in the name of his responsibility for civic order.

The termination of *Oedipus the King* comes with his fulfillment of that punishment against himself. Starting in *Oedipus at Colonus* and moving through the *Antigone* is the story of the destruction of Creon because of Creon's prideful civic morality and his use of it to justify punitiveness. In Table 1 we quoted Creon's speech as an embodiment of Stage 4 civic morality. In the passage Creon: *a.* asserts loyalty to the state as the highest value, *b.* asserts the need to punish and discipline all who do not hold this loyalty, and *c.* equates civic loyalty with discipline and obedience in the family as well as the state and justifies such discipline as necessary to avoid civic disorder.

Creon uses this civic-order morality to justify his own punitiveness. Antigone's morality, which he denies, is a morality of loyalty to kinship and to the Gods who support the norms of kinship. Antigone's morality, while it questions Creon's man-made law, is not a morality of conscience or principle. She says:

Nor did I think your orders were so strong that you, a mortal man, could over-run the gods' unwritten and unfailing laws. So not through fear of any man's proud request would I be likely to neglect these laws, and draw on myself the gods' sure punishment.

Her morality is essentially like that of the Jehovah's Witness who refuses to be drafted, or pledge the flag, or have a blood transfusion, because of God's word and God's authority. The nature of this morality is not conscience but respect for authority and divine sanction. The norms of the morality are not universal principles of human justice and welfare, but respect for the dead expressed in maintaining concrete and arbitrary rules. It is essentially a Stage 4 morality of divine order rather than of civic order.

Creon's blindness, then, was not a blindness to a higher justice, it was the blindness of taking justice into his own hands in the name of civic morality. In the *Antigone*, as in every tragedy, the hero acts out of a misplaced sense of justice. The "lesson" the hero learns through suffering is that he has no right to demand justice or enforce it on others. If he enforces punitive justice on others, he punishes those he loves most and so, eventually, himself. In the *Antigone*, Creon finds that his "justice" leads to the suicide of his wife and son, and only then learns true justice. The *Antigone* ends with Creon:

O crimes of my wicked heart, harshness bringing death.
You see the killer, you see the son he killed.
For you have died too soon.
Oh, you have gone away
Through my fault, not your own.
    Chorus:
You have learned justice, though it comes too late.

We have considered Greek tragedy as embodied in the Agamemnon and the Oedipus cycles. They start with a world in disorder and a tragic hero who will bring order into the world by a passionate act of "justice" where justice is a punitive reaction at one or another moral stage. This act of justice ends by destroying either someone the hero loves or himself, or both. The "wisdom" the hero learns is "judge not, lest you be judged." This wisdom does not bring the hero to the principled moral stage, it only leads him to recognize the error of his misplaced demand for justice.

It is characteristic of almost all tragedies that their heroes are men of conventional morality. An example of a drama with a hero above conventional morality, a principled hero, is Bolt's *A Man for All Seasons*. As quoted in Table 1, the hero, Thomas More, illustrates Stage 6 (or 5B). The drama appeals to our Stage 6 sense of principles of conscience and reaffirms them. A Stage 6 man goes to his death willingly in the service of his principles. The drama is not a tragedy, it is a reaffirmation of Stage 6. It tells us that a man of principle will die for his beliefs and die in calmness. In so doing, it reaffirms our faith in moral principles and in the potential nobility of man. It is not a tragedy because a principled or State 6 hero is one who is able to live with the consequences of his action; there is no wisdom he can attain through suffering; his suffering may redeem others, but he needs no redemption himself. The emotion aroused by *A Man for All Seasons* is similar to that aroused in the *Crito*, by Socrates' calm acceptance of death on behalf of principle (as cited in Table 1). Of this death, Phaedo tells us:

> I could hardly believe that I was present at the death of a friend, and therefore I did not pity him; his mien and language were so noble and fearless in the hour of death that to me he appeared blessed. I was pleased and I was also pained because I knew that he was soon to die and this strange mixture of feelings was shared by us all.

Phaedo's emotion is one response to the death of a principled man; blind shock, as at the death of Martin Luther King, is another. In the first case the emphasis is upon the principled man's acceptance of his fate, in the second case on its wanton undeservedness. In neither case is the reaction that of classical tragedy.

Not only is the hero of a tragedy not initially principled, but the wisdom he learns through suffering is not the wisdom of a higher or principled morality.

The problem tragedy faces is the problem of justice, but the tragic wisdom is not a higher principle of justice, a "right principle," or a better "system of moral values" in Olson's terms. The tragic wisdom is rather religious; it is the resignation of the demand for justice in order to accept life in a cosmos which is just in no humanly understandable sense.

To clarify that the tragic wisdom is the resignation of the demand for personal justice and the acceptance of a cosmos which is both just and unjust, let us turn to Shakespearian tragedy. Shakespearian characters are more concerned with personal justice and less concerned with civic morality justice than the characters of Greek tragedy. As in Greek tragedy, the Shakespearian tragic hero is a person of pride and strength as well as passion, and the tragic action is a result of moral error rather than loss of self-control. It is an act he believes is morally right when he commits it, and only later comes to see as morally wrong. The act in each case is a vengeful act to the person the hero most loves. In Lear, the act is cutting Cordelia out of her estate and his life; in Othello, murder. In both cases, these acts are performed not out of sheer passion, but in the illusion of acting morally in the name of justice to correct the loved one's ingratitude or unfaithfulness. The tragedy terminates with the death of both the loved ones and the self. This termination, however, involves a mutual forgiveness and a recognition of the supremacy of love over justice. It is in this context that forgiveness, the "judge not, lest ye be judged," is presented.

CORDELIA: We are not the first
Who, with best meaning, have incurred the worst.

LEAR: No, no, no, no! Come, let's away to prison;
We two alone will sing like birds i' the cage:
When thou dost ask me blessing I'll kneel down,
And ask of thee forgiveness; so we'll live,
And pray, and sing, and tell old tales, and laugh
At gilded butterflies, and hear poor rogues
Talk of court news; and we'll talk with them too,
Who loses and who wins; who's in, who's out;
And take upon 's the mystery of things,
As if we were God's spies, and we'll wear out,
In a wall'd prison, packs and sets of great ones
That ebb and flow by the moon.

EDMOND: Take them away.

LEAR: Upon such sacrifices, my Cordelia,
The gods themselves throw incense.

Lear tells us not only that he willingly renounces all desire for an influence in state affairs to "ask and give forgiveness," but suggests that he and Cordelia "talk of court news . . . as if we were God's spies." He does not believe in divine justice, he is not one of God's spies, but he renounces his demand for justice, for understanding the mystery of things which dictates who loses, who wins.

We have so far stressed the morality of the protagonists in tragedy, and have only indirectly stressed the morality of the fate which befalls them. On this, it is useful to summarize A. C. Bradley's comments on the Shakespearian view of fate or justice as "alike just and unjust":

In this tragic world, then, where individuals, however great they may be and however decisive their actions may appear, are so evidently not the ultimate power, *what is this power?* It will be agreed that this question must not be answered in "religious" language. Two statements, next, may at once be made regarding the tragic fact as he represents it: one that it is and remains to us something piteous fearful and mysterious; the other, that the representation of it does not leave us crushed, rebellious or desperate. The ultimate power in the tragic world is not adequately described as a law or order which we can see to be just and benevolent,—as, in that sense, a "moral order": for in that case the spectacle of suffering and waste could not seem to us so fearful and mysterious as it does. Neither is the ultimate power adequately described as a fate, whether malicious and cruel, or blind and indifferent to human happiness and goodness; for in that case the spectacle would leave us desperate or rebellious. Yet one or other of these two ideas will be found to govern most accounts of Shakespeare's tragic view or world. These accounts isolate and exaggerate single aspects, either the aspect of action or that of suffering; either the close and unbroken connection of character, will, deed and catastrophe, which, taken alone, shows the individual simply as sinning against, or failing to conform to, the moral order and drawing his just doom on his own head; or else that pressure of outward forces, that sway of accident, and those blind and agonized struggles, which, taken alone, show him as the mere victim of some power which cares neither for his sins nor for his pain.

The sense in which the ultimate power in the tragic world is moral may be argued as follows:

Whatever may be said of accidents, circumstances and the like, human action is, after all, presented to us as the central fact in tragedy, and also as the main cause of the catastrophe. That necessity which so much impresses us is, after all, chiefly the necessary connection of actions and consequences. For these actions we, without even raising a question on the subject, hold the agents responsible; and the tragedy would disappear for us if we did not. The critical action is, in greater or less degree, wrong or bad. The catastrophe is, in the main, the return of this action on the head of the agent. It is an example of justice; and that order which, present alike within the agents and outside them, infallibly brings it about, is therefore just. The rigour of its justice is terrible, no doubt, for a tragedy is a terrible story; but, in spite of fear and pity, we acquiesce, because our sense of justice is satisfied.

Now, if this view is to hold good, the "justice" of which it speaks must be at once distinguished from what is called "poetic justice." We might not object to the statement that Lear deserved to suffer for his folly, selfishness and tyranny; but to assert that he deserved to suffer what he did suffer is to do violence not merely to language but to any healthy moral sense. It is, moreover, to obscure the tragic fact that the consequences of action cannot be limited to that which would appear to us to follow "justly" from them. The idea which this suggests, is that of an order which does not, indeed, award "poetic justice," but which reacts through the necessity of its own "moral" nature both against attacks made upon it and against failure to conform to it. Tragedy, on this view, is the exhibition of that convulsive reaction; and the fact that the spectacle does not leave us rebellious or desperate is due to a more or less distinct perception that the tragic suffering and death arise from collision, not with a fate or blank power, but with a moral power, a power akin to all that we admire and revere in the characters themselves. This perception produces something like a feeling of acquiescence in the catastrophe, though it neither leads us to pass judgment on the characters nor diminishes the pity, the fear, and the sense of waste, which their struggle, suffering and fall evoke. And, finally, this view seems quite able to do justice to those aspects of the tragic fact which give rise to the idea of fate. They would appear as various expressions of the fact that the moral order acts not capriciously or like a human being, but from the necessity of its nature, or, if we prefer the phrase, by general laws,—a necessity or law which, of course, knows no exception and is as "ruthless" as fate.

Bradley here attempts to present the Shakespearian cosmos as a representation of the Hegelian world-order. But the essential statement is accurate, the statement that the tragic world is neither just and moral nor is it morally neutral. In our own view, this view of the cosmos as both just and unjust is an expression of the fact that the human sense of justice is a universal natural emergent in life; it rests on "natural law" in the sense that it is not the arbitrary creation of culture and training. Just because it is "natural," human morality comes into painful and sharp contrast with society's law or society's justice. Just that contrast proves that it has its source in a larger cosmic "law."

While the sense of justice is natural, nature or fate is not bent on reward for justice or morality. The world order, then, is one which has established man's sense of justice and then left it in conflict with the forces of nature and society. In that sense, our view is much closer to Bradley's Hegelian view than to psychoanalytic views of conscience as a cultural creation to restrain amoral impulses, and in that sense, our view of morality supports a larger vision of the "tragic fact" which is still compatible with science.

If what we have said is correct, modern tragedy should present a new vision of the "tragic fact." In Greek and Shakespearian tragedy, the tragic hero's misguided struggle for justice is generated from a conventional morality. The fate which strikes him down, like the hero's own demand for justice, is both just and unjust; and like the hero's, is expressive of the framework of a conventional morality of civic and cosmic order. The modern literary consciousness is one increasingly aware of principled morality, but as we have noted, a principled hero does not make a tragedy. A modern tragic hero, then, will be one who expresses the demand for a justice at a level intermediate between conventional and principled morality, at the level where he can make a principled demand for justice but does not really accept or live by principles. The writer who has most clearly expressed this conception of the tragic hero is Dostoevsky.

If the problem of tragedy is the problem of justice, it reaches its ultimate ideological statement for modern man in Dostoevsky. Dostoevsky's parricidal tragic hero, Ivan Karamazov, says:

With my pitiful, earthly, Euclidian understanding, all I know is that there is suffering and that there are none guilty; that cause follows effect, simply and directly; that everything flows and finds its level—but that's only Euclidian nonsense, I know that, and I can't consent to live by it! What comfort is it to me that there are none guilty and that cause follows effect simply and directly, and that I know it—I must have justice, or I will destroy myself. And not justice in some remote infinite time and space, but here on earth, and that I could see myself.

I understand, of course, what an upheaval of the universe it will be, when everything in heaven and earth blends in one hymn of praise and everything that lives and has lived cries aloud: "Thou art just, O Lord, for Thy ways are revealed." But it's not worth the tears of one tortured child who beat itself on the breast with its little fist and prayed in its stinking outhouse, with its unexpiated tears to "dear, kind God"! It's not worth it, because those tears are unatoned for. They must be atoned for, or there can be no harmony. But how? The sufferings of her tortured child the mother has no right to forgive; she dare not forgive the torturer, even if the child were to forgive him! And if that is so, if they dare not forgive, what becomes of harmony? Is there in the whole world a being who would have the right to forgive and could forgive? I don't want harmony. From love for humanity I don't want it. I would rather remain with my unavenged suffering and unsatisfied indignation, *even if I were wrong*. Besides, too high a price is asked for harmony; it's beyond our means to pay so much to enter on it. And so I hasten to give back my entrance ticket, and if I am an honest man I am bound to give it back as soon as possible. And that I am doing. It's not God that I don't accept, Alyosha, only I most respectfully return Him the ticket.

In one way, Ivan Karamazov has stated the problem of justice in a way which is insolvable. The culmination of moral development is the formation of universal principles of justice before which the law of society is brought to the bar, as in Martin Luther King's statement in Table 1. The construction of moral principles is the construction of ideals which are independent of social and cosmic reality, and by which reality is itself judged. Awareness of moral principle implies an ultimate division or gap between the Is and the Ought, the Real and the Ideal. Ivan Karamazov tells us that "God's law" heals this gap no more than "society's law." Even if there is a God, a moral power in the universe, His morality is not our morality because He has made an unjust world. No Kingdom of Heaven can atone for the injustice of this world.

The problem of the world's justice as it is raised in the name of autonomous moral principle can be compared with the problem as it is raised in the name of conventional (Stage 4) morality in the Book of Job. Job asked Ivan Karamazov's question of justice, but he asked it egocentrically. Job asked the justice question, "Why me? Why should an upright man like me suffer?" Job's morality was a law-maintaining morality premised on divine reward and punishment, or eventually on respect for divine authority. Ultimately, then, Job can be satisfied with God's answer, a reassertion of his authority:

Where wast thou when I laid the foundations of the earth
Declare if thou hast understanding,
Wilt thou disavow my judgment?
Wilt thou condemn me, that thou mayest be justified?

The Book of Job, then, is in a sense an assertion of the "higher" elements in Stage 4 law—maintaining morality. Satan induces Jehovah to test whether Job's uprightness is based on divine reward, or whether it will be maintained in the face of disaster. While Job's morality is not based simply on divine reward and punishment (Stage 1 in our terms) his morality is partly contingent on divine justice, on some equation between uprightness and the events of fate. This contingency is stripped away, leaving a morality of respect for divine authority which no longer demands "justice" because justice is limited, egocentric, human desire for rewards according to one's own scales.

For moderns such as Dostoevsky, the question of justice asked at the principle level cannot be answered by the revelation of a divine authority in the cosmos.

Dostoevsky, of course, attempts to provide a number of answers to the question. One is Christian, that "there is a being who would have the right to forgive and could forgive." But he attempts to answer the question also along the lines of classical tragedy. He claims, that is, that when the sense of justice of the tragic hero dares to go beyond or to violate civil law and religious faith, it leads the hero to murder and self-destruction, in Ivan's case to the classic crime of parricide. The tragic hero's principled sense of justice in Dostoevsky is fused with the notion that morality is relative and arbitrary, with a consequent sense of being beyond good and evil.

In understanding Dostoevsky's tragic heroes, it is helpful to understand that they have real-life counterparts understandable in terms of moral stages. Our longitudinal work has demonstrated that there is a twilight zone in the movement from conventional to principled moral thought. A prerequisite to moving from conventional to principled morality is awareness of the relativity of conventional morality. In the ordinary course of development, dissatisfaction with the arbitrariness of conventional morality leads the individual to search for, or construct, more universal and autonomous ethical principles. A number of the youths we have studied, however, do not move directly from conventional to principled thought. Instead, becoming aware of the relativity of conventional morality, they assume that all possible moralities are relative and arbitrary, that there is no validity to judgments of right and good. These subjects generally oscillate, like Dostoevsky's heroes, between railing at society's injustice and the assertion that all concepts of morality and justice are relative. Sometimes, like Dostoevsky's heroes, they not only question, but they commit crimes to prove they are beyond morality (Kohlberg and Kramer, 1969). Longitudinal study indicates that most of the students eventually progress to principled morality, and indicates that their moral questioning and "crimes" are only transitional to a higher morality.

In Dostoevsky's works, the moral ambivalence and ambiguity of the hero requires that he have a double who collaborates in his crime and who is truly amoral (Kohlberg, 1967). Parallel to Ivan is Smerdyakov, to Raskolnikov, Svidrigailov, to Shatov, Stavrogin. These figures both tempt or lead the tragic hero into crime and reveal that behind their sense of justice, which justifies crime, is not justice but amoralism. The doubles themselves are uninterested in justice and are completely amoral. These figures, too, have their real-life counterparts. In addition to adolescents in ambivalent passage to moral principle, there is another group of individuals in the twilight zone. These individuals, all extremely bright, never fully comprehend or believe in conventional morality and are primarily Stage 2 instrumental egoists throughout early adolescence. In late adolescence, they, too, philosophically discover the relativity of conventional morality. Rather than being torn between demands for justice and amoralism, they use relativity to freeze and harden their basic posture of Stage 2 instrumental egoism.

These individuals, if delinquent, tend to be consistently delinquent rather than to be ideologically delinquent. Thus there are real-life counterparts of Dostoevsky's doubles. An example is the Leopold-Loeb pair in which Leopold was a neurotic transitional figure moving from conventional to principled morality and Loeb was a genuinely amoral instrumental egoist. (In real life, as in Dostoevsky's novel, there was a homosexual counterpart to this ideological alliance.)

Because Dostoevsky's heroes are post-conventional though not principled, and because of their relations to their doubles, Dostoevsky's novels do not fit the formula of tragedy applicable to Greek or Shakespearian drama. But it should be recognized that, ultimately, Dostoevsky presents, like all tragedians, a tragic hero who violates law in a passionate demand for justice. This demand leads him to kill those he loves, to recognize that he was not free or informed, and to recognize that one cannot judge, lest one be judged.

In spite of the complexity of ideology in Dostoevsky's novels, then, his most essential tragic effects, like Shakespeare's, depend on the emotions aroused by the tragic hero's murder, directly or indirectly, of someone he loves. The demand for justice, the questioning of good and evil, can lead only to a murder, which in the end, reasserts the supremacy of love over justice. The tragic hero overvalues justice, and his own honor connected with it, and this leads him to destroy those he loves. In the termination, the hero and the audience recognize the primacy of love over justice, and the hero is willing, too late, to accept life under terms he originally rejected.

In contradiction to the psychoanalytic view, we have presented a view of tragedy as an enactment in moral character, action and fate a dialectic (a sort of ballet) of Hegelian ideas centering around the problem of justice, and have used our moral stages and types to translate moral ideas into characters and action. We have also, however, recognized that the central action of tragedy involves the murder of someone one loves, and suggested the relevance of Freudian ideas to this fact. The fact suggests that the tragic action involves the ultimate primary emotional conflict, the conflict between emotions of love and hate, and their resolution. To understand this aspect of tragedy we need, however, to arrive at a broader notion of emotional conflict and its resolution through catharsis than that presented in the Freudian view. This notion is sketched out in Vygotsky's youthful *Psychology of Art*, in a way compatible with the cognitive-developmental psychology on which our moral theory is based. Vygotsky's theory of catharsis is a general theory of aesthetic conflict, rather than one which depends upon the assumption of repressed impulses and ideas. Vygotsky claims (p. 217) that:

Contradiction is the essential feature of artistic forms and materials. The essential part of aesthetic response is the manifestation of the affective contradiction designated *cartharsis*.*

Vygotsky points out, like the Freudians, the components of catharsis which involve repressed passions:

---

*Excerpts from *The Psychology of Art* by L. S. Vygotsky are reprinted by kind permission of the M.I.T. Press, Cambridge, Massachusetts.

The possibility of releasing into art powerful passions which cannot find expression in moral everyday behavior is the biological basis of art.

Tragedy awakens our most hidden passions, forces them to flow within banks of granite made of completely opposite feelings, and ends this struggle with a catharsis of resolution. The hero feels contradictory passions in the course of the play and we feel contradictory passions toward him. We cannot discharge these passions through action as the hero does; we wait while opposing affects are generated and collide, leading to cathartic discharge.

While a protagonist always fights objects, laws, or forces, the various types of drama are distinguished by what he actually opposes. In tragedy he fights inflexible, absolute laws; in comedy he usually fights social laws; and in farce he struggles against physiological laws. The protagonist of a drama is therefore a character who combines two conflicting effects, that of the norm and that of its violation; this is why we perceive him dynamically, not as an object but as a process. This becomes particularly obvious if we look at the various types of drama. Hence, the prime characteristic of tragedy is maximalism, or the violation of absolute law by absolute strength of heroic struggle.

Because of this fact, Vygotsky claims that inherent contradictions in character are necessary for tragic art (p. 229):

The character of Othello himself is only a point of encounter for the two opposing affects. Let us take a look at the hero. If Shakespeare wanted to describe a tragedy of jealousy, he should have chosen a jealous man, put him together with a woman who would provide him with a motive, and finally would have established between them a relationship in which jealousy could become the inevitable and inseparable companion of love. Instead, he chooses characters and material which make the solution of his problem extremely difficult. "Othello is not jealous by nature; on the contrary, he is trustful," remarked Pushkin. Indeed, Othello's trustfulness is one of the mainsprings of the tragedy. Everything proceeds because Othello is trusting and because there is not a streak of jealousy in his nature. In fact, his character is utterly opposed to that of a jealous person. Similarly, Desdemona is not the type of woman who would cause blind jealousy in a man. Many critics even find her too idealized and pure. Finally, the most important point—Othello's and Desdemona's love appears so platonic that one might think they never really consummated their marriage. The tragedy reaches its climax: the trusting Othello, now violently jealous, kills the innocent Desdemona. The "flight of a machine heavier than air," with which a work of art was compared, is triumphantly achieved in Othello, where the tragedy evolves in two opposing directions and generates conflicting emotions in us. Each step, each action, drags us lower, to abject treason and treachery, while at the same time lifting us to the heights of an ideal character, so that the collision and cathartic purification of the two opposite affects engendered becomes the basis of the tragedy.

We should not look for realism or consistency in character portrayal in tragedy, then; a character need not display "usefulness, appropriateness, likeness, and consistency." The tragic hero is not a realistic type that a psychologist might describe; he must represent humanity in conflict. The resolution of conflict is catharsis.

Catharsis expresses the central fact of aesthetic reaction, according to which painful and unpleasant effects are discharged and transformed into their opposites. Aesthetic reaction as such is nothing but catharsis, that is, a complex transformation of feelings. Though little is known at present about the process of catharsis, we do know, however, that the discharge of nervous energy (which is the essence of any emotion) takes place in a direction which opposes the conventional one, and that art therefore becomes a most powerful means for important and appropriate discharges of nervous energy. But, then, in any work of art there are emotions generated by the material as well as the form; the question is: How do these two kinds of emotion interrelate to each other? We already know the answer, for it derives from our preceding arguments. This relation is one of antagonism; the two kinds of emotion move in opposite directions. The law of aesthetic response is the same for a fable as for a tragedy: *it comprises an affect that develops in two opposite directions but reaches annihilation at its point of termination.*

Finally, Vygotsky stresses the importance of *cognitive* transformation in catharsis. Catharsis is a "transformation and clarification of feeling." Catharsis is not the mere release of energy or passion, it is the overcoming of it:

A sincere feeling taken per se cannot create art. To do this we require the creative overcoming the feeling, resolving it, conquering it. The perception of art requires creativity; it is not enough to experience the feelings of the author; to understand the structure of the work of art, one must also creatively overcome one's own feelings and find one's own catharsis.

It is at this point that emotional conflict theories of catharsis join with the consideration of moral ideas we have outlined in this paper. It is only when the contradictory emotions generated in the course of the dramatic action of tragedy can be resolved with the sense of "Justice so moves that man learns wisdom only through suffering" that the tragic effect is attained.

What is the distinction between Vygotsky's cognitive-developmental doctrine of catharsis and that of Aristotle and Freud? Both doctrines present catharsis as the therapeutic discharge of negative emotion. As Raphael (1960, p. 15) has pointed out, "Aristotle's doctrine is an answer to Plato's criticism of tragedy in *The Republic*. Tragic drama calls forth pity for the distress of its heroes, and this, Plato thinks, will render us liable to self-pity, instead of endurance, when we meet misfortune ourselves. Pity is therefore antagonistic to virtue and the attempt to control pity requires the banishment of the art that fosters it." Accordingly, Raphael notes (p. 82), Plato replaces tragedy with a philosophic tragedy best represented by the trilogy of the death of Socrates (*Apology, Crito, Phaedo*). It has the theme of tragedy, the death of a hero; it has the form of tragic drama, prologue, episodes and choruses. But its effect is intended to be different. Phaedo says, "I did *not pity him* . . . he appeared blessed." In contrast (p. 15): "Aristotle seeks to defend tragedy while retaining Plato's criterion of justification. Harmful emotions must have some outlet; better to let them boil up at mere representation, and then the soul will be less troubled by them on real occasions of misfortune. Aristotle disagrees with Plato about the psychological effect of exciting emotion. In opposition to Plato's view that the capacity for emotion grows with exercise, Aristotle puts forth the doctrine that when our feelings are stirred we blow off steam and so are 'purged.' "

As we have noted, Aristotle's doctrine of catharsis received a powerful new interpretation through Freudian psychology, in which tragedy was seen as the discharge of the negative emotions of antisocial lust and anger and primitive guilt. The debate between Plato and Aristotle as to whether artistic portrayal of negative emotions strengthens them by exercise or weakens them through catharsis has recently been a debate between behaviorists, supporting the Platonic notion, and the Freudians, supporting the Aristotelian notion, and has led to intense experimental inquiry by psychologists studying aggression, effects of the mass media, and so forth (Bandura, 1963; Maccoby, 1965). The results on the whole support the behaviorists and Platonists, and give little comfort to the doctrine of catharsis.

Neither the Platonic-behavioristic or the Aristotelian-Freudian doctrines, then, adequately explain the positive emotional effects of tragedy. As Vygotsky stresses, catharsis is not the purgation of negative feeling, it is "the creative overcoming of the feeling, resolving it, conquering it, the transformation of the feeling into its opposite." This transformation depends upon a conflict "between the violation of absolute law by absolute strength of heroic struggle." This notion is clarified by Raphael (1960, p. 25) who says:

Tragedy always represents a conflict between inevitable power or necessity and the reaction to necessity of self-conscious effort. In the case of tragedy victory always goes to necessity. The tragic hero, however, attracts our admiration because of some grandeur of spirit, a greatness in his effort to resist and our pity for his defeat. The inner conflict of tragedy is between the two forms of the sublime, the awe-inspiring strength of necessity and the grandeur of spirit which inspires admiration. Each triumphs on its own plane.

In our terms, both Fate and the hero are both just and unjust, both are in unresolvable conflict, both are (or achieve) a sublimity above justice.

More specifically, beneath the demand for justice of the hero is hatred and the desire for *death* of another and ultimately the self. Beneath the working of fate is another "justice" which equally represents the force of death. The force of death in the hero leads him in seeking vengeance or "justice" to hurt or kill those he loves. Once he has killed those he loves, he is ready to die himself. Equally, the force of death or Fate kills not only the evil "villain," but the innocent and lovable. In the end, then, the "catharsis" of tragedy is the transformation of emotions of hatred (demand for death of others) and of grief or fear of death into their opposite, love of life. The ultimate emotional source of tragedy is the fact of death, of the unfulfilled desire for immortality (Unamona, 1954). The ultimate demand of justice is the demand that the just shall be immortal. The ultimate tragic fact is that death comes alike to the just and the unjust. Most religious ideologies of divine justice and of immortality deny this tragic fact, and so are inconsistent with tragedy. We have pointed to the fact that the modern consciousness, resting on autonomous human principles of justice and a scientific view of man's mortality, implies a tragic view of life. The effect of tragedy is to abandon our demand for justice, but it is also to abandon our demand for immortality and to love life as it is while accepting death. Tragedy achieves this emotional effect without religious ideology. It presents an unsolvable conflict without an intellectual solution. The fact that an emotional solution is reached without an intellectual solution is what is meant by the mystery of "catharsis." It is what is meant in recognizing that tragedy and its characters are more than our Hegelian ballet of moral ideas around the theme of justice. Tragedy involves emotional conflict as well as intellectual conflict between ideas. In the psychology of Vygotsky and Dewey, however, emotional conflict: (a) has a cognitive component, and (b) leads to transformation and development of emotion, not mere purgation.

Let me, then, summarize the argument. Agreeing with Aristotle and his modern interpreter, Olson, we found tragedy to be a representation of moral action by a hero with a determinate moral character leading to a moral emotion of catharsis. This catharsis was not a mere purging of pity and fear but was a new and in some sense higher attitude to the moral qualities of life: it was a moral insight. We found ourselves, however, unable to explain the moral insight on the basis of the Aristotelian moral psychology and moral philosophy which identify morality with habits of virtue and vice and with prudential practical wisdom.

We turned then to the Freudian moral psychology of unconscious loves and hates in the family as these generate a conflict between impulse and conscience-guilt. In this psychology, the tragic crime, usually a murder of someone in the family, is one which arouses pity (or identification) and fear because it is one which the spectator has unconsciously fantasied. The tragic crime leads to extreme punishment by fate which is both just and unjust because it is a crime which arouses the spectator's own superego, his primitive sense of guilt. The tragedy ends with a reconciliation or integration of impulse and conscience in the spectator on this basis.

We found the Freudian psychology illuminating, but unable to cope with the conscious cognitive component of the moral insight involved in the tragic effect. We found it unsatisfactory also in its description of characters as stock representations of ego, superego and id. These defects became apparent when Freudian psychology is used, as by O'Neill, to write tragedy as well as to psychologize about it. There is a weakness in the moral insight of modern Freudian tragedy because its fundamental view is that there is no moral wisdom except the wisdom that morality is the fate of a social animal bound by the arbitrary, relative standards of his culture.

Accordingly, we turned to the cognitive-developmental moral psychology which defines universal stages of moral ideology. We found this psychology gave us a better description or typology of dramatic characters than did the Aristotelian psychology of habit or the Freudian psychology of drives. Of more importance, we found that it helped clarify the moral insight involved in the tragic effect. It explained why the problem of tragedy is the problem of justice. It explained why the hero, operating from a basis of conventional morality, demands a justice which violates conventional morality but is not truly a principled or higher justice. It explains why, then, the tragic insight is the insight into the limits of conventional-stage conceptions of justice, a realization of the meaning of "Judge not, lest ye be judged" which is yet a moral, rather than a relativistic or amoral, meaning of the "Judge not." It suggests that the problem of modern tragedy, as yet best handled by Dostoevsky, is the problem of the post-conventional tragic hero who demands justice but who cannot live by principles of justice. It suggests that this problem is one which parallels the state of many modern adolescents.

My own interest in tragedy forms part of an interest in literature's role in education, in literature as stimulating human development. For education, the ultimate literature is tragedy because it, alone, can help the individual with life's central problems, not merely help him to cope with suffering, but to develop through suffering. In that sense, the tragic vision is one which every human being needs to feel and understand. The teaching of literature itself depends upon a moral psychology that goes beyond Aristotle and Freud.

There are three educational theories of the moral effects of literature. The first is that literature is valuable because it has a "moral" in the conventional sense, that it conveys true moral and political doctrines and stimulates virtuous habits and emotions—the doctrine of Plato, of Tolstoy, and of the Marxists. The second doctrine, that of Aristotle, retains part of this notion, but stresses "practical wisdom" as opposed to moral ideology and "catharsis" as opposed to stimulation of virtuous emotions. As stated by Olson: "Tragedy promotes perceptions conducive to practical wisdom and a temporary alignment of passion, emotion and desire with right principle." The cognitive-developmental, the third doctrine, stresses that literature stimulates new stages, qualitatively new forms, of moral and aesthetic thought and feeling. The value of tragic literature is that it invests life with a meaning beyond conventional morality and conventional emotion, that it gives a new meaning to morality rather than supporting the old meanings of conventional moral or religious ideologies.

TABLE 1. DEFINITION OF MORAL STAGES
          WITH EXAMPLES FROM LITERATURE.

I. Preconventional level.
At this level the child is responsive to cultural rules and labels of good and bad, right or wrong, but interprets these labels in terms of either

the physical or the hedonistic consequences of action (punishment, reward, exchange of favors) or in terms of the physical power of those who enunciate the rules and labels. The level is divided into the following two stages:

Stage 1: *The punishment and obedience orientation.*
The physical consequences of action determine its goodness or badness regardless of the human meaning or value of these consequences. Avoidance of punishment and unquestioning deference to power are valued in their own right, not in terms of respect for an underlying moral order supported by punishment and authority (the latter being Stage 4).

Guard (in *Antigone*):
I want to tell you first about myself.
I didn't do it, didn't see who did it.
It isn't right for me to get in trouble.

We couldn't see a chance of getting off.
He said we had to tell you all about it.
We couldn't hide the fact.

Stage 2: *The instrumental relativist orientation.*
Right action consists of that which instrumentally satisfies one's own needs and occasionally the needs of others. Human relations are viewed in terms like those of the market place. Elements of fairness, or reciprocity and equal sharing are present, but they are always interpreted in a physical pragmatic way. Reciprocity is a matter of "you scratch my back and I'll scratch yours," not of loyalty, gratitude or justice.

Iago:
I follow him to serve my term upon him;
. . . You shall mark
Many a duteous and knee-crooking knave,
That, doting on his own obsequious bondage
Wears out his time, much like his master's ass,
For naught but provender, and when he's old, cashiered
Whip me such honest knaves. Others there are
Who, trimmed in forms and visages of duty,
Keep yet their hearts attending on themselves,
And throwing but shows of service on their lords
Do well thrive by them and when they have lined their coats
Do themselves homage; these fellows have some soul,
And such a one do I profess myself.

Since I could distinguish betwixt a benefit and an injury, I never found man that knew how to love himself.
Ere I would say I would drown myself for the love of a guinea-hen, I would change my humanity with a baboon. . . .
We have reason to cool our raging motions, our unbitted lusts, whereof I take this that you call love to be a sect or scion. . . .
It is merely a lust of the blood and a permission of the will. . . .
Put money in thy purse.

II. Conventional level.

At this level, maintaining the expectations of the individual's family, group, or nation is perceived as valuable in its own right, regardless of immediate and obvious consequences. The attitude is not only one of *conformity* to personal expectations and social order, but of loyalty to it, of actively *maintaining*, supporting, and justifying the order and of identifying with the persons or group involved in it. At this level, there are the following two stages:

Stage 3. The interpersonal concordance or "good boy—nice girl" orientation.

Good behavior is that which pleases or helps others and is approved by them. There is much conformity to stereotypical images of what is majority or "natural" behavior. Behavior is frequently judged by intention. Being good or moral and being loving are equated.

Ismene (from *Antigone*):

If things have reached this stage, what can I do,
poor sister, that will help to make or mend?

We must remember that we two are women
so not to fight with men.
And that since we are subject to strong power
we must hear these orders, or any that may be worse.
So I shall ask of them beneath the earth
forgiveness, for in these things I am forced,
and shall obey the men in power. I know
that wild and futile action makes no sense.

Go, since you want to. But know this: you go
senseless indeed, but loved by those who love you.

Desdemona:

Do not doubt, Cassio
But I will have my lord and you again
As friendly as you were.

You do love my lord,
You have known him long; and be you well assured
He shall in strangeness stand no further off. . . .
If I do vow a friendship, I'll perform it
To the last article; my lord shall never rest . . .
For thy solicitor shall rather die
Than give thy cause away.

Tell me Emilia, Dost thou in conscience think that
there be women do abuse their husbands
In such gross kind?
Wouldst thou do such a deed for all the world?
In troth I think thou wouldst not.
I do not think there is any such woman.
Beshrew me if I would do such a wrong for the whole world.

Stage 4: *The "law and order" orientation.*
There is orientation toward authority, fixed rules, and the maintenance of the social order. Right behavior consists of doing one's duty, showing respect for authority and maintaining the given social order for its own sake.

Creon (from *Antigone*):

You cannot learn of any man the soul,
the mind, and the intent until he shows
his practise of the government and law.
For I believe that who controls the state
and does not hold to the best plans of all,
but locks his tongue up through some kind of fear,
that he is worst of all who are or were.
And he who counts another greater friend
than his own fatherland, I put him nowhere.

Nor could I count the enemy of the land
friend to myself, not I who know so well
that she it is who saves us, sailing straight,
and only so can we have friends at all.

Such is my mind. Never shall I, myself,
honor the wicked and reject the just.

III. Post-Conventional, Autonomous, or Principled Level.
At this level, there is a clear effort to define moral values and principles which have validity and application apart from the authority of the groups or persons holding these principles and apart from the individual's own identification with these groups. This level again has two stages:

Stage 5A: *The social-contract legalistic orientation.*
Generally with utilitarian overtones. Right action tends to be defined in terms of general individual rights and in terms of standards which have been critically examined and agreed upon by the whole society. There is a clear awareness of the relativism of personal values and opinions and a corresponding emphasis upon procedural rules for reaching consensus. Aside from what is constitutionally and democratically agreed upon, the right is a matter of personal "values" and "opinion." The result is an emphasis upon the "legal point of view," but with an emphasis upon the possibility of changing law in terms of rational considerations of social utility (rather than freezing it in terms of Stage 4 "law and order"). Outside the legal realm, free agreement, and contract is the binding element of obligation. This is the "official" morality of the American government and Constitution.

Socrates (in the *Crito*):
Ought one to fulfill all one's agreements? Socrates asks. Then consider the consequences. Suppose the Laws and Constitution of Athens were to confront us and ask, Socrates, can you deny that by this act you intend so far as you

have power, to destroy us. Do you imagine that a city can continue to exist if the legal judgments which are pronounced by it are nullified and destroyed by private persons? At an earlier time, you made a noble show of indifference if you had to die. Now you show no respect for your earlier professions and no regard for us the laws, trying to run away in spite of the contracts by which you agreed to live as a member of our state. Are we not speaking the truth when we say that you have undertaken in deed, if not in word, to live your life as a citizen in obedience to us? It is a fact then that you are breaking covenants made with us under no compulsion or misunderstanding. You had seventy years in which you could have left the country if you were not satisfied with us or felt that the agreements were unfair.

Stage 5B:

Stage 5A is the "objective" form of Stage 5 thought; it starts with the rational social perspective, the perspective of a rational member of society. Stage 5B is the "subjective" perspective; it starts with the perspective of the individual moral self. Stage 5A stresses society, its laws and its welfare as what is real, as what exists, and what is and can be agreed upon. Stage 5B tends to stress the ideal, the self-oriented to the "higher," to the "ideal self," to the "ideal moral law" or to "higher values." As oriented to society and its "authority" 5B orients to the "authority" of an "ideal society," to Utopia, not to society as it is. Within Stage 5B, there is the 5B "rules and conscience intuitionist" and the 5B "human-realization existentialist."

Socrates (5B):

But perhaps someone will say "Do you feel no compunction, Socrates, at having followed a line of action which puts you in danger of the death-penalty?" I might fairly reply to him "You are mistaken, my friend, if you think that a man who is worth anything ought to spend his time weighing up the prospects of life and death. He has only one thing to consider in performing any action; that is, whether he is acting rightly or wrongly, like a good man or a bad one."

Thomas More in *A Man for All Seasons* (illustrating Stage 5B or Stage 6):

The law is not a "light" for you or any man to see by; the law is not an instrument of any kind. The law is a causeway upon which, so long as he keeps to it, a citizen may walk safely.

I am used to hear bad men misuse the name of God, yet God exists. In matters of conscience, the loyal subject is more bounden to be loyal to his conscience than to any other thing.

Stage 6: *The universal ethical principle orientation.*

Right is defined by the decision of conscience in accord with self-chosen *ethical principles* appealing to logical comprehensiveness, universality, and consistency. These principles are abstract and ethical (the Golden Rule, the categorical imperative), they are not concrete moral rules like the Ten Commandments. At heart, these are universal principles of *justice*, of the *reciprocity* and *equality* of the human *rights*, and of respect for the dignity of human beings as *individual persons*.

Martin Luther King (letter from a Birmingham jail):

One may well ask, "How can you advocate breaking some laws and obeying others?" The answer lies in the fact that there are two types of laws, just and unjust. One has not only a legal but a moral responsibility to obey just laws. One has a moral responsibility to disobey unjust laws. An unjust law is a human law that is not rooted in eternal law and natural law. Any law that uplifts human personality is just, any law that degrades human personality is unjust. An unjust law is a code that a numerical or power majority group compels a minority group to obey but does not make binding on itself. This is difference made legal. I do not advocate evading or defying the law as would the rabid segregationist. That would lead to anarchy. One who breaks an unjust law must do so openly, lovingly, and with a willingness to accept the penalty. An individual who breaks a law that conscience tells him is unjust, and willingly accepts the penalty of imprisonment in order to arouse the conscience of the community over its injustice, is in reality expressing the highest respect for law.

References

Bandura, A. "Aggression." In M. Hoffman and L. Hoffman, eds., *Review of Child Development Research*, vol. 1. New York: Russell Sage, 1963.

Bolt, R. *A Man for All Seasons*. New York: Random House, 1960.

Bradley, A. C. *Shakespearian Tragedy*. London: Macmillan, 1904.

Dewey, J. *Art as Experience*. New York: Minton, Balch, 1937.

Grene, D., and Lattimore, R., eds. *The Complete Greek Tragedies*. Chicago: University of Chicago Press, 1959.

Hobhouse, L. T. *Morals in Evolution*. London: Chapman & Hall, 1906.

Kohlberg, L. "The Child as a Moral Philosopher." *Psychology Today*, 2 (1968): 27.

Kohlberg, L. "Stage and sequence: the cognitive-developmental approach to socialization." In D. Goslin, ed., *Handbook of Socialization Theory and Research*. New York: Rand McNally, 1969.

Kohlberg, L., and Kramer, R. "Continuities and discontinuities in childhood and adult moral development." *Human Development*, 12 (1969), 93–120.

Kohlberg, L., and Turiel, E. *Recent Research in Moral Development*. New York: Holt, Rinehart, and Winston, 1973.

Nietzsche, F. *The Birth of Tragedy from the Spirit of Music in the Philosophy of Nietzsche*. 1948; reprint ed., New York: Modern Library, 1971.

Olson, E. *Tragedy and the Theory of Drama*. Detroit: Wayne State University Press, 1966.

Raphael, D. D. *The Paradox of Tragedy*. London: Allen and Unwin, 1960.

Unamuno, M. *Tragic Sense of Life*. New York: Dover, 1954.

Vygotsky, L. S. *The Psychology of Art*. Cambridge, Massachusetts: M.I.T. Press, 1971.

The *Reeve's Tale* and the Comedy of Limitation

Robert Worth Frank, Jr.

It is poetic justice that a narrative which depends heavily for its comic effect on "place" should find its own reputation affected by its position in the *Canterbury Tales*. The third tale in the opening sequence, the *Reeve's Tale*, coming immediately after the *Miller's Tale* and belonging to the same genre, has been overshadowed by that brilliantly-told narrative. The story has its own lustre and needs no apology, but it has not received the critical attention it deserves, and for this its enormously attractive elder sibling is partly responsible.

The fact that Chaucer does place the *Reeve's Tale* immediately after the *Miller's Tale* is, however, a fact of first importance. By thrusting the Miller's *goliardeys* immediately after the Knight's gracious and elevated narrative, Chaucer has established sequence as a fundamental technique for major aesthetic and thematic effects in the *Canterbury Tales*.[1] By following the Miller's tale with the Reeve's, he confirms this intention. The dramatic personal opposition of the two tales is carefully arranged before the Miller tells his story and thoroughly realized when the Reeve tells his. Chaucer exploits a possibly traditional hostility between reeves and millers[2] to ground the dramatic antagonism in the cultural expectations of his audience. He reinforces this hostility by introducing differences of temperament,[3] physique, and age.

The two narrators are firmly linked, on the other hand, by their lowness of caste and their vulgarity of mind. If the contrast between the Knight and the Miller (and the Reeve) is a comedy of class and nurture, the conflict between the Miller and the Reeve, arising between members of the same class, is a comic reflection of the absurd clashes created by the limitations of human vision. Their conflict occurs, finally, not because of sociological rivalries, but because of human imperfection. This is revealed in the petty personal basis of the quarrel. The Miller's *senex amans* may or may not be a thrust at the aged lecher Oswald the Reeve. What seems to offend him is that Robin's dupe and cuckold is like him a carpenter. Part of his blindness may be to miss the obvious insult for the marginal. Indeed, Robin protests that no offense is intended, and one is tempted to believe him.[4] The clash occurs, nonetheless, essentially because any one so gross as the Miller cannot avoid offending; any one so choleric as the Reeve cannot avoid being offended. Their collision, viewed from this vantage point, may be said to take us more deeply into the comedy of the human condition than any differences between the Miller and the Knight.

The more obvious conflict between the Knight's world and the Miller's, however, is continued in the *Reeve's Tale*. We must not miss the significance of Chaucer's telling not one *fabliau* in the opening moments of the *Canterbury Tales* but two and of having at some stage intended, as the fragmentary *Cook's Tale* reveals, to tell three in one-two-three order. That he reacted with delight to the new possibilities offered by the *fabliau* we cannot doubt; the magnificent imaginative response they elicited is evidence enough. But the tale of John and Aleyn does not follow the tale of Alisoun and Nicholas because, having started on the *fabliau*, he could not stop. The assumption must be that the *Reeve's Tale* takes us still further in the exploration of love begun by the Knight and continued in so surprising a fashion by the Miller.

Before the Reeve's tale we have his Prologue, and this introduces yet another feature of the Canterbury scheme, the "confession." This is an extended utterance by a pilgrim on some aspect of his nature or his experience which will reveal him more fully than the relatively objective portrait in the *General Prologue*. It functions rhetorically to relate tale to teller with special force and to cast on that tale a special light generated by the knowledge provided in the confession. The Reeve's is the first and briefest of the confessions; though not developed with the flair or the intensity of the Wife of Bath's or the Pardoner's, it reveals the potentialities of the form.

As Chaucer used it in the *Tales* the form is original with him—though we need to know more than we do about his sources. The "complaint" might have had some slight influence. More directly relevant are confessions of the sins as in Langland, and the tendency always for a personification, as in the *Roman de la rose*, to speak "confessionally" so as to reveal the range of values or experience covered by the abstraction. We should also remember that Chaucer had a thorough knowledge of Ovid's *Heroides*, which has a strong confessional character, and that he had been using this recently in the *Legend of Good Women*.

The Reeve's confession is a confession of old age, which may seem an inappropriate and undramatic subject for self-revelation. But Chaucer is working with a tradition which goes back to the elegies of Boethius' friend Maximianus.[5] These elegies were part of the medieval curriculum, as Ernst Curtius has reminded us, and they provided for the Middle Ages the authoritative description of old age.[6] Chaucer himself seems to have had some direct knowledge of Maximian's work.[7] By the terms of this tradition, old age is a time of pain and dread: the old man—or woman— laments the decay of physical strength and beauty, the rapid passing of time and the approach of death, the dreariness of the years that remain (he may call on death for release), and the loss of sexual power though sexual desire still stings. This last is given special emphasis in Maximian.[8]

We can see all these themes in the Reeve's Prologue: the loss of strength (3867–70), the swift flow of time (3889–95), the drab future (3896–98),[9] and above all sexual desire combined with sexual impotence (3877–81, 3886–90).

The tradition or topos is sufficiently close to human experience to be powerful and also to mislead, for convention rather than observation is the operating force.[10] If we allow the conventional character of the Reeve's speech—which is not to deny the freshness or poetic vitality of Chaucer's treatment—we can see several matters more clearly than perhaps has been done before. First, repeatedly critics have characterized the Reeve and his Prologue as bitter. A "personal" quality is ascribed to the performance that seems unwarranted.[11] The Reeve is simply talking as one cast in the role of the "old man" should talk. His performance is not an autobiography; it is a rhetorical device. (Old age is not stressed, indeed it may not be present, in the Reeve's portrait in the *General Prologue*, because it is not rhetorically relevant there.)[12] The rhetorical function seems twofold. The "old man" topos, given the proper emphasis, can serve as a kind of *memento mori*. It does so here: not so broodingly as to cause a chill, only enough to cast a cool, ironic air over the tale of comic pride and comic sexuality that follows.

Second, again a matter of emphasis, the "old man" topos can be used to dramatize the strength of "wyl," of sexual desire. This element of the topos is isolated in the Parson's comment on "thise olde dotardes holours, yet wol they kisse, though they may nat do, and smatre hem. / Certes, they been lyk to houndes; for an hound, whan he comth by the roser or by othere [bushes], though he may nat pisse, yet wole he heve up his leg and make a contenaunce to pisse" (I 857–58). This emphasis on desire and impotence, echoing a similar emphasis in Maximian, is in the Reeve's Prologue. It thus gives a clue to the tale: it is, as much as it is a comedy of pride, a comedy of desire. In the old man's mouth, the narrative becomes a wry celebration of desire, certainly not a condemnation of it. We have a telling recognition of its reality and its force from this Priapus emeritus. He is neither a figure of pathos with his "coltes tooth," nor a puritan, a proto-Malvolio as Murray Copland would have him.[13] Too much has been made of his envy and bitterness. True, he is not admirable, but he is comic. Confessing his own impotence, he attests to the powerful attraction of what he can have no more. His tribute to spontaneous and uninhibited amour is a comic confession of human limitation; without dignity himself, he tells of an undignified and unrestrained scratching of the common neural itch.

Since we do not have the exact source Chaucer used for the *Reeve's Tale*, though several analogues in Old French have been identified,[14] we cannot speak as confidently as we should like about his reworking of the original.

The comparison with the analogues done many years ago by Walter Morris Hart stands up well.[15] What needs re-consideration is Hart's stress on character. A principal contrast between Chaucer's work and the *fabliaux*, according to Hart, is his interest in character: The characters seem real people in a real place (p. 11). Simkin is not a type but an individual; "it is not the miller at whom we laugh, but at the man, real, complex, human" (p. 25). This kind of comment on the portraits is endemic. There is no question that the most notable addition by Chaucer to his original is the portraits of Simkin, his wife, and Malyne his daughter at the beginning of the tale.[16] There *is* a question, however, as to what is meant by "character"—to Chaucer and to us. Too much talk has flowed about verisimilitude, "realism," exploration of character.

Certainly the action is not delayed in the opening section in order to *explore* character. The role of several characters must be established for the purpose of the plot, the climax, and the desired comic effect. The miller and his wife must be identified as pretentiously proud people so that their final humbling shall be all the greater. This vice must be established now so that it can be ignored in the narrative proper. For note that nothing is made of their pride during most of the narrative; in fact, it may be said not to exist. The miller might be accused of intellectual pride, or of the ignorant man's feeling of superiority over the learned man, in some of his actions, but this is not the "family pride" introduced in the opening portrait. Nor do we see any of the wife's pride, her "hoker" and "bisemare." The absurd pride of lineage is not part of the original plot and is not functional in Chaucer's plot except for its comic value at the climax. Therefore it is not dramatized and is not referred to until the climax, when Simkin will roar, "Who dorste be so boold to disparage / My doghter, that is come of swich lynage?" (4271–72) Throughout the body of the narrative Simkin performs exclusively in the conventional, explicitly identified role of the thieving miller (3939–40, 3995–98).

There is no psychological consistency here and there is no complexity of character. Scholarly criticism flounders in this area because we have insufficient knowledge on two matters: what "character" was in Chaucer's time and how it was viewed, especially for literary uses. An anthropologically naive assumption that human character is identical in all ages has blinded us to the possibilities of differences between "character" then and today, though there is some evidence for these.[17] Character was viewed, it appears, in its general, typical aspects, conceived of in less dynamic and complex forms than it is today, and seen as discrete rather than psychologically coherent.[18] The *literary* view of character was primarily rhetorical. A character is the agent of an action and is manipulatable for such actions and such effects as the artist desires.[19] Certainly the main implications of *effictio*, portraiture, point to a rhetorical view of character.

The heightening of the comic action and of the climax in the night scene is one rhetorical purpose the portraits serve. Another and possibly more important rhetorical purpose is to establish the "lowness" of the narrative and to reinforce the "low" style appropriate to comedy. One must abandon one's democratic prejudices to properly appreciate a *fabliau* like the *Reeve's Tale*.[20] Part of the fun is the fact that the characters and their actions are, as Professor Higgins said of Eliza Doolittle, "so deliciously low." The very fact that *effictio*, however distorted from the normal pattern, is utilized for such low-born characters underlines their lowness. They are introduced almost like the king and queen and princess in a romance: a miller "dwellynge many a day," "A wyf he hadde, ycomen of noble kyn," "A doghter hadde they"; and this romance echo[21] (there are others) further mocks their lowness. So does the family pride, a parody of the genuine and admired condition of noble birth, based as this is on millerdom, bastardy, and church robbery.

Details are included which give no insight into character and play no part in the action, for example, "Pipen he koude and fisshe, and nettes beete"—their only function seems to be to dirty the miller's hands. Chaucer manages skillfully to include some low details that he can exploit later: "As piled as an ape was his skulle." The image debases, and also the baldness will be useful. Some of the details may create a kind of false suspense. Simkin, bristling like a barbican with his long panade, his joly poppere, his Sheffield thwitel, is a parody warrior. But except possibly for John's remark, "The millere is a perilous man," all the hardware comes to nothing. But we must recognize that *all* the details do make for lowness, directly or by mockery, and that some of the details serve this end alone.

Malyne's portrait is a case in point. It is a mock portrait of a heroine, a lumpy country girl treated for a moment by the narrative like a lovely lady in a romance.[22] So there can be no mistake, she is given two features of romance beauty, "eyen greye as glas" and fair hair. This second gift is presented in a line that could have come from a romance (or *Sir Thopas*), complete with an internal rhyme and a minstrel tag: "But right fair was hire heer, I wol nat lye" (3976). But as attributes of a "wenche thikke" with "kamus nose" and "buttokes brode" and "brestes rounde and hye" they simply go to show how far she misses the mark. So we must not sentimentalize her as Copland tries to do. Her easy acceptance of Aleyn is what we expect from country girls. Echoes of the aubade spotted by Robert Kaske[23] come grotesquely from her mouth and, as he quite correctly observes, check our sympathy by reminding us that this is not the real thing. There is no pathos in Chaucer's final comment on her, as Copland wishes to believe: "And with that word almoost she gan to wepe" (4248).[24] Real romance heroines *really* swoon and weep: it is the sign of genuine emotion. Malyne is not a psychological study or a realistic character. She is at best a type, "crude country wench," and is meant to be interesting not in herself but as a counter in the plot and for the effect she produces, that of "lowness."

This comparative lack of interest in character as such is seen most obviously in the clerks. Their roles are stock and they need no introduction. They are scarcely distinguishable one from the other. The use of dialect is a brilliant device, suggested apparently by the observation in the source that they came from one place,[25] but it does not reveal character. Its primary effect is to label them as "outlanders," if not precisely "low," certainly comic to Chaucer's London audience and disarmingly "sely" to Simkin and possibly "low" in his eyes as well.[26]

More important is the question of why they must be clerks at all. It makes a neater tie with the Miller's tale, to be sure, and increases the impact of the Reeve's tale as a work of rebuttal. The question for the *Reeve's Tale* might be disposed of by noting that, on the evidence of the analogues, the source contained two clerks, though these seem to have been clerks in minor orders. The term after all was an elastic one. Bédier noted years ago that clerks were the favorite heroes of the *fabliaux*, an observation reinforced more recently by Per Nykrog.[27] But an appeal to French practice begs the question for an English poet, and so does an appeal to his sources. Recently Sheila Delany has called attention to the medieval hostility of town to gown, exacerbated by the special privileges enjoyed by university students and officers, particularly "ecclesiastical immunity, or exemption from normal civil judicial process," and by the various connections, political and economic, between the university and the courtly aristocracy. She sees the unusual flexible social position these circumstances created for the medieval clerk as the special reason for Chaucer's use of clerks to "quite" the Miller. The tale "requires a hero whose social position is fluid enough to be considered inferior by the cuckolded miller and at the same time to be recognized as inherently superior by an aristocratic audience."[28]

Two aspects of the student role in late medieval tradition seem especially relevant for Chaucer's decision. The clerk, especially the student, had a reputation as an inveterate and successful sexual adventurer. After all, he wrote, or presumably wrote, much of the love poetry, Latin and vernacular, English included. In "De Clerico et Puella" he triumphs over all considerations of prudence and propriety, wringing from the maiden unconditional surrender: "fader, moder, ant al my kun ne shal me holde so stille / þat y nam þyn ant þou art myn, to don al þi wille."[29] A completely explicit statement of his reputation is provided in the *Interludum de Clerico et Puella*, where initially even lodging is denied him by the girl: "By Crist of heuene and Sant Ione, / Clerc of scole ne kep I non, / For many god wymman haf þai don scam."[30]

The other critical element in the student role is the commitment to study and the exercise of intellect. Aleyn and John's intellectual involvement is at best implied by the miller's comments on their "philosophye" and "lerned art" (4048–56, 4122–26) and by Aleyn's argument on "esement" (4179–86), but since they are "yonge povre scolers" we must assume it. Guilty to some degree of intellectual pride they may be. They do not express their conviction of superiority to the uneducated as overtly as Nicholas does (3299–3300), and their request to handle the milling of the college grain springs from high spirits and a desire for sport, but they clearly feel they are a match for the miller (4004–11) and the miller knows they feel this way (4046–56). So they are outwitted by a simple trick. They respond in kind, urged on by their animal nature and aided by shrewd use of their wits. This contradictory combination of God-given intellect and animal will, true for all human kind, is most sharply expressed in the clerk's role. Here is a primary source, I suspect, of their attraction for Chaucer.

Intelligence in the service of animal nature is the kind of inversion to electrify a moralist, but to charge a comic sensibility. There may even be a positive value perceptible in the inversion, a righting of an imbalance, a recognition of flesh's claim to wit's services. Aldo Scaglione has called attention to the motive of *ingegno* in the earlier French *fabliaux* and in the *Decameron*, that is, of cleverness, "intelligence having the power and therefore the right to prevail against any other value, a natural force destined to triumph beyond good and evil. . . ." In these works, he says, "human ingenuity has found a godly master to serve with exultant readiness: love."[31] There may be some of this in the vigorous career of Aleyn and John. They are rewarded in the action and condemned by no man except the unworthy miller. One thing seems undeniable: if one wished to comment in a comic vein on human desire and human intelligence simultaneously, the medieval student-clerk made an ideal agent.

Agents exist, of course, to serve plot, and plot is the heart of the *fabliau*. It remains the heart here, although, as with the *Miller's Tale*, Chaucer has, by the portraiture and the language, so enhanced his comedy that plot must compete for comic honors. It is a tribute to it that it holds its own. If a zany elaborateness characterizes the Miller's story, simplicity is the key to the Reeve's. A horse is untied and some meal is stolen; in a common bedroom a country girl is swived ("raped" is too strong and "seduced"is too kind; Chaucer's word is best), a cradle is moved, and a wife is swived as well. The element of intrigue is minimal. The first action leads to the second. Motivation is of the simplest. The miller robs because he is a miller; the clerks swive because they are clerks. An overlay of seemingly more sophisticated motivation is provided, but it is nothing of the kind. The miller says he steals because his ability to steal has been challenged. The clerks say they swive because (Aleyn) they have been aggrieved and have some relief coming to them and because (John), having been robbed, they will look like fools if they don't. But only a miller would feel this way, only a clerk would consider swiving a recompense and a saving of face. Why critics persist, in the face of Aleyn's and John's specific statements, in saying their motive is revenge, is a mystery. The mistaken assumption of a revenge motive has darkened interpretation and obscured recognition of the real forces at work in the tale. The vengeful intention of the Reeve, to "quite" the Miller, does not make the tale itself a grim or brooding narrative.

The most dramatic change Chaucer has made in the plot of his original, so far as we can judge, has been to remove completely the preposterous business of the cupboard in which the daughter is locked each night and given the key, an arrangement circumvented by one of the clerks' telling her that an iron ring he has slipped from the andiron enables a girl to remain a virgin no matter how often she strays. The stratagem has a wild ingenuity, but it is cumbersome and inappropriate. Why, if the miller wishes to protect his daughter's honor, does he give her the key? A more telling count against it is that the cradle trick is the pivotal action and its simplicity is the cream of the jest. The girl locked in the closet and the business of the ring are too contrived and involved and rob the simple cradle trick of some of its comic impact. Then too, a second dupe, the daughter, is distracting. It is the miller who must be the only target.[32]

Chaucer's change is a daring one. There is no explanation of *why* Aleyn succeeds, not a whisper, not a promise (4195–97). Perhaps the fact that she was "twenty yeer" of age and still unmarried helped.[33] But Chaucer seems to have relied on his audience's willingness to believe that country girls fall when you push them and that clerks succeed when they try. As a consequence, the simplicity is preserved. Nothing is easier than to cuckold a miller and deflower his daughter. It is the ease and simple ingenuity that twist the knife in the wound.

The fleshing out of the plot is controlled by the same sense of economy and by an equally sensitive feeling for timing and comic effect. The evening in the miller's home, the drinking, and especially the snoring scene are a brilliantly humorous exploitation of vulgarity. But this momentary slowing up, this pause in the action, is necessary, for the second stage of the plot is getting under way and we must not move into it too quickly or it will not achieve its own momentum, and its comic climax will come too soon.

The narrative shifts easily but rapidly from one scene to another, often assisted by a linking rhyme. The dialogue is brief and invariably relates to action. Even the innocent greeting by Aleyn, "Al hayl, Symond, y-fayth! / Hou fares thy faire doghter and thy wyf?" (4022–23) turns out to be an unwitting inquiry about the evening's bill of fare. And note how this first speech, so normal-sounding, misleads expectation, so that the spate of Northern dialect that bursts a moment later from John's mouth (4026–33) smacks the audience like a custard pie. For compression, only Alisoun's "Tehee!" betters Simkin's reply to Aleyn's news that his daughter has been swived three times that night: " 'Ye false harlot,' quod the millere, 'hast?' " Aleyn's whole night's work is comprehended in that "hast." There are even more eloquent and dramatic silences—Aleyn in bed with Malyne, John in bed with the good wife. Where it is not necessary, dialogue or monologue is eschewed, and action is king. For economy, swift forward motion, and sureness of effect the *Reeve's Tale* has no master.

Perhaps the greatest glory of the tale is its style. It is a superbly functional style, fitting the various demands of the tale effortlessly like a sleek and supple skin, above all fitting the narrative demands. It is admittedly difficult to separate Chaucer's control of the narrative movement, a question of action, from the style itself. But a scene such as Aleyn's fight with the miller (4273–85) owes as much to the style, that is, to the syntax and language, as it does to the selection and pacing of event. Here, in a scene that begins as pure action, there is no rhetorical elaboration or retardation. There is a unit of action, contained in a simple clause, in each of the first three lines: "he caughte Aleyn," "he hente hym," "he smoot hym." It is not too important that the pronouns be sorted out exactly; the rapidity of movement and the sense of action and counteraction are what matter. The fourth line, also a clause, but set off from the first three by reversing the order of subject-verb, stops the action momentarily to provide the gory consequences, "Doun ran the blody streem upon his brest." The action resumes in the next line, but moves on from the simple exchange of blows to a confused wrestling, reflected in the more complex and crowded syntax; we get first the changed situation, "And in the floor," and the condition of the antagonists, "with nose and mouth tobroke," and then the main clause, a simple subject and verb but rendered more vivid by a homely comparison, "They walwe as doon two pigges in a poke," followed by another clause in which two adverbs express the whole confusion and uncertainty of the struggle, "And *up* they goon and *doun* agayn anon." In seven lines the comic brouhaha has been set before us. It is time to introduce a new element; the miller stumbles and falls backward on his wife, and wakens her, and she enters the action. In thirteen lines we have twelve verbs and as many clauses, eight of them main clauses. Perhaps more relevant is the fact that the verbs, isolated with their adverbs, are sufficiently concrete and vivid to provide a summary of the action: Caughte, hente, smoot, ran doun, walwe, goon up and doun, sporned, fil doun bakward, wiste, falle aslepe, waked, breyde.

Decorum is another shining virtue of the style. The words just quoted illustrate that it is an appropriately low style. Low style in the Middle Ages is in large part a matter of low referents.[34] The referents for the words cited above, that is, the kinds of action pointed to, are sufficiently low, and so is the language. It is never inappropriately elevated, but is either neutral, allowing the lowness of the referent its full force—"hente," "smote"—or is actively low—"walwe." The lowness is intensified by the referents of other words in the passage, largely because the words are sufficiently specific to point to aspects of experience removed from polite association or actively linked to low life. Simkin catches Aleyn not by the throat but by the "throte-bolle." There are no heroic overtones to "nose and mouth tobroke," or to "in the floor." The inelegant comparison, "walwe as doon two pigges in a poke," needs no comment. The simplicity of the syntax, here and throughout, predominantly simple sentences or the simplest of compound sentences, is not only ideal for rapid narrative but appropriate for a low style.

It is at moments, however, a playful style. Charles Muscatine calls it a naturalistic style,[35] and it is true it does not have the range of the style in the *Miller's Tale*. But it flirts occasionally with other styles, romance style for one.[36] The opening lines have something of that excessive, almost irrelevant specificity that is found in the romance, and the voice of the hack minstrel jogs into view in the fourth line, "And this is verray sooth that I yow telle." Attention has already been called to the echoes of romance diction and manner in the portrait of Malyne. The clerks' dialect, though it contributes to the low style of the tale, introduces a new melody each time it appears, setting it off from the language surrounding it. Its effect is playful, comic, and refreshing. It reverses normal expectation, for the clerk is usually the master of language, the ignorant man (John the carpenter, Harry Bailly) is mastered by it. Here Simkin speaks English competent enough to play with sophistical argument; it is the clerks who speak a tongue uncouth and not quite acceptable. There is other music, too. The voice of the thundering preacher may be heard in the passage on Malyne's heritage: "worthy blood of auncetrye," "hooly chirches good," "hooly chirches blood," "hooly blood," "hooly chirche" (3982–86). The short burst of legal language in the noisy and noisome air of the miller's chamber is doubly incongruous because directed toward a roll in the hay. Robert Correale has found the language of Compline echoing in the night scene.[37] And Robert Kaske hears, curiously distorted, the ritual motifs of the aubade in the parting of two of history's least romantic lovers.[38] Proverbs salt the language at critical moments.[39] There are some puns, though not many.[40] Metaphor is used sparingly, but such metaphors as there are, it has been observed, come almost exclusively from the animal world: peacock, pie, ape, "Wery and weet, as beest is in the reyn," jay, fly, swine's head, pigs. The menagerie includes also the wolf and the mare of the fable, hawks, a cock singing, wild mares, and Bayard the horse. The animality that animates the tale could hardly be more insisted upon by language. John Block Friedman suggests an iconographic significance for much of this detail beyond the merely low and imaginatively playful.[41]

Finally, the style has amazing energy. It is a highly verbal syntax. It is an explosive diction, vigorous, flavorful, experimental, serving the demands of low style while charging it with a crude, demonic energy. Some of the most effective words and phrases are used by Chaucer only in this tale: gras tyme, mowled, open-ers, mullok, stree, grene tayl, sparkles,

chymbe, balke, panade, poppere, thwitel, camus, smoterlich, hoker, bisemare, sokene, craketh boost, hopur, wagges, wehee, step on thy feet,
jossa, warderere, whistle, quakke, on the pose, joly whistle wel ywet,
dwale, bibbed, fnorteth, draf-sak, daf, cokenay, toty, swynes-heed, throte-
bolle, poke, shymeryng. It is a glorious glossary. For all its freshness it
is used with precision and mastery, as A. H. MacLaine's study of a word
from the wine trade, "chymbe" (3895), shows.[42] We need more such
studies of the language of the poem. Chaucer has tapped here a new
tun-ful of language that comes rushing and frothing through his narrative.

We must finally, however, ask, what does the tale have to say? Something,
to begin with, about space and place. Space is undeniably the functional
element in the *Reeve's Tale*. The whole plot hinges on it: the size of the
room, the bedding of all parties in this one room, the shifting of the
cradle. To call attention to the critical nature of space and to hint at
philosophical implications we have Simkin's words:

> Myn hous is streit, but ye han lerned art;
> Ye konne by argumentes make a place
> A myle brood of twenty foot of space.
> Lat se now if this place may suffise,
> Or make it rowm with speche, as is youre gise.
>   (4122–26)

There were probably heated debates on the topic of space at Oxford
and Cambridge in the late fourteenth century—an additional reason, perhaps, for the tale's odd anchoring in academia. As our knowledge, sadly
inadequate, of fourteenth-century English philosophy becomes more
detailed we may be able to point to a specific controversy. This much
can be said now. Behind Simkin's mockery may lie discussions in an-
gelology, some version of the question often cited as the *reductio ad
absurdum* of scholasticism—how many angels can dance on the point
of a pin? The nature of angels was at issue, and the ways in which their
nature differed from human nature: Aquinas asserted that two angels
could not occupy the same place; Duns Scotus asserted the contrary.[43]
Refinements of position on the doctrine of transubstantiation also led to
comments on the nature of space.[44] But more probably Simkin's speech
reflects developments in philosophy associated with William Ockham
and his contemporaries and successors. Fourteenth-century skepticism
and philosophical empiricism, the attacks on Aristotelian physics, particularly Aristotelian doctrines about matter and space and about motion,
and the sometimes extravagant working out of the logical implications of
God's absolute power (*potentia absoluta*) led, among other conclusions,
to some startling speculations about space:[45] That a specifically limited
space was infinitely divisible and "that the same body could be in several
places at once . . . and several bodies in the same place at once. . . ." As

Gordon Leff puts it, "the empirical laws of mechanics and physics could be overridden. . . ."[46] We come very close to what may have agitated the miller's imagination in the statement from the *Centriloquium Theologicum* attributed to Ockham: "in the whole universe there are no more parts than in one bean, because in a bean there is an infinite number of parts."[47]

If the miller is willing to be playful concerning space, reducing it to a fiction, the narrative insistently demonstrates its inescapable reality.[48] Before the tale begins, by what may be odd coincidence, the Host announces that they are at Deptford and Greenwich, and this makes a difference: shrews live there. The very first thing the narrative proper does is to establish *place* with an almost nursery-rhyme precision: at Trumpington, not far from Cambridge, there is a brook, and over that brook a bridge, and on that brook a mill. The actors and actions are constantly being located for us. John will stand by the hopper, Aleyn by the trough; the horse is tied behind the mill, "under a levesel"; he is caught in a ditch; the miller is sitting by the fire when they return; the cradle is at the foot of the miller's bed; the cake made of the stolen half-bushel is behind the mill door. Throughout, by their dialect, the clerks are *placed* in the North. Being in the *wrong* place is fatal, as John and Aleyn discover when they are decoyed away from the hopper and trough, as Aleyn and the wife discover when they are decoyed into the wrong beds, as the miller discovers when the moonlight shining through a crack falls on his bald head. All this might be put down to technique, to the solid grounding of the tale in an unidealized "real world." It is that, but it is so overwhelming that *place* becomes a thematic element in the poem.

Counterposed to the reality of space and place is another reality, that of "wyl"; it appears primarily as sexual desire, though this is not its only form. It is expressed in the wild energy of the tale, an energy we see in both plot and language. (Critics who find the tone of the tale "grey" or depressing simply fail to give themselves to this demonic quality of the narrative.)[49] "Wyl" is a dominant aspect of character, too. The miller is belligerent and ambitious, his wife is ambitious and proud, the clerks are "testif" and sexually aggressive. This energy generated by "wyl" may be seen in the wee-hee of Bayard, the wild chasing through the fen, the determined chicanery of Simkin, the leaping into beds, the fighting and beating. There is nothing admirable about this "wyl" except as a force of nature. Certainly it is not pretty or polite. But it is undeniably powerful.

Its sexual expression here takes "love" a further distance from the romantic conceptions of the *Knight's Tale* than does the *Miller's Tale*. There is less of the romantic to mock; there is no Absolon. What sex destroys here is another, less-elevated form of social restraint: the pragmatic family marriage. Sex is shown in its stripped and animal form. Shown that it may be seen for what we know it in some part to be, hide it from ourselves though we try. Shown to be this, but not necessarily to be condemned. We do know that in this family, where the niceties of courtly love cannot possibly operate, marriage is governed by a rigid though pretentious formula of caste and chattels and the prime goods of virginity. The explosive nature of sex which it hopes to ignore is the very basis of its existence—the wife's bastardy, the incontinence of the priest her father. Though locked out, sex comes bursting through the window and seems, by contrast with the absurdity and artificiality of these schemes for a village *mariage de convenance*, a healthy and an honest form of action.

Indeed, there is a stripping away of all pretensions in the tale, a digging down to bedrock. A kind of common-sense reality is being affirmed. The comic Chaucerian fabliau world tends to be self-corrective; the deviations from sense are halted by actions within the tale and by exposure to ridicule from the audience. Proverbs often carry the simple sense that should guide or that proves therapeutic. In this tale the proverbs speak constantly to one theme: there is no avoiding necessity; indeed, necessity has no peer.[50] Life must be lived close to the bone. The social pretensions of the miller and his wife, the intellectual pretensions of both the miller and the clerks, the distant sophistries of the schools are brought up against the facts they try to deny. The inescapable reality of the real world—a kind of Dr. Johnsonian kicking of Bishop Berkeley's solipsistically generated stone—presses hard against the characters. The equally hard fact of naked human will bears down upon them as well. The clerks triumph, if triumph it is, because they rid themselves first of their pretensions. The reduction of life to the animal aims neither at praising nor condemning the animal but at recognizing it and at exposing the sophistical. We are invited—and by the tale's imaginative force compelled—to laugh at the bare animal we are and to roar at the paragon of birth and intellect we Adam's sons claim to be. We are after all creatures of necessity: as John says, "man sal taa of twa thynges: Slyk as he fyndes, or taa slyk as he brynges." What we find is the hard, real world; what we bring is our will, our creaturely nature. These are what we live with. We forget this to our comic embarrassment.

Notes

1. Charles A. Owen, Jr., "Chaucer's *Canterbury Tales*: Aesthetic Design in Stories of the First Day," *ES*, 35 (April, 1954), 1–8; also W. C. Stokoe, "Structure and Intention in the First Fragment of the *Canterbury Tales*," *UTQ*, 21 (1952), 120–27.
2. Frederick Tupper, "The Quarrels of the Canterbury Pilgrims," *JEGP*, 14 (1915), 265–70; *Types of Society in Medieval Literature* (New York: Henry Holt and Company, 1926), pp. 52–54. It seems reasonable that reeves and millers might clash, but Tupper presented no documentation of a traditional hostility, and I have seen none; perhaps this assumption should be challenged. For information about the responsibilities of the reeve, see H. Y. Moffett, "Oswald the Reeve," *PQ*, 4 (1925), 208–23; H. S. Bennett, "The Reeve and the Manor in the Fourteenth Century," *EHR*, 41 (1926), 358–

65; and his *Life on the English Manor* (Cambridge: Cambridge University Press, 1937), pp. 155 ff., esp. 166–78 and 186–92; George Caspar Homans, *English Villagers in the Thirteenth Century* (Cambridge, Mass.: Harvard University Press, 1941), pp. 296–307; and P. D. A. Harvey, *A Medieval Oxfordshire Village: Cuxham, 1240 to 1400* (Oxford: Oxford University Press. 1965), pp. 53–56, 63–74, an especially revealing study.

3. Walter Clyde Curry, *Chaucer and the Mediaeval Sciences* (New York: Oxford University Press, 1926), pp. 71–90.

4. M. Copland, *"The Reeve's Tale*: Harlotrie or Sermonyng," *MÆ*, 31 (1962), describes the Miller as good-natured and finds the quarrel all Oswald's doing (p. 27).

5. F. J. E. Raby, *A History of Secular Latin Poetry in the Middle Ages* (Oxford: The Clarendon Press, 1934), I, 124–25; George R. Coffman, "Old Age from Horace to Chaucer," *Speculum*, 9 (1934), 249–77.

6. *European Literature and the Latin Middle Ages* (New York: Pantheon Books, 1953), p. 50.

7. George L. Kittredge, "Chaucer and Maximianus," *American Journal of Philology*, 9 (1888), 84–85. "A book of Maximianus" was one of the books left in 1328 to the Almonry School at St. Paul's Cathedral in London, the school which Chaucer may have attended. See Edith Rickert, "Chaucer at School," *MP*, 29 (1931–32), 258–70.

8. There is a convenient summary of Maximian's elegies in Coffman, op. cit., p. 251. Coffman's article is slightly misleading. His purpose was to trace a passage on old age in Horace through late classical and medieval writers. It is Maximian, however, who introduced the theme of sexual desire–sexual impotence in old age, and Maximian clearly lies behind Chaucer. Coffman does not examine the Maximian inheritance in detail and he does not focus on it in Chaucer as sharply as it demands.

9. I take the sense of these somewhat difficult lines to be, "foolish or unknowing persons may say unthinkingly ["rynge and chymbe"] that with old age one has left his troubles behind him; the truth is that for old people all that awaits them is dotage."

10. There are two Middle English paraphrases of Maximian's first elegy: MS. Digby 86, second half of the thirteenth century, *English Lyrics of the XIIIth Century*, ed. Carleton Brown (Oxford: The Clarendon Press, 1932), No. 51, pp. 92–100; and MS. Harley 2253, early fourteenth century, *Reliquae Antiquae*, ed. J. O. Halliwell and T. Wright (London: J. R. Smith, 1841), I, 119–25. Most striking is the number of conventional elements in John Gower's picture of his old age in *Confessio Amantis*, VIII, 2403–37, 2726–2857: the ravages of old age (2824–32), the cheerless prospects (2850–57), and most notably, though genteelly expressed, the retention of desire (2772–79) but the threat of impotence (2410–30). At moments his imagery is close to Chaucer's: "That which was whilom grene gras, / Is welked hey at time now" (2436–37).

11. For example, John Speirs, *Chaucer the Maker* (London: Faber and Faber, 1951), p. 131; Paul Ruggiers, *The Art of the Canterbury Tales* (Madison and Milwaukee: University of Wisconsin Press, 1965), pp. 67, 69 (a sensible discussion of the tale); Trevor Whittock, *A Reading of the Canterbury Tales* (Cambridge, England: Cambridge University Press, 1968), p. 97. Paul Olson says the confession is "rather consistently a generic confession of the sins of old men" and calls the Prologue "a rhetoric of ingratiation" which stresses the Miller's presumption and animality and the Reeve's holiness and potential moral limitations: *"The Reeve's Tale*: Chaucer's Measure for Measure," *SP*, 59 (1962), 6, 7.

12. Brooks Forehand, "Old Age and Chaucer's Reeve," *PMLA*, 69 (1954), 184–89, attempting to refute George Coffman (op. cit., 273, 277), who found the

Reeve middle-aged in the General Prologue, argues not very convincingly that his "rusty blade" is an indication of old age.

13. Pp. 26–27.
14. On the possibility of oral versions as Chaucer's source, see W. W. Heist, "Folklore Study and Chaucer's Fabliau-Like Tales," *PMASAL*, 36 (1950), 251–58. Two texts (A and B) of "Le Meunier et les deux clers," the closest known analogue of the *Reeve's Tale*, are printed by W. M. Hart *in Sources and Analogues of Chaucer's Canterbury Tales*, ed. W. F. Bryan and Germaine Dempster (New York: Humanities Press, 1958), pp. 126–47. They are reprinted more recently in Jean Rychner, *Contribution à l'Étude des Fabliaux: Variantes, Remaniements, Degradations* (Geneva: Faculté des Lettres, 1960), II, 152–60. Rychner discusses the two texts in I, 103–08 (B and C by his system). There is a convenient translation of the A version (B) in *Fabliaux: Ribald Tales from the Old French*, trans. Robert Hellman and Richard O'Gorman (New York: Thomas Y. Crowell, 1965), pp. 51–57. Chaucer's version shows elements from both A (B) and B (C); see *Sources and Analogues*, pp. 124–25, and Germaine Dempster, "On the Source of the *Reeve's Tale*," *JEGP*, 29 (1930), 473–88.
15. "The Reeve's Tale. A Comparative Study of Chaucer's Narrative Art," *PMLA*, 23 (1908), 1–44.
16. See Louis A. Haselmayer, "The Portraits in Chaucer's Fabliaux," *RES*, 14 (1938), 310–14, who observes that the *fabliaux* used the conventional detail and diction of the standardized rhetorical *effictio*, inappropriate though it was to the subject matter of the *fabliaux*. He describes Chaucer's transformation of the *effictio*, however, as governed by considerations of realism.
17. J. Huizinga, *The Waning of the Middle Ages* (Garden City: Doubleday Anchor Books, 1954), passim, but esp. "The Violent Tenor of Life," pp. 9–31; and D. W. Robertson, Jr., *Chaucer's London* (New York: John Wiley and Sons, Inc., 1968), pp. 5–8; also Brandt, below.
18. William J. Brandt, *The Shape of Medieval History: Studies in Modes of Perception* (New Haven: Yale University Press, 1966), passim, but esp. "The Aristocratic View of Human Nature," pp. 106–46, and "The Clerical View of Human Nature," pp. 147–70.
19. Wayne Shumaker, "Alisoun in Wanderland: A Study in Chaucer's Mind and Literary Method," *ELH*, 18 (1951), 77–89. Robert M. Jordan, *Chaucer and the Shape of Creation: The Aesthetic Possibilities of Inorganic Structure* (Cambridge, Mass.: Harvard University Press, 1967), discusses the characterization of the Miller (not Simkin) in terms which are relevant here (pp. 128–29); also the portraits in the *Miller's Tale* (pp. 190–91).
20. Joseph Bédier's thesis that the *fabliaux* were a bourgeois literary form (*Les Fabliaux: Étude de Littérature Populaire et d'Histoire Littéraire du Moyen Âge* [Paris: Librairie Ancienne Édouard Champion, 1893], pp. 371–85, 427–35) has been successfully challenged by Per Nykrog (*Les Fabliaux: Étude d'Histoire Littéraire et de Stylistique Médiévale* [Copenhagen: E. Munksgaard, 1957]), who maintains that they were written primarily for a courtly audience, and must be considered "une sorte de genre courtois" (pp. 18–51, 94, etc.). For some modifications of Nykrog's view, see Rychner, op. cit., I, 145–46, and Alberto Vàrvaro, "I Fabliaux e la Società," *Studi Mediolatini e Volgari*, 8 (1960), 275–99. Nykrog observes that the victims of *fabliau* intrigue are usually from the lower classes: "Le fabliau paraît donc être le genre par lequel les nobles s'amusent au dépens de la 'courtoisie des vilains'" (p. 104). The class attitudes in Chaucer's *fabliaux* are aristocratic and anti-villein. See the illuminating study by D. S. Brewer, "Class Distinction in Chaucer," *Speculum*, 43 (1968), 290–305, esp. 301.
21. Cf. the introduction of the emperor ("Syr Artyus was hys nome"), his wife

Dame Erayne ("Weddedde he had a lady / That was both fayr and semely"), and their daughter Emare ("He hadde but on chyld in hys lyue / Begeten on hys weddedde wyfe"): *Emare*, lines 25–48; *Sir Orfeo*, 25 ff., 49 ff.; *The Earl of Toulouse*, 13 ff., 37 ff.; *Eger and Grime*, 1–8; *Sir Cleges* (Sir Cleges and his wife), 7 ff., 25 ff.; *Havelok the Dane* (Athelwold and his daughter), 106 ff; *King Horn*, 4 ff.: in *Middle English Metrical Romances*, ed. Walter Hoyt French and Charles Brockway Hale (New York: Prentice-Hall, Inc., 1930).

22. The name "Malyne" may have low associations or a pun. See Norman Hinton, "Two Names in *The Reeve's Tale*," *Names*, 9 (1961), 117–18: "Aleyn" and "Malyne" may be from O. F. "alignier" meaning *"arpenter, accoupler, couvrir* (used of animals), and *peupler"*; and O. F. "maligner," meaning *"machiner, trainer, tromper, être trompeur*, and *user de fraude*. . . ."

23. "An Aubade in the *Reeve's Tale*," *ELH*, 26 (1959), 295–310; see 310.

24. Op. cit., 19–22. Chaucerian *pathos* is normally accompanied by excessive weeping.

25. "Ne d'une vile et d'un pais. . . ." *Sources and Analogues*, p. 126, A.2; also in B.

26. Tolkien's study of the clerks' dialect has never been superseded: J. R. R. Tolkien, "Chaucer as a Philologist: *The Reeve's Tale*," *Transactions of the Philological Society 1934*, pp. 1–70. On the comic possibilities of the dialect, see pp. 3–7. On the "low" effect of the dialect, see Charles Muscatine, *Chaucer and the French Tradition* (Berkeley and Los Angeles: University of California Press, 1957), pp. 199–204. Also Sheila Delany, below.

27. Bédier, pp. 333–34; also 389–98; Nykrog, pp. 110, 266–67, but especially 132–33.

28. "Clerks and Quiting in the *Reeve's Tale*," *MS*, 29 (1967), 351–56; see p. 353. Derek Brewer suggests historical reasons for the Cambridge location: "The *Reeve's Tale* and the King's Hall, Cambridge," *Chaucer Review*, 5 (1971), 311–17.

29. *The Harley Lyrics: The Middle English Lyrics of MS. Harley 2253*, ed. G. L. Brook (Manchester: Manchester University Press, 1956), No. 24, lines 35–36 (p. 63).

30. *Early Middle English Verse and Prose*, ed. J. A. W. Bennett and G. V. Smithers (Oxford: Clarendon Press, 1966), p. 198: lines 27–29; cf. 7–10. The successful sexual adventurer of *Dame Sirith* is a clerk: ibid., p. 92, line 348.

31. *Nature and Love in the Late Middle Ages: An Essay on the Cultural Context of the Decameron* (Berkeley and Los Angeles: University of California Press, 1963), pp. 66–67.

32. Germaine Dempster suggested a different reason for the change: "What interest can we find in the clerks' knowledge of the theft, in their mention of it, or in their taking notice of the snoring, if plans for deceiving the girl have been elaborated previously?" "On the Source of the *Reeve's Tale*," p. 487.

33. W. A. Turner, "Chaucer's 'Lusty Malyne'," *N & Q*, 199 (1954), 232, citing a Latin tract on physiognomy, suggests her apelike "camus" nose would be a sign that she was "libidinosus et amans coitum. . . ." Katherine T. Emerson, replying in "The Question of 'Lusty Malyne'," *N & Q*, 202 (1957), 277–78, argues that Aleyn's greeting (4023) means he already knows her. Also, Malyne uses the improper word "lemman" (4240, 4247) and is called a "wenche," that is, a light or wanton girl, by the Reeve (3973, 4167, 4193, 4194) and Aleyn (4178).

34. Nykrog, pp. 232–35; Edmond Faral, *Les Arts Poétiques des XIIe et XIIIe Siècles: Recherches et Documents sur la Technique Littéraire au Moyen Âge* (Paris: É Champion, 1924), pp. 87–88.

35. Op. cit., pp. 197–204.
36. Gardiner Stillwell, "The Language of Love in Chaucer's Miller's and Reeve's Tales and in the Old French Fabliaux," *JEGP*, 54 (1955), 693–99, cites evidence that "the use of would-be-elegant love-diction in ironic contexts was well established in fabliau-literature" (693). See also E. Talbot Donaldson, "Idiom of Popular Poetry in the *Miller's Tale*," pp. 116–140, esp. p. 138, n. 33, in *English Institute Essays 1950*, ed. Alan S. Downer (New York: Columbia University Press, 1951).
37. "Chaucer's Parody of Compline in the *Reeve's Tale*," *Chaucer Review*, 1 (1967), 161–66.
38. Op. cit., pp. 293–310.
39. See Bartlett Jere Whiting, *Chaucer's Use of Proverbs* (Cambridge, Mass.: Harvard University Press, 1934), Harvard Studies in Comparative Literature, 11, pp. 243–64 for a list of proverbs in the *fabliaux*, where, as he notes, they were frequent and often served a structural function (pp. 17–18); on the proverbs in the *Reeve's Prologue* and *Tale*, see pp. 86–87.
40. See Paull F. Baum, "Chaucer's Puns," *PMLA*, 71 (1956), 225–46; and "Chaucer's Puns: A Supplementary List," *PMLA*, 73 (1958), 167; Norman E. Eliason, "Some Word Play in Chaucer's *Reeve's Tale*," *MLN*, 71 (1956), 162–64; Norman Hinton, above, n. 22; and John M. Steadman, "Simkin's Camus Nose: A Latin Pun in the *Reeve's Tale*?" *MLN*, 75 (1960), 4–8; Ian Lancashire, "Sexual Innuendo in the *Reeve's Tale*," *Chaucer Review*, 6 (1972), 168–76.
41. "A Reading of Chaucer's *Reeve's Tale*," *Chaucer Review*, 2 (1967), 8–19.
42. "Chaucer's Wine-Cask Imagery: Word Play in *The Reeve's Prologue*," *MÆ*, 31 (1962), 129 31. There are a few other studies of words or references in the tale: Robert Pratt, "Symkyn Koude 'Turne Coppes': The *Reeve's Tale* 3928," *JEGP*, 59 (1960), 208–11; "Chaucer and the Holy Cross of Bromholm," *MLN*, 70 (1955), 324–25; Edward A. Block, ". . . 'And It Is Half-Way Pryme'," *Speculum*, 32 (1957), 826–33; also Katherine T. Emerson, n. 33 above.
43. A. Vacant, "Angélologie de Saint Thomas d'Aquin et des scholastiques postérieurs," *Dictionnaire de Théologie Catholique* (Paris: Letouzey et Ané, 1903), I, 1231–48, esp. 1231–32; Aquinas, *Summa Theologica*, I, q.52, arts. 1, 2, 3; and q.53; C. R. S. Harris, "Space and Time," in *Duns Scotus* (Oxford: The Clarendon Press, 1927), II, 122–46, esp. 122–23, 128; Scotus, *In II Libr. Sententiarum*, dist. II, quaest. viii, in *Commentaria Oxoniensia*, ed. Marianus Fernandez Garcia (Quaracchi: Collegium S. Bonaventurae, 1914), II, 151–53.
44. *Summa Theologica*, II, q.75, art. 1, obj. 3 and ad. 3; Harris, p. 123.
45. A. C. Crombie, *Augustine to Galileo: The History of Science A.D. 400–1650* (Cambridge, Mass.: Harvard University Press, 1953), pp. 229, 232, 235–44; Gordon Leff, *Heresy in the Later Middle Ages* (Manchester: Manchester University Press, 1967), I, 294–307; also, "The New Cosmology" in *Gregory of Rimini: Tradition and Innovation in Fourteenth Century Thought* (Manchester: Manchester University Press, 1961), pp. 120–54.
46. *Heresy*, I, 206, 300.
47. Crombie, *Augustine to Galileo*, p. 241 (Conclusion 17, C).
48. For a somewhat different view of the role of "space" in the tale, see Gerhard Joseph, "Chaucerian 'Game'-'Ernest' and the 'Argument of Herbergage' in the *Canterbury Tales*," *Chaucer Review*, 5 (1970), 92.
49. Copland, op. cit., p. 30.
50. 4026–28, 4129–30, 4134; cf. also 4205, and 4144–45. My view of the function of the proverbs here differs from that expressed in Donald MacDonald, "Proverbs, *Sententiae* and *Exempla* in Chaucer's Comic Tales: The Function of Comic Misapplication," *Speculum*, 41 (1966), 453–65.

The Interpretation
of Shakespeare
in the   *Joseph G. Price*
Theatre

Three compelling instances from among many demonstrate that Shakespearean criticism has taken a new and promising direction. The International Shakespeare Conference held at Stratford-upon-Avon in August
1970 scheduled for its final session the director, John Barton. Delegates
had attended his Royal Shakespeare Company production of *Measure
for Measure* earlier in the week. Barton led a discussion prompted by
the scholars' questions. Did Mr. Barton subscribe to the Christian interpretation of the play? Is the Duke Divine Providence? Is the prison scene
black comedy? Did Shakespeare fail to integrate the elements of the play?
Is there a structural weakness? Barton replied that *Measure for Measure*
does break in half; in the first acts, the play is essentially realistic, then
moves to fairy tale. For this reason, any single-minded interpretation
such as a Christian allegory failed. "The dominant figure in the play is
the Duke although he gives little sense of divine providence. He is a
man generally in control, but his soliloquies show his uncertain humanity.
He is frequently irritated by the opposition which confronts his plans."
Of course, this session was not the first where a theatre professional subjected himself to an audience of critics, but the discussion's concentration
upon interpretation rather than staging denoted a new respect, a mutual
respect between scholarship and theatre.

Early in 1971 a *New Companion to Shakespearean Studies* was published as a survey which reported the latest findings in all areas of Shakespearean scholarship.[1] In effect, it was an updating of *Companion to
Shakespeare Studies* edited by Granville-Barker and G. B. Harrison in
1934. The interim not only bears witness to a new respect but gives signs
of a fruitful partnership between theatre and scholarship in the future.
As a single illustration, Stanley Wells in assessing Shakespeare criticism
since Bradley argues for "the use in critical work of scholarly investiga-
tions into the history of Shakespeare's plays on the stage." He concludes
his survey with the prediction, "Criticism based on a strong sense of the
play as something that is incomplete until it is performed seems likely
to grow in importance, but it is a difficult area of discussion."[2]

The prediction was borne out almost immediately at the World Shakespeare Congress in August 1971 at Vancouver. Regardless of individual
approaches and interests, the delegates reached a consensus that the play

must be examined in its intended medium, the theatre. This constituted a radically different perspective from that which had formed Shakespearean criticism since the beginning of the nineteenth century. The Romantics had exalted Shakespeare beyond the confines of theatrical practicality, whether in his theatre or theirs. No "Globe" could contain his transcendant spirit; no performance could actualize the beauty; no groundlings could share the sensitivity. Whatever was the Elizabethan reality, for the nineteenth-century critic the Shakespearean characters had outgrown actors, and his moral philosophy had defied stage representation. Only in the study did the reader discover the Shakespearean universe. At the turn of the century, the movement toward realism among critics and naturalism among artists did little to restore dramatic analysis to the theatre. Shaw did lonely battle against fragmented studies of the text and of the playwright. Criticism constructed theories of interpretation either upon Shakespeare's psyche or upon sources, images, poetics, rhetoric, structure, characterization, theme, ritual, or myth. It had valuable results in the study of the canon but was less successful in the explication of one play. Of necessity, the critic moved beyond the theatre and the audience in collecting images and themes, in the psychoanalysis of Hamlet and his creator, in the rhythmic patterns of comic form. Even an experienced director such as G. Wilson Knight divorced his principles of production from his criticism when, along with the text, he elaborated schemes which no performance could sustain. In his essay on *All's Well that Ends Well*, he identifies Helena and Bertram as representatives of Church and State, the Middle Ages and the Renaissance, the East and the West, the occult and science until at last Helena moves beyond all of these to a bisexual plane where she functions "almost as Christ, within the Christian scheme. The play is a microcosm of that scheme."[3]

The scholars who met at Vancouver, representative perhaps of all current schools of criticism, brought interpretation full circle. Whether dealing with dramatic elements or philosophical and psychological significances, criticism was related, more often than not, to the theatre. Topics such as language, formerly treated in isolation, were now brought to bear upon performance. In analyzing imagery, George Hibbard argued for an early failure in *Titus Andronicus* where the stage picture could not accommodate Marcus' long poetic description of his mutilated niece. T. J. B. Spencer spoke of Shakespeare's "careless art" in terms of dramatic construction. Comparisons of Shakespeare with Marlowe and Jonson were made respectively by Wolfgang Clemen and David Bevington in terms of theatrical experimentation and structural forms. Clemen, in particular, made a convincing case that the complex, multi-level form as illustrated in *Richard II* results from theatrical competition with Marlowe and the success of his simple rhythms. Discussion of such subjects frequently led to the aesthetic experience in the modern theatre. The entire Congress had been provoked by Norman Rabkin's extreme attack on the "old criticism:"

Shakespeare criticism is in trouble. If we don't change our critical habits we are likely to betray Shakespeare as badly as did critics who wrote about the girlhood of his heroines. . . . Given a romantic inheritance, given a genuine sense of the integrity of a single poem or play or novel, given a puritanical bias which assumes that the value of literature is moral and familiarly expresses itself in the notion of the professor as lay preacher, given a long history of assumption that art is valuable at least half because of what it teaches, and given an art which is verbal, so that virtually all the patterns, parallels, structural juxtapositions, image clusters, ironic repetitions, variations, and generic conventions a critic can find can be translated into other words, was it not inevitable that the bias toward a criticism that would produce discrete and rational arguments should culminate in the study of meaning?[4]

If the delegates rejected Rabkin's dismissal of meaning, nevertheless the majority supported the new direction made explicit in his critical philosophy, "We need . . . to consider the play as a dynamic interaction between artist and audience, to learn to talk about the process of our involvement rather than our considered view after the aesthetic event."

As perhaps was inevitable the consensus at the Congress was reached in regard to principle rather than to method of implementation. Delegates divided quickly on the roles of critic and director and on the ways theatrical interpretation might increase the understanding of Shakespeare. What were the bounds to legitimate experimentation? When did the production become the director's play rather than Shakespeare's? Bernard Beckerman described the scholar as protective of the text, the director as explorative. Yet one wondered whether the explorations of directors, even when stamped by ego, had carried the text any further than the fanciful theories of critics. This argument, both in the discussion at Vancouver and in its larger ramifications, is examined by Kenneth Muir, "The Critic, the Director, and Liberty of Interpreting."[5] A laboratory test of the question was contrived at Vancouver when actors presented different versions of the same scenes in *Troilus and Cressida* to a panel of scholars. If the contrivance worked against any satisfactory resolution, the Congress received and acknowledged with acclaim one artistic reply. As Kenneth Muir points out, the moment of accord came at an aesthetic experience. It came at a showing of Grigori Kosintsev's new film, *King Lear*, where both cosmic significance and extraordinary perceptions in details conveyed new understanding to scholars as audience. In his address to the Congress Kozintsev also established the premise where critical theory and theatrical interpretation must meet and find common justification: "Shakespeare begins where the logic of sole interpretation ends."

The meeting point is much easier to find today than it was when Tillyard was forced to write of *All's Well*, "Fail the play does, when read: but who of its judges have seen it acted? Not I at any rate."[6] Not only have the plays been presented frequently in production, but today's scholar is likely to have had experience in the theatre, certainly as audience, sometimes as participant. The Vancouver Congress had theatre professionals as delegates, but among its scholar-delegates were Kenneth Muir, T. J. B. Spencer,

Jan Kott, Bernard Beckerman, Daniel Seltzer, Rudolph Stamm, John Russell Brown and others with practical associations with the theatre. Their published work to date reflects theatrical intimacy and knowledge and is a strong factor in the redirection of Shakespearean criticism. It is not surprising that the proposed topic for the 1975 World Congress is "Shakespeare in the Theatre and Film."

Redirection does not mean invention. As with most academic trends, the groundwork has been extensive. As early as *Prefaces to Shakespeare*, Granville-Barker set his criticism in a workable theatrical framework. Arthur Colby Sprague has pioneered in relating the material of theatrical history to the interpretation of Shakespeare. Muriel Bradbrook's tracing of thematic and generic developments in Elizabethan times is rooted in stage tradition. Madeline Doran has treated Renaissance aesthetics with respect for the theatre. John Russell Brown's work in comedy and Shakespeare generally has insisted upon the test of production. Alan Downer and Robert Ball have always applied the same test. Recently, a number of studies which begin as stage histories conclude interpretively. Both Nevill Coghill and Anne Barton indicated paths in their studies of Shakespeare as practical dramatist.[7] Popular editions, in particular the "New Penguin Shakespeare" and the "Signet Shakespeare" have used stage history for explication. In the critical introduction to his edition of *A Midsummer Night's Dream*, Stanley Wells begins with theatrical accounts that reveal much of the play as art.

The relationship between criticism and theatrical interpretation has blossomed to maturity. Definitions have been proposed, often in critical terminology:

Today *any* Shakespeare staging has to come to terms with the tension between Renaissance values and modern evaluations. . . . Viewed from the angle of the drama as a work of art, this contradiction involves an inevitable friction of the various functions of the drama—the friction, that is, between the expressive and the affective aspects, between the significance of what Shakespeare *expressed* in plot and in character, and the changing impact of this on the *affect* of the contemporary spectator. . . . From an abstract point of view this, then, is an essential task of theatrical interpretation: the expressed content has to find its affective equivalent, and this involves, on a different level, a corresponding correlation between the mimesis and the moral qualities of the play. To recreate the *mimetic* and the expressive is impossible without reference to Shakespeare's world and his intentions; to reassess their *affective* and *moral* effects is impossible without reference to our audience and Wirklichkeit.[8]

Critical methodology has evolved in the work of Gareth Lloyd Evans, whose analyses of productions have replaced the more descriptive annual reviews in the *Shakespeare Survey*. In articles such as "Shakespeare and the Actors: Notes towards Interpretations," "Shakespeare, the Twentieth Century and Behaviourism," and "Interpretation or Experience? Shakespeare at Stratford," Evans has drawn fresh insights from performances.[9] Influences are admitted happily between director and critic, between Peter Brook and Jan Kott, and obviously between John Barton and Anne Barton whose program notes to his *Twelfth Night* and *Measure for Measure* elucidate plays and productions. The impetus to a mature relationship may have sprung from a new breed of director and a new concept of his own role. I suspect that the director now identifies his role with that of the influential, if not always the soundest, critic. He wishes to demonstrate the permanent values in Shakespeare in terms of the present. The bald statement has the ring of a commonplace. But I am suggesting a precarious balance that differs at least in intention from criticism and productions which, on the one hand, have sought exclusively the universal or, on the other hand, exclusively the relevant. The balance is a dialectic which, as Robert Weimann argues, makes the modernized Shakespeare as unacceptable as a museum version, "Thus, past significance and present meaning engage in a relationship which, in its interdependence, may illuminate either."[10] Whether the synthesis makes for better Shakespearean production is not my point.[11] What is important is the identification of director with critic as each searches for a contemporary aesthetic experience which is true to the Shakespearean spirit (and less necessary, to the Shakespearean letter). In assuming this role, the director may be distinguished from his immediate predecessors. Evans has characterized the new breed at Stratford-upon-Avon (Trevor Nunn, John Barton, Terry Hands, David Jones, and "in the background" Peter Brook):

They are representative of the "academic" spirit which, both for much good and some ill, has penetrated Shakespearian production. They will turn the bazaars and museums of scholarly exegesis upside down to find a good bargain (the R. S. C. programmes are stuffed with their better buys—Traversi, Wain, Mahood, Salingar, Leech—and with some of their worst). They "know" their texts, even if they do not always use all of them. They are meticulous in historical detail—when they decide to be. You can say now, as you could not, only a few years ago, that Shakespearian production is in the hands of the most knowledgeable directors of all time.[12]

Evans was writing of the 1969 season in which, in an attempt at overall interpretation, the Royal Shakespeare Company produced four plays to link the romantic comedies with the romances. The major success was Barton's *Twelfth Night* where the director had "read his Folio without arrogance and with much wisdom." The result was a fortunate resolution in the dialectic, an "acquired" interpretation where "time and time again the production illuminates the text, not only by the intelligent and lyrical speaking and the sharpness with which the wit is observed, but in by-play and the intelligent placing of lines."[13] It is not without significance that such praise was conferred on a comedy. For, as the critic seeks illumination, there are no greater dangers and no greater rewards than in the theatre's management of comedy. From Elizabethan times to the present, first Shakespeare, then his editors and critics have worried about the integrity of the text. "And let those that play your clowns speak no more than is set down for them: for there be of them that will themselves laugh, to set on some quantity of barren spectators to laugh too; though, in the mean time, some necessary question of the play be then to be considered." The extemporaneous matter of clowns, the inserted lines of prompters and stage managers, the comic stage business that effected textual changes, the explosive farce that smothered dialogue, the gimmickry that disturbed tone, the burlesque that muted lyricism—all have threatened Shakespeare's artistry. Yet today we understand more fully than past critics how that artistry demands to be realized in the theatre, how the verbal sprang from Shakespeare's imagination in extraordinary harmony with the visual. Comedy especially cries out for the actor and the stage. The line lies quiet on the page without the triggering gesture; eavesdropping is lackluster without giggles and whispers; recognition strains credibility without theatrical magic. We yearn to see Malvolio reading his letter, Leontes discovering Hermione, Bottom wearing his ass's head, Benedict being baited. Much of the comedy depends on the staging of Gadshill; perhaps all the humor depends on the staging of the more troublesome tavern scene with Francis.[14] Indeed, too many critical essays on Shakespearean comedy are unconvincing precisely because they isolate the plays from theatrical experiences, from the inevitable consequence of a line for an audience. Critics today are less likely to make that mistake.

Two recent productions of comedies which cannot be ignored by future commentators may illustrate this point. Because of their intelligent and provocative readings, both productions merit inclusion in the critical canon; their explications are as rewarding as any interpretive essay. Each, in fact, contradicted respected opinion, and a reassessment already has set in. Both will alter significantly the criticism and staging of *All's Well that Ends Well* and *A Midsummer Night's Dream*. I am speaking of John Barton's Royal Shakespeare Company production of *All's Well* in 1967 and Peter Brook's 1970 production of the *Dream* with the same company. Both directors were attentive to the text in eliciting Shakespeare's meaning and in making relatively few cuts and alterations. Yet their treatment of the plays differed sharply. Barton mined his text, bringing up riches never before unearthed, for he was exploring an unpopular play long contemned by critics and producers. Brook framed his text, regenerating through an outer form a play long suffocating in excessively romantic encrustments. In a sense, Barton's *All's Well* was the experimental culmination of a slowly evolving stage history; Brook's *Dream* was the rejection of a strangling stage tradition.

All's Well that Ends Well opened on June 1, 1967, at Stratford-upon-Avon before an audience whose expectations could not have been great. Writing in anticipation of seeing this "strange comedy" again, J. C. Trewin, after 50 years of Shakespearean playgoing, expressed his reticence in a quotation from Daniel George, "Attempts to include me in the flock being driven to the high-browsing pastures of the moment will always fail."[15]

I have traced elsewhere the unfortunate history of *All's Well* among critics and in the theatre.[16] To demonstrate the critical consensus, it is enough here to recall the play's identification with Shakespeare's "dark" or "bitter" comedies and the indictments of Helena as a contriving, insolent aggressor, of Bertram as a lecherous snob, of Parolles as a contemptible shadow of Falstaff, of the King and Lafeu as intrusive old fools, of Lavache as the misanthropic clown. To the majority of critics, the play was a failure caused either by Shakespeare's cynicism or his inability to mold diverse plots and tones. Whatever praise the play elicited as literature was in terms of individual strokes or theme. In the theatre, *All's Well* had some success in the eighteenth century in an adaptation that stressed Parolles and farce. It had little success as sentimental drama in the nineteenth century. In the twentieth, it has been staged more frequently and with varying success although most productions have been selective in emphasizing one plot, one character, one tone rather than the totality which the text demands. The most popular production had been Tyrone Guthrie's, which was staged at Stratford-upon-Avon in 1959. He blended high romance with burlesque and achieved his effect by both additions and omissions: he added a fifteen minute farcical pantomime by the military in Florence; he omitted the role of the Clown and modified other realistic elements; the characterization of Diana, the Widow, and Mariana were made comically vulgar. Overall, twentieth-century productions were revealing much more merit to individual scenes and roles than critics were attributing to the play. These components had not yet been integrated in a production which allowed full scope to the text, but certainly the theatrical tradition rather than criticism was developing an explication which would elevate *All's Well* to respectability in the Shakespearean canon.

The first reviews of Barton's production echoed past criticism in such phrases as "one of Shakespeare's worst plays," "the oddest" of all "the odd plays" which Shakespeare wrote, "unwieldy material," "a play that is almost totally unsatisfying," "the wryest, the loneliest" among the comedies. Such notices proved only that the reviewers had done their homework and brought to the theatre all the prejudices of past decades, perhaps past centuries. For, in spite of these charges which crept into the introductory paragraphs, the reviews were favorable and audiences enthusiastic. After discussing "how well simplicity could serve a play which is anything but simple," Robert Speaight concluded, "I don't know whether I have read Mr. Barton's intentions aright—to say nothing of Shakespeare's—but it was an immensely enjoyable evening."[17] There was praise for the "sober, sweet lucidity" which brought out "the play's gravity, its complex architectural and musical beauty," for the realistic qualities—"it is not about humours or puppets; it is about people," for the setting and style—"sophistication and rich baroque grace," for elements of contemporary black comedy—"a harsh scene" when Parolles is exposed, and of course for individual characterizations such as the spirited sense of adventure which Estelle Kohler displayed as Helena.[18]

The variety of praise suggests the full scope which Barton had given to the play's diversity. He treated his heroine and her love as romance. He stressed her attractive traits, especially manifested in the warmth which she enkindled in all her relationships. Obviously, Shakespeare intends Helena to have the support of her future mother-in-law; Barton made this visual in numerous intimacies. On two occasions in her confession of love, Helena knelt to the Countess and was embraced by her. The sick king responded affectionately and approvingly when Helena sat on his couch, then fluffed his pillow as she persuaded him to her cure. Earlier, in the virginity dialogue, Parolles was delighted with Helena as well as himself and twice put his arm around her. Even Bertram showed pleasure at her appearance in court and was concerned until she chose him as her suitor. The Florentine women were sympathetic and eager to help her. What some critics had attacked as masculine aggressiveness, Barton's Helena played as high spirits, repressed occasionally by a genuine humility, nervous when choosing a husband, modest when kneeling with Bertram in his final submission. To highlight romance, the production's single intermission occurred immediately after Helena's soliloquy of resignation.

Matched against this tone was the realism of Bertram, not a social realism assessing class lines nor a Freudian realism depicting "maleness" in conditions of war and lust. That kind of realism had led to the post Ibsen problem comedy. Rather, Ian Richardson portrayed a perfectly understandable youth asserting and testing an adolescent view of manhood. Decorated by a recent and slightly ridiculous mustache, he was eager to seek court and military honor—and certainly sexual conquest. Against both, Helena, whose romance embraced more reality than his realism, became a barrier. Barton here followed a line surely intended by Shakespeare. Bertram, whose inherent virtue has not yet matured, is led astray not by vice nor even viciousness but by the youthful inclination toward the braggart-soldier. Instead of a haughty contempt for his elders, his peers, and his household dependent—as argued by many critics, but nowhere supported with textual evidence—Bertram, at Barton's direction, knelt to receive the Countess' blessing in the first scene. He appeared at court not contemptuous but awkward; Parolles had to restrain and instruct him. The talk of war excited him and led pointedly to his dismay when the King kept him at court, then married him off. Bertram's frequent submissions were threaded visually by Barton. As Bertram had knelt to his mother, so in obeying the King he knelt to Helena as he would kneel again in the last scene.

With Parolles flailing the air with his sword, Bertram decided to escape. As had been done often in production, Barton combined the two military scenes in Florence and added a Guthrie-like display. Instead of laughs however, the military ritual evoked for the audience a martial spirit akin to Bertram's. Bertram became giddy with his success in war, as he would again in his sexual conquest. In fact, he was slightly tipsy when he returned for the trial of Parolles. Barton rearranged this scene to build to a

sobering climax for Bertram. Enraged, Bertram drew his sword on Parolles, was disarmed by Dumain and tripped by his own sword. If the first
half of the play had been directed toward romance, this scene was se-
verely realistic; for some, it was too harsh; for others, it was black
comedy and they laughed. Nevertheless, Parolles bore the brunt of Bertram's maturing. Bertram's own exposure was kept much lighter, partly
through the comic management of a delightful Diana who relished her
role. The audience accepted the final reconciliation, one in which the wisdom of romance overwhelmed the credible shallowness of youth. And
isn't it precisely in this that the joy of *All's Well* resides?

Other motifs were elaborated in the production. The sense of fairy
tale remained in the curing of the king and in the conception of the child.
As the King agreed to be cured, Helena laid her hands on his head and
recited her incantation. Similar verse passages carried the same tone.
Even the reformation of Bertram had a touch of heaven about it, which,
of course, in the theatre need not destroy psychological realism, at least
when the maturity is in virtue. Barton gave good rein to the comedy as
well. The virginity duologue was funny and uninhibited. Bertram's im-
mature imitation of Parolles with such stage business as his choking
on his pipe, his indecorous errors at court, and his clumsy wooing of
Diana brought laughs. Lafeu added his sophisticated humor. Parolles
recovered from his exposure with great comic resiliency in his "Simply
the thing I am" speech. So, too, he added humor in the last scene by
handing Lafeu a very dirty handkerchief to wipe his tears. Unfortunately,
neither director nor actor realized the potential of the Clown, and this
comedy suffered. Guthrie had cut the role, Barton did little with it, yet it
has been played with great success.

The programme suggested the trap which had undone other productions.
The danger lay in the theme. The notes talked about the play in terms of
generation gap, of "crabbed age and youth"; the temptation must have
been great to impose a relevance. But in Shakespeare's play, there is no
generation gap, for the youthful Helena is supported throughout by the
elders, the Countess, the King, Lafeu. The conflict is between the young,
Helena and Bertram. There may be talk of youth and age, but the Countess
recalls her youth by identifying with Helena and, if he contrasts the young
lords with Bertram's father, the King only reflects humanly on the good
old days as he believes that he too faces death. The idea gains no support
from Lafeu, as we might expect were the statement thematic. Happily,
whatever Barton intended, only the programme announced the theme.
Critics found little evidence of it in the production. Themes floated freely
as the lines released them.

Barton had allowed Shakespeare's play to move in the directions dictated by particular scenes. The production was a success. Yet, an uneasiness persisted among reviewers and critics. The play did not quite jell;
the parts were not integrated in an artistic harmony. Perhaps the characteristic assessment was that of B. A. Young in *The Financial Times* on

June 3: "The play is undeniably a slow starter, but once it's got rolling it remains, for me at any rate, particularly attractive right to the end. This production shows it off as well as could be." Perhaps the shades and tones could not be reconciled within a play that was neither fairy tale, romance, farce, satire, nor problem comedy.

The success and popularity of the production, however, grew. The play settled down to the longest run in its stage history. As it did so, it matured as unexpectedly as Bertram. The tones blended, seemingly because actors, recognizing that they were playing very human roles, learned how to enmesh that humanity, to engage each other in spite of the fixed conventions which seemed to bind their generic roles. Helena forgets her father, jokes about virginity, entraps and seduces her beloved because she is human, not a fairy-tale heroine. The King says, "I fill a place; I know it," because he is human, not a medieval authority figure. Parolles wants to exist, "Simply the thing I am," because that existence is human, not a stock role as braggart-soldier. What finally emerged in harmony was a cast consistently human among the inconsistencies of convention . . . or perhaps of life.

Along with *Macbeth*, the production of *All's Well that Ends Well* was taken on tour by the Royal Shakespeare Company to Finland and Russia. Even the reviewer for *Izvestia* whom we expect to be addicted to didactic art stressed the humanity of *All's Well* as the moral for socialism:

The humanism of Shakespeare tells in this comedy with special force: hatred and contempt of class barriers; belief in the worth of a man only in proportion to his personal humaneness; confidence that nature creates all people equal— these progressive ideas command our respect today as well. Thus, Shakespeare, whom the very course of time has united with all generations of defenders of equality, now speaks out together with the followers of the great humanists. And the fact that these ideas are given the form of a comedy in no way diminishes them.[19]

Surprisingly, his major objection to the production was a recurrent criticism, "If only the element of comic nature had been strengthened by the director. . . ."

In a final sifting of emphases, this is exactly what Barton and his cast did. With additional refinements and a new Helena (Lynn Farleigh), the production was brought to London in January 1968. It opened with extraordinary notices. In competition, Tyrone Guthrie produced *Volpone* during the same week. Many critics gave the laurel to *All's Well*: "one of the very finest things the RSC has done," "a production that leaves one all tangled up in superlatives and exclamations," "surely makes this play the most pleasant of Shakespeare's 'unpleasant' comedies," "I am beginning to love the wry comedy that never asks for our affection." Typical was the conversion of J. W. Lambert:

Yet many of these [actors] who failed so dismally in *Macbeth* scored hit after resounding hit in one of the most remarkable Shakespearian achievements I have ever seen: one, in fact, that I never expected to see—an immensely enjoyable production of *All's Well that Ends Well*. . . . I have never before left the theatre without finding it a crabbed and disagreeable bore. This time I felt positively like Saul after his interesting experience on the road to Damascus. It was all true: here *was* the conflict of generations, expressed with subtlety and sardonic wit; here *was* the contrast between the last of feudal France and the brash energy of Renaissance Italy. Here, crabbed or not, *was* a poetry which tossed phrase after meaningful phrase at us, until it seemed by rights the piece should be as full of quotations as *Hamlet*. In the balance and intelligence of John Barton's production all qualms at Helena's tricking Bertram into marriage vanished.[20]

In comparing the production in London with its beginnings in Stratford, reviewers singled out the emergence of comedy: "The actors seem to have found more of the quietly comic moments—Bertram cheering Helena's suitors on, not knowing he is to join them; the recently bedridden king dancing on stage after his cure; Lafeu looking Parolles up and down and inquiring, 'Who's his tailor?' And the encounter between Lafeu and Parolles is still a little masterpiece of comic engineering."[21] Phillip French found the text to be "far better, far wittier, than I thought it."[22] Even the much-maligned reconciliation was justified in critical theory reminiscent of Langer, Frye, and Barber:

And how finely it manages the gentle ritual of the end, when as one discord after another is resolved, "Mine eyes smell onions" exclaims Lafeu, and in that single phrase recognizes the absurdity of the contrivance, smiles at it, yet ratifies our unquenchable insistence—a correct aesthetic demand, not a superficial emotional surrender—for a well-tempered harmony at the last.[23]

What had occurred in the theatre was the achievement of harmony, a tonal blending that may have been beyond the reach of exclusively literary criticism. For as the experience of this production demonstrates, the harmony in *All's Well* depends upon the visual as well as the verbal. This in no way diminishes the artistry of the play any more than calling Shakespeare a man of the theatre reduces the artist. After all, the argument all along has been, is this a good *play*? My judgment upon the play is more restrained than that of Hilary Spurling, "What has happened in the past eight months is a shifting and refining till this most complex, shadowy play now seems, as its heroine did to Bernard Shaw, surely Shakespeare's loveliest work."[24] But, no doubt, critics must now revise the interpretation of *All's Well*.

John Barton had pierced the conventions of *All's Well* to let the individual lights of human characterization shine through. In his Royal Shakespeare Company production of *A Midsummer Night's Dream* which opened in Stratford-upon-Avon in August 1970, Peter Brook transformed the conventions themselves. Brook's method was the more startling, for he threw out the romantic image of the play which critics and audiences had formed over two centuries or more. The *Dream* had been considered Shakespeare's most innocent play, a paean to love and its charming unrealities, an epithalamion—perhaps for an Elizabethan marriage—celebrated by all levels of sixteenth-century society. The lyrical verse played sweetly on themes of lunatic, lover, poet, and airy nothings. Fairy magic evoked the suspension of disbelief, and the reader slipped into the green and dream world where lovers' blindness was miraculously cured. On stage, the green world had been realized with spectacular lushness, thick wooded scenes spotted with dainty fairies in pale moonlight, music by Mendelssohn, opulent costumes, and even live rabbits as in Beerbohm Tree's production. Although twentieth-century Shakespearean staging moved from such lavishness to simplicity, then starkness, the lure of spectacle in the *Dream* usually proved irresistible. Michael Benthall's 1949 production at Stratford was called aptly "floriferous."[25] Even when staged with restraint, productions demanded of their audiences assumptions of romantic love and conventions of fairy tale.

Brook first shattered the visual expectations of his audience by framing the play in an open, gymnasium-like set constructed of three white walls, open at the top and exposing the machinery of the theatre. Around the top ran a catwalk where musicians would play, actors would wait for cues, props would be lowered. Trapezes hung from above and fireman-ladders scaled the wall. Then, actors in white capes, slacks, and shoes moved briskly onto the stage, and the play began. More descriptively, the circus began. In searching for a new frame independent of ancient fairy lore, Brook had found the illusory magic of circus. Since all the tricks, acrobatics, and juggling are performed in full view of a circus audience, Brook added a dimension of theatrical reality to the *Dream*. At all times, the audience and actors were to share the realization that they were participants in a show. The conversion from Shakespearean convention to circus was immediate. The three worlds of Shakespeare's structure became one under the big top when Theseus and Hippolyta reappeared as Oberon and Titania, when lovers and fairies swung on the same trapezes. Fairies flew not in our imagination but as graceful acrobats. Bright gowns of purple, yellow, and green soared across the set. Magic juice came not from the distillation of flowers but from the juggler's spinning wheel. Puck towered above the lovers on stilts as he baited them. They lost each other in entangling coils of wire dangled from above rather than in wooded underbrush. Titania descended on aerial wires that held a gorgeous bed of scarlet ostrich feathers. Bottom, transformed into circus clown into ass, wore button nose, little ass's ears, undershirt, and suspenders. In a carnival revelry splashed out in streamers, confetti, flying plates, and a triumphal wedding march, Bottom with phallic thrusts and sexual hee-haws was led to his "nuptial" bed. The ending too was circus-like. No curtain fell. The performers leaped off-stage, mingled with the audience, shook hands, laughed and joked with mutual delight that the "show" had worked its magic again.

Essentially, criticism has two jobs, explication and reinterpretation. On the one hand, criticism attempts to explain artistic intention and artistic effect, then bridge the gap. On the other hand, it attempts to extricate from the mysterious universality of art the particular significances for a new generation. Barton had done the former, Brook the latter. For Brook, Shakespeare more than any other playwright "offers the actor or director such dynamic elements with which to create a miniature world in all its complexities and richness . . . endless permutations without in the least destroying the basic fabric of the work."[26] His goal then was a modern world in miniature where Shakespearean themes of love, desire, and delusion might be reinterpreted in terms of contemporary beliefs and attitudes. As he used a circus set for his physical frame, Brook used the psychosexual for his conceptual frame. He spoke of the subliminal in the characters, the dualities in their personalities, the secret lives of fantasies that are given release in the woods near Athens. His interpretation of the *Dream*, suggested in part by Jan Kott, is defiant of nineteenth-century sentimentality and of later romantic escapism:

It is a story about love and illusion, love and role playing, love and the different aspects of making love, including the most extraordinary demonic notion of Oberon having his Queen fornicate with a physically repellent object—the Ass. And why does Oberon do it? Not out of sadism, anger or revenge—but out of genuine love. It is as though in a modern sense a husband secured the largest truck driver for his wife to sleep with to smash her illusions about sex and to alleviate the difficulties in their marriage.

Cupid's blindness became Freudian suppression. Subliminal passions first were freed in the sexual rough-and-tumble midsummer madness, then matured in the sexual reality of the marriages which end the play. In mood and staging, Brook stressed this reality; each couple moved toward bed with measured steps, not playful ones.

Structurally too, Brook reinterpreted the *Dream* through the revelations of contemporary psychology. Shakespeare creates his three worlds of courtier, mechanic, and fairy, reflects light upon each from the same Love and its blinding delusions, moves each within the sphere of the others, and at last merges them in the final scene. Shakespeare's audience grows aware of the relationships among the worlds and between its own fantasies and realities. By the end of the play, it is led to recognize that the imaginative world is as real as the sensory. If the modern psyche, however, is an interplay of conscious and subconscious, if the imagination distorts external stimuli as well as fantasizes within, if a man is a composite of his waking and dreaming worlds, then these worlds in *A Midsummer Night's Dream* have no distinctions. For Brook, the modern audience need not grow to a recognition of relationships; it begins with an assumption that sublimated desires and deliberate actions spring from the same psyche. It assumes identities. Consequently, Brook flattened the three worlds into one at the beginning of his production. The same set served for all. The same actors moved from roles to roles until, at last, they left the stage and joined the audience. The identification was complete. Modern men were role-players too, and who could tell the dancers from the dance?

Once more, critics agreed that something had happened in the interpretation of Shakespeare. Praise was lavish: "one of the most beautiful Shakespearean productions of our lifetime," "a milestone in the history of Shakespearean production," "a marvelous evening."[27] Clive Barnes wrote, "This is without any equivocation whatsoever the greatest production of Shakespeare I have seen in my life. . . . It is the most genuinely and deeply original production of Shakespeare in decades."[28] And Brook had got his message through. Criticism changed direction in concept and in its terminology, "Shakespeare evokes love as the primal, protean energy . . . love as possession, as contemplation, as absorption, as degradation, as exaltation, as madness, as sanity."[29] For the first time perhaps, the *Dream* was described as a play "about the frustrations of people who want to make love" and its characters as "flawed people who deal with the disorder of love."[30] The production itself was "contemporary in design, Freudian in tone. . . . Brook and his colleagues have tried to find in Shakespeare modern equivalents for modern audiences."[31] In one of the first critical essays to reassess the play, Donald Richie wrote of Brook's novel reading of the last scene, "These people watching the play within the play, then, are disillusioned adults, they suffer from an ennui which we as audience know all about, for they have become as surfeited and as jaded as we."[32]

So begins the reinterpretation of *A Midsummer Night's Dream*. After an interview with Peter Brook, Margaret Croyden posed the question, "What are the appropriate forms to express the existential and psychological depths beneath the surface of the Shakespearean plays?"[33] Modern criticism, of course, has been absorbed with this problem. It will turn to the theatre for answers more frequently and seriously than it has in the past.

Notes

1. Kenneth Muir and Samuel Schoenbaum, eds., *New Companion to Shakespearean Studies* (Cambridge: Cambridge University Press, 1971).
2. *New Companion*, p. 261.
3. "The Third Eye," *The Sovereign Flower* (New York: Macmillan, 1958), pp. 93–160.
4. I have relied upon the text as reported in the Vancouver *Province* (August) rather than upon my notes taken during the address.
5. The essay will appear in a *Festschrift* which I am editing for Arthur Colby Sprague.
6. *Shakespeare's Problem Plays* (London: Chatto & Windus, 1950).
7. Nevill Coghill, *Shakespeare's Professional Skills* (Cambridge: Cambridge University Press, 1965) and Anne Righter (Barton), *Shakespeare and the Idea of the Play* (London: Chatto & Windus, 1962).

8. Robert Weimann, "Shakespeare on the Modern Stage: Past Significance and Present Meaning," *Shakespeare Survey*, 20 (1967), 113–20.
9. *Shakespeare Survey*, 20 (1967), 21 (1968), 23 (1970).
10. Weimann, p. 117.
11. Arthur Colby Sprague believes that productions over the last two decades have paid less respect to Shakespeare than those immediately preceding. See *New Companion*, pp. 209–10.
12. *Shakespeare Survey*, 23 (1970), 132.
13. Ibid., p. 135.
14. These are obvious examples; for subtler instances where the text requires comic business, see Arthur Colby Sprague, *Shakespeare and the Actors* (Cambridge, Mass.: Harvard University Press, 1944).
15. The *Birmingham Post*, 3 June 1967.
16. *The Unfortunate Comedy* (Liverpool: University of Liverpool Press, 1968).
17. "Shakespeare in Britain," *Shakespeare Quarterly*, 18 (Autumn, 1967), 389–97.
18. For each category, see respectively Hilary Spurling, *The Spectator*, 9 June 1967; B. A. Young, *The Financial Times*, 3 June 1967; John Peter, *The Times* (London), 2 June 1967; D. A. N. Jones, *The New Statesman*, 9 June 1967 and again Young; W. A. Darlington, *The Daily Telegraph*, 2 June 1967.
19. S. Giatsintova, *Izvestia*, 15 December 1967. The English translation was prepared by Richard P. Martin, Pennsylvania State University. I am also grateful to Gerald Burnsteel who sought out reviews and to Marie Tarsitano who worked with the Barton *All's Well* promptbook at the Shakespeare Library, Stratford-upon-Avon.
20. See respectively Hilary Spurling, *The Spectator*, 28 Jan. 1968; Peter Roberts, *Plays and Players*, Mar., 1968; Henry Popkin, *The Times* (London), 18 Jan. 1968; J. C. Trewin, *Illustrated London News*, 27 Jan. 1968; J. W. Lambert, *Drama*, 88 (Spring, 1968), 16–27.
21. Popkin.
22. *The New Statesman*, 26 Jan. 1968.
23. Lambert.
24. Spurling.
25. Arthur Colby Sprague and J. C. Trewin, *Shakespeare's Plays Today* (London: Sidgwick and Jackson, 1970).
26. Quotations from Brook are taken from an interview conducted by Margaret Croyden and reported in the *New York Times*, 17 Jan. 1971.
27. See respectively Jack Kroll, *Newsweek*, 1 Feb. 1970; Henry Hewes, *Saturday Review*, 6 Feb. 1971; Irving Wardle, *The Times* (London), 28 Aug. 1970.
28. *New York Times*, 22 Jan. 1971.
29. Kroll.
30. Hewes.
31. Margaret Croyden, *New York Times*, 17 Jan. 1971.
32. *TDR*, 15 (Spring, 1971), 330–34.
33. Croyden. It should be noted that in the critical debate which has followed Brook's interpretation there have been many dissenters. After testing my response twice, at productions in Stratford and in the States, I count myself among them.

Time
Dancer

Jack McManis

Your joys and your tears,
unweary Ben Jonson,
wear out the years
as you sing
heart-wiry and ring
fire new and air sweet;
oh foot the chanson
on diamond feet
till you hoof it to heaven
and angels throng
around crying amen!
cry encore! encore Ben!
Divine dance and song—
ancient Ben, your life leaven
turns full time's star-trysts
and crystal twists
of the sun
other lyrists
begin, but leave undone.

Milton's Gawdy-Day with Lawrence

Ralph W. Condee

> Lawrence of virtuous Father virtuous Son,
>   Now that the Fields are dank and ways are mire,
>   Where shall we sometimes meet and by the fire
>   Help waste a sullen day, what may be won
> From the hard Season gaining? Time will run
>   On smoother till *Favonius* re-inspire
>   The frozen earth, and clothe in fresh attire
>   The Lily and Rose, that neither sow'd nor spun.
> What neat repast shall feast us, light and choice,
>   Of Attic taste, with Wine, whence we may rise
>   To hear the Lute well toucht, or artful voice
> Warble immortal Notes and *Tuscan* Air?
>   He who of those delights can judge and spare
>   To interpose them oft, is not unwise.[1]

Milton's sonnet to Edward Lawrence is one of his masterpieces in its skillful integration of the extra-poetic situation, by which I mean dinner with Lawrence,[2] with the poem, the verbal construct, which invites Lawrence. The poem creates its unique character as a poem by means of an integration of its literary techniques with the non-literary situation which called it into being; that is, the poem is what it says. In accomplishing this it resembles in its small way the major poems on which Milton's chief fame rests—"Lycidas," "Epitaphium Damonis," *Samson Agonistes*, and the two great epics. Thus "Lycidas," for example, is written in the pastoral tradition, but its pastoralism is more than a convention; it memorializes Edward King, but it is more than a memorial to King. The extra-poetic fact of King's death fuses with the literary tradition of pastoralism in order for "Lycidas" to exist as the unique creation that it is. So also *Paradise Lost* and *Paradise Regained* deal with, among other things, the extra-poetic concepts of the true nature of heroic virtue; but they do so by means of, in terms of, and completely integrated with the literary, epic, "heroic" tradition descended from Homer and Vergil. The poem to Lawrence, in 14 lines, accomplishes a similar integration of what it says on the one hand and what it is on the other.

In addition to being an invitation to dinner, the sonnet is a winter-poem, concerned with the extra-poetic experience of the cold outdoors and the comfortable indoors; "the Fields are dank and ways are mire," the days are sullen, the season is hard, the earth is frozen. But sheltered from the sodden English winter, John Milton and Edward Lawrence will find warmth and comfort by the fire. And beyond this, there is also the warmth of memory and anticipation—Favonius, the west wind of spring, brought lilies and roses in the past and will bring them again. In physical terms, this is the situation set forth in the first eight lines.

But the snug contrast of those first eight lines, of the two warm friends surrounded by the cold and wet, derives far more from the metaphoric warmth of their companionship than it does from the explicit hearth that keeps off the chill. The "Lily . . . that neither sow'd nor spun" is of course rooted in the Gospel according to St. Matthew, and Lawrence needed no footnote, as modern readers apparently do, to put the quotation into its precise Biblical context in Matthew. As J. R. Green remarks of Milton's time, "England became the people of a book, and that book was the Bible."[3] Thus the image of the lily calls up to them not only the warmth of the spring which Milton and Lawrence anticipate after the dank English winter; as a literary image it brings with it its own aura of the small, English, Protestant, Bible-reading community of Milton, the Lawrences, and other supporters of the Commonwealth, besieged by the outside hostile world of Catholic France and Spain and the English Royalists eager to avenge the execution of King Charles. For a brief moment in the sonnet the Biblical Protestantism serves a function similar to that of the reverberations of the Homeric-Vergilian tradition with *Paradise Lost* and *Paradise Regained*: the Bible acts as a resonator in the literary-cultural tradition to create echoes which the sonnet makes use of. There are, of course, important differences, most of them too obvious to stop over. But one of the differences is that in *Paradise Lost* Milton uses the images, the ideas, even the structure of the Aeneid as a pattern of metaphors expressing the superiority of true Christian heroism to pagan heroism; in the Lawrence sonnet Milton uses the quotation from Matthew as an opportunity for a momentary glimpse of one basis for the warm companionship with Lawrence.

This Protestant, Biblical context of the Lawrence sonnet should perhaps remind us that Milton, in his poem in praise of the Roman Catholic Manso, written some 15 years before the Lawrence sonnet, kept the poem completely pagan in its imagery and allusions. Even the beatific vision with which the poem closed was specifically Greco-Roman and non-Christian. His admiration for Manso was quite different from his feeling of warm kinship with Lawrence.

One might wonder at the opening line of the sonnet: why, in a poem which can afford only 14 pentameter lines, does Milton begin with what looks like a pedantic circumlocution: "Lawrence of virtuous Father virtuous Son." The father Henry (1600–1664) was Lord President of the Council under Cromwell and Edward his son was soon to be a member of Cromwell's Parliament. And an inherent element in the total poem is Milton's spiritual, ideological kinship with the father and the son, spanning the two generations. Milton, revolutionary and defender of regicides, had more at stake than his career in the success of the Commonwealth cause; for all he knew he had gambled his life on his beliefs, and the Lawrences were his allies. The warmth of friendship and community which brought Milton and Edward Lawrence together was a bond of deeply, dangerously held political and religious beliefs.

One must not overstate these implications in the poem; it would be a simplistic over-reading to say "fire" (line 3) = "Protestantism" and "sullen day" (line 4) = "Catholic/Stuart Royalism." But it is under-reading the poem to imagine that Milton's friendship with Lawrence is a random acquaintance based on a mutual love of good food. Their ties were close, were linked to their firmest convictions concerning God and Man, and were held in the face of the gravest of dangers. The warmth of the poem comes not only from the fire and the hope of spring but from mutual devotion to their highest ideals in perilous times.

Other seeming circumlocutions in the sonnet are similarly functional: "Favonius," as countless editors have noted, is the west wind invoked by Horace in his ode on spring (I.iv), and Milton's first line has overtones that are more than political; it echoes another passage from Horace, also an opening line—"O matre pulchra filia pulchrior" ("O mother lovelier than your lovely daughter," I.xvi); and these recollections of Horace,[4] to a seventeenth-century reader, were hardly pedantic tags. They were poems every schoolboy knew, as we today share a common background of overworked quotations from Shakespeare.

Edward Lawrence would have known his Horace as well as he knew his Bible; in fact there is some evidence that Edward may have been a schoolboy under Milton's tutelage. Masson[5] thought Edward's brother Henry studied under Milton; we know that Edward's sister Martha married Richard Barry, who was certainly one of Milton's pupils.[6] But whether Edward learned the odes as Milton's student or not, the common heritage between them was rich and complex, and Milton is warmly recalling some of its delightful aspects as he invites his friend. The sonnet is working, in a low-keyed way, with its Biblical and Horatian overtones just as "Epitaphium Damonis," with much more fervor, united its deep grief and its beatific vision with the Theocritean-Vergilian pastoral.[7] And as "Epitaphium Damonis" used the literary tradition of pastoralism as a poetic tool to arrive at its Christian vision of Diodati in Heaven, so in a smaller way the Lawrence sonnet not only states Milton's friendship with Lawrence, it implies it by means of the metaphoric, allusive images which united them in friendship.

There may be more significance in the sestet, with its reference to "Attic taste, with wine," the lute, the artful voice, and the Tuscan air, than we now know; the conversations of close friends usually have overtones that we outsiders miss. But we should be bad readers if we overlooked the sensuous pleasure that Milton, and presumably Lawrence, looked forward to: good food, good wine, good music—the warmth of pleasure as well as physical and spiritual warmth in this cold winter of

Cromwell's second year as Lord Protector. Sir Walter Raleigh certainly misread the sonnet in saying, "It is impossible to take one's ease with Milton, to induce him to forget his principles for a moment in the name of social pleasure. . . . But the qualities that make Milton a poor boon-companion are precisely those which combine to raise his style to an un-exampled loftiness, a dignity that bears itself easily in society greater than human."[8]

But Raleigh made Milton into a kind of Puritan that he never really was. The same Milton who wrote *Paradise Lost* had also described the ageing Ovid, miserable and thirsty in his exile to the barren plains of Tomis on the Black Sea:

> Naso Corallaeis mala carmina misit ab agris;
>   Non illic epulae, non sata vitis erat.
> Quid nisi vina, rosasque racemiferumque Lyaeum
>   Cantavit brevibus Teia Musa modis?
>   (El. VI, 19–22)

[Ovid sent bad verses from the Corallian fields because there were no banquets in that land and the vine had not been planted. O what but wine and roses and Lyaeus wreathed with clusters did [Anacreon] sing in his short measures?—Trans. M. Y. Hughes]

And in the same poem, when his friend Diodati had apologized for sending a bad poem to Milton because of overindulgence, Milton answered,

> Quid quereris refugam vino dapibusque poesin?
> Carmen amat Bacchum, Carmina Bacchus amat.
>   (13–14)

[But why do you complain that poetry is a fugitive from wine and feasting? Song loves Bacchus and Bacchus loves songs.]

Milton was 25 years younger when he wrote the sixth elegy; but while one must not think of Milton as a drunken reveller either at 21, when he wrote the sixth elegy, or at 46, when he wrote the Lawrence sonnet, still his love of wine, music, and beautiful women recurs throughout his poetry over a 40-year span.

The date of the Lawrence sonnet is generally agreed to be approximately 1654/5,[9] and this fact bears on the total meaning of the poem: Milton was 46 on 9 December 1654. Edward Lawrence at 21 was about 25 years Milton's junior. But see how delicately Milton manages the tone with which he addresses his young friend. The sonnet is in four sentences and two of these are questions—"Where shall we sometimes meet . . . ?" "What neat repast shall feast us . . . ?" The deference that Cromwell's Secretary for Foreign Languages shows to his friend less than half his age is part of the warm, friendly climate of the whole poem.

This deference—purposeful informality, if you will—is an integral part not only of the invitation-to-dinner but also of the poem-embodying-the-invitation-to-dinner. And it is an unobtrusive counterpart of the same sort of fusion that integrates *Paradise Lost*: *Paradise Lost* is epic, heroic, the tale of our Grand Parents' greatest adventure. But *Paradise Lost* exists also as a structure built out of Milton's concept of true heroism as patience, heroic martyrdom, and obedience to the will of God. In *Paradise Lost*, "epicness" is not merely a literary technique but also an ideal of self-sacrifice. So in the Lawrence sonnet, at a greatly diminished emotional pitch, this companionship at dinner exists as a close kinship of mutual ideals and aims, regardless of age or station, and this extra-poetic experience of friendship and community, of spiritual kinship, is indivisibly fused with the poem by its imagery, its allusions, and even its syntax.

This amalgamation of the extra-poetic dinner invitation with the sonnet which gives it a poetic entity extends even to the line-endings of this poem which transcends age, position, and formality: lines 1 and 2 are end-stopped, giving us the proper Petrarchan orientation. They begin the announcement that this is a sonnet, a rigidly-organized ritual. But immediately the formality of the pentameters loosens with a series of run-on lines—"Where shall we sometimes meet and by the fire / Help waste a sullen day?" "Time will run / On smoother [the line runs on] till *Favonius* re-inspire / The frozen earth." The interplay between the formalism of the Petrarchan rhyme-scheme and the friendly, conversational quality of these fluid lines harmonizes quietly with the ritual of the invitation to the feast, a ritual warmed and enlivened by the bonds of friendship and mutual pleasures uniting the middle-aged government official and his young guest.

Similarly, in later years, *Paradise Regained* will use the interaction between Christ's spiritual combat with Satan in the desert and the literary tradition of epic battle to create a union of the poetically heroic (an epic poem) with extra-poetic heroism (Christ's victory over Satan), thus integrating the events and the poem in *Paradise Regained*. *Paradise Regained* and the Lawrence sonnet are obviously vastly different poems; but both in *Paradise Regained* and in this sonnet Milton creates a poem which becomes what it says, which embodies itself in its texture while using the texture to express itself. In *Paradise Regained* the fusion embodies an epic which creates what Milton meant by a truly heroic poem; in the Lawrence sonnet the ritual of the feast unites with the warmth of true friendship, and the ritual of the sonnet unites with the easy grace of a poem which echoes their bonds of union.

The "sonnetness" of the poem reinforces this: it is, as we have seen, strictly Petrarchan; unlike many of Milton's sonnets it scrupulously observes a full stop after the eighth line, with a shift in subject (to the "neat repast" itself) in the sestet. Yet in spite of this formal rigor, only five of the 14 lines are end-stopped, imparting the conversational tone we have just noted. Milton and Lawrence will dine formally, but, Raleigh to the contrary notwithstanding, they will dine as boon-companions. The sonnet, in its overt statement, its rhyme scheme, its images, and its sentence structure, says so, and clearly.

Van Doren points out the skill with which Milton manages the sensuous sound of the sestet:

"What neat repast shall feast us"—only the teeth and lips are required for pronouncing that, as only the teeth and lips will taste and sip the delicacies of the day. "Of Attic taste"—there it is again, "with wine": all light and choice, and fragile as the air these gentlemen will grace by breathing it. As music is mentioned the sound of the words grows deeper and richer—"hear the lute," and "warble immortal notes"—yet it will not grow hoarse; nothing in this poem will ever disturb the clear, smiling calm, the knowing and cultivated courtesy that Milton imagined for its medium.[10]

Lest this analysis lead us to think of Milton and Lawrence as so over-ly precious that an access of strong emotion might induce fainting among the two diners, let us remember that Milton was not always so gentle a man. The Lawrence sonnet was written only shortly after Milton's *Defensio Secunda*, in which he attacked the Reverend Alexander More in such bludgeoning terms as "obscuri cujuspiam nebulonis" ("skulking and drivelling miscreant"),[11] "tu igitur iste é gurgustio clamator" ("thou brawler from the stews"), "semper enim in ancillis prolabitur libido hominis" ("for the fellow's lust is always inflamed by cooks and waiting maids"). And, perhaps four years earlier, Milton had heaped incredible invectives on the head of Salmasius: "Veterator," ("you old rogue") he called him.[12] "Eunuchus," "professor triobolarus et extraneus" ("cheap, barbaric pedant"), "sine terra et lare homo nihili et stramineus eques" ("landless, homeless, worthless, straw-stuffed scarecrow knight"), "bi-pedum nequissime" ("most worthless of two-legged creatures"), "sine sale, sine genio proclamator et rabula" ("senseless, witless, bawling pettifogger") are some of Milton's gentle terms for the aged scholar—who had been no less crudely insulting. Taine says of the controversy between Milton and Salmasius, "We fancy we are listening to the bel-lowing of two bulls."[13] Milton, in writings not only like the two *Defences*, but in *Samson Agonistes* and *Paradise Lost*, reminds one of the kind of poet Yeats confessed he had admired—

> . . . When I was young,
> I had not given a penny for a song
> Did not the poet sing it with such airs
> That one believed he had a sword upstairs.[14]

But Milton did not always choose to write as if he had a sword up-stairs. In the Lawrence sonnet, written in the midst of Milton's vituperative defences of the Commonwealth, a different side of his complex character appears. It is a side of Milton that his nephew Edward Phillips described, speaking of Milton in the 1640s:

He would drop into the society of some young sparks of his acquaintance. . . .
With these gentlemen he would so far make bold with his body as now and
then to keep a gawdy-day.[15]

This is not Raleigh's Milton, but it is surely the Milton of the Lawrence
sonnet, that serene and gentle masterpiece which ends with a quiet under-
statement.

> He who of those delights can judge and spare[16]
> To interpose them oft, is not unwise.

The litotes of "not unwise" suppresses the jar of the slight moralizing;
the double negative softens the Horatian "carpe diem" to a pianissimo
cadence. It is this quiet warmth which pervades the whole texture of
Milton's invitation to young Lawrence.

Notes

1. I use the text of M. Y. Hughes, *Complete Poems and Major Prose* (New
   York: Odyssey Press, 1957).
2. E. A. J. Honigmann, in *Milton's Sonnets* (New York: St. Martin's Press,
   1966), p. 52, argues that the poem is not intended as an invitation "but
   rather to suggest a closer friendship, or at least to forestall the slackening
   of friendship." I think the poem is more specific than that.
3. *A Short History of the English People. The World's Great Classics* (New
   York: Colonial Press, 1899), II, 139.
4. For Milton's fourth line cf. Horace, *Odes* II. vii. 6–7: "morantem saepe diem
   mero / fregi" ("with whom I often shortened the day with wine").
5. David Masson, *The Life of John Milton* (Cambridge and London: Macmillan, 1854–1894) III, 657–60.
6. William Riley Parker, *Milton: A Biography* (Oxford: Clarendon Press,
   1968), II, 922–24.
7. Ralph W. Condee, "The Structure of Milton's 'Epitaphium Damonis,'"
   Studies in Philology, LXII (1965), 577–94.
8. Sir Walter Raleigh, *Milton* (New York: Putnam, 1900), p. 8.
9. Parker, II, 1044. Honigmann (p.178) suggests a date as early as perhaps
   "before 1652."
10. Mark Van Doren, *Introduction to Poetry* (New York: Sloane, 1951), pp.
    124–25.
11. Milton was mistakenly attacking More as the author of the anonymous
    Regii Sanguinis Clamor ad Coelum ("A Cry to Heaven of the King's
    Blood"), which was not by More but by Peter Du Moulin; but Milton
    seems not to have been mistaken in his estimate of More's character. I use
    the Latin of the Columbia edition (New York: Columbia University Press,
    1932), VIII, 22 ff., but the translations of Robert Fellowes as reprinted in
    Hughes, 821 ff.
12. Columbia edition, VII, 12 ff. Trans. adapted from that of Samuel Lee Wolff.
13. H. A. Taine, *History of English Literature* (New York: Henry Holt, 1886),
    trans. H. Van Laun, I, 491.
14. "All Things Can Tempt Me," ll. 5–8.
15. In Hughes, *The Life of Milton*, p. 1030.
16. The reading "spare" = "afford" seems best. See Honigmann, pp. 180–81,
    for a summary of the controversy.

Fact and Factuality in Literature

Frank Brady

In one of his essays G. K. Chesterton remarks, "When we are very young children we do not need fairy tales: we only need tales. Mere life is interesting enough. A child of seven is excited by being told that Tommy opened a door and saw a dragon. But a child of three is excited by being told that Tommy opened a door. Boys like romantic tales; but babies like realistic tales—because they find them romantic." This contrast leads Chesterton to conclude, "A baby is about the only person, I should think, to whom a modern realistic novel could be read without boring him."[1]

This distinction between the realistic and the romantic, or essentially between the factual and the imaginative, will not elicit agreement on all points; even Wordsworth was not sure whether "the visionary gleam" belonged to a four-years' or a six-years' darling, while Coleridge was quite certain that no child had prophetic attributes. And, as the *Intimations Ode* itself shows, the factual and the imaginative can interact in ways difficult to define. Chesterton, however, has isolated two extreme attitudes, two mental sets, which literature draws together, even coalesces, often in similarly complex combinations. In giving the preference to the imaginative, Chesterton was a grandchild of his period.

Such a preference, of course, is not an historical absolute. Addison might defend and Joseph Warton exalt "the fairy way of writing," but the eighteenth century remained predominantly an Age of Fact in which the powers and pleasures of the imagination commonly met with an active mistrust.[2] Dr. Johnson is a characteristic, if extreme, exponent of this attitude when he writes of Collins, in the *Lives of the Poets:*

He had employed his mind chiefly upon works of fiction and subjects of fancy, and by indulging some peculiar habits of thought was eminently delighted with those flights of imagination which pass the bounds of nature. . . . He loved fairies, genii, giants, and monsters; he delighted to rove through the meanders of enchantment, to gaze on the magnificence of golden palaces, to repose by the waterfalls of Elysian gardens.

Looked at more harshly, this is the realm of neurotic symptoms Pope portrays in the Cave of Spleen or of those phantasmagoria dear to Dullness. To justify the "peculiar habits of thought" which produced the first Gothic novel, Horace Walpole felt compelled to insist that it was conceived in a dream. The well-established moment at which fact and imagination stand poised in balance with each other—in retrospect, the moment of crossover in critical respectability—occurs in the Preface to *Lyrical Ballads*: Wordsworth's principal purpose, he says, was to throw the coloring of imagination over ordinary incidents and situations. He domesticated the imagination, which the eighteenth century had so often equated with the fantastic; at the same time he hardened the distinction beween Poetry and Matter of Fact or Science. And this shift found its imprimatur in Coleridge's definition of the secondary imagination.

This allusion to a complicated theoretical development serves only to recall the origins of the usual view taken today of factual and imaginative literary forms. This view is stated simply in René Wellek and Austin Warren's *Theory of Literature*. "It would be a narrow conception of literature," they admit:

> to exclude all propaganda art or didactic and satirical poetry. We have to recognize transitional forms like the essay, biography, and much rhetorical literature. . . . The center of literary art is obviously to be found in the traditional genres of the lyric, the epic, the drama. In all of them, the reference is to a world of fiction, of imagination. The statements in a novel, in a poem, or in a drama are not literally true; they are not logical propositions. There is a central and important difference between a statement, even in a historical novel or a novel by Balzac which seems to convey "information" about actual happenings, and the same information appearing in a book of history or sociology.[3]

W. K. Wimsatt epitomizes this attitude when he says, "Poetry is truth of 'coherence', rather than truth of 'correspondence', as the matter is sometimes phrased nowadays."[4] Nor is this attitude restricted to formalist criticism. Northrop Frye likewise differentiates between descriptive or assertive writing where "the *final* direction of meaning is outward" and "all literary verbal structures [where] the final direction of meaning is inward. . . . In literature, questions of fact or truth are subordinated to the primary literary aim of producing a structure of words for its own sake."[5]

Agreement on this point between formalist and archetypal criticism finds its basis in Aristotle's distinction between the poetic universal and the historical particular; its English touchstone is Sidney's statement that "for the poet he nothing affirms, and therefore never lieth."[6] Yet some critical uneasiness persists. Despite Sidney, poets and novelists do seem to be affirming something, and if they do not lie they may be mistaken. There is a troublesome conflict, Mr. Wimsatt notes, between the claim for an autonomous art and the assertion of its ethical content.[7] On the other hand, factual and quasi-factual works can demand to be considered as literature. At least one critic, Murray Krieger, has tried to establish the theoretical relationship between coherence and correspondence: the literary work functions simultaneously as a window onto the world and as a world enclosed by endlessly faceted mirrors . . . so that the mirrors somehow become windows opening again upon our everyday world, although through them that world never again can appear to us as it did before the mirrors originally shut us off from it.[8]

Kreiger shows admirable determination and ingenuity in struggling with so difficult a problem, and if his solution seems illusionistic I have no better one to offer. This essay will attempt nothing so ambitious. It starts from the premise that by grandly ignoring the factual aspects of literature, modern theorists have left the nature and role of one of its essential elements obscure. Further, as Mr. Krieger has pointed out, and as is plain from the statement from Wellek and Warren just quoted, quasi-factual forms, like the allegorical, the satiric, and the didactic, have been slighted.[9] Since the factual presents such a range of critical problems, I can discuss only one here as an entry to this general subject, that being "What are the roles of historic fact and factuality in a literary work?"

Definitions first, and it is symptomatic of modern critical emphasis that while definitions and discussions of the imagination are endless, almost no literary critic has ever tried to define fact. (Philosophical definitions are at best helpful tangentially.) A fact, as ordinarily understood, is something that exists or occurs in the present or has in the past; this is "historic fact" of the "Columbus crossed the Atlantic in 1492" variety. But most statements commonly called factual in a literary work are not of this kind. Instead they represent the ordinary circumstances of everyday life: "Mary washed the dishes in the sink, dried them, and put them on the shelves." This second type of factual statement will be designated "factuality" here; it exemplifies what the philosophers call "sense" without "reference" to historical fact. A third type of the factual is made up of those laws or general statements, called "universals," such as "all men are mortal," though they are usually proportional or statistical in nature.[10] One critic who did try to define fact actually illuminated the connection between universals and the first two types of factual statement just differentiated: "A fact is a specific manifestation of a general law: this general law is the truth because of which that fact has come to be." The falling apple is the fact that manifests the law of gravitation.[11] The usefulness of this definition is in suggesting that our three types form a spectrum with factuality as the middle term. Specified as historic or referential, factuality becomes fact (our term from now on for "historic fact"). Generalized, factuality turns into universals.

The basic use of fact or factuality in other than non-fictional literature is to establish authenticity, to ensure conviction.[12] A common example is the realistic description of setting, which prepares the reader to accept what is to come and indeed to furnish unprovided details from his own experience. "Imagine," I say to my students, "a painting of a cottage and its front lawn, with a hedge that partly blocks both. What lies behind the hedge?" Invariably they say, "More of the cottage and lawn," and feel cheated when I answer, "Nothing lies behind the hedge." This exercise serves, obviously enough, to insist that they stick to the data given in the text and discourages speculation on the relevance of Hamlet's studies at Wittenberg. But my insistence is pragmatically rather than theoretically correct, since any selection of detail sketches a gestalt that the reader fills out for himself.

It is easy to see that the factual helps to establish credibility, but harder to explain why it does so. Johnson asserted that our response to fiction depended basically on our recognizing it as fictional, while Coleridge thought "the willing suspension of disbelief" was fundamental to this process. A modern critic argues that both may be right at different levels of the mind.[13] Another means of reconciling these two positions is to work from the philosopher's distinction between belief and acceptance: "we believe or disbelieve what we take to be factual statements, but we accept or reject what we take to be fictional statements."[14] Then the role of the factual is to convert acceptance, so far as possible, into belief. It is one of the techniques that the poet (any writer of fiction) uses. Henry James remarks that the reader will realize that certain things cannot happen unless he is successfully drugged: "there are drugs enough, clearly—it is all a question of applying them with tact; in which case the way things don't happen may be artfully made to pass for the way things do."[15]

In terms of our spectrum, fact—factuality—universals, it becomes apparent that the heavier the use of fact, the greater the credibility of the work. Consider three possible openings to a novel:

1. Once upon a time, in the reign of a certain king . . .
2. In the reign of a medieval king of England . . .
3. In the reign of Edward II, a few days before the battle of Bannockburn, the town of Falkirk . . .

The first opening suggests legend or fairy tale, the second is too vague to establish conviction by itself, but the third gives the reader a specific time and place to focus on.[16] This last example suggests the opening of an historical novel, a form which raises with special force the issue of credibility and in turn the question, "How important is factual accuracy to fiction?"

Rather than starting with an historical novel for a test case, let us choose a work which poses the question in a simpler form. If Keats's "On First Looking into Chapman's Homer" is the basis for discussion, the formalist may say, "Does it matter if Keats confused Cortez and Balboa?" No, because they are essentially interchangeable examples of the explorer-commander, but if Keats had stuck George III on that peak in Darien it would. Yes, replies the formalist, and if the last line of the sonnet had read, "Silent as Orator Henley on his tub," the poem's meaning would have been altered too: the role of historic (or proper) referents is no different here from that of common referents, such as "surmise" and "peak." In short, fiction can absorb *incidental* factual inaccuracy, just as Aristotle said in the *Poetics*.

One doubt may linger: "How are we justified, theoretically, in substituting Balboa for Cortez?" The meaning of the sonnet's last four lines depends on a piece of historical information which cannot be educed from the poem itself. Perhaps common sense disposes of this particular case by saying that the last three lines show Keats must have had Balboa in mind. But the meaning of historical allusions is not always so clear. Take, for example, "Stetson! / You who were with me in the ships at Mylae!" A well-known anthology identifies Mylae as a battle in the First Punic War "which, like World War I, was fought for economic reasons," and says of Stetson, "presumably representing the 'average businessman.' "[17] No doubt a respectable gloss, but the margin for error has grown. What emerges, in little, is the kind of problem in referentiality that formal theory finds troublesome. Yet it is certainly possible to maintain that the problem of assigning the correct significance to incidental fact in fiction may be no different in kind than any other problem in interpretation, such as whether the last two lines of the "Ode on a Grecian Urn" have a determinate meaning.

The larger version of this problem, and one less easily disposed of, now appears: "How important is factual accuracy in significant cases to fiction?" J. M. Cameron presents one extreme answer to it when he says if Marvell's account of the execution of Charles I in the "Horatian Ode" is accurate, that is accidental so far as the poem is concerned.[18] To this point Margaret Macdonald replies—the specific connection is accidental— that a story which departs wildly from history "will not have verisimilitude which appears to be its object and will be implausible and tedious. Or if, nevertheless, interesting will provoke the question, 'But why call this character Oliver Cromwell, Lord Protector of England?' "[19]

The opposite extreme to Mr. Cameron's view is stated by Mary McCarthy with her usual clarity and briskness:

If we read a novel, say, about conditions in postwar Germany, we expect it to be an accurate report of conditions in postwar Germany; if we find out that it is not, the novel is discredited. This is not the case with a play or a poem. Dante can be wrong in *The Divine Comedy*; it does not matter, with Shakespeare, that Bohemia has no sea coast, but if Tolstoy was all wrong about the Battle of Borodino or the character of Napoleon, *War and Peace* would suffer.[20]

Mary McCarthy's statement arouses two reservations: referential accuracy in a poem or play can matter—think of Rolf Hochhuth's *The Deputy*; and "all wrong" qualifies her point about Tolstoy so strongly as almost to negate it. Still, the main thrust of her argument is hard to reject, and it can be clarified by distinguishing three uses of referentiality: (1) incidental use, as in the Keats and T. S. Eliot examples discussed earlier. These allusions serve a coherential rather than correspondential function in that they make a point within the structure of the poem rather than reinforcing its credibility. (2) Enhancing use, as in Effie Deans' interview with the Duke of Argyle and Queen Caroline in *The Heart of Mid-Lothian*. Why did Scott use a real nobleman as Effie's intercessor instead of inventing, say, a Duke of Ayrshire? The answer seems to be that for any reader with even a slight knowledge of Scottish history Argyle, the virtual ruler of Scotland, has an aura about him; he is a figure who combines strong, ready-made associations of power and benevolence. Also he fits Scott's general re-creation of the Scottish past with its firm, often feudal ties between the rulers and the ruled, here between a great nobleman and a humble, but honest and courageous girl. Scott may heighten Argyle's character somewhat, but he does not contradict what history says of him. If Argyle actually had been a mean courtier, the effect of the scene would be rather spoiled for the knowledgeable reader; as it stands, the effect is enhanced. (3) Authenticating use, as in Marvell's "Horatian Ode." In spite of Mr. Cameron's brave statement, I have never read a discussion of the poem that did not get at least indirectly wound up in the problem of what Cromwell and Charles I were really like. And presumably if Marvell had not been concerned with what they were like he would not have written the poem. In cases of this kind referential accuracy assumes considerable importance: at a minimum Marvell must present a *tenable* view of their characters or the poem would be seriously damaged.

Two overlapping forces can modify the impact of truth of correspondence: distance in time, and loss of interest in the facts involved. Were the Greeks really the valiant defenders of freedom and the Persians the hubristic barbarians depicted in Aeschylus's *The Persians*? Most of us are content to accept this characterization as the play's *donnée* without worrying about its historical truth. We tend to dissolve the specific circumstances into a basic struggle between tyranny and freedom. Also, truth of correspondence becomes an almost meaningless standard when applied to figures like Julius Caesar or Napoleon, about whose merits historians as well as writers of fiction may disagree forever. But present a play in which Lincoln is portrayed as an unfeeling egotist, or the Nazis as the virtuous exponents of a virile Aryanism, and no matter how "coherent" the work it will be attacked as untrue to the facts.[21] From this discussion of the importance of fact in fiction one general conclusion emerges: truth of correspondence provides the groundwork for truth of coherence.[22]

This conclusion also holds true for factuality, but before pursuing its implications the concept of factuality itself must be examined more carefully. First, it must not be confused with "reality" or even that "literary representation of reality in European culture,"[23] which Erich Auerbach studied so brilliantly in *Mimesis*. Factuality is only one level of mimesis in Auerbach's sense, and even so it is hard to define with any precision. Tentatively it may be described as the factual material through or on which the writer's imagination or perception works, this material consisting in external description (of people, places, and events), internal description (of thoughts and feelings), dialogue, and commentary (by author or character).

Second, the example given earlier of factuality, Mary's dishwashing, illustrates only one of its possible levels of presentation. Some critics seem implicitly to equate factuality with Henry James's "solidity of specification," but this is misleading if James's phrase is taken simply to mean "concreteness" or "particularity." In an important essay, "The Substantive Level," Mr. Wimsatt remarks that James himself "may be adduced as the master of several systematic forms of abstractness," and goes on to distinguish three levels of concreteness: the abstract, the minimum concrete or substantive, and the extra-concrete. Examples on a scale of these levels are implement, spade, and rusty garden spade.[24] Factuality encompasses the last two levels, and evidently can be a quantitative as well as qualitative aspect of fiction. It seems paradoxical, however, to speak of the factuality of the abstract. Abstraction and generalization are not identical, of course, but both in fiction may be classed among those universals touched on previously. They appear, for instance, in the form of philosophical or moral generalization, as in the opening sentences of *Rasselas* and *Pride and Prejudice,* setting the tonality or establishing the angle of vision of such works rather than being instruments of conviction.

To the extent that the use of factuality in fiction is governed by rules— "tendencies" might be a more accurate term—they are the rules of emphasis and, as already remarked, credibility. Emphasis, of course, is one of the fundamental principles operating in any literary form, and its connection to factuality may be self-evident; but it is useful to look briefly at one area in which factuality occurs, setting in the early novel, to specify what forms factuality can take and on what substantive levels it appears. The eighteenth-century novel pays little attention to setting in iself. It is what Robinson Crusoe does with his island rather than what it looks like that is important. As critics have noted, when Defoe emphasizes setting it is to make a moral or psychological point: the careful naming of Moll's route across London after she steals the child's necklace stresses her physical acuteness and moral blur; psychologically, it represents the displacement onto physical detail sometimes induced by shock. (Similarly, in *Madame Bovary,* Emma counts the threads in her napkin after learning that Rodolphe has deserted her.) The tracing of a geographical route is a common eighteenth-century substitution for setting, as in *Tom Jones* and in volume seven of *Tristram Shandy*: action and change are the concerns here. What factual description of setting appears is usually at the substantive level, as in *Clarissa* where the layout of Mother Sinclair's house is important to the plot.[25] An exception to this rule is Fielding's detailed description of the grounds and view at Paradise Hall (*Tom Jones,* I.iv), which exemplifies the rural ideal. But this setting remains an awkward and unintegrated factor in the novel. In contrast, while descriptions of setting in *Emma* mostly remain at the substantive level, houses and places now become expressive of character; significantly, their names acquire importance, and it would be possible to chart the novel thematically in terms of Hartfield, Highbury, Randalls, Donwell Abbey and so forth, to say nothing of the offstage shadow of Maple Grove. In Dickens, as often remarked, the settings acquire extra-concrete particularity and full symbolic value.

This development suggests asking whether there is an intrinsic connection between extra-concrete particularity and symbolic setting. In theory, perhaps not; and in practice our second main factor also operates, the use of factuality to establish credibility. As a general tendency, the more imaginative or improbable the setting, the heavier is the use of particularity. The eighteenth-century novels just mentioned made no demand for particularity in setting because, at least in part, they were inherently factual in basic attitude as well as in style.[26] But the romance, in its various forms, does need to validate the credentials of the imagination through detail. Whoever read of a magician's eyrie that was not a clutter of disorganized junk? Science fiction bemuses the reader with mystifying detail about the universe. The latter-day romance of chivalry often provides very detailed setting, while the *Morte d'Arthur*, accepting similar material as realistic and contemporary, is descriptively sparse. "Had my title," says Scott, "borne 'Waverley, a Romance from the German,' what head so obtuse as not to image forth a profligate abbot, an oppressive duke, a secret and mysterious association of Rosicrucians and Illuminati, with all their properties of black cowls, caverns, daggers, electrical machines, trap doors, and dark-lanterns?" (ch. 1). Scott was not above taking his own hints, as in *The Antiquary*.[27] The elaborate factual description of Wuthering Heights serves as a solid basis for the imaginative story to come. But it is useless to multiply examples. Henry James's well-known analogy can summarize this point:

the balloon of experience is in fact of course tied to the earth, and under that necessity we swing, thanks to a rope of remarkable length, in the more or less commodious car of the imagination; but it is by the rope we know where we are. . . . The art of the romance is, "for the fun of it," insidiously to cut the cable, to cut it without our detecting him.[28]

Setting is only one aspect of the role of factuality in fiction; clearly if other areas in which factuality operates, such as dialogue, were explored different conclusions about forms of factuality and substantative levels might be reached.[29] Also the overall shift in interest from the general to the particular would have to be taken into account. But I am primarily interested here in the theoretical aspects of factuality, and at this point in an issue mentioned earlier: the affinity of factuality for those kinds of fiction—the allegorical, the didactic, and the satiric—which formalist criticism has difficulty in responding to because of their basic referentiality. In studying these genres, beside the factors of referentiality and substantive level already discussed to some extent, the question of relatedness among factual details becomes important. The allegorical demands the greatest amount of relatedness among the details themselves, since by the nature of allegory detail must show significant coherence on at least two levels. (The details themselves may be fantastic—enchantresses and dragons and wells of life—but they are presented as if they were factual.) The substantive level of allegory will vary according to the weight of meaning the detail is made to bear, Dante and Spenser being more concrete than Bunyan. In the didactic, where ideas are expressed directly rather than embodied, detail becomes subordinate and illustrative, often taking the form of fact (historical allusion) as in the *Essay on Man*, since fact is a compressive device: a reference to, say, Julius Caesar, not only illustrates a generalization but reinforces it through the strength of its historical example.

As we shift from the allegorical and didactic toward the satiric, referentiality becomes increasingly important. Pope's persona and interlocutor debate in various poems whether it is better to use generic or real names, but the essence of satire is contradicted if we rest content with "harmless characters that no one hit." Yet it is certainly possible to understand the *Epistle to Arbuthnot* without knowing whom Atticus and Sporus shadow forth; the formalist may well argue that it hardly matters if the description of Sporus is unfair to Lord Hervey; what matters is, for example, the place of Sporus as a climactic portrait in the poem's structure. Here can be developed somewhat further the formalist's objections to criteria based on correspondence. Once the critic gets involved in disputes about historical accuracy, he will inevitably find himself bogged down in those dreary biographical and intentional arguments which ignore the poem's coherence, and both interpret and evaluate it on extra-literary grounds. This line of reasoning must command respect, but it frames the coherence-correspondence relationship too much as an "either-or" proposition. Can we ignore the poem's "intention," however we define that term? Pope did mean Sporus to bear a recognizable relationship to Hervey, he did mean to damn his character to posterity, and—except for a few scholars—he succeeded brilliantly. Like Scott in his portrait of Argyle, Pope heightened, or blackened, Hervey's character, but it is a tenable construct. It can be argued, of course, that we are interested in Sporus and "Pope" as types of evil and good men rather than as historical persons, generalizing them as we do the characters in *The Persians*. To do so adds to the universalizing effect of the *Epistle to Arbuthnot* at the cost of some of its substance and edge. As far as I can see, we are always forced to read satire with both coherential and correspondential attitudes.

Tangentially, it seems that whenever possible formalist criticism dissolves truth of correspondence into truth of coherence through such mediatory terms as complexity, maturity, and sentimentality. These are values, and about values there is no disputing. I do not want to enter into the question of how poetry is related to value except to point out that the formalist position always seems to involve some "givens" about the ideal reader which are reminiscent of Hume's attempt to solve the question by using certain self-evident judgments as limits:

whoever would assert an equality of genius and elegance between Ogilby and Milton, or Bunyan and Addison, would be thought to defend no less an extravagance than if he had maintained a molehill to be as high as Tenerife or a pond as extensive as the ocean.[30]

If Hume's second example seems merely unfortunate, it is possible to find similar comparisons: who today would think it had ever been possible to value Homer and Ossian equally? Or to dismiss Milton as a highly overrated poet of harmful influence?

To return to satire and factuality. As we pass through the three phases of satire differentiated by Mr. Frye—from the reassertion of the conventional and commonsensical to the triumph of chaos—factual coherence or interrelatedness naturally diminishes.[31] Already in the second phase, in which theory or system is set against the experience it is supposed to explain, illusion and reality intermingle uneasily, as in *Don Quixote*. A. B. Kernan demonstrates that "the scene of satire is always disorderly and crowded,"[32] and it becomes more so in Mr. Frye's third phase. Here, where the moral, social, and intellectual orders collapse, discontinuous detail piles up, one of the great examples being *The Dunciad*; and the scene in that case can be illuminated by looking at its epic counterpart, the landscape in Book II of *Paradise Lost*. Milton's Hell, we know, is a type of disorder, "rocks, caves, lakes, fens," and so forth, a substantively factual but incoherent landscape; in Chaos the factual is reduced to non-dimensional elements identified not by substance but by warring "accidents": "hot, cold, moist, and dry." Of such, too, is the kingdom of Dullness. To pick one similarity, substance in the form of the young Grand Tourist at last "turned *air*, the echo of a sound."

Factuality never seems, however, to constitute a genre in itself. Dead-center realism, "pure mime," is uncommon, and when Zola tried to reduce the novel to uninterpreted observation or report, it slipped apart historically, and perhaps inevitably, into the opposite extremes of symbolism and naturalism.[33] Further, it can be argued that any massing of detail, even in Balzac, occurs less for the sake of transcribing reality than for structural purposes within the work itself; detail turns into symbol.[34] At least we can agree on the basic principle that any selection of detail *a priori* involves interpretation. But this principle leads to the troublesome problem of how to decide when detail is irrelevant. Leslie Stephen remarked of Balzac's novels that

we meet with artifices like those by which Defoe cheats us into forgetfulness of his true character. One of the best known is the insertion of superfluous bits of information, by way of entrapping his readers into the inference that they could only have been given because they were true.[35]

Though Stephen disapproved of this practice, he provided its theoretical justification: if factuality establishes credibility, irrelevant factuality enhances it. Such realism imitates the unfinishedness of life rather than the smoothness of art. Taking a similar position, F. W. Bateson asserts that "the plethora of concrete detail (the convention of phenomenal particularity)" ensures the fictional compact between author and reader. For example, in Katherine Mansfield's "The Fly," the boss's armchair is a functional consequence of plot and characterization: "it is the addition of greenness to the chair, a non-functional detail, that is the mark of the realistic convention." Suppress the detail and the convention collapses.[36] Yet, as the earlier discussion of settings indicated, extra-concrete particularity is *not* characteristic of eighteenth-century fictional descriptions of setting. Particularity is much more likely to appear there in the form of dialogue, and few critics would justify non-functional dialogue—though it is hard to see, in theoretical terms, why it should be treated any differently from descriptive detail. At this point we are left without any way of establishing irrelevance, and perhaps so long as factuality is conceived of as a transcription of reality it will never be possible to distinguish theoretically between the authenticating and the superfluous detail.[37]

The problem looks curiously different if the phenomenal surface is itself treated as "reality" rather than as a mimetic representation of it. Some such effect appears in the novels of Jean-Paul Sartre with their "notations qui rendent sensible jusqu'à l'hallucination ou l'obsession la présence, l'existence horrible et fascinante des choses."[38] The moral disappears with the mimetic; no longer is it a question of whatever is, is right or wrong, but as Alain Robbe-Grillet puts it in his discussion of the *nouveau roman*, "cella *est*, et c'est tout." His shift from a mimetic to an expressionistic view of his own work leads M. Robbe-Grillet to say, "Je ne transcris pas, je construis." Verisimilitude is irrelevant, and indeed "the false" becomes a privileged point of view for the modern writer; the authenticating detail is replaced by "le petit détail qui fait *faux*." He illustrates this point by separating the surface presentation of things in Kafka from their allegorical meanings, leading him to conclude that what remains is "cette signification immédiate des choses (descriptive, partielle, toujours contestée)."[39] Detail can be fragmentary, unrelated, but never irrelevant, just as a diary, theoretically speaking, never includes irrelevant detail, for all is governed by the diarist's immediate sense of significance.[40]

If factuality, like imagination, is too broad a classification to constitute a genre, it is still possible to imitate Addison and categorize its pleasures. It would be neat if they were the simple inverse of the pleasures of the imagination, the evocation of the small, the ugly, and the commonplace; they are not, though such elements move through them. The first of the pleasures of factuality is the providing of information. Referring to a Balzac novel which includes an "irrelevant" chapter on the process of making paper, Mary McCarthy says, "The passion for fact in a raw state is a peculiarity of the novelist. Most of the great novels contain blocks and lumps of fact—refractory lumps in the porridge of the story."[41] Such informational material may be an artistic defect which Flaubert or Henry James would deplore, but the novel refuses to assimilate itself to the stricter models of poetry or drama; in its imitation or construction of life, it requires less coherence or admits more pure referentiality than these forms. One can extend Yvor Winters' comment on history as literature to the novel at least: "the historical work has the advantage of dealing with accomplished and influential facts. One may argue that an interest in such facts is not a literary interest, but I do not believe we can make this distinction."[42] What is intrinsically "literary" about the imaginative and "non-literary" about the factual? To approach the question in a different way: the assumption that contemplative disinterest is the only proper approach to literature ignores a fundamental element in our response to it. In reading we learn and relearn about ourselves, others, and the world. If this were not true, literature would be a minor and esoteric art. The providing of information is part of what we learn.

A second pleasure of factuality is representation, seen most clearly in verisimilitude. Hugh Kenner, deriving the fall of modern man from his absorption with fact, speaks of "the taxidermal tranquility of *trompe l'oeil*";[43] and Mr. Cameron claims it provides "only a perverse pleasure";[44] yet verisimilitude, at various substantive levels, has persistently fascinated certain writers and readers. One has only to think of the account of mass burials in Defoe's *Journal of the Plague Year* or the description of a girl going in and out of a drugstore door in John Updike's "A Sense of Shelter." Chaucer's detailed evocations of certain of his pilgrims no doubt have symbolic value, possibly layers of it, but what first strikes, and remains with, the reader is the vividness of their portrayal. Nor are "truth-about" and "truth-to" something always so distinct as aestheticians like to assert.

A third pleasure of factuality is truthfulness, in the sense of "this is the way things are." Looked at in respect to fact, this might be called the resonance of the specific. To an inhabitant of the Upper West Side of Manhattan, Saul Bellow's *Seize the Day* renders the scene—Broadway, the Hotel Ansonia, and so on—with a powerful circumstantiality that arouses a practically autotelic pleasure. If this seems a provincial example, consider a different kind of case involving geographical fact, the reader of Dickens who visits London for the first time. All those moving but somewhat indistinct descriptions suddenly take on specificity: even if buildings and streets have changed, the fog remains the same. To the formalist such accidents of experience should not affect our response to *Bleak House*; in practice they cannot help modifying it to some slight degree. Life and art become mutually reinforcing.

The resonance of fact is a special instance of truthfulness. Take as an example of the general case the opening lines of Dryden's portrait of Og:

Now stop your noses, readers, all and some,
For here's a tun of midnight work to come,
Og, from a treason-tavern rowling home.
Round as a globe, and liquored every chink,
Goodly and great, he sails behind his link. . . .

The firmness and vitality of this portrait do not depend on verisimilitude
or extra-concrete particularity, and to the extent that Og is a more than
life-size portrait of Shadwell the imagination plays its part. Dryden in-
flates Og the better to puncture him, and what we basically respond to, I
think, is the commonsensical attitude Dryden deploys in this process with
extraordinary force. As T. S. Eliot said, he "states immensely,"[45] and
statement seems allied to factuality as suggestion is to imagination.
Truthfulness of this kind, the sense that the writer is operating at the
level of ordinary thought and feeling, is hard to pin down; but just as
there is a visionary tradition in English poetry that includes Spenser,
Blake, Shelley, and Yeats, so there is a factual tradition that includes
Chaucer, Jonson, Dryden, Crabbe, and in some of his poetry W. H.
Auden. These poets are of this world, worldly. Of course the great embodiment of the factual among English writers is Dr. Johnson.

Factuality, then, extends much beyond Pooh-Bah's "merely corrobora-
tive detail, intended to give artistic verisimilitude to an otherwise bald
and unconvincing narrative." But bad factual writing remains at this
level. There is no need here to explore its depressingly various causes:
the fallacy of misplaced concreteness, the simpleminded accumulation of
particulars, the attempt to make inert detail do the work of the intelligence and the imagination. Its one theoretical justification, Zola's "experimental novel," is as impossible a goal as Ranke's desire to record
history "as it actually happened." Objectivity at most presents an interesting theoretical limit. In practice, Fielding observed, it is necessary to
provide what he calls "poetical embellishments":

without interruptions of this kind, the best narrative of plain matter of fact
must overpower every reader; for nothing but the everlasting watchfulness,
which Homer has ascribed only to Jove himself, can be proof against a newspaper of many volumes. (Tom Jones, IV. i)

Even Chesterton's baby will nod.

Factuality and imagination need each other: their interaction is a central
and insufficiently studied literary process, of which I can try to offer only
a few samples. At one extreme is the imaginative work which uses mini-
mal factuality as a cable tying it to experience. A good instance is Stevens'
"The Idea of Order at Key West," which includes two "facts," the place
"Key West" specified only in the title, and the name "Ramon Fernandez."
Neither of these apparently firm details withstands much examination.
"The glassy lights, / The lights in the fishing boats at anchor there," are

a property common to any fishing village, and whoever looks for "the ever-hooded, tragic-gestured sea" at Key West will find it actually quite placid. Stevens had read the French critic, Ramon Fernandez, but denied that he was referring to him in the poem.[46] These two facts provide an "irrelevant" specificity that helps to keep the balloon from flying away.

More often, factuality and imagination are used disjunctively. They can establish a work's structure, as in Keats's "Ode to a Nightingale" or, as in the same poem, they can furnish its theme.[47] The question which the "Ode" moves toward, "Was it a vision, or a waking dream?" is resolved clearly in "The Eve of St. Agnes." Poising factual against imaginative in one of its most common oppositions, realistic against romantic, Keats turns the romantic into the real. Though the lovers "glide, like phantoms" in their escape, the threatening storm outside is an "elfin-storm . . . Of haggard seeming"; while their enemies inside are "sleeping dragons" who have receded in power and substance to the level of "the arras, rich with horseman, hawk, and hound."

Disjunction is not easily separable from juxtaposition. In *Hard Times* when Mr. Gradgrind fills his little vessels with facts and more facts, Dickens prepares the reader to reject the view of things that takes a horse to be a graminiverous quadruped in favor of the view, at once more playful and more serious, that the world is a circus. Milton manipulates levels of imagination in a more complicated way in *Paradise Lost*. His basic problem was to liken "spiritual to corporal forms" (v. 573), essentially the problem of the allegorist, but except for Sin and Death he avoids allegory in order to create the denser, more concrete world of the epic. As Dickens condemns the dry-as-dust mentality of the factual, Milton—it hardly comes as news—disparages the physical level of epic and romance with its "tilting furniture" and "tinsel trappings" to praise the spiritual qualities of "patience and heroic martyrdom" (ix. 32–36). But also he reduces classical myth to an imaginative backdrop against which his spiritual-corporal world achieves solidity, as in his summary of Hell where . . .

> Nature breeds
> Perverse, all monstrous, all prodigious things,
> Abominable, inutterable, and worse
> Than fables yet have feigned, or fear conceived,
> Gorgons and hydras and chimeras dire.   (ii. 624–628)

Or one further example, the beautiful description of Mulciber's fall from Heaven becomes simply a distortion of the truth: "thus they relate, / Erring" (i. 746–747). The Christian knows the facts. Both these cases of juxtaposition fall within that enormous system of factual-imaginative relationships which finds complicated forms in the juxtaposing, comparing, and contrasting of the physical-moral, spiritual-material, internal-external, and abstract-concrete, and extending throughout the poem comprise its basic imagistic technique. Finally, from the most complex study in juxtaposition, *Don Quixote*, we can isolate one aspect to mention, the way in which the imaginative authenticates the factual. As one critic puts the point, "the undeniable physical fact of the book, Part I, cause[s] events in Part II, thereby making them seem 'truer.' "[48]

Like disjunction and juxtaposition, modulation between the factual and the imaginative is a common technique. One of the finest aspects of the Waverley novels is Scott's ability to modulate smoothly from the vigorous dialect of Lowland peasants and shopkeepers to the Gaelic-tinged, high-flown language of Highland history and romance, in part through the old-fashioned speech that exemplifies the outlook of transitional figures like Jonathan Oldbuck and the Baron of Bradwardine. In this case modulation suggests that the factual and the imaginative essentially form part of the same world. It is more difficult to modulate between the fantastic and the factual, which are usually taken as disjunctive. The veracity and even the existence of the Ghost in *Hamlet* are problematic, but there is at least sleight-of-hand modulation in *Macbeth* in the literal fulfillment of fantastic prophecy. A fine example of disjunction disguised as modulation occurs at the beginning of *Gulliver's Travels*. Swift sticks as close to the semblance of facts as he can: Gulliver grows up in Nottinghamshire, attends Emmanuel College, Cambridge, sets up practice in the Old Jury, and so forth. The first voyage and shipwreck slip into factuality. Not until Gulliver finds himself bound with "several slender ligatures" and perceives "a human creature not six inches high" is the reader clearly in the world of the fantastic—as Gulliver never is. Yet retrospectively the reader can pick out a couple of details that anticipate this transition: the slight declivity of the ocean bottom which forces Gulliver to walk nearly a mile to shore, and the "very short and soft" grass on which he sleeps.[49]

The use of diminution and magnification in *Gulliver's Travels* in turn recalls how often fantasy depends on alteration in scale, obvious examples being *Gargantua and Pantagruel* and *Alice in Wonderland*, though to different ends: in *Gargantua*, the fantastic liberates the individual will from the demands of society—"Do as you please"; in *Alice*, the representative of the factual, Alice, resists the fantastic forms the world takes —"You are all a pack of cards." A particularly skillful balancing of the fantastic and the factual involving alteration in scale occurs in Walter De La Mare's *Memoirs of a Midget*, where Miss M. resolutely maintains her human nature in defiance of the Big People's efforts to treat her as a toy.

The factual and the imaginative do not always mesh properly, of course; failure appears in disjunction, juxtaposition, or modulation. Positively, this failure is a major source of the comic, as in Sir Epicure Mammon's aureate vision of Dol Common:

She shall feel gold, taste gold, hear gold, sleep gold;
Nay, we will *concumbere* gold.

Sir Epicure has the visionary gleam, with a difference.[50] Here the comic provides the necessary, and otherwise inappropriate, connection between the imaginative and the material. Negatively, the inappropriate remains just its awkward self. Hugh Kenner remarks that "Fact . . . continues to creep up the slopes of Parnassus like crab grass, and it is finally Wordsworth, of all people, who is the very alembicator of Fact":

it is clear that he feels haunted by a sense of responsibility toward mere data; nor would he have us suppose him insensible to the primary function of the real language of men, which is to convey information. But the decorum of the factual is comic, because one can never tell from what direction a new fact may impinge.[51]

Mr. Kenner is certainly right about inappropriate juncture in Wordsworth's poetry, though possibly he gives the wrong reasons.[52] Nor does he explain those passages, as in *Tintern Abbey* or *The Prelude*, where Wordsworth modulates with marvelous effect from the factual to the imaginative. But these are problems in historical or formal analysis.

The most complex way of interweaving factual and imaginative occurs in those much discussed "frame" structures that dramatists from Shakespeare to Pirandello, for example, have been fond of.[53] These might be called reversible reactions (factual $\rightleftarrows$ imaginative), since what they share is a tendency toward being read in either direction: they can assert either the authenticity or unreality of either side of the equation. For instance, the "mousetrap" in *Hamlet* may imply either that all involved, from the Player King and Queen to the audience watching *Hamlet*, are players of parts, or that all are equally "real." Or even that both propositions are true in some paradoxical way.[54] This well-known effect can also be disjunctive: Prospero's "Our revels now are ended" portrays the whole world as a vision; yet his Epilogue puts himself and the play at the mercy of the audience's critical judgment.

And the audience can vary like Prospero. At one moment we feel with Yeats

That this pragmatical, preposterous pig of a world, its farrow that
  so solid seem,
Must vanish on the instant if the mind but change its theme.

At another, we kick the stone and refute Berkeley. But these are extremes. The imaginative orders the factual; the factual sustains the imaginative. They are inextricably connected.

Notes

1. "The Ethics of Elfland," in *G. K. Chesterton: A Selection from His Non-Fictional Prose*, ed. W. H. Auden (London: Faber, 1970), pp. 180–81.

2. Hugh Kenner stresses this aspect of the eighteenth century in his perceptive and amusing study, *The Counterfeiters* (Bloomington: Indiana University Press, 1968).

3. *Theory of Literature* (New York: Harcourt, Brace, 1949), pp. 14–15. Messrs. Wellek and Warren's uneasiness in dealing with this point appears in an uncharacteristic confusion of literal truth and logical propositions. A lighthearted response might be that either in life or in a novel when X says to Y, "I love you," the statement may be literally true and it may be a proposition, but it is not a logical proposition.

4. W. K. Wimsatt and Cleanth Brooks, *Literary Criticism: A Short History* (New York: Alfred A. Knopf, 1957), p. 748. This statement may be put alongside Mr. Wimsatt's earlier definition: "Poetry is that type of verbal structure where truth of reference or correspondence reaches a maximum degree of fusion with truth of coherence—or where external and internal relation are intimately mutual reflections."—"The Substantive Level," in *The Verbal Icon* (Lexington, Ky.: University of Kentucky Press, 1954), p. 149.

5. *Anatomy of Criticism* (Princeton: Princeton University Press, 1957), p. 74.

6. Gerald Graff comments on the contextual meaning of this saying in *Poetic Statement and Critical Dogma* (Evanston: Northwestern University Press, 1970), appendix B.

7. See Murray Krieger, *The Play and Place of Criticism* (Baltimore: Johns Hopkins University Press, 1967), p. 210.

8. *A Window to Criticism* (Princeton: Princeton University Press, 1964), p. 28.

9. Murray Krieger, *The Play and Place of Criticism*, p. 167.

10. See J. P. Day, "Artistic Verisimilitude," *Dialogue*, 1 (1962), 167.

11. Clayton Hamilton, *The Art of Fiction* (New York: Doubleday, Doran, 1939), p. 4.

12. A full discussion of the purpose appears in Mary McCarthy, "The Fact in Fiction," in *On the Contrary* (New York: Farrar, Straus, and Giroux, 1961).

13. H. Osborne, "On Artistic Illusion," *British Journal of Aesthetics*, 9 (1969), 218.

14. Day, p. 283.

15. *The Art of the Novel*, ed. R. P. Blackmur (New York: Charles Scribner's Sons, 1934), p. 34.

16. See Mary McCarthy, *On the Contrary*, pp. 255–56.

17. *The Norton Anthology of English Literature*, ed. M. H. Abrams et al. (New York: W. W. Norton, 1962), ii. 1784, notes 5, 6.

18. *Poetry and Dialectic* (Leeds: Leeds University Press, 1961), pp. 5–6.

19. "The Language of Fiction," in *Perspectives on Fiction*, eds. J. L. Calderwood and H. E. Toliver (New York: Oxford University Press, 1968), p. 67.

20. *On the Contrary*, p. 263. This statement is part of Miss McCarthy's argument that the novel is "continuous with real life" (ibid.). For a contrasting view, see David Lodge, *The Language of Fiction* (London: Routledge and Kegan Paul, 1966), p. 42.

21. Gerald Graff discusses an actual example, Ezra Pound's *Cantos*, in *Poetic Statement and Critical Dogma*, appendix. A. M. C. Beardsley's attack on the anti-Semitism of the *Cantos* wavers between coherential and correspondential arguments—*Aesthetics* (New York: Harcourt, Brace, 1958), pp. 427f.

22. John Hospers's position is somewhat similar to this, though he argues that prose is essentially referential and poetry nonreferential. Even so, he asserts that "the referential function of language in poetry . . . is important as a *prerequisite*."—*Meaning and Truth in the Arts* (Chapel Hill: University of North Carolina Press, 1946) pp. 126f. Mr. Graff claims that the critic's

beliefs, his ethical and philosophical attitudes, must govern the extrinsic criteria by which he judges the "ground-consequent" relationship presented in a literary work (*Poetic Statement and Critical Dogma*, pp. 144f.). I am happy to avoid the question of how fiction is related to the reader's religious and ethical views.

23. Erich Auerbach, *Mimesis*, trans. W. R. Trask (Princeton: Princeton University Press, 1953), p. 23.
24. *The Verbal Icon*, pp. 135, 138.
25. Specific description of setting does occur in *Clarissa*, as in Belford's letter to Lovelace of "Monday, July 17," but it is rather unusual.
26. Biblical writers also felt no need to provide detail, since what they presented was literally true (see *Mimesis*, pp. 14–21). It is apparent, of course, that there are obvious exceptions to what is said here about the eighteenth-century novel, such as the "romance" element in *Clarissa*; and, of course, *Tristram Shandy* is a case by itself.
27. See C. O. Parsons, *Witchcraft and Demonology in Scott's Fiction* (Edinburgh: Oliver and Boyd, 1964), in particular pp. 92–95.
28. *The Art of the Novel*, pp. 33–34.
29. For example, Leo Braudy provides a good account of Fielding's use of factuality from a quite different angle in *Narrative Form in History and Fiction: Hume, Fielding, and Gibbon* (Princeton: Princeton University Press, 1970).
30. "Of the Standard of Taste."
31. *Anatomy of Criticism*, pp. 223–239.
32. *The Cankered Muse* (New Haven: Yale University Press, 1959), p. 7.
33. See Mr. Frye's suggestive comments in *Anatomy of Criticism*, pp. 49, 79–80, 285.
34. So Maurice Blanchot claims in "L'Art du roman chez Balzac," in *Faux Pas* (Paris: Gallimard, 1943), pp. 211–16.
35. "Balzac's Novels," in *Hours in a Library* (London: Smith, Elder, 1909), i. 190.
36. F. W. Bateson and B. Shahevitch, "Katherine Mansfield's 'The Fly': A Critical Exercise" and the ensuing discussion between Mr. Bateson and E. B. Greenwood in "The Critical Forum," *Essays in Criticism*, 12 (1962), 39–53, 341–51, 448–52; quotations on pp. 348f.
37. Martin Price suggests the less pessimistic view that in the novel relevance itself expands "to require new detail, and the irrelevant detail becomes the boundary at the limit of expansion" ("The Irrelevant Detail and the Emergence of Form," in *Aspects of Narrative*, ed. J. Hillis Miller, New York: Columbia University Press, 1971, p. 75). This essay as a whole bears on a number of points considered in the present discussion; see, in particular, pp. 87–91. Mr. Day makes an interesting attempt at a related distinction between "insignificant" and "incidental" detail ("Artistic Verisimilitude," p. 290).
38. Jean-Louis Curtis, *Haute École* (Paris: R. Julliard, 1950), p. 198.
39. Alain Robbe-Grillet, "Du réalisme à la réalité," in *Pour un nouveau roman* (Paris: Éditions de Minuit, 1963), pp. 135–44.
40. I have expanded this point in a review of the new edition of Pepys's *Diary* in the *Yale Review*, 60 (1971), 269–71.
41. *On the Contrary*, pp. 257–58.
42. "Problems for the Modern Critic of Literature," *Hudson Review*, 9 (1956), 361.
43. *The Counterfeiters*, p. 96.
44. *Poetry and Dialectic*, p. 22.
45. "John Dryden," in *Selected Essays* (New York: Harcourt, Brace, 1950), p. 273.

46. *Letters of Wallace Stevens*, ed. Holly Stevens (New York: Alfred A. Knopf, 1966), p. 798.
47. See Robert M. Adams, *Strains of Discord* (Ithaca: Cornell University Press, 1958), pp. 65–67. Mr. Adams discusses many examples of what he calls "real life-imagination" contrast.
48. Norman N. Holland, "The 'Willing Suspension of Disbelief' Revisited," *Centennial Review*, 11 (1967), 19–20.
49. I have suggested some other relationships between the factual and the fantastic in *Gulliver's Travels* in the introduction to *Twentieth-Century Interpretations of "Gulliver's Travels"* (Englewood Cliffs: Prentice-Hall, 1968), pp. 5–11. See also *The Counterfeiters*, pp. 128–42; and Robert C. Elliott, *The Power of Satire* (Princeton: Princeton University Press, 1960), pp. 197–200.
50. There are comparable serious effects, as in Milton's Mammon, whose imagination turns everything into dross.
51. *The Counterfeiters*, pp. 64–65.
52. For an alternative explanation, see F. A. Pottle, *The Idiom of Poetry* (Ithaca: Cornell University Press, 1946), chap. 6.
53. A recent discussion appears in *Strains of Discord*, chap. 4.
54. See, among others, J. Hillis Miller, "Three Problems of Fictional Form: First Person Narration in *David Copperfield* and *Huckleberry Finn*," in *Experience in the Novel*, ed. Roy Harvey Pearce (New York: Columbia University Press, 1968), pp. 28–30.

The Novel's
Original Sin
F. W. Bateson

It is announced from time to time—by V. S. Pritchett, for example, or Lionel Trilling, or some other critical bigwig—that the novel is dead. Or if not actually dead as good as dead, in its last painful and pathetic agonies. The process of dissolution set in, it seems, with Gustave Flaubert, became more acute in Henry James's later novels and short stories, and was completed without possibility of cure by the great experimentalists of the first quarter or third of this century—Gide, Proust, Mann, Joyce, Lawrence and the decidedly less great Virginia Woolf. After their masterpieces, or all-but masterpieces, a failure of nerve set in; apparently there was nothing significant left for the novelist to say and no interesting new way in which to say it. I need not elaborate the familiar obituary notice. Alas, poor Yorick! I knew him—well, too well, especially when I was in my twenties and (critically) deplorably liable to be led by the nose.

My own attitude to the novel today is rather different from the tale of literary decline and fall I have just summarized, though perhaps it is even more disparaging. The heresy that I am proposing to advance, put as bluntly as possible, is not that the serious novel is dead but that, with the exception of the satiric novel, it *ought* to be. It is certainly true that would-be serious and nonsatiric novels continue to be written and even read, but I deplore both facts. In a word, I regard the novel as *per se* an inferior art-form, one hopelessly vitiated by an internal technical self-contradiction.

I begin with the aesthetic problem posed by the length of the average novel. It is impossible for the human memory to retain in its original freshness and detail each episode in the preceding chapters as a novel progresses. At best we retain a vague outline of what occurred before, and though it is theoretically possible, no doubt, to refer back to a related passage in an earlier chapter, how often do we do so? Unlike the historian, the novelist does not even provide indexes; the list of characters at the beginning of a Dickens novel is the nearest we get to one.

Sometimes the chapters have headings or brief outlines, but no novelist that I can think of gives us the detailed summaries that Milton added to each book of *Paradise Lost*. Unlike the lyric too—which is continually sending us back to earlier stanzas by its repetitions of phrasing or imagery

—the novel is in effect a One-Way form of literary traffic. Poetry has been defined as memorable words; a novel, on the other hand consists of immemorable words. *Qua* novel it makes little or no difference whether the writing is finished or slovenly. Novels, after all, translate, and within certain limits it does not seem to matter how competent the particular translation is. No doubt that is why the translator's name is so often omitted. But the crucial self-contradiction implicit in the novel form is not the deficiency in any unity of impression that its immemorability imposes.

I want to dig deeper into the hideous, ultimate nature of the novel. Before doing so, however, let me throw at the novel-addict a dictum of E. M. Forster's in *Aspects of the Novel*. According to Forster, who was after all not at all a bad novelist himself, a novel can *never* achieve the final beauty of form that is obtainable in a play. Never, never, never—however much you struggle with *le mot juste* or some subtle and delicate shade in your characterisation or plot. The remark is made more or less *en passant*, and Forster shows no awareness of its devastating implications. He may not, perhaps, have realized the strict critical consequence of his admission. For surely if a literary genre is necessarily, by its very nature, incapable of the sort of perfection that is attainable in such a closely related genre as the drama its life cannot be expected to be a long one. Is it not even our duty, as responsible literary critics, to administer forthwith the fatal destructive *coup de grace*?

As I have already admitted, I am prepared to allow one species of the genus an exemption from this universal condemnation. But with this one exception the rigor of my Puritanic logic will not allow me to condone the practice either of serious novel-writing or of serious novel-reading. Frivolous novels are, of course, another matter. It is not a literary sin to read or to write a thriller or a detective story. I am myself a P. G. Wodehouse fan. But we are not concerned with such subliterature. I am shooting now at the big stuff—*War and Peace, Moby Dick, David Copperfield, Middlemarch, The Ambassadors, Women in Love, Ulysses*—et hoc genus omne.

Let us begin, then, by asking what a novel is—or is supposed to be. A novel is first of all, I suppose, a narrative in prose of a certain length (40,000 words has been suggested by Forster as the minimum); it is also, obviously, something more. "Realism" must be superimposed on "story." "The first thing we normally ask of a novel," Walter Allen has said, "is that it shall give us a recognizably faithful picture of the life of its times." A novel, then, is a kind of social history. But that history must be pseudo-history. For the second thing that we normally ask of a novel is that it shall be *fiction*, a "life of the times" enacted by characters who have never existed, proceeding from situation to situation that are all equally unverifiable historically.

The contradiction could hardly be more complete: the untrue masquerading as the true! Or, to put it in another way, an omniscient narrator disguising himself as a biographer or social historian, but without the unfortunate historian's limitation that his researches will always be incomplete. Now it is precisely in attempting to persuade us to suspend our disbelief in the reality of its characters by providing them with a background and a setting that are recognizable and familiar that the novel commits what I call its original sin. The reader ought surely to be convinced of the quasi-reality of a novel's characters from his own social or introspective experience, as he is convinced of it in a good play, narrative poem or romance. But the novelist adds to the evidence from intersubjective human probability the objective minutiae of real life—landscapes, houses, costumes, professions, incomes, etc. And the effect of the latter is supposed somehow to confirm the former. "Improbable, my dear reader, though my heroine's behaviour may seem," the novelist insinuates, "it did really happen. I know, because I can tell you how many windows there were on each floor of my heroine's uncle's house, the Rectory of Hogsbottom Episcopi, in the county of Somerset in the year 1867." But in fact the one kind of knowledge (the illusion of psychological probability) has no necessary connection with such information as is provided in the *Victoria County History of Somerset* or a *Penguin Guide*. The knowledge provided by a novelist is really a mode of rhetoric; it is only by rhetoric, the art of persuasion, that he can hope to convince us he does know all about the windows of Hogsbottom Rectory in 1867. But this rhetorical omniscience, though it is intended to look like history, is not history because it is not verifiable from historical documents. You can explore every acre of Somerset without finding a Hogsbottom Episcopi in any one of them. In other words, *the novel is fiction posing as fact*.

The point is worth elaborating. The novel is distinguished from other narrative genres—such as drama or the epic—by its wealth of plausible incidental detail, its general function being to encourage the reader to believe himself in a world similar in all its external aspects to that in which we have our daily being. Instead of the mere willing suspension of disbelief that poetry or fantasy demands from its readers, the novel-reader finds himself cajoled into accepting the events described in a novel as of almost the same order of reality as the events he meets in the newspaper. The two worlds become coterminous. That at least seems to be the novelist's intention.

Consider the case of the first English novelist—Daniel Defoe. Having begun as a genuine journalist in his *Review* he had no difficulty in concocting his *Journal of the Plague Year*, which was for a long time considered an authentic contemporary account of the Great Plague of 1665 —just as he had no difficulty in passing himself off as a Whig in Edinburgh when he was in fact a Tory spy in the pay of Harley. *The Journal of the Plague Year* is now classified as a historical novel. On the other hand, Defoe's *True Relation of the Apparition of Mrs. Veal*, after having been first accepted at its face value as a journalist's report on certain psychic phenomena at Canterbury and then re-classified as just one more of Defoe's fabrications ("the first ghost story in English"), has recently been vindicated as an accurate account of what his Canterbury informants believed to be literally true—though presumably the ghost's recommendation of *Drelincourt On Death* was an advertising trick devised by Defoe to push the sales of that dreary treatise.

The history of the novel is full of similar episodes, some of them involving highly respected scholars. Thus George Sherburn's excellent early article in *Modern Philology* on various appreciations of Milton's minor poems instances Edmund Waller's recommendation of *Lycidas* to Saint-Evremond, which he dated *c.* 1673. His source is *Letters supposed to have passed between M. de St. Evremond and Mr. Waller,* which was only published in 1769 and is in fact the work of the poet John Langhorne and is a sort of historical novel. More recently a Miss King-Hall wrote another historical novel, largely based on Horace Walpole's letters, called *The Diary of a Young Lady of Fashion,* which several reviewers, including one in the *Spectator,* absurdly mistook for the authentic memoirs of an eighteenth-century aristocrat. Though surprised, Miss King-Hall (who had not intended to deceive anybody) was naturally delighted. For a historical novelist such an error constitutes the sincerest form of flattery. And even when a confusion with history proper does not occur, a near-miss, as it were, will be chalked up by the critics in the novel's favor. Consider this tribute that Max Beerbohm once paid to Trollope's novels:

> Reading him, I soon forget that I am reading about fictitious characters and careers: quite soon do I feel that I am collating intimate memoirs and diaries. For sheer conviction of truth give me Trollope.[1]

And here is an extract from a review in the *New York Times* of a novel called *The Kentuckians:*

> . . . consistent and persuasive: instead of a current novel by Janice Holt Giles, it might almost be a word-for-word printing of a manuscript found by her among the archives.

The logical implication of such eulogies is clear: the closer the novelist gets to persuading his readers that what they are reading is not *his* invention but solid historical fact, the more satisfied they ought to be.

The orthodox reply to such objections as I have been making is that the novel's realism is a literary convention. It is only children, or simple souls like Partridge in *Tom Jones,* who confuse the actors on the stage with real men and women in a real human situation. And no doubt there *is* an element of convention in even the most naturalistic novel. But the convention that the novel uses is different—in degree if not in kind— from any other literary convention: it is *the convention of doing without conventions*—one that minimizes the aesthetic distance between the world of art and the world of things. "Illusion" trembles in it on the edge of "delusion."

A useful parallel might be drawn with the conventions of the painter.

An "academy" portrait often approximates to a photograph in color. The difference between Queen Victoria as she was seen by her subjects and a portrait of her by Winterhalter or Herkomer was that they *immobilized* her, eliminating the real-life complexities imposed by time, while at the same time reducing the three spatial dimensions of phenomenal actuality to two, a certain area surrounded by a gilt frame. But the virtual identity of such pictures with a large photograph is certainly critically disturbing. Take the frame away and you get the *trompe l'oeil* French and Dutch painters of the seventeenth century. (You know the sort of thing. The fly that you instinctively brush from the cake in the corner of the room is not a real fly but a painted one—and the cake isn't real either!)

No doubt a great painter is able to create the illusion of actuality by his pigments as a medium for nonrepresentational statement (the abstract patterns in color and shape that used to be called "Significant Form"). But the novelist's original sin will remain a constant temptation for the painter too. Aristotle would clearly have been a great novel-reader if only he had had the opportunity. Chapter 4 of the *Poetics* gives him away:

Imitation is natural to man from childhood, one of his advantages over the lower animals being this, that he is the most imitative creature in the world. . . . And it is also natural for all to delight in works of imagination. . . . Though the objects themselves may be painful to see, we delight to view the most realistic representations of them in art, the forms for example of the lowest animals and of dead bodies.[2]

Zeuxis, the painter whose grapes were so much like the real thing that birds pecked them, was a contemporary of Aristotle's, and the latter's doctrine of mimesis seems to me to confirm Aristotle's obvious lack of real literary sense. In any case a painter usually puts a frame round his picture, and the viewer cannot see the painting without seeing the frame. The effect is to remind us that we are not looking at real cakes or grapes. And the painter does not insert real cakes and grapes into his pictures, except for those occasional modernistic experiments which are rarely successful. But this is just what in effect the novelist does do. If he does not disguise his novel to look like biography (the Defoe formula), he may unblushingly insert large chunks of unacknowledged history, as Shorthouse inserts extracts from Lady Fanshawe's *Memoirs* in *John Inglesant*. Or he may try to pass off autobiography as prose fiction. If in *The Way of All Flesh*, for example, you substitute "Samuel Butler" for "Ernest Pontifex," the book stops being a novel and immediately becomes an unusual autobiography. And similar substitutions can be made in parts of some of the best English novels, among them *David Copperfield, The Mill on the Floss, Sons and Lovers* and *A Portrait of the Artist as a Young Man*.

The case against the novel's realism, then, is that it deliberately confuses, or at best juxtaposes, two orders of reality—the world of art and the world of things. The reader is never certain whether he is looking at painted grapes or real grapes. And this means that he does not know what criterion of value he is entitled to apply. Is an autobiographical novel to be read as autobiography or as a novel? An autobiography is a kind of biography, which is a kind of history; the names are real, the dates can be authenticated, the places can be found in an atlas. In a novel, on the other hand, real names, dates and places—the "1831" of *Middlemarch* for example—tend to be embarrassments because they distract the reader's attention from the sequences of internal causes and effect in the characters' impressions and evolution that the narrative art is principally concerned with.

Sons and Lovers provides an elementary example of such confusions. When Paul wins the first prize in the winter exhibition at Nottingham Castle, are we to treat this as historical fact (D. H. Lawrence had after all been an undergraduate at Nottingham University, and he was also a painter of some talent), or as an episode in the career of the fictitious hero? Or is it perhaps both—in which case we should like a date provided so that we can check the historical accuracy of the event in, for example, a contemporary Nottingham newspaper? An episode near the end of *Sons and Lovers* raises a similar problem as it were, in reverse. This is the curious friendship that is supposed to develop between Paul and the ailing Baxter Dawes. In terms of the necessary and probable I do not believe in this episode. Nothing that Lawrence has told us about either Paul or Baxter makes the reconciliation plausible. But if the episode is *autobiographical*—a reflection perhaps of some ultimate reconciliation between Lawrence and Frieda's first husband—I shall have to believe in it, improbable though it seems in terms of the novel, because Lawrence can presumably be relied upon on such a point as a historian of his own life.

I need not labor this point. *Madame Bovary*, to take another example, is a great novel, but *le Bovarysme*, the real-life psychological equivalent produced by a diet of sentimental romances such as those Emma Bovary subsisted on is fact. Edith Thompson, one of the most celebrated of modern English murderesses, was a clear case of *Bovarysme*.

I have admitted that one kind of novel evades the general criticism I have levelled against the genre. Why should there be no similar theoretical objection to the satirical novel? *Gulliver's Travels* exhibits the proliferation of pseudo-factual detail that characterizes the common-or-garden novel, but the alleged facts are continually being disproved by Swift's central overriding formulas. The elaborate descriptions of nature and social life in Lilliput and Brobdingnag defy credibility because we do not believe for one moment that their inhabitants and their physical objects are respectively one-twelfth and twelve times the dimensions of their European equivalents. In Book IV the formula is not an arithmetical but a moral or cultural ratio: the Houyhnhnms have the rational qualities of human nature in animal form, the Yahoos who look like human beings have the animal without the rational. Swift, however, does not ask us to *believe* in the curious worlds he creates (Book III is muddled), but to accept his formulas simply as satiric premises. And the abstractness of the premises continuously permeates the concrete "realistic" examples by which they are illustrated.

Animal Farm operates in much the same way. The animals never achieve zoological actuality because the reader is aware all the time of the human political forces that they represent. And, in satiric novels, generally the more a character is conceptualized, the more a sort of allegory is approached, the less the danger grows of fiction being confused with fact. The realistic novel's original sin lies in its accumulation of things at the expense of values; the satiric novel reverses the process: values deflate things.

Jane Austen will provide an example. You will remember Sir Walter Elliot of *Persuasion*. Like myself he was not a great reader of novels, but he did do some reading. His peculiar habits are described in the first sentence of the first chapter:

Sir Walter Elliot, of Kellynch-Hall, in Somersetshire, was a man who, for his own amusement, never took up any book but the Baronetage. . . . [And] this was the page at which the favourite volume always opened:
ELLIOT OF KENNYNCH-HALL
Walter Elliot, born March 1, 1760, married, July 15, 1784 Elizabeth, daughter of James Stevenson Esq., of South Park in the county of Gloucester; by which lady (who died 1800) he has issue Elizabeth, born June 1, 1785; Anne, born August 9, 1787; a still-born son, Nov. 5, 1789; Mary, born Nov. 20, 1791.

Jane Austen always knew when to stop, and from this point the entry is only summarized: "first settled in Cheshire . . . mentioned in Dugdale . . . dignity of baronet, in the first year of Charles II . . ." (etc.). What or whose this *Baronetage* was is not specified, but the various phrases and formulas are exactly those used by John Debrett in his *Baronetage of England* (2 volumes, 1808), and the detailed exactness of the fictitious entry provides a large part of the satirical point. The genealogical minutiae supplied by Jane Austen from this imaginary entry in a real book exhibit Sir Walter's beginning and end in vanity, and so they acquire an implicitly symbolic character. The days of the month on which Sir Walter's four children were born serve no narrative purpose, but the implication clearly is that they interest him not as *birthdays*, the occasions of family festivals and the distribution of presents, but as a satisfaction of his vanity from their tabulation in print in the Baronetage. The gap between the importance he attaches to the 9th of August, Anne's birthday, as two printed words, and its natural human importance to Anne as one frustrated 9th of August followed another, neatly impales Sir Walter's moral inadequacy on Jane Austen's satiric pin. The realistic detail is here serving a serious literary purpose as a comment upon human society. No reader of *Persuasion* ever finds himself consulting an early Debrett to see if the

Elliot entry is really there; but the meticulous accuracy with which Debrett's style is copied is a part of the satire. Sir Walter may be a fictitious character, but there are plenty of people in the real world whose self-importance finds a similar reassurance—though today it is more likely to be in the pages of *Who's Who,* or *The Landed Gentry*—and who deservedly share in the ridicule the reader will continue to bestow on their fictitious exemplars.

Unlike a mere "story" ("Yes—oh, dear, yes—the novel tells a story"), the satiric novel points to a verifiable external world. The non-satiric novel, on the other hand, though it may use aspects of the external world, is essentially subjective, appealing primarily to the reader's curiosity ("What happened next?"), or the reader's latent sentimentality or escapism, all of them self-indulgent mental habits. An escape-route from such self-indulgences may be thought to be provided by what is loosely called symbolism. If the satirical novel may be—indeed, must be—symbolical, why should symbolism not be permissible and respectable in other forms of the novel?

A general answer to this question might be that the atomized fragments of phenomenal reality upon which the novel depends to achieve "realism" cannot bear the moral weight that the non-satiric novelist must put on them. They have to be both casual and significant, trivial and supremely important. The contradiction between what the symbols seem superficially to be—mere brick and mortar, so much physical or organic matter— and the moral immensities that they are supposed to represent is too gross.

E. M. Forster's *Howards End* will illustrate the point. The book is concerned with serious themes and its epigraph "Only connect . . ." has almost become a slogan for a cure of the ills of the modern world. The England that it describes is divided between four disconnected classes— an almost extinct peasantry (Howards End had once been a farm), the philistine world of London business (represented by the Wilcox family), a cultered class (represented by the Schlegel sisters) and a lower middle-class with aspirations to higher things (represented by the clerk Leonard Bast). On the plot level "connections" are certainly made, though often in defiance of psychological probability. Thus the first Mrs. Henry Wilcox is the last surviving member of the family who had actually farmed Howards End. The marriage is not a happy one, but Mrs. Wilcox becomes the intimate friend of Margaret Schlegel who on Mrs. Wilcox's death in due course marries a humbler Henry as his second wife. At the same time Helen Schlegel has a child by Leonard Bast, much to the annoyance of the lesser members of the Wilcox family. But the plot has to be desperately reinforced by symbols. Thus the garden of the old farmhouse has an ancient wych-elm in which pigs' teeth have been imbedded— relics, we are given to understand, of some primitive cult and which somehow authenticate the mystical powers of the first Mrs. Wilcox. An even more grotesque symbol of the urban nature of the other members of the Wilcox clan is their liability to hay fever—an allergy from which the

Schlegels are significantly free. The book ends with Helen's baby by Leonard Bast being carried triumphantly through the hay-field:

"The field's cut!" Helen cried excitedly—"the big meadow! We've seen to the very end, and it'll be such a crop of hay as never!"

Poor Bast is dead by now, but he has "connected" through his baby and the hay-field both with the Schlegels' rather affected London culture and the primeval wisdom of the countryside.

There is more to be said for *Howards End* than this. It has brilliant passages and in Tibby, the Schlegels' absurd brother, satire is achieved of the highest comic character. But the pigs' teeth and the symbolic hay-fever were a mistake. No doubt other novelists have done better— Dickens's fogs, Melville's white whale, the silver in *Nostromo*. But even at its best symbolism seems to be uncomfortable in the novel—forced, unnatural, an invasion from the territory of poetry. An image can only become a symbol by continuous verbal repetition. And prose, the natural linguistic medium of the novel, resists verbal repetition, whereas, poetry thrives on it. Forster's wych-elm has therefore to be given encore after encore as though it was an albatross. It soon becomes a nuisance.

What are we left with? Let me count the survivors. The satiric novel is safe. I read every novel by Aldous Huxley and every novel by Evelyn Waugh as they came out—from the first page to the last. The frivolous novel, what used to be called "railway-reading," is also safe if it is well enough done. If there were really such a thing as what Leavis calls "the dramatic poem in prose" I would be glad to salute it too, as the drama and poetry clearly constitute the highest peaks of European literature; but I suspect that the only dramatic poem possible in prose is the short story. The human memory cannot retain more than at most 10,000 words at a single reading without such aids as metre or rhyme—just as the human eye can only register a limited area of painting at one glance, however prolonged the glance is. As for the historical novel, the inter-cultural novel (*à la* Henry James), the documentary novel, or the autobiographical novel, I prefer my history, my clash of cultures, my reporting and my autobiography to be "straight"—the real thing and not fact confused with fiction. After all, as the great Bishop Butler put it, "Things are what they are; their consequences will be what they will be. Why then should we deceive ourselves?"

But the novel-addict *wishes* to deceive himself.

Notes

1. From the essay on "Servants" in *And Even Now* (1920).
2. Ingram Bywater's translation (1909).

Edward Taylor's Sources

Harrison T. Meserole

Recent scholarship has done much to broaden our knowledge of Taylor's sources. The annual list of published notes, articles, dissertations, and monographs classified under American II Taylor in the *MLA International Bibliography* provides consistent evidence of the kind of careful and imaginative reading of individual poems that has spurred an inquisitive student to a hunt for the particular passage or the particular volume Taylor alludes to in a given line or stanza. The result is that we know now that Taylor read in the works of at least a dozen Renaissance and seventeenth-century poets besides George Herbert, Francis Quarles, George Wither, and Anne Bradstreet. We know now that Taylor's familiarity with contemporary compendia of marvellous facts, general histories of the world, and encyclopaedias of general learning was not limited to Peter Heylyn's *Cosmographie* or William Turner's *Compleat History of the Most Remarkable Providences, Both of Judgement and Mercy Which Have Happened in This Present Age*. . . . We know now from which sources Taylor derived his gaming imagery, what precise event moved him to write, in Donald Stanford's words, "one of the most remarkable poems in the history of American literature," "The Description of the great Bones dug up at Clavarack on the Banks of Hudsons River A.D. 1705," and what role the *Magdeburg Centuries* plays in the *Metrical History of Christianity*.

Yet despite these and other substantial contributions to Taylor studies, much remains to be done. One area largely unexplored to date concerns the poet's interest in and knowledge of folklore. For example, Taylor opens *Meditation* 2.67[B] with the lines,

> Doe Fables say, the Rising Sun doth Dance
> On Easter Day for joy, thou didst ascende.

It is possible that Taylor's source here is Nicholas Breton, who wrote in *Fantasticks serving for a Perpetuall Prognostication* (London, 1626): "I conclude it [i.e. Easter Sunday] is a day of much delightfulnesse: the Sunnes dancing day, and the Earth's holy-day." Or it may have been the eighth stanza of Sir John Suckling's "Ballad upon a Wedding," published in his *Last Remains* (1659):

> Her feet beneath her petticoat,
> Like little mice, stole in and out,
>   As if they fear'd the light;
> But O, she dances such a way!
> No sun upon an Easter-day
>   Is half so fine a sight.

Or Taylor may have read the passage in Sir Thomas Browne's *Pseudodoxia Epidemica* (1646) in which that physician of widely eccentric learning remarks, "We shall not, I hope, disparage the Resurrection of our Redeemer, if we say [that] the Sun doth not dance on Easter day." Browne adds that he cannot "conceive therein any more than a Tropical expression." And certainly there were other contemporary sources for this superstition. In *Observations on Popular Antiquities* (1777) John Brand paraphrases an unidentified seventeenth-century writer in declaring that

> It is a common Custom among the Vulgar and uneducated Part of the World, to rise before the Sun on Easter-day, and walk into the Fields: The Reason of which is to see the Sun Dance; which they have been told, from an Old Tradition, always dances as upon that Day. . . . If therefore this Tradition hath any Meaning, it must be a metaphorical one.

Whatever Taylor's source for this particular superstition, and it may be that because of its nature we shall not be able to assign a precise source, there can be no doubt that he was intrigued by such folk material, as attested to by some forty other quite similar allusions in the *Meditations* to folk medicine, folk beliefs in relation to specific foods or drinks, and folk customs. I should add that a paper soon to be published by Professor Robert Arner of the University of Cincinnati will bring further evidence to bear on this matter, particularly on Taylor's employment of folk metaphor in *Meditation* 1.40. The point is, however, that this is an aspect of Taylor scholarship that requires attention, particularly by scholars with some formal training in folklore.

Similarly, we need more information than we now possess on Taylor's reading in fields other than those that principally occupied him. What books did he use to educate himself in those humanistic and scientific disciplines from which he draws much of his imagery? I have in mind here, for example, metallurgy, alchemy, music, and gemmology. This is not, obviously, mere source-hunting for source-hunting's sake. What we shall find, I think, when we can identify additional volumes that Taylor was able to lay hands on, is that these sources do more than merely link an allusion to a specific author or event.

One example may serve to develop the point. In editing *Meditation* 2.56 for my *Seventeenth-Century American Poetry* (1968), I found that earlier editors had annotated all of the natural wonders and mechanical marvels catalogued in that poem except two: the allusions to "Turrian's Wooden Sparrows in a Flight" (l. 33) and to "Mark Scaliota's Lock and Key and Chain/Drawn by a Flea, in our Queen Betties reign" (ll. 35–36); and in one other instance had provided only a tentative elucidation: for Taylor's reference to "Dresdens Table-sight" (l. 31). Having tracked down the missing items, I began investigation of the Dresden allusion, using as a point of departure Thomas Johnson's provisional explanation of it in *Poetical Works of Edward Taylor* (1939): "Possibly a reference to a collection of Chinese porcelains belonging to Augustus II, elector of Saxony (1670–1733)."

In 1682/3, Tobias Beuteln published in Dresden a folio volume, magnificently bound in full calf with extra gilt tooling, and written in both Latin and German (on facing pages). Its title, like that of many another seventeenth-century folio, occupies an entire page, so I shall give only a portion of it here:

Electorale Saxonicum, perpetuo viridans densissimum & celsissimum CEDRETUM. In Fundo & Solo semper viridis Rutæ, Sive BREVIS DELINEATIO, Electoralium Saxonicorum Celsissimorum OPERUM REGALIUM, Nimirum, Illius ornatissimi Theatri rerum artificialium, & aliorum inæstimabilium Operum, quæ in Electorali Dresda sunt. . . .

On F₁ recto appears the passage that is of interest to Taylor scholars. It is in prose, although Beuteln follows the seventeenth-century custom of inserting bits of verse as he deems appropriate. I print here only the German text (although Taylor probably read the Latin version) because after study of both versions, I consider the German both syntactically and metaphorically more communicative than the Latin.

> Die andere Kammer
> Kostbare Trinck-Geschirre.
> Hier leuchtet scheint und schimmers gantz
> Von Gold- und Silbern-Becher-Glantz
> Von Becken die hell auspoliret
> Und andern Dingen mehr gezieret
> Darunter auch zwar Holtz und Bein
> Doch viel von Gold und Edelstein.

Es seynd zufőrderst vier *Repositoria*, oder Schräncke mit sehr vielen kostbaren Trinck-Geschirren besetzt:

Das erste *Repositorium* begreifft in sich Edelgestein-Geschirre die seynd aus Crystall, Topaz, und Achat mit Golde beschlagen, und mit Rubinen, Smaragden, und anderen Edelgesteinen versetzt, welche nicht allein vor dem seel. Absterben Chürfurstlichen Durchleuchtigsten Herrn Vaters, in vielen Stücken (alss dem grossen Becher von Nephrit-Stein, und andern viel Edelgestein-Geschirren) sondern auch von itzt regierender Churfürstlichen Durchleuchtigsten vermehret, wie an der kostbaren Kanne von Crystall, Gold, und Edelstein zu sehen. Weiter ein Crucifix, und ein Kleinod, von Crystall, Gold, Rubinen, ein Gold- und Silberner Becher, darauf die *Genealogia* des Hauses Oesterreich in Brust-Bildern aus *Chama* gestochen, eine grosse und rare Crystall-Kugel und absonderlich zwey herrliche Geschirre aus Crystall, das eine von itzt regierender Römischer Keyserlicher Majestät *Leopoldo I.* das andere von Dero

Glorwürdigsten Herrn Vatern *Ferdinando III.* anhero præsentirt; und viel andere dergleichen Kostbarkeiten, so in diesem Repositorio über 60. tausend Thaler hoch kommen. Der darunter befindlich-künstlich-geschnittenen und andern Venetianischen Gläser nicht zu gedencken.

Im andern *Repositorio* stehen viel silberne, vergüldete Becher, mit Corall gezieret; auch ein Crucifix aus Corall geschnitten, darunter Messer, Gabel, Löffel, und andere Dinge, die an Hefften und sonst auch von solcher *Materia.* Vom Corall sagt *Ovidius*:

> Wenn Corall an die Lufft erstkommt, so härtets gleich,
> Da unterm Wasser es erst wuchs, wie Kraut so weich.

Im dritten sind Muschel- und Perl-Mutter-Geschirre in Silber, Gold, und Edelgestein gefasset, in welcher eine (so die Durchleuchtigste Churfürstin mit aus Dennemarck gebracht, und hieher præsentirt) der *Neptunus, Delphinen,* und anders zierlich geschnitten. Messer, Gabel, und Löffel von Muscheln und Edelgestein an Hefften, oder durchaus. Es liegen hier auch etliche Land-Perlen, so man in Teichen gefunden.

Im vierdten *Repositorio* sind Straussen-Eyer und Indianische Nutz-Schalen-Geschirre, mit vergüldetem Silber beschlagen, und zum theil künstlich geschnitten und gemahlt. Unter diesen ist ein gross Geschirr aus einer Maldivischen Nutz-Schale, daher mann dergleichen gar selten bringen kan, weil in selbige Insulen nicht wohl zu kommen, die Leuthe wilde und grausam, die Früchte seltzam, und sehr heilsam, und wider Gifft dienlich, desswegen vor etlichen Jahren durch Holländer diss Stück allhier auff zehen tausend Gülden geschäzt worden.

Hernach stehen auff einer langen Taffel viel kostbare Giess-Kannen und Giess-Becken, von vergüldetem Silber, Perl-Mutter, und Edelgestein.

Weiter stehen in dieser Kammer zween Tische von Perl-Mutter (und andern *Materiis* eingelegt) und darauf auch Trinck-Geschirre, und ein kostbar silbern Giess-Becken.

Auff den Schräncken stehen Geschirre von Metall-Schaum, und andern *Materiis,* darunter zwo Greiffen-Klauen, Item Chur-Fürst *Augusti* gedrechsselte Becher.[1]

And Beuteln goes on at length, describing in detail the rooms, alcoves, niches, and display tables holding the innumerable treasures in the royal residence.

Beuteln's volume was well known among European intellectuals of the age and was frequently referred to by other compilers of encyclopaedias and universal histories. Early in the eighteenth century, for example, Caspar Neickelius credited "Herr Tob. Beutels Cedreto" as his source for material on Dresden in his *Museographia oder Anleitung. Zum rechten Begriff und nützlicher Anlegung der MUSEORUM, oder Raritäten Kammern. . . .* (Leipzig und Breslau, 1727) as he paraphrased Beuteln's description of the "Sächsische Kunst-Kammer." In his account, Neickelius added:

Die erste Kammer begreifft mechanische Werckzeuge, als: Goldschmied, Schlösser-Drechsler-Arbeit, Barbierer- oder chirurgische Instrumenta, allerleh Waag-Hebe- und Brech-Zeug, allerleh Schreiner-Arbeit, mathematische Instrumenten, auch einige rare Gemählde zc.

Es möchte mancher wol diss halten für geringe,
Bloss als nur Hand-Arbeit, da doch vergleichen Dinge
Durch Kraffte, Marck und Bein ganz schwere Arbeit machen,
Dass fast ein iedes Glied Darüber möchte krachen:
    In solchen Künsten hat die grosse Müh and Fleiss
    Fur ihren sauren Schweis auch ihren Ruhm und Preis. (p. 191)

I suggest, therefore, that Taylor's allusion in "Dresdens Table-sight" is not to Chinese porcelains but to the tables in the *Repositoria* groaning under the weight of the jewel-encrusted plates, cups, and other vessels of silver and gold, flanked by the knives, forks, spoons, and other serving and eating utensils fashioned out of crystal, agate, and precious metal, in turn inset with pearls, rubies, and emeralds. That this is indeed Taylor's reference is further strengthened by the description of the mechanical implements and chirurgical and mathematical instruments summarized by Neickelius from Beuteln's more elaborate account, for at least three of Taylor's other allusions in *Meditation* 2.56 are to just such mechanical and mathematical devices.

To one who could have viewed the Dresden treasure in person, its brilliance must clearly have outshone the crown jewels. To Taylor, who is at his best when his poetic images are those that appeal to the eye, reading this passage was as memorable an experience as seeing the treasure first hand. It is not in *Meditation* 2.56, however, that Taylor develops this scintillating image. In this poem, already weighted with a long catalogue of natural wonders and mechanical marvels, the simple phrase "Dresdens Table-sight" was enough. But in *Meditation* 2.109, which begins with a description of three lavish feasts, stanza two reads:

Suppose a Feast in such a Room is kept
    Thats deckt in flaming Guildings every where,
And richest Fare in China Chargers deckt
    And set on golden Tables. Waiters there
    In flaming robes waite pouring Royall wine
    In Jasper Cups out. Oh! what glories shine?

And we can find similarly glittering images of jewels, gold, ornaments encrusted with gems, and cabinets inlaid with gems or gold in 30 other of the meditations.

Beuteln's description of the Dresden treasure house, therefore, represents more than a mere annotation for an unfamiliar allusion in a given poem. It provided Taylor with the material out of which he could fashion a metaphor to put to good use, and, moreover, to repeat this use on a significant number of occasions in the *Meditations*. (We know he did repeat favorite metaphors, of course. Psammitych's labyrinth, another of the marvels in the catalogue in 2.56, turns up again in 2.113, and as Calvin Israel demonstrates in *American Notes & Queries* [1966] "barley-breaks" appears five times.) Symbolically, the Dresden treasure represents the acme of earthly value—riches beyond comprehension that sparkle and gleam even in a darkened chamber. This suited Taylor's purpose exactly. As he strove to express the inexpressible, he sought in every direction for the most exquisite and rarest treasures, those things most inordinately prized by man, to place metaphorically in comparison with Christ. When in the comparison such treasures proved to be dross, the shock effect achieved the force Taylor wanted. Thus, the mortal feast in stanza two of 2.109, though lavish by earthly standards, scintillates only for a passing moment, for when compared to Christ's Feast, the sacrament of communion, in stanza three,

> But all this Glorious Feast seems but a Cloud,
> My Lord, unto the Feast thou makst for thine.

From the quality and number of titles in his library, the personal documents he left us, and the testimony of such friends and correspondents as Samuel Sewall, we know that Taylor was a persistent and inquisitive reader. And even a cursory scan of what Taylor wrote makes clear that the Westfield poet-minister-physician did not limit his reading to theology, medicine, and school texts—the three sorts of titles which predominate in his personal collection of books and pamphlets. What we need is more conclusive evidence of the comprehensive range of Taylor's reading: the kind of evidence that modern scholarship has begun to provide in tracing to specific sources the extraordinary variety and number of allusions in the *Preparatory Meditations, Gods Determinations,* the *Metrical History of Christianity,* and Taylor's other poems. Such evidence can be of material value to our fuller understanding of Edward Taylor's poetics.

Notes

1. I have not provided a translation of this and the next passage in German because in the paragraphs that follow in the text I have paraphrased in English a number of the key portions of the original. Moreover, much of the German vocabulary, particularly names of precious stones, metals, and implements, will communicate itself without translation even to readers unfamiliar with the language.

Blake's Creation Myths as Archetypes of Art

W. T. Jewkes

I must Create a System, or be enslav'd by another Man's.
I will not Reason & Compare: my business is to Create.
                                        Blake, *Jerusalem*

"What shall I sing?" queried the cowherd Caedmon of the apparition in his dream that fateful night, and the mysterious visitor replied, "Sing me Creation." A song of creation was to be the proof of his qualifications as a poet. And, the Venerable Bede tells us, although the humble brother doubted his capability, he launched forth bravely on what has become, along with the first lines of *Beowulf*, the best memorized passage of Old English poetry.

Caedmon got his myth of creation from the Book of Genesis, which conforms to the genus of philosophical myths like those we find in Ovid, Plato, and Lucian. These myths describe creation as essentially the act of a preexisting divine figure—Jehovah, or the Demiourgos of *The Timaeus*, or the *deus* or *melior natura* of Ovid, arranging and setting the universe in order. In these accounts, this preexisting Creator apparently already had something to work with. In the opening passage of the *Metamorphoses*, the Creator began with a "face of nature" (*naturae vultus*), as Ovid puts it, "which men call Chaos," all "crude and lumpy matter" (*rudis indigesta moles*), nothing but "bulk" (*pondus*), "lifeless" (*iners*), whose confusion was manifest in discordant atoms (*discordia semina*), and where the various elements, although they already existed, had not realized their essential nature—"land on which no man could stand, water no man could swim in." The beginning of the world (*origine mundi*), the poet tells us, came about when this Creator sorted out the confusion, "settled all argument" (*litem . . . diremit*), "separated" (*abscidit*) heaven from earth, water from land, so that each thing was "set in its own place, bound in firm harmony" (*dissociata locis concordi pace ligavit*). Then the elements realized their essential properties and assumed their hierarchical posture. And so it was that "whichever of the gods it was" brought order to the universe. Then he began to work on the earth. He made it into a globe, shaped the terrain into a landscape, and established the hot, cold, and temperate zones after the "same design and pattern" as that which was to be found in the heavens.

The whole picture Ovid paints for us shows the Creator of the universe behaving much as a technological man would: giving orders, shaping masses, dividing and subdividing, setting zones and boundaries, engineering a landscape, establishing hierarchies.

The myth of creation in the Bible has similar features. Again a pre-existing Creator is seen as engaged in making order out of disorder. The earth apparently already exists, but it is "without form and void," covered with darkness. God's first act is to separate light from darkness. Next, he separates "the water under the vault from the water above," and the waters from the dry land. He distinguishes one species of fruit tree from another, the sea animals from the land animals and animals of the air. He gives them names, classifies them, establishes a hierarchy of relationships. The greater light is to "govern" the day, and the lesser light the night. Man and woman are to be greater than the other animals, and to "rule" them.

So here again Creation is depicted as a task primarily of dividing, classifying, and ordering something already there but previously formless and void. Few unambiguous acts of spontaneous creation are attributed to God. We are told specifically that he "made" heaven and earth, the "vault" or "firmament," and the "two great lights in the vault of heaven." We are told also that he "created" the "great sea monsters and all living creatures. . . ." And finally he "created" man "in his own image, male and female created he them." Yet apart from this last act of creation, most of these procedures seem almost identical with those of ordering and regulating the universe. The lights created actually are the way day and night are differentiated. The "vault" occurs when water is separated from water. Moreover, in many cases, the act of creation seems identical with a command: "God said, 'Let there be a vault'. . . . So God made the vault"; "God said, 'Let there be lights'. . . . So God made the two great lights"; "God said, 'Let the waters teem'. . . . So God created the great sea monsters. . . ." In some cases, the appearance of these phenomena is merely by command: " 'Let there be light' . . . and there was light . . ." " 'Let the waters . . . appear' . . . and so it was. . . ." And in one instance, the creation of plants, their appearance occurs as a direct result of the earth obeying God's command, rather than God himself: "Then God said, 'Let the earth produce fresh growth'. . . . So it was; and the earth yielded fresh growth. . . ." Only in the case of man does God command himself directly: "Let us make man in our image and likeness." And even in this case, he makes man not out of nothing at all, but out of water, earth, and air. The same distinction is to be found in Ovid, where man is "born" (natus est), either "made" (fecit) by the god who made everything else, "of his own divine seed" (divino semine), or else produced from earth in a manner similar to the way Iapetus mixed the seeds of the sky (semina caeli) with running water and molded (finxit) them into the form of the all-controlling gods.

Both these philosophical creation myths lay heavy stress, then, on the ordering and regulating acts of a divine figure in creating the universe, and are correspondingly vague about the origin and nature of other kinds of creative acts. Only in the case of man does the act of creation seem to be more mysterious, more like the work of a Pygmalion fashioning his statue of Galatea from material already to hand into a totally new form.

Beside the philosophical creation myths, the classical world gives us another genus of creation story that might be labelled "genetic," since it describes the creation of all things as a process of conception and birth. This kind of myth is very widespread in the Mediterranean (in fact, it is world-wide), but the central document for my purpose here is Hesiod's *Theogony*, a much earlier and more circumstantial account than the prosaic redaction of Apollodorus. In general, Hesiod pictures the creation of all parts of the universe in terms of the emergence of a whole dynasty of divine beings, "born out of" (ἐξεγένοντο) Gaia, Ouranos, and Night, and apparently reared (ἔτρεφε) by Pontos. At first sight, Hesiod's myth would seem to greatly increase the sense both of the mystery and the spontaneity of the beginning of things. Hesiod discerns three kinds of "birth": the parthenogenetic, the asexual, and the sexual. To begin with, Chaos is an even vaguer notion than it is in either Ovid or Genesis. Chaos seems to be the start of the whole dynasty, but it is by no means clear whether Chaos is a person or a place. Apparently Chaos had no parents, and seems to have given birth to himself (itself?)—the phrase is γένετ' αὐτῶν (l.115)—as do the clearly anthropomorphic Gaia and Eros subsequently. Elsewhere in the *Theogony* Chaos appears to have been burnt up in the conflagration attendant on the war of the Gods (καῦμα δὲ θεσπέσιον κατεχεν Χάος, ll. 700–703), and again it is unclear whether Chaos is a personage or a place. The final mention suggests that it is clearly a place, standing between the earth and Tartaros, for the Titans are settled "on the other side of gloomy Chaos" (πέρην Χάεος ζοφεροῖο, l.814). At any rate, whether person or place, from Chaos emerge (ἐγένοντο, l.123) Erebos and Night, who immediately proceed to copulate in "love" (φιλότητι, l.125) and so produce the first true offspring, Aether and Hemera. Next, Gaia gives birth to Ouranos and the Hills and Forests (Ourea). In this case, no consort is mentioned, but her next children specifically have no father, for she bears Pontos "without any sweet act of love" (ατερ φιλοτητος ἐφιμέρον, l.132). Night performs a similar feat, giving birth to fifteen children specifically without any divine consort (οὔ τινι κοιμηθεῖσα θεὰ τεκε Νὺξ ερεβεννή, l.213). No consort is mentioned for Pontos when he "fathered" (γείνατο, l.234) Nereus; however, his other children were conceived "when he lay with Gaia" (Γαίη μισγόμενος, l.238). From this point on in the poem follows a long line of more or less regular procreation, apart from such anomalies as the birth of Aphrodite from the genitals of her father and Athene from the head of Zeus.

Despite the biologically mysterious nature of some of these acts of giving birth, the total effect of Hesiod's myth is in the end like that produced by the philosophical myths—a picture of higher forms creating lower forms. In Hesiod, the more mysterious acts of parthenogenesis and asexual generation give way steadily to more normal unions to produce immortal offspring, and eventually the gods even begin uniting with mortals to father a race of human heroes. All three myths also correspond in following the story of Creation by an account of the cosmos falling into division, murder, and war.

These three mythological accounts of Creation are the principal archetypes to influence Western literature for more than two thousand years. Poets as late as Shakespeare and Milton still use them as the basis of their own myths of creation. Yet, though they reveal the process of imagination as it goes about its characteristic task of humanizing the external world of nature, by giving the vast powers of nature human lineaments and forming them into a human society, they are not adequate to explain the process of creation that occurs in the imagination of the artist. That is to say, they do not constitute a myth *of* that process, and so they cannot serve as adequate archetypes of art in human civilization. And this basic inadequacy is not really perceived until the late eighteenth century, when Blake sets himself to work on his prophetic poems. The greatness of Blake's imaginative achievement cannot be fully understood until what he created in his prophetic books, and especially in *Milton* and *Jerusalem*, is measured against the myths he inherited. In the process of recreating a myth of creation to satisfy himself, Blake discovered what was missing from the ancient stories of creation, and by a great burst of imaginative power, he was able to produce the first truly archetypal myth of art.

In the Preface to *Milton*, Blake takes a strong line against "the Stolen and Perverted writings of Homer and Ovid: of Plato and Cicero . . . which are set up by artifice against the Sublime of the Bible . . ." and promises that the New Age will be one in which "those Grand Works of the more ancient & consciously & professedly Inspired Men will hold their proper ranks, & the Daughters of Memory shall become the Daughters of Inspiration." According to Blake, even Shakespeare and Milton were "both curbed by the general malady & infection from the silly Greek and Latin slaves of the Sword." Undoubtedly this kind of pontification gets Blake very much disliked by those who know him only as the poet of some charming short lyric poems. Yet despite its strong note of righteousness, this pronouncement does not come from one who is unfamiliar with Greek and Roman writers, nor from one who had not already wrestled several times with the problems of mythmaking. Blake could not have been without some sympathy for those writers he condemns, since he seems dissatisfied also with his own earlier attempts to devise a myth of creation (some of his irony is clearly directed at himself). Before *Milton* he had already constructed an elaborate creation myth, briefly and cryptically worked out in "The Mental Traveller," and then retold in at least four more extended epic versions, in the Books of Urizen, Ahania, and Los, and in *The Four Zoas*. And although these mythic poems address themselves in part to some of the defects in the ancient creation myths, a comparison of them with *Milton* reveals that they had created problems of their own which Blake did not resolve until he wrote *Milton*.

Some problems Blake had already resolved in the four earlier epic poems. At the center of his myth of creation (fall) he had placed four symbolic characters, or "Giant forms," Urizen, Luvah (Orc), Urthona (Los), and Tharmas (the names in parenthesis are pseudonyms used interchangeably when we encounter these forms in their fallen or earthly state). These forms represent categories, or powers, or faculties of the human mind and body, and as such are radically different from the gods in earlier creation stories, who are simply personifications of the vast forces in nature, or of the imagined laws of the universe. The equivalents of some of these characters can be found in some of the old myths, but never with the richness of ambiguity that Blake is able to give them. Urizen, in his fallen state, Blake himself equates with Jehovah (and with Satan), though he might also fit the function of Ouranos, or Cronos, or Zeus as well, an oppressive sky-god, cosmic artificer, a parody of the Demiourgos of Plato, one who limits desire by freezing up life and imprisoning it in rigid boundaries. Gaia, as Mother Earth, is more like Blake's Enitharmon (Los' other half, a kind of *alter ego*), the projection of the fallen and limited spatial universe into which all men tumble when they are born. Prometheus, who in some myths (though not in Hesiod) is supposed to have created man, is actually closer to Orc (the fallen Luvah), at least when he is working for Enitharmon. Then he represents organic energy turned downward to the production of technological feats that lead ultimately to the Iron Age and war—a suffering and dying god.

But though equivalents for some of the "Giant forms" in their fallen states can be dug out of the older myths of creation, there seem to be no counterparts for Los and Tharmas. Tharmas remains a shadowy figure until Blake's later work, but from the start, Los is destined to be a central figure. Los is not just an archetype of the artist, like Pygmalion and Orpheus. He is the symbolic form of art itself, the total form of the creative acts and visions that individual artists evolve in the course of their lives, the power of the human imagination itself, working in space and time, but producing a total vision that exists in that unity of space and time which is eternal and infinite, and has both being and non-being. Los is the imagination in this sense—something, to use Gulley Jimson's phrase, that "goes on going on." No such Titan appears in the earlier creation myths.

A second primordial deficiency that Blake's own early creation myths cleared up was the problem of the beginning of beginnings. This was commonly not pressed beyond Chaos, and even that, as I have already noted, was always a singularly elusive notion. We have seen how in Hesiod Chaos cannot be clearly discerned as either a personage or a place. In the Bible ("without form and void") and in Ovid ("all crude and lumpy matter") it seems to denote the state of a preexisting mass on which a preexisting Creator worked. Inevitably the question presses forward: who created Chaos? Northrop Frye sees Chaos in the Bible as having emerged from a flood prior to Noah's, but I find that a difficult notion to accept, based on a reading of the first few sentences of Genesis, where three things seem to co-exist, "earth," "the face of the abyss," and "the surface of the waters," though in Homer the primal void does seem to have been water, "Oceanos, from whom they [the gods] are all sprung" ('Ωκεανοῦ ὅς περ γένεσις πάντεσσι τέτυκται, Iliad 14.246). The problem occurs in other myths as well. In the Pelasgian creation myth, Eurynome "rises" from Chaos (clearly a place), and couples with the serpent Ophion to produce the World Egg. In the Chandogya Upanishad we are told even more vaguely. "In the beginning the world was merely non-being. Then it was existent. It developed. It turned into an egg."

None of these vague formulations will do for Blake. As he put it, the concept that "before the Creation All was Solitude & Chaos . . . is the most pernicious idea that can enter the Mind." For him, as for Wallace Stevens, the imagination cannot submit to the idea of chaos because the imagination can perceive its opposite. For Blake, the beginning of beginnings should not be envisaged as Chaos, or a void, but rather as a lifeless state in which life was buried, as it is "buried" in a dead seed in the winter, or in the barren desert soil from which a plant grows. His notion is similar to, but more precise than, what we find in the Norse Voluspá, where all things begin with Ginnungagap, literally a "yawning gap," which is nevertheless pregnant with the potential of created life. The Olympian myth of creation goes part of the way here, because the idea of generation is at least connected with the process by which a work of art grows out of traditional forms, just as when the germ of life grows, it reproduces its "buried" form.

In the Book of Urizen, instead of beginning with a Chaos, from which gods were created or "sprang," Blake begins with the four Eternals themselves (they appropriately serve as his Muses in this poem). These "Giant forms," at a time that is neither past, present, nor future, begin as one being, Universal Man. So the fall of Urizen constitutes a revolt of God against man, one of the many reversals of mythic direction Blake sets about creating. It is from this act that Chaos then springs. When Urizen revolts against his brothers by withdrawing into himself he appears to them to have become a void or vacuum. Then Urizen moves to a whole series of acts of invention—the idea of the holy, of a menacing future, of a hostile space, and so on.

By setting up his myth in this way, Blake overcomes a notion that is unacceptable to the imagination. For the imagination can see that it springs neither out of nothing nor out of Chaos. It takes life in a world where all things are identical and any form of division is an act of negative creativity. The same phenomenon is again allegorized by Blake in the Book of Los, which begins with the "Times remote," when all things were one, until this unity was broken by Covet, Envy, Wrath, and Wantonness, who bound Los in flames "hard as adamant, Black as marble," much as Zeus binds Prometheus, until finally the prophetic wrath breaks forth and creates a vacuum, followed by the fall of Los into the world.

In the Books of Urizen, Ahania, and Los, Blake devotes his main narrative to tracing the history of this negative creation, and in so doing he lays bare the inadequacies of earlier creation myths by rehearsing in his own terms their principal line of narrative. Urizen is the chief figure, the instigator of the fall. It is he who creates the idea of the holy, which produces a division in space between subject and object and foists on us the notion of higher forms creating lower forms, as the creator becomes more and more of a mystery to us. These myths explain the origin of religion and of Newtonian science, but they do not account for art. In fact they are the antithesis of art, especially of what Blake called "prophetic art," a fact which Neitzsche later explained as contributing to the death of tragic art through Euripides' introduction of Socratic thought, the belief that reason can impose order on life, with the result that "character must no longer be broadened so as to become a permanent type, but on the contrary, must be so finely individualized . . . that the spectator ceases to be aware of myth at all."

Moreover, the fall of Urizen divides time into a nostalgic past (like the Golden Age), a fallen present, and a menacing future. The fall of the gods into a world of solid obstruction creates a barrier to creative energy, as Urizen begins his desperate labors of digging up mountains and hills to shut off the vision of eternity. So even Los is misled into a futile effort to save Urizen by reshaping him, and his failure to accomplish this impossible task leads him to join the fallen Urizen in despair. Los then creates clock time, and subsequently splits himself into two, and couples with his other half, Enitharmon (here Eve) to produce his son Orc. From this point on, Los is bound in the chains of familial jealousy, like the chains that bind Loki in the Prose Edda. In the *Book of Ahania*, Los' son Fuzon revolts against this process of fall, but by the end of the poem he too is nailed to the Tree of Mystery, recalling both Christ on the cross and Odin on the Tree.

But in rehearsing the earlier creation stories with his own cast of characters, Blake had not yet done much more than replot the defects of those myths. In all of them, creation is immediately followed by an apparently irreversible process of fall. In fact, in Ovid and Genesis, the act of creation, being itself one of division, is the first step in the fall. The same is really true of the Olympian creation myth also, perhaps less obviously. Here, though the gods unite to produce offspring, they reveal in this genetic process what Auden calls "the germ cell's primary division." So too with the Pelasgian, Egyptian, Finnish, Buddhistic, Japanese and Maori creation myths, in which the World Egg splits into two parts which form heaven and earth, and from which then spring all forms of the natural world.

But as Blake sees it, creation cannot come into being *until* the fall has occurred. First there is the state of One-ness in which the Eternals exist:

Four Mighty Ones are in every Man: a Perfect Unity
Cannot exist but from the Universal Brotherhood of Eden
The Universal Man, to Whom be Glory Evermore. Amen.
The Four Zoas, ll.4–6

Next there is the fall caused by Urizen's act of negative creativity. Only then can creation proper begin. It is this story that Blake yet must envision. And it is in *The Four Zoas*, a great but imperfect poem which he eventually seems to have abandoned, that Blake sets about this task. Los is the central figure in this poem, and Blake early outlines a more comprehensive creation story than he had previously written, concerning Los' "fall into Division & his Resurrection to Unity:/ His fall into the Generation of decay & death & his/ Regeneration by the Resurrection from the dead."

For Blake, as I have remarked before, the early creation myths fail to explain how higher forms of civilization seem to have developed out of lower forms, and this phenomenon is essentially what the Orc cycle is designed to account for. Space dictates here an admittedly reductive treatment of this great poem, but it is the overall growth and evolution of Blake's mythological imagination that we are concerned with, rather than a detailed analysis of the poems. *The Four Zoas* is divided into nine "Nights," the first six of which might be said to be a compendium of Blake's previous myths of fall. Three of the four principal characters we have already met and watched them fall: Urizen, Luvah (as Orc), and Urthona (as Los). One new fall is enacted in the first "Night" of this poem—the fall of Tharmas, the personification of the human instinct toward unity. His fall is also naturally an act of self-division, and it is then followed by the falls of Luvah-Orc, and Urizen. Los then attempts unsuccessfully to reshape Urizen, as he did in the Books of Urizen and Los, and subsequently joins Urizen in his fall, splits into two, and engenders his son Orc on Enitharmon. So the Orc cycle begins again. The cry of young red Orc moves Urizen to pity him, but he is defended from this danger by the Spectres of Urthona and Tharmas. So far, Nights I–VI have taken us through what for Blake is now familiar territory.

In Night VII, however, a new hero takes the center of the stage, At the point where Urizen's pity has succeeded in chaining Orc in Promethean defiance, Los now finds a way to break through back to a vision of the Eternal world from which he fell. So the first potentially creative act is prefigured as Los surrenders his lust, his desire as subject to possess or dominate an object:

Enitharmon told the tale
Of Urthona. Los embrac'd the Spectre, first as a brother,
Then as another Self, astonish'd, humanizing & in tears,
In Self abasement Giving up his Domineering lust.

The first step in reuniting the divided parts of nature has been taken in an act which unites the will and the imagination. From this point on, the rebuilding of Jerusalem with the aid of Enitharmon can begin. Los now desires to "fabricate embodied semblances," the artifices of eternity, and his first creations, Rintrah and Palambron, immediately comfort the bound Orc and the divided Tharmas.

This first creative impulse is not without provoking a violent reaction from Urizen, and this finally leads to an apocalypse in the ninth "Night" of the poem in which, while all of the fallen natural world is convulsed by cataclysmic wars and natural calamities, Los begins his first overt creative act, the destruction of the divided heaven and earth, the reuniting of the two sundered halves of the Universal Egg, the split between the holy and the profane, the I-Thou dichotomy:

> Terrified at Non-Existence,
> For such they deem'd the death of the body, Los his vegetable hands
> Outstretch'd; his right hand branching out in fibrous strength
> Seiz'd the Sun; His left hand like the dark roots cover'd the Moon,
> And tore them down cracking the heavens across from immense to immense.

As a result of this act, Space and Time disappear into shadows, and the latent hero of the poem, Albion, greater Adam, a man who contains all reality in himself and is therefore both human and divine, male and female, and a fourfold balance of the human faculties of intellect, imagination, emotion and instinct, is now raised from the sleep in which he has been sunk throughout the poem. His arousal from sleep produces in turn the reintegration of Urizen, focuses on the mission of Luvah-Orc, and revives the primal spirit of Innocence as Tharmas is reborn into the world. The whole action of the poem is then summed up in the following great passage:

> If Gods combine against Man, setting their dominion above
> The Human form Divine, Thrown down from their high station
> In the Eternal heavens of Human Imagination: buried beneath
> In dark Oblivion with incessant pangs, ages on ages
> In enmity and war first weaken'd, then in stern repentance
> They must renew their brightness & their disorganized functions
> Again reorganize, till they resume the image of the human,
> Cooperating in the bliss of Man, obeying his Will,
> Servants to the infinite & Eternal of the Human form.

Then the poem closes with a vision of Albion and his sons sitting down to a great feast, the product of the harvest and vintage of Urizen and his sons, who have set themselves enthusiastically to their new task of plowing up all of nature into a fresh profusion of forms.

In *The Four Zoas*, then, Blake's creation myth is first fully sketched out. For him, creation does not precede fall, it follows fall. The fall, which is what the earlier myths were really about, involves a division of the self into subject and object, and this in turn perverts desire to the "female will," the desire of the subject to possess and dominate the object. This in turn leads steadily downward to Armageddon. Only when the fall has occurred can creation really begin, and it begins first of all in a moment of recognition, where the will is reunited with the imagination in an act of annihilation of self, the renouncing of lust, where the image of desire is made to fulfill the will, and the beloved becomes a creature, not a thing. It is the same illumination that Gulley Jimson urges on the young man he sees walking with his sweetheart: "Look out, Puggy, that isn't a maiden you see before you, it's a work of the imagination." The will, working now in a new direction in the activity of Los and his sons, attempts to unite everything previously divided by the fall. So the creative act is really one that sets out to destroy *the* Creation, the earlier myths about which, as Blake has discovered, were really creations of the fallen Urizen.

But Blake appears to have abandoned *The Four Zoas*, and while the reasons for this may have been many, some of them come to light, I think, when Blake's next epic poem, *Milton*, is placed alongside it. Here again, space dictates only an eagle's eye view of this complex and lengthy poem. Book I divides itself roughly into three parts: 1) the Bard's Song of the fall; 2) Milton's descent and union with Blake; and 3) the journey of Blake and Los toward Golgonooza, where Blake presents his vision of the world to Los.

The Bard's Song recapitulates many of the former motifs of mythic fall we have been considering. It recounts the fall of Urizen through the Seven Ages, the division of Los, and the birth of his children—all a very compressed recension of the story Blake had developed in the Books of Urizen and Los, and in the earlier "Nights" of *The Four Zoas*. The Bard's Song then moves to a quarrel between Palambron (the Orc of this poem) and Satan, caused because Satan had persuaded Palambron to trade his work with the Harrow, breaking up nature into a greater profusion of living forms, for a day's work in Satan's mills:

Next morning Palambron rose: the horses of the Harrow
Were madden'd with tormenting fury, & the servants of the Harrow,
The Gnomes, accus'd Satan with indignation, fury and fire.
Then Palambron, reddening like the Moon in an eclipse,
Spoke, saying: "You know Satan's mildness and his self-imposition,
Seeming a brother, being a tyrant, even thinking himself a brother
While he is murdering the just: prophetic I behold
His future course thro' darkness and despair to eternal death.
But we must not be tyrants also: he hath assum'd my place
For one whole day under the pretence of pity and love to me.
My horses hath he madden'd and my fellow servants injur'd.
How should he, he, know the duties of another? O foolish forebearance!"

The Bard's Song then closes with a more subjective account of the dispute, as Leutha, Satan's emanation, explains his motives of mixed hate and love for making the deal with Palambron.

Blake does two new things here in his fifth myth of fall. In the first place, it now constitutes a smaller Song within a larger epic poem. Secondly, and even more significant, it has become an allegory of Blake's own personal experience with his patron Hayley, during his stay at Felpham while he was engaged in writing *Milton*. The story of fall has become very much more self-conscious as we follow the disturbing effect of Hayley's attempts to conventionalize Blake as a poet, and the confrontation between Palambron (Blake) and Satan (Hayley) can be seen as Blake's very act of writing the poem *Milton* against Hayley's advice.

In the second section of the poem, the Bard's Song provokes a creative response, as Milton descends from Eden. Only he in all Eternity will undertake to cast out pity from Palambron and possessive love from Leutha. So he throws off his Puritanism and descends to aid Blake. Blake requires this example of "self-annihilation and the grandeur of Inspiration" because he needs the strength of Milton to face his own task as prophet-poet.

Milton's descent involves two major actions: a wrestling match with Urizen, in which the human form divine struggles with the body of law, as Jacob wrestled with the Angel of Jehovah. But as Harold Bloom cleverly notes, Milton in Blake's poem does not make Jacob's mistake—he wants to re-form God, not just extract a promise from him. And so he sets about his second act, as he overlays the cold bones of the fallen Urizen with the Adamic clay of Succoth. In other words, he makes God in the image of man. All is set now for the union of Blake and Milton, which occurs in one of the most striking images in the poem:

But Milton entering my Foot, I saw in the nether
Regions of the Imagination—also all men on Earth
And all in Heaven saw in the nether regions of the Imagination
In Ulro beneath Beulah—the vast breach of Milton's descent.
But I knew not that it was Milton, for man cannot know
What passes in his members till periods of Space & Time
Reveal the secrets of Eternity: for more extensive
Than any other earthly things are Man's earthly lineaments.
And all this Vegetable World appear'd on my left Foot
As a bright sandal form'd immortal of precious stones & gold.
I stooped down & bound it on to walk forward thro' Eternity. . . .
And Los behind me stood, a terrible flaming Sun, just close
Behind my back. I turned round in terror, and behold!
Los stood in that fierce glowing fire; & he also stoop'd down
And bound my sandals on in Udan-Adan; trembling I stood
Exceedingly with fear & terror, standing in the Vale
Of Lambeth; but he kissed me and wished me health,
And I became One Man with him arising in my strength.
'Twas too late now to recede: Los had enter'd into my soul:
His terrors now possess'd me whole! I arose in fury & strength.

In the last section of Book I, Blake and Los set out for the city of Golgonooza, but are prevented from entering it by Los' sons, who still think that Blake-Milton is the old puritanical poet. In self-defense, Blake begins a description of Los' world, which is nature contained by the imagination in a process in which all dialectical constructs are constantly being destroyed and recreated by the imagination. Los is the divine smith, building artifices of Eternity, sculptures that the fires of fresher vision will again melt and remold. The book closes with a vision of the sky not as a net shut down over man by the Immortals (as in the Book of Urizen), but as an imperishable tent built up by the sons of Los, among whom Blake now clearly takes his place. Book II need not concern us much here, since clearly the major action of the poem is concentrated in a few moments of charged decision in Book I. It is concerned with the "redemption" of Milton and his emanation Ololon, creator and creature, in the land of Beulah. She too descends, and must undergo an act of self-annihilation. There is one speech that Milton addresses to her, however, which sums up so well what the truly creative act involves that it is worth quoting here:

To bathe in the Waters of Life, to wash off the Not Human,
I come in Self-annihilation & the grandeur of Inspiration,
To cast off Rational Demonstration by faith in the Saviour,
To cast off the rotten rags of Memory by Inspiration,
To cast off Bacon, Locke & Newton from Albion's covering.
To take off his filthy garments & clothe him with Imagination,
To cast aside from Poetry all that is not Inspiration,
That it no longer shall dare to mock with the aspersion of Madness
Cast on the Inspired by the tame high finisher of paltry Blots
Indefinite, or paltry Rhymes, or paltry Harmonies,
Who creeps into State Government like a catterpiller to destroy;
To cast off the idiot Questioner who is always questioning
But never capable of answering, who sits with a sly grin
Silently plotting when to question, like a thief in a cave.

In *Milton*, Blake has made several significant steps beyond his earlier formulations toward a creation myth that is really adequate as an archetype of the function of art in human civilization. In the first place, he greatly condenses the myth of the fall, reducing it in proportionate significance as compared to his succeeding myth of creation. This effect is also reinforced by making it a Song within a Song. Then he has made part of that song of fall an allegory of his own frustrated experience in trying to write *Milton* while under the patronage of Hayley. And he has clearly identified himself as a son of Los.

Biographical allegory, however, is clearly not enough for Blake. It is the first step in moving from impersonal accounts of fall and recovery toward a more subjective myth. But for Blake, the subjective elements still remain to be dramatized. Allegory for him is too abstract; it has the disadvantage that simile has in relation to metaphor, the subject and object are merely yoked together, not fused into one. That is why Blake moves on in the poem to further stages. The Bard's allegorical-biographical song of creation (fall) in turn provokes an act of creation within the poem at large, which is Milton's willingness to annihilate his self and show Blake a model of the poet-prophet's central act by giving human form to the abstract anatomical Urizen. The two great poets then fuse into one, and Blake gains his vision of the true work of a son of Los, the resurrection of the fallen Albion. In this manner we begin to understand the imagination as springing from a vision of something eternal, out of time and space, resurrected in the work of each individual, inspired poet as he reshapes the vision of earlier poets. So Milton is reborn in Blake, and so we can see the process stretching out into the future, where Blake's Jerusalem is identical with the Byzantium of Yeats, and where a work like *The Horse's Mouth* becomes Joyce Cary's own *Milton*.

A highly reductive synthesis like this has many disadvantages, but it is helpful in revealing the uniqueness of what Blake did. By a series of great imaginative feats, he singlehandedly forged a new creation myth to account for how the imagination works in man, helping him to build a civilization by turning lower forms into higher ones. His myth is also a more inclusive one than the earlier creation stories because it contains within its cyclic boundaries those earlier, tragic, myths of negative creation that lead to fall. And as we study them in sequence, we can watch Blake wrestling, as Milton wrestles with Urizen, with the inadequacies of the older forms, as he shapes a new one for himself. In *Milton* this new myth fully emerges, and in the process it has become subjective, internalized, biographic, and dramatic.

Since for Blake, true imaginative creation involves a reversal of the process of fall, it is not surprising that Blake's vision of the activity of art in human civilization reverses several older formulations. For him, creation follows fall, rather than precedes it. The Word is not made Flesh; rather in a work of art, Flesh becomes Word. And man is not made by God in the image of God. Instead, it is the other way around: God is made by man in the image of man. For, as Wallace Stevens puts it, "God and the imagination are one," energy and consciousness are united in the poet's work, where his creative effort is inseparable from a knowledge of what it is doing.

Though Blake was to go on in *Jerusalem* to an even richer and more complex version of his myth of creation, nowhere in his poetry is it more directly presented than in Book I of *Milton*. There, in a biographical, subjective, internalized structure Blake is able to dramatize with startling clarity the process by virtue of which the poet produces, in Baudelaire's words, "a suggestive magic including at the same time subject and object, the world outside the artist and the artist himself." The biographical form of the myth allows us to see from the inside how creation originates in a moment of total recognition, a moment which Blake describes in one of his most serenely poignant passages:

There is a moment in each Day that Satan cannot find,
Nor can his Watch Fiends find it; but the Industrious find
This Moment & it multiply: & when it once is found
It renovates every Moment of the Day if rightly placed.

This is the moment when the true work of creation is done, when form is identified with meaning in an instant illumination, an *Augenblick*, in the mind of the poet. It constitutes a moment of recognition in which, as Stevens again put it, the artist (and the inspired reader) is "like a man returning from Nowhere to his village . . . which he has come to cherish and wants to be near"—like Marcel returning to Cambray after tasting the *madeleine* dipped in tea. In this instant all places become one place. The poet Caedmon is the Adam Kadmon of Cabbalistic tradition, the Divine Man, who is also Albion awake from his dream of time. In that moment, past, present and future time become one fully charged instant. And there, Hesiod's song of "what is, what is to be, and what was before now," Blake's vision of "the Past, Present and Future all existing before me," and the chant of Yeats's golden bird "of what is past, or passing, or to come" are all one.

Above Grasmere, October 4, 1969

Deborah Austin

"I lay upon the steep of Loughrigg, my heart dissolved in what I saw."
    —Dorothy Wordsworth, *Grasmere Journal*, June 1, 1800.

It was October when I did the same.
A century and sixty-nine more years
fell to the four months between yours and mine.
I had your journal with me. Held it, only,
not reading—as in my New Hampshire hills
men gifted so walk soberly, both hands
holding the twin prongs of a hazel-fork,
waiting to feel it quiver and turn down.

Grasmere below was steely-blue at first.
Then a light wind pushed mist down Rydal Fell,
out, like a smoke-puff; twirled it; Helm Crag grew
faint as a phantom, holding all its shape,
then vanished. Then mist touched me, and rain fell.
Big drops at first, for minutes; drizzle, then.
The curtain swayed toward Easedale. Quietly,
the sun looked slant along the swirling drops
until the light broke into all its parts

and built a gentle-colored bow that bent
its pure arc side-to-side across the lake—
rose, orange-lemon, violet—colors dim
as dream, opaled by mist, yet each secure
in its own place, by that celestial gaze
tensed out of mist-milk into harmony,
resolving from rain-chaos to a span
so firm feet could have climbed it—all of air,
light, water, only . . .

             Oh, then I could feel
New England tears wet on my cheek. Through these,
and by them, rain-colors arched across to bind
my mountains to your own: my mountains, gray
granite and blueberries; yours, brackened fells.

The lake was yours and mine at once; the book
there in my hand fell open like a wound
along your side, which entering, I could
for the bow's life see with your eyes and mine.
My heart dissolved, dissolved in what I saw.

The Story
of the
Missing Man

Philip Young

If Peter Rugg, thought I, has been travelling since the Boston Massacre, there is no reason why he should not travel to the end of time. If the present generation know little of him, the next will know less; and Peter and his child will have no hold on this world.

—Jonathan Dunwell

Peter Rugg, the missing man, is nearly everywhere missing. For every citizen who has heard of him at all, ten thousand, or a hundred thousand, have heard of Rip Van Winkle—to whom, indeed, Peter owes a small and obvious debt. But he was once well known and perhaps should be again, as the dwindling few who remember him all seem to believe. It would be good, in short, if Peter could strengthen his hold on a spinning world that has a place for him.

On the 10th of September in 1824, the New England *Galaxy*, a Boston newspaper, contained many matters of moment. For one thing, Lafayette was in the city at the time, and the paper was full of what he said, and what was said about him. On the communications-to-the-editor page was a fine piece of Johnsonian invective directed against the restrictions placed on the use of carriages in the main streets of the city during the General's visit. And near it was the curious report of a man who signed himself Jonathan Dunwell. This had nothing at all to do with Lafayette. It posed as a reply to a friend who had asked for information on a peculiar subject, and was called "Some Account of Peter Rugg, the Missing Man, Late of Boston, New-England."

Dunwell goes about his business in a straightforward way. He first encountered Rugg, he explains, while travelling in a stage outside Providence, Rhode Island, in the summer of 1820. He saw a man, with a little girl beside him, going in great haste in a weather-beaten carriage that was drawn by a large black horse. The man looked dejected, but anxious and desperate as well; he appeared to be a man in great trouble, and that was all that Dunwell saw. But his driver knew at least this about him—that the man never stops longer than to ask the way to Boston, and to mutter that he must be there by nightfall. The driver also said that in his travels he himself had seen this Peter Rugg on the highways better than a hundred times, and often headed directly *away* from that city. He is always followed by a storm, moreover, which often catches and drenches him and the girl; but when the thunder claps near him the great black horse just increases the frantic pace, and off they go. A peddler submitted to Dunwell that he too had seen this man and his daughter, each time asking the way to Boston, in four states. But he did not wish to see them again: "they do not look to me as though they belonged to this world."

While in Hartford three years later, Dunwell continues, he suddenly heard someone cry out "there goes Peter Rugg and his child! . . . wet and weary, and farther from Boston than ever." The man was already a legend, he learned from a stranger; he had been travelling for more than 20 years to Boston—all the while growing older and wearier while his horse grew stronger. The stranger himself had had a typical exchange with Peter, he said. He told him it was a hundred miles to Boston, and Rugg gave his usual reply: "how can you deceive me so? It is cruel . . . I have lost my way." The man repeated: "one hundred miles." And Rugg objected: "I was told last evening it was but fifty, and I have travelled all night." But, said the man, "you are travelling from Boston. You must turn back." "Alas," said Rugg, "it is all turn back! Boston shifts with the wind . . ." and he was off in a clatter.

Finally Dunwell met Rugg in person, and talked with him. But he learned only that Peter used to live on Middle Street in Boston, and thought he was in Newburyport (it was still Hartford). Then with a cry—"Ah, that fatal oath!"—he was off again. But Dunwell is soon in Boston himself, and he looks up an aged lady in Middle Street. She reports the surprising news that Rugg had indeed been there one evening a summer ago, and had asked for his wife. On being told that she had been dead for better than twenty years, and on seeing how changed were the streets, the people, the whole town, he had concluded, "Some other Mrs. Rugg, some other Middle Street . . . no home tonight," and had disappeared. At that point Dunwell decided Peter Rugg was losing his hold on this world entirely.

And that evening he got, from a gentleman at the hotel where he was staying, the last pieces of information he was able to gather. Peter, it turns out, had been a good, comfortable man with a wife and daughter and only one flaw, a terrible temper. One morning he took the little girl on a trip to Concord, and on his way back he was overtaken by a violent storm. In what is now West Cambridge a friend asked him to stop over. But Rugg cried out with a fearful oath, "Let the storm increase; I will see home tonight . . . or may I never see home!" For a while after this his wife on stormy nights thought she saw him doing everything in his power to stop his horse while racing past his own door. But soon her neighbors, who had been cooperative, refused to watch for him any more, and would say nothing about him. His friends, too, gave him up. One day they would hear of him in New Hampshire, the next in Connecticut, then in Rhode Island again. And there was what the toll-gatherer on the bridge between Charlestown and Boston had claimed. A horse and carriage had been rattling through the gate, in defiance of the charges, and once the man had tried to stop them, and had thrown his three-legged stool. But it was as if the missile had gone right through, he said, and he did not wish to discuss the matter any more either. This, concludes Dunwell, was all that he was able to learn.

The editor of the newspaper that published this communication knew no Jonathan Dunwell, and had no notion what the somewhat self-congratulatory name might be pseudonymous for. Swamped during four months with demands for information about him, he finally pleaded in his columns that it might be quite true that Peter Rugg could not get to Boston, but could his creator not get to the *Galaxy* office for the purpose of giving up his identity? The author never did. The story was reprinted in many books, often attributed to people who had not written it, and it was not for 17 years that an edition appeared under the name of the man who had.

That man was William Austin, a nearly forgotten citizen of Boston who deserves better of posterity. William would have represented the fifth generation of Austins born since 1638 in Charlestown, Massachusetts, except that the British intervened by burning that town, and his father's house, in connection with the event known (somewhat inaccurately, since the fight was on Breed's Hill, nearby) as the Battle of Bunker Hill. And so William was born, on March 2, 1778, in Lunenburg, Massachusetts. His father, Nathaniel, though a most prominent citizen, should perhaps be remembered for the fact that he once had the opportunity to say gallantly to a woman (as she fled in panic from the burning city of Charlestown with most of her possessions in her arms), "You've dropped your baby, ma'am!" whereupon he presented her with it. William's mother, Margaret, was of an old Tory family, and never failed to remind her son on Bunker Hill Day that they were commemorating a tragedy.

Austin went to school under the Reverend John Shaw (eventually the grandfather of Mrs. Herman Melville), and then went through Harvard College, where he had a good record and belonged to the best clubs— but not to Phi Beta Kappa, which he declined to join. He disapproved at the time of Harvard itself, and was distinguished there for an attack which he wrote on that institution in which he remarked, among many other things, that "should Homer himself revive and enter the university, he would turn in disgust from the Iliad, and Locke would detest his own essay." He intended to study law upon graduation, but needing money first he got a job with the U. S. Navy as a schoolmaster and soon became, in addition, the first man appointed by government commission as a Navy Chaplain. He served on the famous "Constitution," and in 1800 a case involving salvage arose and turned out fortunately for the temporary clergyman-schoolmaster.

Legal advice was needed, and Austin was sent to Alexander Hamilton to study the matter. Here he impressed Hamilton, got some money for his efforts, and Hamilton's commendation, and he went off to Lincoln's Inn to study law. In England he entertained himself with Washington

Allston and wrote the *Letters from London*—on "men, morals, politics and literature"—which as a book were once widely read and (except by Federalists, who were already alarmed by his liberal views) enthusiastically praised. He attacked slavery, very early saw the dangers of large corporations, and soon got himself into real and highly illegal political trouble back in this country. A staunch Jeffersonian Republican, he attacked in a newspaper article the "pompous imbecility" of a prominent Federalist, Major General Simon Elliot. The General's son, James, expressed the wish to Austin that "you will give me an opportunity to take your life." Austin told his second to get some pistols ("Mother—I suppose—has hidden mine"), and fought a duel in March of 1806—which was two years after the duel in which Hamilton had become involved. Austin fared better than his legal mentor, but unwell. Two shots were to be fired by each of the adversaries, at the murderous distance of ten yards, and feelings were so bitter that each fired an extra shot. Austin managed to miss with all three, and to get hit twice, but he recovered, and the event was kept very quiet. His own children learned of it for the first time after his death, when they found the record among his papers.

The rest of his career was less colorful. A highly successful lawyer, twice married and the father of 14 children, he also held various political offices as a Jacksonian Democrat. Despite his Tory background, his money and his relatives (he was related directly or by marriage to the most aristocratic families of New England's first 200 years—to Bradstreets, Dudleys, Cottons, Adamses, and Channing, Parkman, and Holmes) he remained until he died, in 1841, a progressive democrat.

As far as he was concerned, Austin's stories were a minor sideline. He wrote only five of them, apparently, and never took money for them or kept copies when they were published. But willy-nilly he was a pioneer in the development of American literature. He was, for one thing, a writer who "anticipates" Hawthorne in more ways than have been recognized. Like Hawthorne (and before Hawthorne, who read him, and like Henry James, later) he was able to give to events a quality whereby they seem neither real nor quite unreal. He gives in Peter Rugg a precedent for one kind of outcast that fascinated Hawthorne, as in "Wakefield," and his other first-rate story, "The Man with the Cloaks," is about a fellow who is a prototype for one of the principal figures in Hawthorne's work: the "unpardonable sinner," whose trouble is that his heart has "withered away."[1]

But Austin is of interest not simply as a precursor of Hawthorne or an estimable citizen but as a writer whose work deserves serious attention for its own sake, and he is the first American writer of short fiction but one, Irving, about whom this may confidently be said. In his own day his work was by no means unknown. "Peter Rugg" enjoyed a perfectly enormous poularity; the literary figures of the period—Longfellow, Higginson, Duyckinck and others—concurred in or promoted the general enthusiasm; E. C. Stedman, the poet, described himself as "daft" on the subject.

A few American writers have paid the story an even higher tribute by putting its "legendary quality" to their own use. And before they did, Austin himself, and a man who signed himself simply "Platt," attempted independently of each other to continue the tale of Peter's troubles. Published in three issues of the *Norfolk Republican* (of Roxbury, Massachusetts) in September 1827, Platt's efforts violate the spirit of the original and are of no interest. Austin's continuation is a good deal better, but it does not add much that is memorable either, except a final scene where Peter does get to Boston just as his estate is being auctioned. Here he is told by a voice from the crowd that "there is nothing strange here but yourself, Mr. Rugg. . . . Your home is gone, and you can never have another home in this world."

It is as a forlorn and hopeless man that Peter turns up next, as a part of Hawthorne's "Virtuoso's Collection" (1846). This story is about a fabulous museum which contains the manuscript of the Koran, Don Quixote's lance, the Flying Dutchman's autograph, and other treasures. It is presided over by the Wandering Jew himself, and when the narrator of the tale is asked the way to Boston by the establishment's doorkeeper he knows who asks the question. Much more recently, in *John Brown's Body* (1927), Stephen Vincent Benet also remembered the Jew and Peter together. When John Vilas and his daughter (and her child) wander in a horse and buggy in the backwash of the Civil War in search of the child's father,

> The story had gone on ahead of them . . .
> That made a fable of their journeying,
> Until you heard John Vilas was that same
> Lost Jew that wanders . . .
> But cannot die . . . being cursed.

Vilas' own association, however, is more fitting:

> . . . it almost seems to me
> As if I were no longer what I am
> But the deluded shade of Peter Rugg
> Still looking for Boston through the storm. . . .

Two of America's better-known lady poets, both associated with Boston, both spinsters, and a generation apart, have given Austin's story their own full treatment. Louise Imogen Guiney's "Peter Rugg, the Bostonian" (1891) is a long ballad which adequately retells the tale. Caught in a storm, Peter's fiery horse gets off the route and he goes "forward and backward like a stone/ The tides have in their hold." In the end he pleads to get home "GOD WILLING"—a chastened man upon whom a Catholic poet has bestowed repentance. Miss Guiney's ballad brought the wrath of those faithful to Peter down on her head, but the objections were not to her poetry, where they belong, or her piety, but to the fact that she had made a few apparently innocuous changes in the story—had given Rugg a son, for instance, instead of a daughter.

"A legend is something which . . . anybody is at liberty to rewrite," said Amy Lowell in the preface to her book *Legends* (1921). And in that book she printed "Before the Storm," her "polyphonic-prose" version of this particular "legend." She had been haunted by the tale, she says, from her childhood, when she had naturally thought of it as unauthored, and had had an "abiding fear" of the situation it describes. Her piece is better than Miss Guiney's, and preserves some of the force of the original. It also brings the story up to date; in the best scene, a pitifully comic one, Peter gets to Boston and is taken as a quaint advertisement, perhaps for some cereal product.[2]

More up to date still is the "Phantom Flivver" (*Saturday Evening Post*, January 28, 1950) of Frank Luther Mott, who as an authority on best sellers and magazine fiction could be expected to recognize a tale with popular appeal when he saw one. In his version the narrator, driving fast across Kansas a few years after World War II, passes and then a couple of hours later is startled to repass an old Model-T Ford. ("I feel queer," says his wife.) Later still, echoing Austin, the Ford goes right through the newer car. Piecemeal the man gets the story: the phantom driver is a "hant" named Peter Rugg who, accompanied by a small boy, has been driving nearly 40 years in search of a discontinued part for his beloved car, having vowed to drive all over America to find it, and not to come home till he does. Even an accident in which man, boy, and Ford are drowned in a river does not stay him; the part is finally located; Peter "sez thanks."

No other significant treatments of this story are known, and as happened in the case of Irving's "Rip Van Winkle" no one has come near equalling, let alone improving on, the virtues of the original telling. There have been, however, two successes with the same elements as make up Austin's tale, and they suggest how great an appeal these elements must inherently have. The first was Edward Everett Hale's famous *Man without a Country* (1863). Born on the site of the present Parker House in Boston in 1822, a bookish boy who grew up in the period of Peter's greatest fame, Hale could hardly have escaped knowing about him. In any event the theme of the best known of his many works is the same: defiance in an oath of the powers that be, and a condemnation to wander far from the place where the defier wishes to be. In Hale's story an officer named Nolan cries out in court, "D—n the United States! I wish I may never hear of the United States again!" and is sentenced accordingly. For 45 years he is transferred from ship to ship in the Navy, and never permitted to see in print even a reference to his homeland. So real did Hale make his account of Nolan's misfortune seem that a great many people took the thing as fact, and some claimed to have heard before of the man and his sad career. But the temptation to preach patriotism got not the feeblest resistance from the author, and for literate taste his didacticism overwhelms in the end the air of reality.

Peter's other popular reappearance, this time in deeper and probably unwitting disguise, came in a pleasing and widely publicized 1959 revival, by a group called the "Kingston Trio," of a politically inspired song opposing an increase in the Boston subway rates. The song, called "M. T. A." (Metropolitan Transit Authority), is about a man who got on the subway without the extra nickel and can't get off. Each day at one of the stops his wife hands in food from the platform.

> Will he never return? No he never returned,
> And his fate is still unlearned.
> He will ride forever 'neath the streets of Boston,
> He's the man who never returned.

This ballad owes a good deal to one of the nineteenth century called "The Ship that Never Returned," which was based on the unfortunate experience of an actual ship called the "Olive Branch," but Peter Rugg is at least a spiritual father of it.[3]

It is doubtful that patriotism and credibility will account for the great fame Hale's story once enjoyed, or that politics and three ingratiating singers with a good traditional tune will explain the presence of "M. T. A." on even a depraved Hit Parade. The missing part of the explanation for these successes lies somewhere in or near our response to such desperate and protracted wanderings as we also encounter, so much more forcefully, in "Peter Rugg."

People have of course responded to that state of affairs for a very long time, as to the myth of the Wandering Jew, which is alive and still being rewritten. This is, of course, the widespread story of a Jew, often a shoemaker, who has various names—Ahasuerus, Cartaphilus, Buttadaeus, Laquedem, and many others—who refused Jesus rest at his door when Jesus was carrying the cross to Calvary. As he pushed the Lord away he cried "go on!" And to this received the sad reply: "Truly I go, and that quickly, but tarry thou till I come," or: "It is thou who shalt go on, till the end of time." And so the Jew has done, a desperate, homeless man who can stop only to tell his story.[4] In some places his arrival is heralded by violent storms, and in several he has a specific inability in his wandering to get back to Jerusalem—but did once, and found everything so changed he couldn't recognize it.

Thus many of the elements that appeal to us in "Peter Rugg" have appealed to people for many hundreds of years. The story of the Wandering Jew had its first popular telling in 1602, in a widely printed and oft-reprinted four-page pamphlet which spread out from Germany to France, England, Scandinavia and elsewhere; the tale was generally taken to be true, and many said that they had talked to the poor man. But by 1602 the story was already old. In 1228 Roger of

Wendover had written in his *Flores Historiarum* that an Armenian arch-bishop then in England was asked by some monks about Joseph of Arimathea, who had spoken to Jesus and was said to be living still. (The bishop replied that he himself had seen Joseph; his name before baptism was Cartaphilus; he confessed to having taunted the Lord.) And long before that a sixth-century monk named Moschos referred briefly but unmistakably to the same figure.

Nor does some sort of highly limited credence in the man appear to have entirely died out. Around 1800 a multilingual imposter in England was believed by many until he was exposed by learned men and disappeared; indeed the Wandering Jew is supposed to have reappeared as late as 1870 in Muddy Valley, Utah, to a Morman named Michael O'Grady. Most recently George K. Anderson, author of the monumental *Legend of the Wandering Jew* (1965), remarks that he himself was introduced in 1948 to "a Wall Street broker [*caveat emptor*] who considered himself Ahasuerus." And he is still very much with us in literature; Par Lagerkvist devoted a whole tetralogy to him. In our own country he is Vachel Lindsay's "Scissors Grinder"; appears dimly in Hawthorne's "Ethan Brand," and prominently in O. Henry's "The Door of Unrest"; crops up in original versions by Ben Hecht, Maude Hutchins, Howard Nemerov, and so on.

Rugg was not Jewish, however, but of Dutch extraction, and the famous Flying Dutchman is perhaps his even more direct ancestor; most of the important elements of his story that are not in the religious myth are here. The Flying Dutchman of course concerns a ghost ship which is seen in stormy weather around the Cape of Good Hope, and is ominous of bad luck. In some versions this ship is doomed because of a foul murder committed on board. But in a commoner form, the one Wagner used in his opera, the trouble was that an old Dutch sea captain, Vanderdecken, in the middle of a storm had sworn an oath to round the Cape if it took him eternity. His curse can be lifted only if he finds a woman who will sacrifice everything for him. The helplessness of Peter to control his horse is anticipated by the fact that the ship of one Captain von Falkenburg, condemned to sail the North Sea forever, has neither steersman nor helm.[5]

The stories of the Wandering Jew and the Flying Dutchman, both very widely known, are both obvious sources for "Peter Rugg." But the figure of the condemned wanderer is of course far older than these. The antecedents for the Jew are where one would expect to find them—in the Bible and in Christian lore generally. There is first of all the notable example of Cain, with his sentence ("a fugitive and a vagabond shalt thou be in the earth") and his mark, which he bore lest any encountering him should mistakenly put him to death (the Jew has a cross on his forehead, or on the sole of his boot). And according to John (21:22), Christ did say to Peter of another disciple, "If I will that he tarry till I come, what is that to thee?" There are or have been other myths as well of the eternal wanderings of Biblical characters—Ishmael, Elijah, Judas Iscariot, St. Peter, and Jesus himself and Satan himself among them.

There is a Wandering Jewess as well—Herodias, who in one version of her tale was Miriamne before marrying Herod, and was punished because she showed contempt for the Magi when they passed Jerusalem on their way to the manger (in Sue's *Wandering Jew* she is Ahaseurus' half-sister, and suffers his fate); and there is Kundry of von Eschenbach's (and Wagner's) *Parzifal*, who is condemned to live forever because she laughed at Jesus. Closer to home there is Miriam, the temptress of Hawthorne's *Marble Faun*, who from one angle appears to be that Jewess herself in deep disguise.

In addition there are myths about dancers who were rude to the Saviour and are cursed to dance till Judgment Day, about the wanderings of the Gypsies as punishment for their refusal to shelter the Virgin and her child, about Samiri, the sculptor of the golden calf, and there are Odysseus, Coleridge's Ancient Mariner, and many others like them. Peter's relation to Christian tradition suggests also that his vaguely Satanic hue may have to do with a recurrent notion that the devil travels vigorously by horse and buggy. (Which association might help explain the somewhat mysterious fact that people weren't particularly sympathetic to Peter, and didn't want to have much to do with him after his fall.)

The chief prototype of the Flying Dutchman, in turn, is probably Woden in his role as leader of the Wild Huntsmen—those restless, wandering night-riders who arrive in or presage a storm, as do Peter and the Jew, and who probably trace back to ancient belief in the night-wandering dead. There is a mingling of Teutonic and Christian lore here, for in medieval superstition these spirits were often not men but Woden's avenging maidens, and therefore easily associated with witches, who ride in the night on brooms or goats. One of their leaders was Diana, goddess of the hunt in classical myth—which adds a Roman element to the Norse-Christian mix. The other witch queen was Herodias, the Wandering Jewess herself: she was sweeping, according to one story, when she showed contempt for the Magi, and she has travelled her broomstick ever since.

Stories of unending punishment and frustrated activity go back of course at least as far as Greek mythology, where their ancestors are to be found in the tales of such as Sisyphus, who was condemned to Hades eternally to roll a great stone over the top of a hill, its weight always driving him back just as he approaches the summit; and Ixion, who for aspiring to the love of Zeus's wife turns endlessly on a wheel in Tartarus, the depths of hell; and Callisto, who was placed by Zeus in the sky as a bear with her son Arcas, the little bear, and because of the jealousy of Hera, who persuaded the god of the sea to arrange it, is forbidden ever to descend into the ocean, and goes with her son, as Peter with his daughter, wheeling eternally about the sky, one of the few constellations that never set.

The last of these myths is a story that directly explains a natural phenomenon, and although the theory that it is proper so to interpret myths is distinctly out of fashion, it is impossible to get around the fact that whatever their origins some myths are very suggestive of great natural processes. Sisyphus's stone may once have been, á la Robert Graves, a sun disk with some very special meanings, but his endless, hopeless task naturally puts one in mind of the ocean tide anyway—or of the waves, inexorably ascending the naked shingles of the world toward an unattainable highest reach, and as inexorably withdrawing. Ixion on his eternal wheel, and placed next to Sisyphus in Tartarus, just as naturally suggests the sun as it appears to our eyes, revolving forever about the earth. In the same way, then, and related to his function as a breeder of storms, Peter Rugg—whirling about the countryside, approaching now from one direction and now another but endlessly headed somewhere—might be taken to represent the wind. Then, by extension, just as Sisyphus, especially, has become a ready and fairly eloquent symbol of the futility of human endeavor, or of life itself, so Peter can seem an expression of the aimless or rootless life—or American life, if we will—where things fall apart, the center cannot hold, and we are buffeted about by forces before which we are helpless.

Such notions may point to overtones to Austin's story that are in it, and ones which people have very faintly responded to in reading it. But they are much too simple, and will not adequately explain either its once-great appeal, which is not necessarily gone for good, or its function. Partly the matter of its appeal, first, is a matter of Austin's skill: very surprisingly the telling is fresh, and does not smell of the lamp at all. Apparently relaxed in style it is in fact spare, selective, and unembellished; its distinction lies in the way a desperate situation is related calmly, even somewhat whimsically, and altogether unsentimentally. Further, since Peter's punishment is highly disproportionate to his crime, our participation in his misfortune is perhaps enhanced: the void produced by an inexplicably excessive penalty may allow at least some to fill it with their own nameless anxiety. Indeed there are ways in which "Peter Rugg" is superior to the stories of both the Wandering Jew and the Flying Dutchman. It does not have their epic quality or sweep, but it conveys with more intensity and detail a sense of dreadful helplessness. It can almost stand comparison with Kafka, and especially calls to mind his "Country Doctor": "exposed to the frost of this most unhappy of ages, with an earthly vehicle, unearthly horses, old man that I am I wander astray."

The fact that inferior accounts of Peter Rugg have themselves been at least somewhat effective suggests, however, that the story's ability to attract cannot be explained in literary terms alone. Clearly the tale has the crude, obvious function of the sort that gives most very popular stories a part of their currency. The Flying Dutchman is a warning about the folly of pride and the needless tempting of fate; it reflects superstitions concerning the relation between naming a thing and, by sympathetic magic, bringing it about—an ancient superstition that is intact today in the notion of the "jinx." The Wandering Jew obviously functions as a fable of Christian instruction, and clearly implies a warning too: one should not in any way renounce Christ—look what can happen. And although propagators of this myth have remembered, for the most part, what Edward Everett Hale forgot—that insistence on a moral wrecks it, that on being pointed at certain messages vanish—in the Middle Ages the myth was used as sharply pointed propaganda, as testimony to the power and truth of Christianity as opposed to the error of Judaism. "Peter Rugg" clearly repeats the Flying Dutchman superstition and its orthodox lesson about pride—a New-English sin, as it were. But a good deal that is more subtle than this finds expression in Austin's story, and another reading of the myth of the Wandering Jew leads to some of it.

This figure has impressed many people as a strikingly apt, and by no means unsympathetic, personification of what long seemed the historical fate of the Jews, from the beginnings of the Diaspora, at the end of the Captivity, to the recent past. In the myth a symbolic account of their dispersion in the very early Christian era—first along the shores of the Mediterranean, then throughout the Greco-Roman world, and finally throughout Christendom and beyond it—is powerfully signified. The specific inability of Ahasuerus to return to Palestine, as Peter to Boston, is a sharp reminder of the time when the Jews themselves were expressly prohibited from entering that city, then in Roman hands, on pain of death.

In the same way Peter Rugg, galloping about the countryside north, south, and west of Boston, plausibly personifies what may (perhaps for the first time but legitimately) be called the "New England Diaspora." He is a symbol of the great waves of emigration that began just before Austin wrote the story—waves which broke first from Boston out across New England itself; then, after 1782 and the end of the Revolution, swept across New York and northern Pennsylvania; and then after 1812 and the next war rolled across Ohio, northern Indiana and Illinois, eventually to reach the Pacific. The tendency of the Jews after their scattering to hold fast to their own ways and their own culture helped to remind people that their true roots were elsewhere, and thus may have helped in turn to keep alive a myth which expressed that fact. In much the same way the tendency of New Englanders was to reproduce in their new locations a culture and a setting which were as much as possible like the ones they had known before. They often simply transplanted themselves, and built anew the towns (with Puritan traditions and tidy white homes and steepled meeting-houses around elm-shaded public squares) that are visible today hundreds and thousands of miles from their origins. In its own day the story of Peter Rugg must have been redolent of these tidal waves.

And so it would not seem exactly coincidental that the period of Peter's creation and greatest vogue was the very period, 1820–1840, of the most vigorous exodus from New England. The story was born of the complex of feelings this exodus aroused, and it gave voice to them. New Englanders were very touchy on the subject; they were intensely patriotic about their region, and greatly alarmed over its "depopulization." (Of course there are no exact figures on the emigration, but relative to the population levels of the times it is known to have been vast.) The people who didn't go disapproved, rather helplessly but deeply, of those who did; they felt a silent reproach to their own ways and allegiances, hence to themselves, in all this departure. This feeling emerges in the story rather forcefully in the fact that people were unsympathetic to Peter, and it explains what would otherwise be a mystery in the affair—especially in the harsh ending of Austin's continuation—that no fairly weak association of Peter with the devil or storms will entirely account for. The story indirectly but firmly disapproves of Peter Rugg. The modern reader's natural sympathy for him must oppose a forget-about-him feeling that is in the tale itself, for there Peter has become the black sheep who has deserted the fold, his name no longer spoken in family circles.

The passing of time, and the tremendous, homogenizing changes which have swept across the country in recent decades, have obscured what might be called the diasporac level in Austin's tale. But this loss has been erased by a promotion of its protagonist from regional to national stature, for there has been an enormous gain in the validity of a remark Count Alexis de Toqueville made about Americans, not just New Englanders, back in 1835. Peter Rugg, that is, personifies very well a quality to which de Toqueville, in his extraordinary *Democracy in America*, gave a whole chapter: "The Restless Spirit of the Americans." An American, observes de Toqueville,

settles in a place, which he soon afterward leaves . . . and if at the end of a year of unremitting labor he finds he has a few days' vacation, his eager curiosity whirls him over the vast extent of the United States. . . . Death at length overtakes him, but it is before he is weary of his bootless chase of that complete felicity which is forever on the wing.

Death has not yet quite caught up with Peter, and he typifies even better than restlessness the "anxiety, fear, and regret" which, de Toqueville went on to say, keep the collective national mind "in ceaseless trepidation." No transplanted Dutchman or Jew, and no longer simply a New-Englander, Peter is an American.

Such interpretations as these, however, cannot account entirely for the hold the story once had on people, or for the spell it still casts on readers who are exposed to it today. The impelling image that is at the heart of the tale is not reckoned with by them: the image of a powerful horse racing away with a desperate, helpless man and his little girl as a black cloud hovers over, signalling disaster. That is what distinguishes the story from its sources; it is that image that does most to arouse the story's emotional charge, the feelings on which rest its basic appeal.

Clearly these feelings are primarily of anxiety—of fear combined (now that it's no longer possible to care about nineteenth-century emigration) with pity, and both unpurged. The problem is how the image goes about arousing these emotions.

As vivid, irrational narratives, myths often bear a close resemblance to dreams. Very closely allied in primitive cultures, the two are similar enough to suggest the possibility, however limited, of examining myths that people have responded to and remembered as though they were really dreams they had experienced and been able to reconstruct. If we are attracted to it, then, we could look at a myth as an expression—however dim and rendered always into symbols—of something that is going on in us. The events of the myth become external happenings with internal meanings, in somewhat the same way that our private desires and fears may be dramatized in our dreams.

Many myths, like the one of Pocahontas, are for the most part wish fulfillments, the kind of daydreams we have asleep. Some myths are nightmares, the moving pictures of our fears; and many, like the story of Rip Van Winkle, are complex mixtures of the two. In the bewildering and somewhat frightening way Boston seems to Peter to shift location, and in the way familiar scenes distort themselves, as well as in the central image, "Peter Rugg" is clearly a nightmare.

One modern theory of dreams posits a whole class of nightmares which come not from the fear of something external to us, but from a fear of our own impulses. In this type of nightmare a roaring lion, for instance, represents no retributive father or anything of that sort, but the feared outcropping of the anger that is normally buried in us. It is possible, then, to speak of the myth of Peter Rugg as though it were, for those who have responded to it, a nightmare which they themselves have had vicariously, and to think of it as a nightmare which produces an anxiety that comes to people as a fear of their own impulses.

Now the association of nightmares and sex is immemorial. The whole and specific aim of the *mara*,[6] the incubus or succubus to which nightmares were for so long attributed, was sexual abuse of the dreamer. If we turn for help to Freudian psychology, which has been no more reluctant in relating bad dreams to sexual problems than folk-belief, we are offered a choice of weapons, and a book *On the Nightmare* (1931) by Freud's biographer, Ernest Jones, comes readily to hand. Here Dr. Jones lays down a dogma (or, his term, a "formula"), to wit and flatly: *"an attack of the Nightmare is an expression of a mental conflict over an incestuous desire."* He claims further that the presence of an animal in a dream reinforces the theme of incest; further still that "dreams of *travelling* are almost constantly associated with sexual motives, such as . . . escaping with the loved parent away from the competing one. . . ." He submits both dreams and myths to exactly the same sort of analysis,[7] and thus it looks very much as if he would have to say here that "Peter Rugg" is, like other nightmares, an expression of the Oedipus Complex (or, despite the misnomer, the Electra Complex?), and presents us with a striking picture of a father and daughter in wish-fulfilling but *Angst*-ridden escape of the mother.

One of the most important consequences of the Oedipal situation is the sense of castration, remote from the ordinary consciousness of adults, but large in the unconscious mind. The notion of castration comes, of course, as a response, compounded of fear, guilt and the need for punishment, to the Oedipal wishes. Indeed Jones ingeniously connects a wealth of mythological beliefs about specifically—and of all things—horses with the whole problem of castration. Should we then take another tack and say that the essential anxiety in "Peter Rugg" is over castration? Should we gravely reconsider in this light Austin's request that his second get him a pistol: "Mother—I suppose—has hidden mine"? Is Peter's daughter now a substitute cast up by the machinery of censorship for his mother ("Some other Mrs. Rugg")?—or a curious symbol ("Peter") of the detached member?—or of both? And is her reproach now really the mother's reproach to Peter's infantile striving toward her? Or his wandering a search instead—for his mother, home, Middle Street, and the harbor of Boston?

As fast as that the amateur finds himself in murky water, over his head and unsnorkled. Fumbling around in the darkness, however, a few things may fuzzily emerge. For one thing, Jones's book, itself a bit of a nightmare, was written in those grand free-wheeling days before Freudian doctrine had undergone real testing, qualification and revision. It would not be unfair to say that his hypotheses are a bit unguarded. For another, we are searching for the story's appeal to the reader, not for what it might reveal about the writer; and in this context about all we could say is that the appeal is remotely to our own Oedipal guilt—which, if it exists at all, is buried so deep that most people, unable to detect even the existence of what's being appealed to, will hesitate to believe that any such communication is taking place.

Of course it may be that in the end we cannot really locate or explain the source of anxiety in "Peter Rugg." Indeed it may be that—as opposed to fear, where we know what we fear—anxiety is dread unable to identify its origins. It might even be that in pursuing Peter feverishly we have contracted his disease, and can't get home with the project. But in the ordinary rules of sport three strikes are allowed the batter: if incest and castration are a pair of misses then a third swing ought to be permissible. (If not, we can imitate Austin in his duel and shoot anyway.) Turning in but not from Freud, it just might do to make use, finally, of his other trinity—somewhat more "available" than the Oedipus triangle: his three-part view of the human psyche. It's conceivable that this may seem, to return to a previous metaphor, a little like coming up for air.

For Freud the basic cause of anxiety is the fear of being overwhelmed by instinct, or appetite—the fear that the forces we normally subdue by repression will get out of hand and break through our defenses to destroy us. When for any reason the struggle between appetite and repression becomes intense, and pent-up drives threaten to break loose, people suffer from anxiety—especially because they fear not only disgrace or destruction in the eyes or at the hands of others; they fear as much the power of their own disapproval, of their "consciences." Anxiety, then, comes when we fear that the instincts, or the normally repressed unconscious forces in general (a crude description of the "id"), will overwhelm consciousness (the "ego"), and then our consciences (the "supergo") will rise up and condemn us.

Subject to certain variations this theory is quite widely accepted, and it may throw light on the source of the anxiety that the central image of Peter Rugg occasions. This image presents an extraordinary vision of the destruction of control, of the usual self's precarious balance between appetite and conscience suddenly shattered. The looming and mythically powerful horse is passion, born of Peter's cosmic defiance, and broken out in spasms of vengeance for its normal suppression. Peter is the self, tied to the horse and hopelessly out of control. And the little girl increases his sense of guilt in sitting mutely by and providing a witness to the shameful display; her very presence is a grim reproach; she is, in short, conscience. The image presents a vivid and classic picture of the situation that produces anxiety. The horse, id, overwhelms Peter, ego, while the little girl, superego, sits in silent but terrible judgment. The horse and the girl are thus externalized aspects of Peter himself, and vicariously they are all symbolic aspects of ourselves. There, perhaps, is our nightmare.

Of course it is probable that for Freudians the horse in this nightmare would be a sexual symbol of appetite,[8] whereas the passion that got out of Peter's control was rage or anger—his "terrible temper." But Freudian revisionists like Karen Horney have argued persuasively that the fear that rage or anger will break loose and destroy us can produce anxiety every bit as effectively as the fear of a loss of sexual control can do. Anxiety comes when *any* of our basic defenses against the onslaught of irrational impulse are seriously threatened. The anxiety that visits a man who, say, hates some superior and fears lest his anger burst out and cost him the position his false affability and compliance have built is extremely common. Peter's horse, then, is the symbol of Peter's rage, and this outbreak is no less awesome or terrible to behold than a loss of sexual control (to which our own dreams have accustomed us) would be. We see in Peter a man who, for the momentary breakdown of discipline and the defiance of superior power, has fallen clean out of comfort, home, place and time—and most of the other relationships which map our routes and define our roles. He has exploded right out of the grooves of his life. Anyone secretly knows how delicate is the balance whereby he maintains his security; anyone can participate through Austin's symbols in the anxiety of the man who was suddenly missing. Pity, we suspect, comes chiefly from the ability to see ourselves in the misfortunes of others, and when the horse and the little girl and Peter Rugg go riotously by in all the wrong directions we pity Peter because our own anxieties tell us that there, but for the precarious grace of control, go we.

Notes

1. It is worth noting that the "moral" to Hawthorne's story about the outcast "Wakefield" would serve as well for "Peter Rugg":

   Amid the seeming confusion of our mysterious world, individuals are so nicely adjusted to a system, and systems to one another and to a whole, that by stepping aside for a moment a man exposes himself to a fearful risk of losing his place forever. Like Wakefield, he may become, as it were, the outcast of the universe.

   "The Man with the Cloaks," one of the very best early American short stories and almost completely forgotten, concerns a fellow who refused his extra cloak to a man who had none; in the chill of his guilt he has to put on another coat each day until before very long he is much too big for a room and must look out in misery at the world through the long tunnel of all his collars. Such a theme also suggests Hawthorne.

2. Miss Guiney's and Miss Lowell's versions of "Peter Rugg," as well as the story itself, "The Man with the Cloaks," two other Austin stories, Platt's additions, and an account of Austin's life, are all conveniently to be found in Walter Austin's *William Austin, the Creator of Peter Rugg*, Boston: M. Jones, 1925.

3. Peter might claim another offspring in Joe Btfsplk, "the world's worst jinx" in Al Capp's "L'il Abner." Joe travels under a black cloud, and gets to Boston, where he brings bad luck to the Red Sox.

4. Most Teutonic versions of the Wandering Jew myth stress his inability to die—*der ewige Jude*—where the Romance emphasize his wandering—*le Juif errant*. Our versions apparently derive more from the latter.

5. The myth of the Flying Dutchman seems also congenial to the American imagination. In *Life on the Mississippi* Mark Twain reports a tradition about a steamboat that couldn't round a bend that had been cut off when, as occasionally happened, the river suddenly shortened itself and took a new, more direct course to the sea. The pilots tempted fate with their oaths, and Twain says that when he was an apprentice pilot watchmen told him that they had themselves seen the "phantom steamer," "still trying to find her way out."

6. The "mare" in nightmare is etymologically distinct from our term for a horse of female gender. It originally meant "fiend" and is derived from the Anglo-Saxon *mara*—an incubus or succubus believed to be the source of bad dreams and derived in turn from the verb *merran*, to crush, cognate with Icelandic *mara*, Danish *mare*, Old High German *mara*, and so on (even into French, where the hag shows up in *cauchmar*?). Our mare is from Anglo-Saxon *mere*, the female of *mearh*, a horse. But by some obscure process mare and *mara*, horse and fiend, became associated in the imagination. Thus it is possible to say, remembering his horse, that "Peter Rugg" has doubly to do with nightmare. See Ernest Jones, *On the Nightmare*, new ed., New York: Grove Press, 1959, especially Part III, "The Mare and the *Mara*."

7. Jones, pp. 44, 70, 204 and 66.

8. Jung might well agree. In a chapter on "Dream Analysis" in his *Modern Man in Search of a Soul* he remarks that in myth and folklore generally the horse "carries one away like a surge of instinct"; it "represents the lower part of the body and the animal drives that take their rise from there." (Plato, in a startling section of the *Phaedrus*, said substantially the same thing.) For Freud all dreams of flight have sexual significance, and there are myths of flight comparable to "Peter Rugg" (Europa carried off by a bull, for instance) that seem transparently sexual. Some verse about another "Wild Ride" by the spinster Louise Imogen Guiney, written a few years before the poem about Peter's, has a refrain in which horses clearly suggest desire:

> I hear in my heart, I hear in its ominous pulses,
> All day, the commotion of sinewy, mane-tossing horses;
> All night, from their cells, the importunate tramping
> and neighing.

There Warn't No Home
Like a Raft
Floating Down the Mississippi,
or Like a Raft
Floating Down the Neckar,
or Like a Balloon
Ballooning Across
the Sahara:
Mark Twain as
Improviser

Chadwick Hansen

Mark Twain wrote *A Tramp Abroad* during the period when he had put aside the uncompleted manuscript of *Huckleberry Finn*. Thus it is scarcely surprising, as Walter Blair has pointed out, to find echoes of the major work in the minor one.[1] The most obvious of these echoes occurs when the persona of *A Tramp Abroad* decides, capriciously enough, to complete one section of the abortive walking tour of Europe around which the book is loosely organized by descending the Neckar on a raft, from Heilbronn to Heidelberg. The experience is, as in *Huckleberry Finn*, idyllic:

Germany, in the summer, is the perfection of the beautiful, but nobody has understood, and realized, and enjoyed the utmost possibility of this soft and peaceful beauty unless he has voyaged down the Neckar on a raft. The motion of a raft is the needful motion; it is gentle, and gliding, and smooth, and noiseless; it calms down all feverish activities, it soothes to sleep all hurry and impatience; under its restful influence all the troubles and vexations and sorrows that harass the mind vanish away, and existence becomes a dream, a charm, a deep and tranquil ecstasy. How it contrasts with hot and perspiring pedestrianism, and dusty and deafening railroad rush, and tedious jolting behind tired horses over blinding white roads!

As in the not yet written celebration of the raft in Chapter XIX of *Huckleberry Finn*, rafting is associated with the rising of the sun; the persona and his companion set off down the Neckar "as the gray east began to redden and the mysterious solemnity and silence of the dawn to give place to the joy-songs of the birds." Huck, one recalls, would end his description of a Mississippi sunrise with "the song-birds just going it!"

It would seem that themes from his uncompleted masterpiece were nagging at the back of Mark Twain's mind, and they continued to do so. The voyage down the Neckar begins in Chapter XIV of Volume I of *A Tramp Abroad*; in Chapter XV, entitled "Down the River," one finds the following:

As the morning advanced and the weather grew hot, we took off our outside clothing and sat in a row along the edge of the raft and enjoyed the scenery, with our sun-umbrellas over our heads and our legs dangling in the water. Every now and then we plunged in and had a swim. Every projecting grassy cape had its joyous group of naked children, the boys to themselves and the girls to themselves, the latter usually in care of some motherly dame who sat in the shade of a tree with her knitting. The little boys swam out to us, sometimes, but the little maids stood knee-deep in the water and stopped their splashing and frolicking to inspect the raft with their innocent eyes as it drifted by. Once we turned a corner suddenly and surprised a slender girl of twelve years or upward, just stepping into the water. She had not time to run, but she did what answered just as well; she promptly drew a lithe young willow bough athwart her white body with one hand, and then contemplated us with a simple and untroubled interest. Thus she stood while we glided by. She was a pretty creature, and she and her willow bough made a very pretty picture, and one which could not offend the modesty of the most fastidious spectator. Her white skin had a low bank of fresh green willows for background and effective contrast—for she stood against them—and above and out of them projected the eager faces and white shoulders of two smaller girls.

The passage is genteel, and afflicted by that sick prettiness which the idea of a naked girl on the verge of pubescence too often evoked from Victorian sensibilities. But in the present context its importance lies in its also being idyllic, and even, before the appearance of that twelve-year-old Eve, Edenic. As in the not yet written Chapter XIX of *Huckleberry Finn*, the raft has taken us into a world where the children (and the Black slaves, if there had been any?) are innocently and joyously naked, and one is reminded that throughout *Huckleberry Finn* the uncomfortableness of clothes is the commonest and most constant evidence of the restrictiveness of civilization.

Further down the Neckar, in Chapter XVII, the raft passes by cliffs where laborers are blasting a way for a railroad, and the persona thinks himself in mortal danger.

It appeared certain that we must perish, but even that was not the bitterest thought; no, the abjectly unheroic nature of the death—that was the sting—that and the bizarre wording of the resulting obituary: *"Shot with a rock, on a raft."* There would be no poetry written about it. None *could* be written about it. Example:

> *Not* by war's shock, or war's shaft,—
> *Shot*, with a rock, on a raft.

The association here, of course, is with the satire on obituary verse in another not yet written chapter of *Huckleberry Finn*, Chapter XVII, which was to follow immediately the smashing of the raft in that novel. But "shot with a rock on a raft" is a distressingly inept bit of satire compared to Emmeline Grangerford's "Ode to Stephen Dowling Bots, Dec'd." Indeed, rafting down the Neckar was in general so inferior to rafting down the Mississippi as an imaginative experience for Mark Twain that he could not keep his mind on it; he is forever forgetting the voyage and inserting irrelevant digressions in a sorry attempt to flesh out his narrative.

Even in the digressions, however, one finds echoes and anticipations of *Huckleberry Finn*, particularly in the last of them, the "legend of Dilsberg Castle." A young knight, Conrad von Geisberg, is persuaded by Catharina, the girl he is to marry, to sleep in a room of which it is said that anyone sleeping there will fall asleep for 50 years. During the night the girl and their friends carry him to a "ruined chamber" and dress him in decayed rags (they had first given him a "sleeping-draught"). When he awakens, his disguised friends persuade him that he has indeed slept for 50 years, that all his friends are dead, and that his "lost Catharina" died of grief over what had happened to him nearly 50 years ago. He is convinced, mourns his Catharina, who "never wittingly did a hurtful thing in all the little summer of her life," and announces that he will repay "her loving debt" by dying of grief for her. At this point the girl laughs, throws her arms around his neck, and invites him to join in the laughter because it was "all a jest." But he cannot be aroused out of his "hallucination." Continuing to believe her dead, he pines away and dies, to be followed, after many years of repentance, by the desolate Catharina.

This is, of course, a variation on the legend Irving used in Rip Van Winkle. Mark Twain's chief contribution to it has been to make it into a practical joke which turns appallingly serious, and it is that which connects it to *Huckleberry Finn*—connects it to those episodes in which Huck discovers that playing tricks on Jim results in pain rather than laughter, both for himself and Jim.[2]

Perhaps it is significant that immediately after giving us this soured practical joke, with its evocation of one of the central themes of *Huckleberry Finn*, Mark Twain finds himself unable to continue his fictional voyage. And he rids himself of the Neckar raft in the same way he had temporarily rid himself of the Mississippi raft. The persona decides to pilot the raft. He takes the steering-pole, and

we went tearing along in a most exhilarating way, and I performed the delicate duties of my office very well indeed for a first attempt [!]; but perceiving, presently, that I was really going to shoot the bridge itself instead of the archway under it, I judiciously stepped ashore. The next moment I had my long-coveted desire: I saw a raft wrecked. [When the Neckar rafts first appear in the book, in Chapter XIV of Volume I, the persona tells us that he used to spend hours watching them from his window in the Schloss Hotel, idly hoping to see one smash itself on a bridge-pier.] It hit the pier in the center and went all to smash and scatteration like a box of matches struck by lightning.

After the smashing of the raft at Heidelberg there are few evocations of *Huckleberry Finn* in the remaining chapters of Volume I of *A Tramp Abroad*, and there are no echoes of it at all in Volume II, a sorry performance in which Clemens tried unsuccessfully to persuade himself that he was interested in rhapsodizing over Alpine scenery, and in plagiarizing other people's guidebooks, and in satirizing old-world civilization as he had done in *The Innocents Abroad*. It would seem, then, that the echoes of *Huckleberry Finn* in *A Tramp Abroad* may be explained by the line of reasoning I have so far adopted; the themes of Mark Twain's shelved and incomplete masterpiece were nagging at the back of his mind; they surfaced here in the inappropriate context of a European travel book; he laid them to rest temporarily as he had done once before, by smashing the raft which was their vehicle, but he would not fully be rid of them until he had mastered them by completing the manuscript of *Huckleberry Finn*.

There is some truth to this argument, but it is only a partial truth, and just how partial it is may be seen by examining *Tom Sawyer Abroad*, which Mark Twain finished in 1893, a full decade after he had finished *Huckleberry Finn*, and in which some of these themes occur once more. The events of the story follow those of *Huckleberry Finn*, just as the latter had followed the events in *Tom Sawyer*.[3] Tom, hankering for more adventures, has got himself and Huck (who is the narrator once more) and Jim aboard a balloon which crosses the country and then the Atlantic. In Chapter VII, while they are crossing the Sahara, Huck celebrates the delights of living in a balloon, which are disconcertingly similar to those of living on a raft:

We was used to the balloon now, and not afraid any more, and didn't want to be anywheres else. Why, it seemed just like home; it 'most seemed as if I had been born and raised in it, and Jim and Tom said the same. And always I had had hateful people around me, a-nagging at me, and pestering of me, and scolding, and finding fault, and fussing and bothering, and sticking to me, and keeping after me, and making me do this, and making me do that and t'other, and always selecting out the things I didn't want to do, and then giving me Sam Hill because I shirked and done something else, and just aggravating the *life* out of a body all the time; but up here in the sky it was so still, and sunshiny and lovely, and plenty to eat, and plenty of sleep, and strange things to see, and no nagging and no pestering, and no good people, and just holiday all the time. Land, I warn't in no hurry to git out and buck at civilization again. Now, one of the worst things about civilization is that anybody that gits a letter with trouble in it comes and tells you all about it, and makes you feel bad, and the newspapers fetches you the troubles of everybody all over the world, and keeps you down-hearted and dismal 'most all the time, and it's such a heavy load for a person. I hate them newspapers; and I hate letters; and if I had my way I wouldn't allow nobody to load his troubles onto other folks he ain't acquainted with, on t'other side of the world, that way. Well, up in a balloon there ain't any of that, and it's the darlingest place there is.

We had supper, and that night was one of the prettiest nights I ever see. The moon made it just like daylight, only a heap softer; and once we see a lion standing all alone by himself, just all alone on the earth, it seemed like, and his shadder laid on the sand by him like a puddle of ink. That's the kind of moonlight to have.

Mainly we laid on our backs and talked; we didn't want to go to sleep.[4]

The dawn is missing this time, and the complaint against newspapers and the mails is out of character for Huck, but otherwise the situation is thoroughly familiar: we are on a journey which has taken us out of the restrictions and irritations of civilization and into a realm of personal freedom. One isn't surprised to discover, in the next chapter, that nobody is wearing clothes:

they went down and had a swim, and then Tom come up and spelled me, and me and Jim had a swim, and then Jim spelled Tom, and me and Tom had a foot-race and a boxing-mill, and I don't reckon I ever had such a good time in my life. It warn't so very hot, because it was close on to evening, and we hadn't any clothes on, anyway. Clothes is well enough in school, and in towns, and at balls, too, but there ain't no sense in them when there ain't no civilization nor other kinds of bothers and fussiness around.

Nor is it surprising to find Tom, three chapters later, playing a trick on Jim, although it is more than a little startling to find how easily, and cruelly, and offensively he succeeds. Jim is tricked into shovelling most of a load of sand out of the balloon,

and he made all that part of Africa damp, he sweated so. We couldn't work good, we was so full of laugh, and Jim he kept fretting and wanting to know what tickled us so, and we had to keep making things up to account for it, and they was pretty poor inventions, but they done well enough, Jim didn't see through them. At last when we got done we was 'most dead, but not with work but with laughing. By and by Jim was most dead too, but it was with work; then we took turns and spelled him, and he was as thankful as he could be, and would set on the gunnel and swab the sweat, and heave and pant, and say how good we was to a poor old nigger, and he wouldn't ever forgit us. He was always the gratefulest nigger I ever see, for any little thing you done for him. He was only nigger outside; inside he was as white as you be.

How are we to account for such tired and/or hideous parodies of themes we know better from *Huckleberry Finn*? By the 1890s some of Mark Twain's themes were becoming obsessive, but these are clearly not so, if only because they are handled so superficially as to be quite lacking in the emotional intensity one expects of any self-respecting obsession. We cannot find an adequate explanation for these passages in Mark Twain's psyche, but we may find one in his methods of composition.

Mark Twain's favorite narrative structure was the episodic journey, which he used both in his fictionalized travel books and in his fiction.

Within that loose and general structure he was very much an improviser. That is not to say that he made everything up afresh as he went along. Like the improviser in any art he had a stock of themes and subjects, a few of them original, but the majority adopted wherever he could find them, and whenever he reached a point where he could use one, he got it out and did a variation on it. That is, he would start a character or characters travelling off to Europe, or down the Mississippi, or back in time to Arthur's England, and when he found a convenient point to do a sunrise, he would do one.[5] Or do a celebration of travel as an escape from the cares of civilization.[6] Or point out that some or all of the characters are innocently naked. Or set two characters who speak different dialects talking to each other.[7] Or do a practical joke, which might or might not backfire.

Such a process does make for an abundance of repetition from book to book, but it is not the same thing as writing the same book over and over again. If only because the themes on which Mark Twain constructed his variations are so brief they are fundamentally different from, for example, the Jamesian *donnée*, a subject which implies an entire book. The subjects of Mark Twain's variations generally imply no more than a chapter—a fact which may help to account for the huge number of incomplete manuscripts which he left, and which also helps to account for the fact that he quoted himself and others as unselfconsciously as Mozart.

The analogy to improvisation on traditional themes in the music of Mozart and his predecessors is useful, but less useful perhaps than an analogy to jazz, an art which, like Mark Twain's, has strong roots both in folk and in non-folk sources. Certainly there are many points of comparison between the jazz musician and Clemens. The former refers to polite music and to the artist who plays it as "legitimate" (and implies, of course, that his own music and he himself are somehow illegitimate). Mark Twain's ambivalence toward the world of polite letters is too well known to need much documentation, but it is worth noticing that on one occasion he protested that he was not a "born-and-trained novelist" but a "jack-leg."[8] The *Dictionary of American English* defines "jackleg" as "an impostor, incompetent workman, or shyster" and adds that it is "often used of lawyers."[9] *Webster's Third* provides somewhat more adequate definitions:

1a: characterized by lack of skill or training: AMATEUR. . . .
  b: characterized by unscrupulousness, dishonesty, or lack of professional standards. . . .
2: designed for use as a temporary expedient: MAKESHIFT. . . .

Neither the *DAE* nor *Webster's*, however, gets at the full meaning of the word as Mark Twain used it, and as it is still used in the modern Black community. In the latter it refers most often to a preacher, of the sort to be found on the street-corner or in the store-front church, who has never attended a theological seminary and whose preaching, therefore, depends on an accumulated store of folk religious themes and the inspiration of the moment. There is a jazz tune called "Jackleg,"[10] and the music, as recorded by the Adderley brothers' band on Mercury MG36100, shows no trace of condescension toward its subject; it is a celebration of the earthiness and spontaneity of the Black church arts, which provide many of the roots of jazz.

Mark Twain was a jackleg in that sense, a man without an educated background in his art, but with the accumulated stock of themes and the creative energy to improvise upon them which are typical of the folk artist.[11] He shared with the jackleg preacher and the jazz musician both the virtues and the defects of the improviser, and as anyone who has listened much to jazz will know, the chief defect is the uneven quality of the performances. You can't be inspired every night, as a particularly articulate musician once said to me,[12] and the result is that many improvisations, perhaps most of them, will be perfunctory or worse. But sometimes you get lucky. And that is what justifies the whole process, because at such times you discover, to your mingled joy and wonder, that what you are descending is not the Neckar but a monstrous big river, and next you've got the full day, and everything smiling in the sun, and the songbirds just going it!

Notes

1. I follow Blair's revision of Bernard DeVoto's chronology for the writing of *Huckleberry Finn*: "When Was *Huckleberry Finn* Written?" *American Literature*, XXX (1958), 1–25. I extend his remarks on the relationships between the two books in Chapter 12 of *Mark Twain & Huck Finn* (Berkeley: University of California Press, 1962).
2. The consequences of trying to "make a fool uv ole Jim wid a lie" are explored in my essay on "The Character of Jim and the Ending of *Huckleberry Finn*," *Massachusetts Review*, V (1963), 45–66.
3. This was, of course, one of several attempts by Mark Twain to get more literary mileage out of the characters of *Huckleberry Finn*. *Tom Sawyer, Detective* also begins as a sequel to that novel, as do the recently published adventures of Tom and Huck among the Indians.
4. I wish to thank O. M. Brack, Jr., of the Center for Textual Studies at the University of Iowa for checking this and the following quotations from *Tom Sawyer Abroad* against the text of the forthcoming Iowa-California edition of that short novel and for making the necessary corrections.
5. One thinks here, of course, of the three Mississippi River sunrises analyzed so tellingly by Leo Marx in "The Pilot and the Passenger: Landscape Conventions and the Style of *Huckleberry Finn*," *American Literature*, XXVIII (1956), 129–146. But there are many more sunrises in Mark Twain; in Volume I of *A Tramp Abroad*, for example, one finds not only the Neckar sunrise previously mentioned but the series of burlesqued sunrises in the final chapters.
6. The reader may wish to consult at this point the passage from Chapter III of *Roughing It* in which the narrator sets off in a stage-coach, at sunrise,

across the Western plains, and celebrates the "ecstasy" of the journey as opposed to "the years of tiresome city life that had gone before it," and the passage from Chapter IV in which, "there being no ladies," the narrator and his companions strip to their underclothing. I thought at one time of treating these passages in the body of my essay, but rejected the idea on the ground that adding a stage-coach careening across the Western plains to my title would have made it (the title) unwieldy.

7. This was one of his favorite themes, and it has interesting implications for his understanding of cultural differences. The humor of these conversations, however, is apt to be forced and mechanical. See, for example, the conversation between Scotty Briggs and the clergyman in *Roughing It* or those between the Boss and Sandy (when he is speaking a Yankee vernacular and she is speaking like Malory) in *A Connecticut Yankee*. Improvising variations on a theme was a favorite method of composition for Mark Twain not only from one book to another but within single books, as Frank Baldanza has shown in "The Structure of *Huckleberry Finn*," *American Literature*, XXVII (1955), 347–355.

8. In his preface to *Those Extraordinary Twins*.

9. It is this pejorative meaning which Robert A. Wiggins assigns the word in *Mark Twain: Jackleg Novelist*. As John Lydenberg has pointed out, this book quickly becomes one more "account of novel after novel, and the jackleg thesis . . . gets lost."

10. Written by Samuel Hurt, who was a trombonist in Dizzy Gillespie's big band.

11. The word is used in this same sense by the journalist Tom Wolfe, who has looked into many of the unexplored corners of American culture: "From out the black hole of the garage comes the sound of a record by Bob Dylan with his raunchy harmonica and Ernest Tubbs' voice raunching and rheuming in the old jack-legged chants. . . ." Tom Wolfe, "The Chief and his Merry Pranksters Take a Trip with Electric Kool-Aid," New York: *The World Journal Tribune Magazine* (January 29, 1967), p. 7.

12. He was speaking of the late Charles Ellsworth "Pee Wee" Russell, a notoriously uneven performer.

The Ring and the Book:
"Underthought"

Maurice B. Cramer

I owe a twofold debt to T. H. Jones and his 1960 article, "The Disposition of Images in Browning's *The Ring and the Book*."[1] In the first place, he repeats the familiar proposition that in Browning's poem "the ring metaphor is essentially confused if not confusing." Since Paul A. Cundiff's 1948 article, "The Clarity of Browning's Ring Metaphor,"[2] this proposition has been outmoded, even though it is not widely enough known to be so. I need to take my turn discussing the ring metaphor as central form-giving image for the poem, and shall do so as though it were brilliantly clear and illuminating. In the second place, Jones suggests a method of reading *The Ring and the Book* that otherwise might not have occurred to me to apply; Jones asserts that it cannot be applied because Browning's poem is too superficial and static for it to be applicable. I shall attempt to apply it, however, and believe that in this case the method is exceptionally fruitful. The following summary paragraph from Jones's article, then, can serve as point of departure for my attempt:

This flaw in the structure of the poem does imply a defect in the imagery used. There is nothing of what Hopkins called 'underthought' in *The Ring and the Book*. The imagery is . . . all external and on the surface. In particular, the gold and ring figures seem extraneous and imposed, used arbitrarily instead of arising out of poetic necessity. It seems more appropriate to attribute this to a failure in technique rather than to the essential superficiality of Browning's mind. Semantic activity is noticeably absent from all of Browning's poetry; in *The Ring and the Book* the most remarkable defect . . . is the absence of metaphoric activity: his images do not, in general, become symbols, nor does his imagery as a whole attain the stature of myth. Not only does Browning lack the mythopoeic faculty: he seems to have no conception of the nature and necessity of myth in poetry. In a sense his poetry is the most private ever written, because all of his images are essentially private. (p. 68)

The first thing to do is to go to the passage in the letter to Baillie, 14 January 1883, in which Gerard Manley Hopkins makes his interesting distinction between "underthought" and "overthought":

there are . . . two strains of thought running together and like counterpointed; the overthought that which everybody, editors, see . . . and which might for instance be abridged or paraphrased . . . ; the other, the underthought, conveyed chiefly in the choice of metaphors etc used and often only half realised by the poet himself, not necessarily having any connection with the subject in hand but usually having a connection and suggested by some circumstance of the scene or of the story. . . . The underthought is commonly an echo or shadow of the overthought . . . an undercurrent of thought governing the choice of images used.[3]

I shall try to apply this distinction between the two streams of thought to *The Ring and the Book*, especially Book I, first of all paraphrasing overthought but watching for premonitory underthought signals, and then seeking to prepare for that great outburst where underthought for a moment overwhelms overthought, where quickly the two join and flow on together almost as equals to create the splendid coda and cadence with which Book I closes (ll. 1330–1416).[4]

In my experience the secret of happy and fruitful reading of the two most controversial books of *The Ring and the Book* (I and XII) is to assume that Browning's mind is at least as clear, intelligent, and profound as one's own, that he is an effective artist, that he understood poetic structure, and that the verse paragraphs that greet one unmistakably on page after page are carefully constructed to be unified new moments in an unfolding process, and are an invaluable key to total poetic experience and meaning. As important as recognizing the integrity of each paragraph and its individual contribution to the evolving whole that is Book I or Book XII, is the recognition that paragraphs can be grouped and that these groups (often indicated by Browning) mark larger contributions to the process, more important stages in the process than any one integer. Thus in discussing structure, while it would be possible although tedious to justify every paragraph, one can move more rapidly and with profit by evoking chiefly the groups.

In my experience another secret of happy and fruitful reading of Books I and XII is to be as leisurely and open-minded as possible (perhaps I should say, as Robert Browning) with regard to identifying definitively, inflexibly the central speaker, the persona, the "I," the poet in the poem. Sometimes the writer does appear to take it for granted that you know him to have been one partner in the famous marriage in which the other partner was a celebrated poet, that elopement and Italian sojourn were necessities, that the poet-wife is now dead, that he did buy an old book in June in Florence, that he actually possesses a ring or rings created recently by a well-known Roman jeweller. More often, however, the speaker seems to move away from that Robert Browning, and, if one persists in rigid identification, one tends to find the poem a gross misinterpretation of history, to be tempted to write on margins, "error," "mistake," "liar," and the like; commentators have moved in this direction. The poet's lack of regard for historical accuracy begins at once in the first full paragraph; neither of the Castellani rings that may have been prototypes of the ring that is the central form-giving image of the poem is embossed with lilies; the ring of the poem has ten shapely lilies adorning the rondure from one edge of the bezel to the opposite edge. The historical inaccuracies continue and increase when the speaker narrates some of his adventures with the Book. Personally I've long doubted that he "had mastered the contents, knew the whole truth" (I, 117)[5] by the time he got back to the cool shade of Casa Guidi, walking in the fierce noon sunshine from the Square where he bought the Book. Two hundred and sixty-two pages of bad print and worse Latin—to say nothing of handwritten Italian—don't in my opinion lend themselves to that kind of mastery. Certainly it took the Pope, acting as supreme court, and me longer than that. I do, however, understand why the speaker makes the claim: to move in an hour or so from the purchase under the blazing sun to mastery in the cool darkness adds to the condensed and unified swiftness, vividness, excitement of the narrative; these are the indispensable stylistic qualities of Book I. "Print three-fifths, written supplement the rest" (l. 119): "A very strange inaccuracy," writes A. K. Cook against this line in his useful *Commentary*.[6] Strange indeed since any right-minded historian can go at once to the original Book on display at Balliol or to Hodell's photo-reproduction in any good library[7] and count that of the 262 pages "not more than 14 are written." Again, I think I can explain why the speaker miscounts; he is eager to bring the reader into as living intimacy with his own experience and with those seventeenth-century events as possible. Manuscript seems warmer, more vitally human than print. He says of one of the letters he uses:

> . . . part fresh as penned,
> The sand, that dried the ink, not rubbed away,
> Though penned the day whereof it tells the deed. (XII, 233-35)

Immediately after this egregious miscounting, the speaker proceeds to translate the Italian of the Book's title page. "Word for word," he claims, not meaning by this, evidently, exact word order; but he does a fairly accurate job except with regard to the date. He cannot resist slipping in an extra phrase. Instead of writing, "At Rome on February Twenty Two/ Sixteen Ninety Eight," he writes, "At Rome on February Twenty Two/ Since our salvation Sixteen Ninety Eight." Now one can attribute this to Victorian piety or to the metrist's need for filling out the blank verse line; I prefer to think it is the first muted hint of one of the poem's important concerns, the relation between the events of the Franceschini story and the context of world history. Browning was interested in exploring crises in the history of Christianity, as, for example, the death of St. John in "A Death in the Desert" (published 1864). The Pope and his monologue exist in *The Ring and the Book* partly at least to evoke this much later crisis: the conjunction of Innocent's reign and Voltaire's birth is emphasized by being given a paragraph all to itself in Book XII. Many times in Book X the Pope points up the ironic contrast between Christian hope and love and the horrors of the case he must contemplate: "The best yield of the latest time, this year/ The seventeen-hundredth since God died for man" (X, 1533-34).

Even worse from the point of view of an honorable historian is what the speaker does when he attempts to give an impression of the Book's contents. The actual Book begins with 36 pages of defense argument, involving several speakers, and continues with 32 pages of prosecution argument, involving several speakers. Browning got his notion of alternating arguments and differing points of view from the small chaos of the Book; he writes accurately enough, "Thus wrangled, brangled, jangled they a month" (I, 241). But he's done a sharper, swifter job than the Book. He begins his account with the chief prosecutor, since his language could be biting and dramatic, and then quickly passes to the chief defense lawyer, so that charge and answer can be juxtaposed immediately. Then he proceeds to alternate defense and prosecution adjunct speakers, giving, in rapid-fire, staccato exchange, two or three lines to each. The speaker is evoking the confused chaos of materials out of which an art work emerged, but it's a carefully planned chaos, the artistic illusion of chaos rather than the long-winded turmoil of the original; one is even reminded a bit of the explosively effective stichomythias of Euripidean tragedy. We have not yet been invited to enter the artist's studio, but shape is already being given to his materials, even though the illusion of shapelessness is intended.

Well then, we've got to about line 241 of Book I and discovered that there is a ring or two, there is a Book, and there are Mr. and Mrs. Robert Browning. On the spectrum of historicity the speaker sometimes approaches the point where these items repose in pure actuality, and sometimes he is far, far away toward the opposite point. (Perhaps I should add here that *The Ring and the Book* contains hundreds of facts derived accurately from the Book; Hodell, Vol. II, has 43 double-columned pages of notes on this subject.) If now we ransack Book I structurally from beginning to end, expressing overthought as briefly as possible and touching on underthought, we shall then be in a better position later to summarize as richly as possible the speaker's personality, his intellectual and spiritual traits that make up one of the most memorable and attractive experiences to be carried away from Browning's masterpiece.

Book I opens with an abrupt question, and two-fifths of a blank verse line: "Do you see this Ring?" This is printed so as to be almost a verse paragraph in itself, but also so as to be not quite a verse paragraph. In any case it alerts the reader to the fact that the speaker is already assuming a role, is already creating a relationship between himself and his audience. This situation continues and ripens. "Do you see this square old yellow Book?" (l. 33); "Here it is, this I toss and take again" (l. 84); "Give it me back!" (l. 89). The speaker is clearly attempting to involve the reader intimately with objects he is discussing; all appear to be in the same room together. In the fifth paragraph from the end of Book I, he says, "I point you the wide prospect round" (l. 1333). In the fourth from the end he exclaims, "See it for yourselves!" (l. 1364); alongside this on the margin years ago I scribbled, "He sounds like a barker at a fair." Since then I've read Daniel Stempel's 1965 article, "Browning's *Sordello*: The Art of the Makers-See" (*PMLA*, 80, 554–61), and I find it impossible not to trace stray beams of his illuminations in *The Ring and the Book*. "The Makers-see" is a phrase describing the poets who help mankind by keeping heaven's windows from being slammed fast (*Sordello* III, 928–30). The least good poets say they've seen; the next best poets describe what they saw; the best poets "Impart the gift of seeing" to mankind (III, 866–68). The speaker in *Sordello* assumes the role of a lecturer in the rotunda of a diorama or phantasmagoria, who takes up his pointing-pole, and as the illumined paintings are displayed and move on, one image melting into the next, keeps up a running commentary and calls attention to outstanding items. The speaker of Books I and XII of *The Ring and the Book* is less like a lecturer in a well-known Victorian commercial enterprise than he is like a private gentleman in his own drawing room, handing objects around, perhaps showing images with the aid of his own magic lantern, keeping up a constant commentary to his guest or guests in his earnest attempt to make them too see the visions he regards as so important. The speaker switches hats now and again, as we shall see, but this is one dominant impression from Books I and XII.

Book I continues with a packed paragraph (ll. 2–32) describing an image that moves toward metaphor and symbol and that is dynamic or resonant enough to be the central form-giving image for Book I and perhaps for the entire poem of 21,000 lines, its echoes still brightly audible at the end both of Book I and Book XII. The image has perhaps two parts —of the perfected ring itself, and of the perfecting process whereby the marvel was turned out. The Roman jeweller Castellani was the maker; he had rediscovered the process whereby the ancient Etruscans made their rings and proceeded to imitate in his studio rings of theirs found at Chiusi. There is first of all virgin gold, too soft to manage. There is a harder metal, gold's alloy (shall we say copper?) to mingle with the gold so that it can be managed, hammered and filed into desired shape and decoration. The speaker doesn't specifically mention the lost wax process (*cera perduta*), in which a model of the ring is made in wax and then enclosed in a clay mould and mounted on clay; the wax is then burnt out, leaving a vacant mould into which the molten alloyed metal can be poured and so take the shape previously designed in wax.[8] But when the speaker says in a subordinate metaphor, "the artificer melts up wax / With honey, so to speak" (ll. 18–19), perhaps one should think of the lost wax process; perhaps a seeker after underthought can be forgiven for mentioning the honey and wax, the sweetness and light of Swift's *The Battle of the Books*, which Arnold exploits in *Culture and Anarchy*, Chapter I ("Sweetness and Light") of which was first published in *Cornhill Magazine* July 1867. In any case, it is time for the clay mould to be broken away, and the ring to be worked on; it is "malleolable" to use a word that Browning coined in line 702 as being more exact than the "malleable" that readers expect; the speaker wishes to emphasize the fact that the ring is now neither too soft nor too hard, but just right for the little hammer (*malleolus*) of the jeweller and his file to "widen out the round" in order to make the bezel that eventually will receive the posy (I, 1390) and to emboss the ten lilies that will glorify the remaining smoothed rondure. Thus having accumulated his gold and alloyed it, having created his design and shaped the ring in accordance, having hammered, filed, decorated, the jeweller has a penultimate operation: repristination or blanching by quick exposure to an acid that will remove traces of the alloy from the ring's surface so that it can give the illusion of consisting only of pure soft gold which, as we know, is only one of the original and essential ingredients.

The opening ring paragraph has to do most obviously with art and art making, but it has also a well authenticated historical background, which, since it may throw light on various levels of poetic interpretation, may as well be summarized here. The Brownings had actual connections with Castellani; in 1859 they visited his showroom in Rome and were received "most flatteringly as poets and lovers of Italy." [9] Isa Blagden, whom before Mrs. Browning's death Browning called "our best & dearest friend" (*Dearest Isa*, p. 71) and to whom after Mrs. Browning's death he said, "no human being can give me one hand—with the feeling on my part that the other holds that of my own Ba—as you can & do" (*Dearest Isa*, p. 85), presented each of them a Castellani "Etrurian" ring. Mrs. Browning's ring has no embossed lilies, but on its bezel is engraved AEI (the Greek translated by Liddell and Scott as "always," by Mrs. Browning as "for ever," and by the speaker of Book I perhaps as "evermore" in line 28). In thanking the giver Mrs. Browning wrote, "I can't wait till tonight to thank you my dearest Isa for the exquisite little ring—shall I not keep it for ever, as a memorial of what must last as long—my true love for you, dear?" (*Dearest Isa*, pp. 10–11). After Mrs. Browning's death Browning wore this tiny ring on his watch chain along with a 20-lire coin dated 1848, a piece of the first money struck in Venice to record the lifting of Austrian dominion and associated by Browning with his wife because of her passionate interest in the cause of Italian unity and freedom.[10] It was said of Browning that "during his last illness the poet kissed the ring with all affection before composing himself for his night's rest" (Hodell, II, 337–38). This ring and coin are now on display at the British Museum. Browning alludes to *his* Castellani ring in a letter to Isa Blagden discussing the design for his wife's grave monument: "You gave me a ring (which I shall wear to my dying-day) and gave orders for it *at Rome*" (*Dearest Isa*, p. 198). The posy on the bezel of Browning's ring, *Vis Mea* (cf. Psalm 28:7, "The Lord is my strength"), is that on the ring of Geoffrey Wentworth, the hero of Isa Blagden's novel, *Agnes Tremorne* (*Dearest Isa*, p. 200). There are no lilies on this ring either, but on each side of the bezel "where the ring begins to swell there are two thin vertical bas-relief bands. One of these vertical bands is slightly thicker and might suggest a cord, but the vertical bands are non-representational." [11] The lily is a fairly common motif in ancient Mediterranean art; it is possible that this slight embossing of his ring was the initiative that led to the ten lilies of the ring in *The Ring and the Book*. I cannot say whether Browning had or had not seen an Etrurian ring so decorated. His Castellani ring is on display at Balliol College along with the Old Yellow Book and a medallion of Innocent XII, the Pope of the poem.

There is another British Museum ring that might be touched on in this gathering of historical associations: "Gold finger ring, oval bezel engraved 'Ba.' The interior is inscribed, 'God bless you June 29, 1861.' Hair is set behind glass at the back of the bezel. The ring was worn by Robert Browning." "Ba," as every one knows, is the pet-name by which Mrs. Browning was addressed by her intimates. The date is that of her death. "God bless you," is what she kept repeating to her husband the night of her dying. A few fragments from a letter written by Browning to his sister on June 30 will add to this web of association: "I said you know me? 'My Robert—my heavens, my beloved'—kissing me. . . . 'Our lives are held by God.' . . . She put her arms round me 'God bless you' repeatedly. . . . I only put in a thing or two out of the many in my heart of hearts. . . . A. [Annunziata, their maid] cried 'Quest' anima benedetta é passata!' It was so. She is with God, who takes from me the life of my life. . . . I shall now go in and sit with herself—my Ba, forever." [12]

This little history of rings may suggest several things. There is no single, unmistakable, actual prototype for the poem's ring. More than one ring may have contributed. Connotations, vibrations surrounding posies like AEI, *Vis Mea*, "God bless you," "Ba," and phrases from letters like "for ever," "Robert—my heavens," "heart of hearts," "anima benedetta," "the life of my life," "My Ba, forever" suggest, first of all, what I suppose few have doubted, that knowledge gained from that unusually successful marriage of the two poets is an important thematic element in *The Ring and the Book* (I am not at all saying that Ba is Pompilia, any more than I said that her ring is The Ring), that the eternity of art, the eternity of love springing from physical as well as from spiritual union,[13] the eternity of God are among the resonances of which one must be aware in the ring figure. Indeed, since lurking under the lilied loveliness of the ring's surface there is a story of love/sex gone wrong and leading to anguish and murder, a story that gains in dramatic blackness by its contrast with love/sex gone right and vibrating in these ring resonances, a story that is treated with a bleak, sometimes sordid realism and yet eventuates in exalted idealism so that more than one commentator has been reminded of what goes on in both parts of Goethe's *Faust*, I cannot help wondering whether with the word "symbol" (". . . 'Tis a figure, a symbol, say," l. 31) at the end of this ring paragraph, the poem's first, we do not approach the first two lines of Chorus Mysticus at the very end of *Faust* II: "Alles Vergängliche/ Ist nur ein Gleichniss," or even the more famous last two lines of the Chorus, "Das Ewig-Weibliche/ Zieht uns hinan." [14]

By now we have slipped over from history to interpretation; perhaps I should add a few more "underthought" hints gathered from contemplating the vibrations set up by the poem's opening paragraph. I have been teaching *The Ring and the Book* for many years in graduate seminars. I often begin discussion by reading this ring paragraph aloud and asking for associations that may occur to seminar members. Somebody is almost always ready with the notion of the ring, the circle, the sphere as symbols of eternity, perfection, divinity. I have had students start quoting Vaughan's "The World":

> I saw eternity the other night
> Like a great ring of pure and endless light,
>   All calm as it was bright.

The last time this occurred one student protested that it was inadmissible to linger there and not move on at once to the sublunary world (like the sordid Franceschini world Browning commences to evoke about line 120) that Vaughan at once contrasts with his opening vision: "time in hours, days, years," "The doting lover," "The darksome statesman," "blood and tears," "poor despisèd truth,"—all the circumstances of the world of becoming whereby most men avoid "A way where you might tread the sun" (cf. Browning's epithet for Shelley, "Sun-treader," *Pauline*, l. 151, l. 1020), until

> One whispered thus:
> This ring the bridegroom did for none provide
>   But for his bride.

Thus we find ourselves in the presence of an ancient tradition—the erotic union of man and woman used as a metaphor for the union between God and mankind. Browning uses the metaphor in the last long paragraph of "A Death in the Desert": Christ (says the unnamed scholiast) "conceived of life as love,/ Conceived of love as what must enter in,/ Fill up, make one with His each soul He loved"; conceived that in the end there would be "Groom for each bride! Can a mere man do this?" This is the ultimate or divine psyche-epipsyche relationship generally preceded by or based on a prior human psyche-epipsyche relationship between man and woman.[15] The notion owes much to Aristophanes' speech in Plato's *Symposium* in which human beings are described as halves of divided spheres seeking their better halves through the world in order to heal the original severance. Dante gave momentum to the tradition in expressing his love for Beatrice in *La Vita Nuova* and the *Commedia*.[16] Donne revelled in it: "Our two soules therefore, which are one" ("A Valediction: Forbidding Mourning," l. 21);

> When love, with one another so
>   Interinanimates two soules,
> That abler soule, which thence doth flow,
>   Defects of lonelinesse controules.
> Wee then, who are this new soule, know,
>   Of what we are compos'd, and made.   ("The Extasie," ll. 41–46)
> · · · · · · · · · · · · · ·

> Our bodies why doe wee forbeare?
> They are ours, though they are not wee, Wee are
> The intelligences, they the spheare.　　(ll. 50–52)
> . . . .
> Loves mysteries in soules doe grow,
> But yet the body is his booke.　　(ll. 71–72)

The tradition's energy has carried it into the twentieth century. Yeats, writing in "The Serpent's Mouth," says, "If it be true that God is a circle whose centre is everywhere, the saint goes to the centre, the poet and artist to the ring where everything comes round again. The poet must not seek for what is still and fixed . . . but be content to find his pleasure in all that is for ever passing away that it may come again . . ." (*Essays and Introductions*, p. 287). Still later in "Among School Children" he writes:

> . . . our two natures blent
> Into a sphere from youthful sympathy,
> Or else, to alter Plato's parable,
> Into the yolk and white of the one shell.

Yeats said of himself as a young man in London, "I was in all things a pre-Raphaelite," and the most condensed expression of the tradition I know is to be found in a sonnet by that early outstanding Browningite, D. G. Rossetti, "Heart's Hope" (V from "The House of Life"): "Thy soul I know not from thy body, nor/ Thee from myself, neither our love from God." To go farther back in the nineteenth century, it is possible that in Shelley's prose fragment "On Love" and in "Epipsychidion," his poem celebrating the psyche-epipsyche relationship, there is an epistemological emphasis carrying over into the accumulation. Souls copulate via the body, and so get to know each other ("Adam knew Eve his wife; and she conceived," Genesis 4:1); minds copulate with the universe, including Godhead, and so get to know all they are capable of knowing. Body and soul are equally necessary in true human love and the eternalizing relation with God that results; content and form are equally necessary in true art and its eternalizing process ("Forever wilt thou love, and she be fair!" says Keats of the lovers on the Grecian Urn). Aspects of this conglomerate keep turning up in the nineteenth century. It is an important theme in Wordsworth's *The Prelude*, Tennyson's *The Princess* and *In Memoriam* ("I, the divided half of such/ A friendship as had mastered Time," ll. 1655–56), in Swinburne's "The Triumph of Time" (ll. 30–48). *The Ring and the Book* is perhaps Browning's fullest expression of it, but it appears in many earlier poems, sometimes as an aspiration that fails ("Two in the Campagna"), sometimes as an infinite moment in which two souls become one soul and roll on together toward a goal of transcendent knowledge and transcendent life ("By the Fireside"). Browning could have caught the germ from most of the writers named above: Plato, Dante, Donne, Shelley are indispensable elements making up the personality either of the historic Browning or of the poet created in *The Ring and the Book.*

The "Maker-see" who has made us see the ring and feel, perhaps, these vibrations, proceeds to make us see the Book: "Do you see this square old yellow Book . . . ?/ Examine it yourselves!" (ll. 33 and 38). In the process the gentleman-lecturer dons and lays aside a metaphorical mask or two. The paragraphs carefully grouped in lines 33–678 narrate the story of a bargain-hunter poking around in the market square of San Lorenzo in Florence among the stalls of second-hand goods; he finds a cheap book that attracts him, buys it, and on his way home reads at it. We have already seen that in summarizing the contents he gives a push here and there so that in recreating the chaos of the Book, it is actually no formless chaos that comes across. The speaker here might be called a gold-adventurer; he prospects, he finds a likely location, he mines and accumulates what seems to be gold; as he digs and works, an ingot of possible gold takes shape so that it can be transported to an assay-office and tested for its contents. Mining goes on until perhaps line 363. Then begins the assay that continues to about line 460. On his own he finds the mass too soft to be of immediate use; he takes the Franceschini tale to Rome (as Shelley had done with his Cenci material) and the Romans are skeptical of its value. But this gold prospector and miner is stubborn, and in the end reports that he "Assayed and knew my piece-meal gain was gold." John Killham is a bit dubious of the speaker's language here: "assaying it (whatever that means)."[17] When one consults an unabridged dictionary on the word, one finds it to be a technical and essential part of gold processing; Browning uses the word exactly in 1842 in discussing a review "of me and mine . . . a sub-editor has been allowed to travel over and spoil . . . the Ms. was forwarded to me, by a friend of the unnamed penman, to *assay* my good nature—which is virgin gold when these matters are concerned."[18] In other words, in the inventorying and assaying process, the gold worker has convinced himself that he has found two things: pure, virgin gold (poet's gold), but a metal that has yet much to be done to it before it can be coaxed from ingot shape to art shape. And so from line 461 to line 678 the gold worker is a busy metallurgist preparing his find for "smithcraft" by hardening it with an alloying metal. When the speaker says, "I looked," "I felt," "I fared," "I found," "I saw," "I knew," throughout these lines, while at the same time retelling the Franceschini story with dramatic and poetically beautiful vividness, we know that the whole soul of the man is being brought into activity (will, sense, understanding, passion, judgment, enthusiasm), while (as Coleridge puts it), "He diffuses a tone and spirit of unity, that blends, and (as it were) *fuses*, each into each, by that synthetic and magical power, to which we have exclusively appropriated the name imagination" (*Biographia Literaria*, XIV). Thus the soft pure gold becomes alloyed, hardened, malleolable. Poet's gold is on its way to poem.

Suddenly, as the end of the alloying process approaches, the metal-

lurgist, attempting to explain the situation and evaluate his accomplishment, turns into an archaeologist who has stumbled on the ruins of an
ancient building, a pillar almost totally disintegrated by the touch of
time:

> Ever and ever more diminutive,
> Base gone, shaft lost, only entablature,
> Dwindled into no bigger than a book,
> Lay of the column; and that little, left
> By the roadside 'mid ordure, shards and weeds,
> Until I haply, wandering that way,
> Kicked it up, turned it over, and recognized,
> For all the crumblement, this abacus,
> This square old yellow book,—could calculate
> By this the lost proportions of the style.   (ll. 670–79)

I would finesse this passage were it not for the possibility that it contributes an underthought expansion to the overthought central form-
giving image of Book I. The scholar has discovered the last relic of the
entablature of a classical building, and, using a technical term, calls it the
"abacus," which as I understand the architectural situation is the element
that transmits the upward energy of the column to the downward thrust
of architrave, frieze, cornice, pediment—the upper wall and roof of whatever structure it may be. Ex pede Herculem: using knowledge and imagination the speaker is able to evoke something like the original building—the
life of seventeenth-century Italy, of the Franceschini, Pompilia, Caponsacchi, and Innocent XII. If the ring figure is the overthought central
form-giving image, perhaps in this edifice of the past, palace of art,
temple of love, house of fame or of life, or whatever it may be, the
speaker is feeling his way toward an underthought central form-giving
image. Perhaps it resembles the Pantheon at Rome with its rotunda and
dome, its Corinthian portico—each column with abacus in place. Perhaps
it resembles Palladio's Villa Rotonda near Vicenza with its dome and
Ionic porticoes—each column with its abacus in place. After all, there is
the dominating ring; there is a possible parallel with *Sordello* and its
speaker, the Maker-see lecturer in the rotunda of a diorama. As with the
ring, so with the abacus here, there is history in the background. The
abacus shape in the classical orders I have glanced at resembles much
the shape of the Old Yellow Book Browning holds in the portrait of him
painted by his son, excellently reproduced as frontispiece in Hodell's *The
Old Yellow Book*, Volume I. Hodell's Volume I, a complete photo-
reproduction of Browning's chief source, was deliberately sized and
shaped to resemble the original volume as depicted in the portrait and as
displayed at Balliol College.

At this point in Book I occurs a group of paragraphs (ll. 679–779) that
at first sight may seem more difficult to relate to the central gold-
processing. These paragraphs express an aesthetic with differing facets
not necessarily irreconcilable. The first might be called the plastic: "This

was it from, my fancy with those facts," ". . . such alloy,/ Such substance of me interfused the gold/ Which, wrought into a shapely ring . . ./ Lay ready . . ." (ll. 679–85). Such emphasis on form and matter may recall Aristotle: "from art proceed the things of which the form is in the soul of the artist . . . the matter is present in the process and it is this that becomes something . . . there is a brazen sphere, this we make. For we make it out of brass and the sphere; we bring the form into this particular matter, and the result is a brazen sphere" (*Metaphysics*, Book VII, chapters 7–9). This plastic or Aristotelian emphasis is not out of harmony with Croce's emphasis on a mutual coherence of images ani- mated by a dominant feeling. It is the artist's intuition or imagination that has expressed the ring-making process with its connotations and set it up as the central form-giving energy of the poem (see the opening paragraphs of Croce, "Aesthetics," *Encyclopaedia Britannica* 1944). These Book I paragraphs (ll. 679–779) also show concern with truth—the truth of history, the truth of art—which since it grows more prominent as the poem progresses may as well be ticketed here as Platonic. Plato in *Phaedrus* shows a similar interest in the relation between truth, love, and literature; the dialogue moves, as does *The Ring and the Book*, from facts that are lies or half true and half deceptive, to facts that are true, to truths, to that Truth that makes a man wise unto salvation. The aes- thetic notion that occupies the majority of these 100 lines cannot be labeled quite so glibly, perhaps. I shall initially call it the resuscitative theory. It commences with the premise that God is the original and sole true creator, and that man with an innate instinct toward growth, "Re- peats God's process in man's due degree":

> Creates, no, but resuscitates, perhaps.
> . . . .
> May so project his surplusage of soul
> In search of body, so add self to self
> By owning what lay ownerless before,—
> So find, so fill full, so appropriate forms—
> That, although nothing which had never life
> Shall get life from him, be, not having been,
> Yet, something dead may get to live again,
>
> . . . .
> —Mimic creation, galvanism for life.
> . . . .
> Why did the mage say . . .
>   'I raise a ghost'?
> 'Because,' he taught adepts, 'man makes not man.
> 'Yet by a special gift, an art of arts,
> 'I can detach from me, commission forth
> 'Half of my soul; which in its pilgrimage
> 'O'er old unwandered waste ways of the world,
> 'May chance upon some fragment of a whole,
>
> . . . .

```
                              . . . prompt therein
          'I enter, spark-like, put old powers to play.
          'Push lines out to the limit, lead forth last
          '(By a moonrise through a ruin of a crypt)
          'What shall be mistily seen, murmuringly heard,
          'Mistakenly felt. . . .'                              (ll. 717–59)
```

These are not the clearest lines in Book I, but their Faustian overtones
may help. The mage quoted above can possibly be regarded as another
mask of Book I's central speaker; he seems not totally unaware of the
archaeologist who, chancing upon an abacus, was able to calculate the
lost proportions of the style and so restore the edifice of past life. Here
the mage chances on a "rag of flesh" and "starts the dead alive." But this
is what Goethe did with Faust, Gretchen, et al.; when he took up resuscitative work on *Faust* again after the lapse of years, he wrote at the opening
of "Zueignung": "Ihr naht euch wieder, schwankende Gestalten" ("Again
you come, you wavering forms"). Book I's speaker, who quotes the mage
to validate what he himself has been doing with Guido, Pompilia, et al.,
speaks of appropriating "forms" already created but needing resuscita-
tion. This too is the process that Faust must employ when, instructed by
Mephistopheles, he dares to visit the mysterious, dangerous realm of the
Mothers who control such unappropriated forms so that he can lead
forth at last at the Emperor's palace Paris and Helena. In doing this Faust
calls himself "Magier" or mage, and he had a pilgrimage to make, "O'er
old unwandered waste ways of the world." [19] "Form" or "forms" used in
this sense occurs several times in the Helena scenes of *Faust* II both in
Act I and Act III. Similarly in the Helena scenes words like ghost or
phantom, mist or cloud or murmur recur often enough to contribute to
the atmosphere of Goethe's poem and to be recalled here when the mage
says, " 'I raise a ghost,' " or I " 'lead forth last/ (By a moonrise through
a ruin of a crypt)/ What shall be mistily seen, murmuringly heard,/
Mistakenly felt.' " One can hardly avoid thinking of the mystifications,
the glooming and gleaming chiaroscuro of the Helena scenes.

    The Faust legend and Goethe's *Faust* were important ingredients in the
development of Browning as poet, and of the speaker in Book I. Like
Goethe Browning meditated on these matters from an early age. He said
of his father that he "seemed to have known Paracelsus, Faustus . . .
personally." [20] As Goethe's Faust figure was influenced by the career of
Paracelsus, so Browning's *Paracelsus* (1835) has Faustian aspects. Browning was in his twenties when sometime before 1839 (Griffin and Minchin,
p. 136) he got to know Carlyle, that volcano of Goethe enthusiasm, who
wrote and talked about his hero endlessly. In 1842 Browning writes: "I
don't well know what Carlyle is doing. I spent an evening with him last
week: he talked nobly—seemed to love Goethe more than ever. Do you
prosecute German-study? I read pretty well now." In 1843 he writes that
he reads German "tolerably," and at once adds, "I have not seen Carlyle
lately . . . but I will see him" (*Browning and Domett*, pp. 49 and 52).

German, Goethe, and Carlyle seem inextricably associated in his mind. Goethe's *Helena: A Classico-Romantic Phantasmagoria*, which later became part of Act III of *Faust* II, was published in 1827. In 1828 in *Foreign Review* Carlyle wrote about it, filling about 50 pages with commentary and translation and using phrases and ideas that remind one of *The Ring and the Book*. I mention this since, when one reads *Faust* II, one feels a kind of dioramic or phantasmagoric ebb and flow in the imagery, and we have already found a possible connection between the speaker of Book I and a lecturer at a diorama or phantasmagoria. Browning had some acquaintance with at least three other *Faust* translators, Sir Theodore Martin, Dr. John Anster, Bayard Taylor (whose translation is listed in the Sotheby Catalogue of the 1913 Browning auction).[21] He also knew in 1843 Abraham Hayward's prose translation.[22]

To return to the passage that expresses what I initially called a resuscitative aesthetic: when the mage has said his say about his unusual insight and outsight that enable him to bring the dead back to life, he concludes complacently, "then write my name with Faust's!" Thus the connection is unexceptionable. But then the central speaker makes his comment: "Oh, Faust, why Faust? Was not Elisha once?" He then proceeds to describe in language very close to the Biblical account how Elisha resuscitated the Shunammite's dead child (II Kings 4:34). One might interpret this as repudiation of the Faustian aesthetic in favor of a more orthodox and divine inspiration. Mephistopheles is, of course, a devil; it is, therefore, fiendish or infernal inspiration that sent Faust to the Mothers "O'er old unwandered waste ways of the world" so that he might "appropriate forms" and lead forth Paris and Helena. But in Goethe's *Faust* Mephistopheles is also a kind of confidential agent or colleague of the Lord, and so his inspiration has a divine dimension. Moreover the Faustian undercurrent is too strongly established in these lines to be discarded; indeed the triple iteration in lines 759–60, "'. . . Faust's!'/ Oh, Faust, why Faust?" strikes me as an unmistakable signal that we must not forget *Faust* as we go on in our reading; the myth has now been given ineradicable status in the underthought of Book I.

This is not to say that the 12 lines (760–72) devoted to Elisha ("God is salvation") and his resuscitative miracle are unfunctional. It is true that the Faust who discusses with Mephistopheles the lonely untrodden way ("Kein Weg! In's Unbetretene") he must pursue to the Mothers, is Faust *schaudernd*, as the text directs, and that in feeling this awe he throws out the famous line, "Das Schaudern ist der Menschheit bestes Theil" (*Faust*, l. 6272). Nevertheless the speaker of Book I, who attributed his chancing on the Old Yellow Book to the push of "a Hand,/ Always above my shoulder" (I, 40–41), might find the role of a Hebrew prophet more congenial than that of "Magier" or mage, might regard it as a smoother or more tactful transition to the final touch of aesthetic theory, the supernal inspiration expressed in the concluding paragraph of the four:

                        Enough of me!
        The Book! I turn its medicinable[23] leaves
        In London now till, as in Florence erst,
        A spirit laughs and leaps through every limb,
        And lights my eye, and lifts me by the hair,
        Letting me have my will again with these
        —How title I the dead alive once more?   (ll. 773–79)

The speaker of these lines may remind one of the ecstatically resuscitative
poet of Coleridge's "Kubla Khan":

        Could I revive within me
        Her symphony and song
        To such a deep delight 'twould win me,
        That with music loud and long,
        I would build that dome in air . . .
        And all should cry, Beware! Beware!
        His flashing eyes, his floating hair!

As we have seen, the speaker of Book I has long been intent on building,
as it were, a "dome in air," at least some sort of annular structure, using
an abacus to restore "the lost proportions of the style" (l. 678). In any
case, years ago Elisabeth Schneider connected the possessed poet of
"Kubla Khan" with Plato's *Ion*.[24] Thus Socrates says to Ion: "poets utter
all those fine poems not from art, but as inspired and possessed. . . .
God takes away the mind of these men and uses them as his ministers,
just as he does soothsayers and godly seers, in order that we who hear
them may know that it is not they who utter these words of great price,
when they are out of their wits, but that it is God himself who speaks
and addresses us through them." Ion agrees: "When I relate a tale of
woe, my eyes are filled with tears; and when it is of fear or awe, my hair
stands on end with terror, and my heart leaps." Socrates adds: "and your
soul dances, and you have plenty to say . . . not by art . . . but by divine
dispensation."[25] Thus we find Plato doubly present in this aesthetic,
with regard to the relation between truth, love, and art, with regard to
the divine inspiration of artists.[26]

    We are now ready to return to the problem with which this discussion
of the four paragraphs on aesthetic theory opened. Why do we have
here this impressive constellation of aesthetic points of view? How are
we to connect it with the central form-giving image of Book I? By now
the answer is obvious, since by now the gold artisan has become the
artist in gold. We have left behind us the confusion and heat of flea-
market gold-mining, of the assaying/alloying laboratory, have been given
entry into the cultured decorum of the artist's studio and insight into
the standards whereby the art work will be wrought.

    No sooner have we grown aware of this coherence than there bursts
upon our consciousness a dramatically singular paragraph (ll. 780–823)
—in itself one of the radiantly clear paragraphs of Book I (should I say,
in itself giving the artistic illusion of brilliant translucence?), in itself

helpful, perhaps calming and reassuring, to the reader because of its definite structure of a beginning, middle, and end. Nevertheless it is momentarily puzzling as to its connection with ring-making. The chief characters are named, and located geographically and societally: Count Guido of Arezzo, Pompilia of Rome, Caponsacchi of Arezzo and of nobler birth than Guido, the Comparini, Innocent XII. The beginning consists of the four-year marriage between Guido and Pompilia; the middle of the reversal when she and her parents discover their mistake and leave Arezzo for Rome and peace, she later than Pietro and Violante and under the protection of Caponsacchi. A second reversal occurs when Pompilia and her parents discover that what they had fled to regain has come to an end since Guido and his accomplices burst in to kill them in their refuge. A third reversal/discovery occurs when Guido is captured, put on trial, and learns that law court and Pope will not allow him to get away with his violence. Pompilia's innocence is reaffirmed; Guido is executed. The speaker has told us these details before, but never with such active action, with such pattern, economy, unity, coherence. Each previous time he had a different purpose: for the sake of inventorying the seemingly chaotic contents of the Old Yellow Book, for the sake of assaying the weaknesses and flaws of the find, for the sake of showing how raw gold can be made more "malleolable" by being alloyed with the activated faculties of the poet's whole soul. There had been form present in the earlier tellings since he had to shape the relatively unplanned chaos of the find in order even to suggest the illusion of chaos in a poem, in order later to suggest the emergence of an ingot. The alloying process could not be allowed to fly into bits and pieces; it trembles with pity and fear and exaltation, but it is shaped on a simple geographical round, the journeys from Rome to Arezzo and back to Rome. Now the speaker has a different purpose in mind. He gives us a plot summary with complicating and resolving actions, discoveries and reversals. One recalls the condensed plot summaries that illuminate Aristotle's *Poetics*, of Euripides' *Iphigenia*, of Homer's *Odyssey* (Ch. XVII), each with complicating and resolving actions, discoveries and reversals pointed up. We recall the importance attached by Aristotle to the presence in plot of discoveries and reversals, that to him plot is the object of imitation, "the first essential and the soul of tragedy" (Ch. VI). Plot then is the form of tragedy. Browning's speaker is intent on displaying essential form as compellingly but briefly as possible, perhaps the initial pattern of the ring whose outline was shaped in his imagination, perhaps the wax model to be used in the lost wax process to mould the molten gold, perhaps the fundamental rondure that in the next and longest groupings of paragraphs will underlie the hammering, filing, fingering, shaping, embossing process that will in the end produce the unique and beautiful ring. In any case, this paragraph seems to me a moment of dynamic poise, a steadying, clarifying introduction to the ten closely interrelated paragraphs that follow (I, 838–1329).

These ten paragraphs make up the longest coherent section of Book I (almost 500 lines, practically a third of the Book), but they are so plainly expressive of overthought, so obviously connected with the central ring-making that their impact can be summed up more succinctly than most other sections of Book I. They make up not the totality but the major portion of the ring's rondure; they are also the ten lily-flowers that decorate the ring between one edge of the bezel and the other edge. Each paragraph is a summary of one of the ten books of dramatic monologues to follow. Three paragraphs summarize "Rome and rumour; smoke," three ordinary citizens reporting what they've heard. Three summarize "tongues of flame . . . each with appropriate tinge," what the chief actors have to say: Guido, Caponsacchi, Pompilia. Three summarize ". . . law, the recognized machine/ . . . pipe and wheel," the words of those involved in the legal process of the murder trial: the defense lawyer, the prose-cuting lawyer, the supreme judge (except for you and me)—Innocent XII. The final paragraph summarizes Book XI, Guido's long outburst just before execution, "the true words shone last," as Browning put line 1281 in a revised version. Each summary contains a roughly similar number of lines; in each are repeated certain circumstances like age of the speaker, time of monologue in relation to the murder, location and audience of speaker. Many introductory phrases are identical or parallel, and each summary ends with a formula: "How Half-Rome found for Guido much excuse" (l. 882), "How Guido, after being tortured, spoke" (l. 1015), "How the Fisc vindicates Pompilia's fame" (l. 1219), and so on. Thus is imitated the structural roundness of the ring and the formal flowers that decorate its surface. These summaries are not perfunctory; they contain vivid and skillful writing; there is human interest, music, poetry, feeling in them and they make useful background commentary for the later reading of their corresponding Books. In the General Prologue to Chau-cer's *Canterbury Tales* there are such traits too along with clear para-graphing as the lines move from one pilgrim to another, a tendency to formulaic repetitive phrases for introductions and conclusions that helps keep the reader oriented as to what is happening. Several commentators on Browning's Book I have been reminded of Chaucer's Prologue. Per-haps all this should embolden me to add that there are parallels also between "Prelude in the Theatre" and "Prologue in Heaven" of Goethe's *Faust* I and Book I of *The Ring and the Book*.

In these ten paragraphs summarizing ten Books there is only one hint from underthought that I'll touch on here. In attempting to express the varying points of view in Rome with regard to the all-engrossing scandal, the speaker uses the following metaphor:

> . . . First, the world's outcry
> Around the rush and ripple of any fact
> Fallen stonewise, plumb on the smooth face of things;
> The world's guess, as it crowds the bank o' the pool,
> At what were figure and substance, by their splash:
> Then, by vibrations in the general mind,
> At depth of deed already out of reach. (ll. 839–45)

There are ring resonances in these lines. Perhaps the pool is round, en-
circled by the crowd; certainly the ripples going out in rings across the
sensitive water from the effect of the stone (or event) are round. Once
more, then, there is a suggestion of spatial extension and structure at
the poem's heart larger than the tiny finger-ring with which Book I opens.
One recalls the anecdote about Browning repeated by DeVane with regard
to the gestation and bringing to birth of *The Ring and the Book*: "I
went for a walk, gathered twelve pebbles from the road, and put them at
equal distances on the parapet that bordered it. These represented the
twelve chapters into which the poem is divided" (*A Browning Handbook*,
New York, 1955, p. 322). Now if these equal distances are linear, 12
pebbles in a row have little significance for us. But if Browning is indi-
cating a circle of pebbles, "a closed plane curve every point of which
is equidistant from a fixed point within the curve" (*Webster's* on "circle"),
we have again, as in the circling ripples caused by the stone in the still
pool, a hint of a structure within the poem more spacious than a finger-
ring. Like the figure used by Wordsworth's speaker in *The Prelude*, "I was
as sensitive as waters are" (III, 139), the metaphor here too seems to have
an epistemological dimension: within the enclosure of crowd and pool
banks (or of pebbles), within or beneath the circling ripples, some experience or meaning or truth *is*, toward which the bystanders reach, seeking
to apprehend what it is, and from which vibrations emanate, seeking
apprehension in the consciousness of those outside the enclosure. Different
kinds of reaches, different responses to vibrations result in differing ap-
prehensions and differing points of view. Perhaps one grows even more
convinced of the substantiality of the latent image structure, of the vi-
brantly expanding metaphorical activity of these lines if one recalls the
eagle's "scientific" midflight explanation in Chaucer's *The House of Fame*
of how all earth sounds reach the House of Fame whose "every wal/ . . .
and flor, and roof, and al/ Was plated half a foote thikke/ Of gold . . .
(*The Complete Works of Geoffrey Chaucer*, ed., F. N. Robinson [Boston,
1933], ll. 1343–46, p. 345). The eagle too uses an epistemological metaphor of stone and rippling water to represent what happens with sound
waves:

> . . . for yf that thow
> Throwe on water now a stoon,
> Wel wost thou, hyt wol make anoon
> A litel roundell as a sercle,
> Paraunter brod as a covercle;
> And ryght anoon thow shalt see wel,
> That whel wol cause another whel,
> And that the thridde, and so forth, brother,
> Every sercle causynge other
> Wydder than hymselve was;
> And thus fro roundel to compas,
> Ech aboute other goynge
> Causeth of othres sterynge
> And multiplyinge ever moo,

Till that it be so fer ygoo,
That hyt at bothe brynkes bee.

(Robinson, ll. 788–803, pp. 339–40)

There is an eagle in the fifth paragraph from the end of Book I of *The Ring and the Book* (ll. 1342–45), and six lines later at the opening of the fourth paragraph from the end the speaker begins to redecorate "the House of Fame" (l. 1351), using it for his own metaphorical purposes but establishing it firmly in the poem's underthought while at the same time adding another touch to that latent edifice we have for some time watched abuilding in Book I, an edifice with greater potentiality for extension in space than the overthought central form-giving image of the ring, despite the ring's domineering power throughout the poem. I don't doubt that Browning had the Chaucer lines quoted above, the image and the experience hidden deep under water and ripples, in mind, whether consciously or not, and that they have value for interpreting *The Ring and the Book*. We cannot here discuss the negative theme of Browning's poem, but I believe it to be connected in verbal expression and imagery with Chaucer's poem. More appropriate for this moment in the present essay is the following observation. Chaucer's poem probably seems at first reading dominantly light or comic, but after meditation one cannot doubt its deeply serious central meaning. Browning's poem is predominantly serious in atmosphere, style, and meaning, but after meditation one cannot doubt a strong, attractive undercurrent of wry, mocking, or comic treatment of various topics, including some that Browning held most sacred. Browning's speaker is a major source in Books I and XII for this effective undercurrent of contrast, and it is partly because his personality owes something to the style of Chaucer's *The House of Fame*. The combination in him of profound learning, rich culture, high seriousness with a vein of humor and comedy is one of the memorable experiences we take away from Books I and XII. It was a stroke of something more than talent, perhaps, that led Browning to cradle in the consciousness of such a person the tragic Franceschini story with its potentiality for being too sordid or depressing. This personality is strongly established in Book I, and reappears in Book XII. With regard to the intervening Books he creates the illusion of his disappearance, expressing it in his ring-making metaphor by the term "repristination." This is the ring-maker's penultimate act of blanching that occurs when the ring, complete except for its posy, is briefly exposed to an acid that removes traces of alloy from the surface. Thus we are left with the illusion of a pure gold ring, although we know that just under the pure film the two original, essential ingredients, gold and gold's alloy, are still there as before, inextricably fused. So with the poet in the poem in Books II–XI; he may seem to be "refined out of existence, indifferent, paring his fingernails"; nevertheless he is still around, and his presence can be felt, although it is not he who speaks.[27]

The value of these points can be established only by a full discussion of what may be the richest underthought passage of the 21,000 lines, two related paragraphs, the fifth and the fourth from the end of Book I (ll. 1330–78). Although these lines have baffled able commentators, they seem to me effective and beautiful, and along with the three following overthought paragraphs to form a strong conclusion to a great Book. But if the reader has not been taught by T. H. Jones and *AUMLA* to make the Hopkinsian distinction between overthought and underthought, it might be possible for him to miss not only their power and beauty, but even their common sense. He may lose, too, the full emotional and artistic effect of the last three paragraphs, the final one of which ("O lyric Love") is one of Browning's supremely functional, yet most anthologized passages. These five paragraphs create the climax of Book I; they move together as an interinanimated power; to miss any one aspect is to diminish a valuable experience.

We have reached the exact point where we are ready to tackle the crucial lines (I, 1330–78), since they start immediately after the ten paragraphs summarizing the ten central monologues that we have discussed. Indeed the lines commence as though they were going to be a paragraph of summary corresponding to Book XII. But no summary resembling the previous ten formal summaries eventuates, and, despite the fact that there is also no summary paragraph for Book I, we are surprised. The surprise is salutary; we are led to recognize that Books I and XII are not lily-flowers embossing the ring's rondure; they have a different function, and a different location on the ring. Something unexpected has happened. To discuss all this, however, requires an essay as long as the present one even though it would concentrate only on the last five paragraphs of Book I, with a glance or two at relevant paragraphs in Book XII. This second, complementary essay is already written since its overthought and underthought concerns are so intimately and organically intertwined with what we have been discussing that both essays had to arrive at expression almost simultaneously.

The duties of the present essay, however, have been discharged. By articulating as coherent a vision as I could manage of Book I, lines 1–1329, I have completed the preparation necessary for a coherent discussion of lines 1330–1416. Without some such preparation the last five paragraphs of Book I will fall short of their potential efflorescence. We have perhaps also accumulated enough evidence to qualify T. H. Jones's argument that in Browning's poem overthought is confused, underthought is nonexistent, semantic and metaphoric activity is absent. I may even venture the assertion that in Books I and XII of *The Ring and the Book* the underthought is so important and active, although often muted and subtle, that it is not possible to express fully the chief meaning and value of the poem without using it as interpretive tool and guide.

Notes

1. *AUMLA*, Number Thirteen (May 1960), pp. 55–69.
2. *PMLA*, LXIII, 1276–82. In addition to this article I am indebted to Professor Cundiff, University of Delaware, for a vast quantity of Browning illumination in print, in letters, in conversation.
3. *Further Letters of Gerard Manley Hopkins*, ed. C. C. Abbott (London, 1938), pp. 105–06.
4. I am indebted to Professor Henry W. Sams, Head, Department of English, and to The Pennsylvania State University, for arranging leaves during which I was able to overthink and underthink about *The Ring and the Book*.
5. My quotations and line numbers are all taken from the Oxford Standard Authors edition of the poem: Robert Browning, *The Ring and the Book*, with an introduction by E. Dowden, notes by A. K. Cook (London, 1940).
6. A. K. Cook, *A Commentary upon Browning's The Ring and the Book* (London, 1920).
7. Charles W. Hodell, *The Old Yellow Book, Source of Browning's "The Ring and the Book"* (Washington, D.C., 1908); Vol. I, Complete Photo-Reproduction; Vol. II, Translation, Essay, and Notes.
8. I am indebted to Professor Deborah S. Austin, Department of English, The Pennsylvania State University, for obtaining for me a private letter dated 18 January 1962, explaining this process and written by a friend of hers who is a scholarly artificer of such objects.
9. *The Letters of Elizabeth Barrett Browning*, ed. F. G. Kenyon (New York, 1897), II, 354–55. See also *Dearest Isa: Robert Browning's Letters to Isa Blagden*, ed. E. C. McAleer (Austin, 1951), pp. 54–55; hereafter referred to in the text as *Dearest Isa*.
10. Katharine C. de K. Bronson, "Browning in Venice," *Century Magazine*, February 1902, LXIII (NS XLI), p. 573.
11. For whatever is clearest and most accurate in my account of Browning rings I am indebted to generous acts of colleagueship on the part of Professor Robert W. Frank, Jr., Department of English, The Pennsylvania State University. He visited the Browning exhibits at Balliol College and the British Museum, talked with curators, described exactly what he heard, saw, and read, drew me sketches of rondure and bezel for the two most relevant rings, and answered my questions in two private letters dated 4 November 1965 and 8 November 1965. I've seldom had uncertainty cleared up so swiftly and pleasantly.
12. *Letters of Robert Browning*, ed. Thurman L. Hood (New Haven, 1933), pp. 62–63.
13. I am indebted to Professor Gordon M. Shedd, Department of English, The Pennsylvania State University, for urging, in a discussion of the ring metaphor, that if the metaphor suggests the balanced union of content and form in art, it should also be considered to suggest the balanced union of body and soul in the love of man and woman.
14. *Goethe's Faust*, ed. Calvin Thomas (Boston, 1892, 1897), ll. 12104–05, ll. 12110–12. In this edition The First Part and The Second Part occupy separate volumes, but the line numbering is continuous.
15. For a useful discussion of these ideas in connection with a poet whose influence on Browning is very significant, see Carlos Baker, *Shelley's Major Poetry* (Princeton, 1948); the index has many references to "epipsyche."
16. Browning said of Dante, 3 May 1845, that he had "all of him in my head and heart," *The Letters of Robert Browning and Elizabeth Barrett Barrett 1845–1846*, ed. Elvan Kintner (Cambridge, Mass., 1969), p. 54. J. E. Shaw in his valuable 1926 article, "The 'Donna Angelicata' in *The Ring and the Book*" (*PMLA*, XLI, 55–81), has accumulated enough textual evidence from

Dante and Browning to be able to say persuasively that *The Ring and the Book* is Browning's dramatic exposition of his theory of love and that "this theory of love is fundamentally identical with that of Dante."

17. *The Major Victorian Poets: Reconsiderations*, ed. Isobel Armstrong (Lincoln, Neb., 1969), p. 161.
18. *Robert Browning and Alfred Domett*, ed. F. G. Kenyon (London, 1906), p. 45.
19. Cf. the words of Mephistopheles to Faust about going to the Mothers: "Kein Weg! In's Unbetretene," "Hast du Begriff von Öd' und Einsamkeit?" (*Faust*, ll. 6222–27).
20. W. H. Griffin and H. C. Minchin, *The Life of Robert Browning* (New York, 1910), p. 22.
21. Sotheby, *The Browning Collections. Catalogue . . .* (London, 1913), item #768. Most of the books and authors mentioned in my essay are listed in this *Catalogue*, and thus probably were on Browning book shelves at one time or another, and can be regarded as likely candidates for reading and study by one of the two poets. I am indebted to Dr. Jack W. Herring, Director of the Armstrong Browning Library, Baylor University, for an opportunity to study this useful document, to him, Mrs. Veva Wood, and the library staff for outgoing assistance during the invaluable weeks I spent at that Browning treasury in Waco, Texas.
22. *New Letters of Robert Browning*, ed. W. C. DeVane and K. L. Knickerbocker (London, 1951), p. 32.
23. There's a touch of alchemical medicine here perhaps. Earlier the speaker had said of the Book, "the thing's restorative" (l. 89), thus echoing the alchemical sentence at the end of Donne's Elegie XI ("The Bracelet"): "Gold is restorative."
24. "The 'Dream' of *Kubla Khan*," *PMLA* (September 1945), LX, 784–801.
25. Plato (The Loeb Classical Library), *The Statesman, Philebus, Ion* (London, 1925); *Ion* translated by W. R. M. Lamb; pp. 421–429.
26. *Ion* is full of rings as metaphor for poetic structure, for connecting the poet with the muses, the poem with its reciter (rhapsode or actor), the reciter with his audience, "a mighty chain" of rings. In *Ion* the rings are magnetized and iron, not gold. Yet one wonders about a possible connection with Browning's ring-haunted poem. Important rings have already been mentioned but there are at least eight others in the poem. There's the javelin metaphor that helps start off and explain the alloying process whereby pure gold is turned into poet's gold:

> . . . fancy has informed, transpierced,
> Thridded and so thrown fast the facts else free,
> As right through ring and ring runs the djereed
> And binds the loose, one bar without a break. (I, 465–68)

There's the geographical "round from Rome to Rome" (I, 526) created by the journeyings of the principal characters from Rome to Arezzo and back to Rome. There's the ring formed by the Franceschini in their attempt to hold the Comparini captive in Arezzo (I, 574), and the "obscene ring" (I, 581) made by the Franceschini around Pompilia when she was left behind and they were hoping to torment her to death. There's a "wellbred ring" of listeners around the speaker of Book IV (I, 938). Pompilia's listeners "Encircle the low pallet where she lies" (I, 1084). There's the metaphor of the wheel used for law's machinery (I, 1111, 1115). There's the ring of vision, "the wide prospect round" (I, 1333) that the Maker-see points to from the hilltop, and the wheel that comes full circle in the same paragraph when the reader, who has been guided to the summit, is guided down again to the plain. There's the especially memorable ring of the last three lines of the poem, Lyric Love's "rare gold ring of verse (the poet praised)/ Linking our England to his Italy!" (XII, 868–70). This is an allusion to the inscription composed by the Italian critic and poet, Niccolò Tommaseo (1803–1874), for the tablet in memory of Mrs. Browning placed on the wall of Casa Guidi. Thus at poem's end the presence of three poets and their work may add a Wordsworthian touch to the aesthetic of *The Ring and the Book*; the Poet, in Wordsworth's 1802 Preface, is "the rock of defense of human nature; an upholder and preserver, carrying every where with him relationship and love. In spite of difference of soil and climate, of language and manners, of laws and customs, in spite of things silently gone out of mind and things violently destroyed, the Poet binds together by passion and knowledge the vast empire of human society, as it is spread over the whole earth, and over all time." This dizzy multiplication of rings may be accidental; on the other hand, it may be additional evidence for the speaker's aesthetic sophistication, and for the influence of *Ion* on lines 773–79 of Book I.

27. The quotation comes from Joyce, *A Portrait of the Artist* (Compass Books, The Viking Press, New York, 1956), p. 215; the context from which it is taken makes an interesting gloss on what Browning is doing with repristination in *The Ring and the Book*, I, 1379–89, and elsewhere.

Conrad:
On Atlantis

John Haag

I have to get there
but the last man who knew the way
died at sea—sank
with the map tattooed on his eyeball
—and lies down now, this prince
of lassitude, in a shroud of silt,
while his indifferent gaze
suffers the lamprey
to enter
at his nose.

This sea dream
tells me my sole hope
slides down a scavenger's
gullet, and I must catch and eat
this sea-beast that feeds
on my guide's mind matter,
then dream the secret eye
alive—and match it,
blood for blood.

The Utopian
Dream

Arthur O. Lewis, Jr.

It is somewhat paradoxical that utopian proposals—frequently the most rational of human schemes—should so often be associated with that most irrational state of mind, the dream; and yet, in critical writings few terms are more commonly used to characterize the perfect world and its inventors than *dream* and *dreamers* and their synonyms. Examples of this usage are numerous: "Utopia—The Everlasting Dream";[1] "Utopia . . . represents mankind's dream of happiness";[2] "vain dreams of perfection in a Never-Never Land";[3] "In constructing a utopia . . . [one must] confront a flexible dream with reality";[4] book titles use the terms: Vernon L. Parrington, Jr., *American Dreams* (1947); Stewart H. Holbrook, *Dreamers of the American Dream* (1957); René Dubos, *The Dreams of Reason: Science and Utopia* (1961); and, of course, the other side of the coin: Chad Walsh, *From Utopia to Nightmare* (1962); and Mark Hillegas, *The Future As Nightmare* (1967). The utopian writers, too, have frequently acknowledged the association in their titles: J. D. Beresford, *What Dreams May Come* (1941); Arthur Bird, *Looking Forward—A Dream of the United States of the Americas in 1999* (1899); Paul Devinne, *The Day of Prosperity: A Vision of the Century to Come* (1902); David A. Moore, *The Age of Progress; or, A Panorama of Time in Four Visions* (New York: Sheldon, Blakeman, 1856); and many others. Beyond acknowledgment in titles, dreams (and visions, fantasies, reveries, and trances, which, despite minor differences in meaning, may be used interchangeably in this context) have been an important tool for utopian writers when used, as has frequently been the case, as the literary vehicle through which the reader is transported to utopia, or as a means for enriching the story once arrived there. For ease of reference the first use may be called *dream vehicle* and the second *dream episode*.

The writer's choice of the dream vehicle as his method for describing utopia is an important one and throws significant light on his attitude toward his ideal state. Other devices have been at least equally successful and more frequently employed. The most obvious way to convey the idea of a perfect society is simply to describe what it would be like or what steps need to be taken to attain it. Plato's *Republic* (ca. 380 B.C.) is still the best example of this approach, and his use of a dialogue among interested persons has its descendants in much utopian writing through the device of conversations between the narrator and his mentor which explain the operation of the new society. However, despite Plato's success, fictional methods have been, on the whole, more commonly used.

Besides the dream there are four basic fictional means for attaining utopia. Probably the earliest is the voyage—usually unplanned—to some unknown land; among the more successful utopias employing this device are Thomas More, *Utopia* (1516), Gabriel de Foigné, *La Terre Australe connue* (1699), and Austin Tappan Wright, *Islandia* (1942). An important variation is the journey by a group of pioneers to an unsettled land for the purpose of creating a better society according to some preconceived plan, as in Theodor Hertzka's *Freiland* (1890). A second means is to present our own society through the eyes of a stranger. Thus in Voltaire's *Micromegas* (1752) and W. D. Howells' *A Traveler from Altruria* (1894) a visitor from another, hitherto unknown society describes his homeland. Annihilation of time (to give utopia time to develop from present society) through a long sleep, or through some kind of suspended animation, provides the framework for Edward Bellamy, *Looking Backward, 2000–1887* (1888), H. G. Wells, *When the Sleeper Wakes* (1899), and Granville Hicks and Richard M. Bennett, *The First to Awaken* (1940); closely related is the long sleep which is revealed to have been only a dream, as in Sebastien Mercier's *L'An deux mille quatre cent quarante* (1770) and William Morris' *News from Nowhere* (1890). Finally, more and more in recent years the utopian writer has plunged into the middle of things and assumed that utopia has been achieved somewhere in the future of his own society, as in Solomon Schindler's *Young West* (1894) and Hermann Hesse's *Das Glasperlenspiel* (1945); in such works the narrator is a member of the ideal society, and his adventures are used to describe its characteristics. A kind of subcategory assumes the existing future society chiefly in order to permit a "historical" explanation of how it came about; American writers at the turn of the century were particularly interested in this approach: for example, Bert J. Wellman, *The Legal Revolution of 1902* (1898), H. Pereira Mendes, *Looking Ahead* (1899), and Charles William Wooldridge, *Perfecting the Earth* (1902). Further, among anti-utopian writers, such as Eugene Zamiatin, *We* (1924), Aldous Huxley, *Brave New World* (1932), and Ayn Rand, *Anthem* (1946), the existing society has frequently been adopted as a vehicle.

Each of these methods has had both successes and failures, but some are now more frequently used than others. Even Plato was dissatisfied with pure discussion as the way to describe utopia and apparently intended to adopt a fictional approach in the unfinished *Critias*, which was to have described life in a state like that proposed in *The Republic*. As exploration of the earth reduced the number of out-of-the-way places, unknown societies seemed less likely to be discovered. Thus, although nonfiction proposals are still put forward and the moon, the planets, and the stars continue to be available for the voyage and foreign-visitor vehicles, writers of the last hundred years have more often chosen the long sleep, the existing society, and the dream as ways of traveling to utopia.

Doubtless it would be a useful critical contribution to examine the advantages and disadvantages of the several methods, but it is only necessary to point out that the chief advantage of the dream vehicle is as a concession to nonbelievers who would not willingly read about such a society when it is postulated as possible but who will accept the fantastic and "nonserious" version implied by this approach. The chief disadvantage is that by choosing the dream as his literary vehicle the utopian writer has already accepted the improbability of achieving his perfect world; where all the other methods have the implicit sentiment that "somewhere" or "tomorrow" utopia exists, the dream says only, "When you wake up, you will know it isn't so."

After the narrator has arrived in utopia—by whatever means—dreams are frequently employed to enhance the story. The simplest usage is to forward the action: the narrator dreams of something which affects his later activities. A second usage is to make the narrator's character more believable or interesting: in dreams his true reactions to the strange new world can be demonstrated. Finally, the narrator's dreams can intensify the criticism of those things in the real world the utopia is supposed to correct, or, in the case of the anti-utopian work, those aspects of the new world which are distasteful to the writer. As might be expected, all three usages are sometimes combined in the same dream. Of special interest are those works in which dream episodes appear within the dream used as a vehicle for attaining utopia. The remainder of the present exercise is an attempt to identify some of these varying uses of the utopian dream and to comment briefly on their literary effectiveness.

Of considerable interest, and antecedent to any serious study of the literary merit of the utopian dream, is consideration of the method by which it is introduced. In this respect utopian writers have attained various levels of craftsmanship. As with any literary device, much depends upon the plausibility of the dream, and this plausibility depends in large part on the way in which the dream is introduced. Generally, the effectiveness of the dream is directly proportional to the strength of the ties between the dream and its external surroundings. That is, the more closely events within the dream reflect the concerns stated by the writer-dreamer prior to beginning the dream the more reasonable the utopia seems to be as a solution to these concerns. Where the dream occurs after the narrator's arrival in utopia, its usefulness in forwarding the writer's intentions depends in large part upon the circumstances surrounding its appearance.

Perhaps the least effective approach is the long sleep that is discovered to be a dream. Such works may justifiably be treated as examples of the dream vehicle rather than of the long sleep. Initially the "long sleep" enhances the credibility of the work, but in most instances at the point where the dream is revealed most readers are disappointed and sense that they have been unfairly led astray—if not cheated. Mary Griffith's "Three Hundred Years Hence" (1836) is a good example of the long sleep which is acknowledged, on the last page, to have been a dream. Throughout most of this long short story there is little to indicate the true nature of the literary device. Edgar Hastings sets out on a business trip and while awaiting passage across the river, "closed his eyes . . . in less than five minutes he was fast asleep."[5] His awakening 300 years later and the circumstances of his long sleep, while unusual in themselves, are explained quietly and sensibly. A subsequent journey through the new world offers no major surprises, but it is reasonable that upon returning from these travels the weary hero should pause to rest in the same chair where he had slept. What is unexpected is the sound of his father-in-law's voice: "Edgar Hastings—hast thou been sleeping?" and his realization, "Oh, my father, what a dream!"[6] For twentieth-century readers the chief interest of this work is as a possible source for Edward Bellamy's much more believable utopia and as an early example of a feminist-influenced society. The dream device is naive, a means for saying something about Griffith's ideal world, adding no real literary merit. Other practitioners of this approach have sometimes presented more interesting proposals, but none has succeeded any better in producing a work of art.

Very different is the cause of the dream in Chauncey Thomas' *The Crystal Button*: Paul Prognosis, a Boston contractor and inventor of mechanical devices, is seriously injured while rescuing an employe from drowning. He lies in a trance for 10 years, occasionally addressing those around him by names they do not recognize, asking strange questions, "unintelligible to his hearers." The reader knows what Paul's family and friends only dare to hope, "that life still flickered in the paralyzed brain,"[7] and that he and his dog Smudge (who never leaves his side) are alive and well, though often puzzled by what they see and hear, in the forty-ninth century city of Tone. Where those around him know only that "To his imagination a waste-basket became a colossal tower; a toy wagon a railway train; his wife's jewel-box, a mammoth tenement house,"[8] the reader knows that the dreamer is seeing the tower, the train, and the tenement house. Upon his recovery from the trance, Paul's sleeping hours continue to be spent in the dream city, and he feels as if some day he may return permanently. The effect of his alternation of real and dream worlds is to raise the possibility in the mind of the reader that perhaps Paul has broken the veil of time; Tone may well be Boston 3000 years hence.

The simplest approach to the dream utopia is a direct one, and most writers have chosen to use it. The chief differences among them lie in the thoroughness of their discussion of the problems which are to be solved or criticized in the dream and in the complexity of the process by which the dreamer falls into his dream. Calvin Blanchard begins *The Art of Real Pleasure* by stating his disagreement with the idea that "life can, at best, be only a sort of half and half of pain and pleasure."[9] Not at all, he goes on, life can be *"pure delight,"* and he will show his reader how: "And now, without further preliminary, imagine yourself and myself in a palace."[10] Edward Kent, called upon for a contribution to the "Bangor book," procrastinates until it is almost too late: "Must I write! and if so, what shall I write? I was in a fix, and as a last resort I went to bed . . . I have an indistinct remembrance of a half-sleeping and half-waking vision of a ragged and suffering orphan who . . . asked me, in plaintive tones, to write."[11] In *Looking Backward and What I Saw* W. W. Satterlee carries the preparation for the dream a little further. His narrator, following a day "full of anxious thought, concerning the social problems which were agitating the minds of my countrymen,"[12] has difficulty in sleeping. Musing over his past life, he has forebodings: "If suddenly I should be called to die, my family would be cast on the cold charities of a self-seeking world."[13] But at last, comforted by his trust in God, he "slept and dreamed . . . moving through space in that indescribable Dream-land way."[14] One of the most thorough introductions to the dream is that of James Cowan, who devoted the entire first chapter of *Daybreak* to the background of his dreamer. Following a long shipboard conversation with his fiancée, Walter is left alone in his deck chair:

I fell into a deep reverie. My mind was filled with contending emotions, and such opposing objects as rolling worlds and lovely maidens flitted in dim images across my mental vision. I loved the best woman on the earth, and I wondered if any of those other globes contained her equal. If so, then perhaps some other man was as fortunate as myself. I was drowsy, but determined to keep awake and pursue this fancy. I remember feeling confident that I could not sleep if I kept my eyes open, and so I said I would keep them fixed on the bright face of the moon. But how large it looked. Surely something must be wrong with it . . . it was growing bigger every minute. It was coming nearer, too. Nearer, larger—why, it was monstrous. I could not turn my eyes away now, and everything else was forgotten, swallowed up in that one awful sight.[15]

What follows is a conversation with other onlookers in the street where Walter now finds himself and the discovery that "the moon is certain to come into collision with the earth in a very short time."[16] The dream has become full grown, and Walter's further adventures on the moon and Mars are the framework upon which Cowan hangs his vision of man's ideal society of the future.

The impact of these dreams is, as noted earlier, greatly influenced by the relationship of events within the dream to those events of the real world which have been drawn to the reader's attention prior to the beginning of the dream. Obviously, the society described will reflect the writer's solutions to problems raised earlier as well as his objections to solutions proposed by others, but some dreams are more believable than others. Thus, Calvin Blanchard was concerned with obtaining the greatest pleasure from life, and in "the Good Time" everyone enjoys life to the full.[17] But, because there has been no characterization of the narrator, no statement of his personal situation, no real discussion of the problems with which he is concerned, the reader never really visualizes him in the new society. Any of the other literary vehicles would have served as well as the dream, and, in fact, Blanchard appears to forget the device he has employed, for the narrator never leaves the imaginary world. The book concludes with a series of appendices and summaries of Blanchard's work; the reader is left with the feeling that he has been reading nonfiction polemic rather than a work of fiction.

At the other end of the scale Cowan's dream is carefully prepared for, and events within it reflect what the reader already knows about the narrator's character: Walter has been engaged to Margaret for years but, despite the nearness of their wedding day, is too reserved to tell her of his love except in unimpassioned terms; she suggests he needs some shaking up, and they jokingly discuss the possibility that he ought to undergo wild adventures or fall in love with "some pretty girl." He has a perfect ear for music, he is a harsh critic, and having long ago criticized Margaret's singing (she has since spent years in voice train- ing), he now finds her unwilling to sing for him; he has just decided to try once more to have her do so. Both are interested in astronomy and the possibility of life on other worlds; perhaps, they lightly agree, the adventures and the other woman can be found on some other planet. Thus, when Walter rides the moon to Mars, falls in love successively with Mona and Avis because of their beautiful voices, pleads with them passionately to no avail, and finds a superior civilization on Mars, the reader finds these matters to be most appropriate. It comes as some- thing of a shock when, while discussing a possible return to earth, Walter feels a dull pain in his head and finds himself in the wreckage of his deck chair, with Margaret solicitously inquiring whether he has been hurt. Throughout the dream there have been times when the beauti- ful voices of Mona and Avis have penetrated even Walter's dreams within the dream, and it seems only natural to learn that Margaret has been sing- ing to him while he slept. In this work the dream vehicle is an integral and fitting part of a story which would have been very different if the writer had used another approach to utopia.

As the examples above demonstrate, the effectiveness of the dream used as vehicle for attaining utopia generally depends upon anteced- ent events. When used within utopia, its effectiveness more often than not depends upon subsequent events. In *Daybreak* Walter (suffering from partial loss of memory) has been trying to understand why his doctor-companion constantly refers to the lost Mona, whose existence he doubts, and this effort is clearly the cause of the dream in which he hears and begins to fall in love with a beautiful voice. But of much greater importance to the plot is his later discovery of Avis, the possessor of the voice, as well as restoration of his memory of Mona and his de- mand that an intensified search for her be set under way. Similarly, R. E. Former, the narrator-hero of *Looking Backward and What I Saw*, un- dergoes five dreams or visions within the main dream. Each such dream episode is triggered by new knowledge of the horrors to which the country has been subjected during the twentieth-century. Far more important, however, is the fact that each dream episode drives Former to further study of "history," permitting Satterlee further opportunity to criticize the utopian schemes to which he objects and to present his own proposal in a better light.[18]

The importance of the dream episode to the over-all literary quality of the utopian work can be demonstrated by a brief view of its appearance in Alvarado M. Fuller's *A. D. 2000* and Edward Bellamy's *Looking Backward*, the first almost unknown, the second probably the most widely read utopian novel of all time. Both use the long sleep vehicle, both are set in the year 2000, both portray societies which have made great strides technologically, both have heroes who long for their nineteenth-century sweethearts but who later marry and become full-fledged useful citizens of the new world, and both use dream episodes to forward the plot. There are other similarities, so many that Fuller felt the need to point out that he had finished writing his book by November 1887, several months before Bellamy's was published.

Unlike Bellamy's Julian West, whose long sleep was entirely accidental, Fuller's hero, Junius Cobb, is a young army lieutenant who uses himself as guinea pig in an experiment half scientific and half intended to overcome slow promotion in the army: "With wealth and rank, I can again enter the world in a position to gratify my ambitions and desires."[19] His awakening in the year 2000 is marred only by the knowledge that he has left his beloved Marie Colchis forever behind him. Early in his new life he dreams of her grave; then the scene changes, and an angel leads him to his lost Marie, saying, "Though years and years have fled and passed, yet life shall once again renew her heart."[20] This dream, which occurs with no antecedent action or discussion, appears to have no purpose other than to intensify Junius' sorrow, until another of the unexpected occurrences with which the book abounds reveals Marie alive and well following a long sleep into which her father had put her to prevent her death from a broken heart after Junius' disappearance. The novel is an attractive one in many ways,[21] but handling of the dream episode is not one of them. In this one aspect of the work Fuller shows little sense of literary craftsmanship.

Bellamy's treatment of the dream episode near the end of *Looking Backward* reveals a more masterful touch and goes far to explain the popularity of his novel. The immediate stimulus of the dream is the powerful emotional state in which Julian finds himself following Mr. Barton's sermon, "with its constant implication of the vast moral gap between the century to which I belonged and that in which I found myself,"[22] and the subsequent exchange of vows with Edith Leete (now for the first time identified as great granddaughter of his nineteenth-century fiancée). Bellamy later described the dream:

His cup of happiness now being full, he had an experience in which it seemed to be dashed from his lips. As he lay on his bed in Dr. Leete's house he was oppressed by a hideous nightmare. It seemed to him that he opened his eyes to find himself on his bed in the underground chamber where the mesmerizer had put him to sleep. Sawyer was just completing the passes to break the hypnotic influence. He called for the morning paper and read on the date line May 31, 1887. Then he knew that all this wonderful matter about the year 2000, its happy, care-free world of brothers and the fair girl he had met there were but fragments of a dream. His brain in a whirl, he went forth into the city. He saw everything with new eyes, contrasting it with what he had seen in the Boston of the year 2000. . . . He felt like a sane man shut up by accident in a madhouse. After a day of this wandering he found himself at nightfall in a company of his former companions . . . told them of his dream and what it had taught him of the possibilities of a juster, nobler, wiser social system. . . . At first they derided him, but, seeing his earnestness, grew angry, and denounced him as a pestilent fellow, an anarchist, and enemy of society, and drove him from them.[23]

The reader despairs: there is no utopia, only the same ugly world that led Bellamy to write his book in the first place. Mercier, Griffith, Macnie had all played the same trick. But Bellamy has contrasted "the Black Hole of Calcutta"—Mr. Barton's phrase—and the "golden century"—Julian West's grateful summation—for the last time: "I . . . found myself sitting upright in my room in Dr. Leete's house."[24] The dramatic confrontation between life as it was in Bellamy's day and life as Bellamy wished it to be is convincing. Probably it helped to make the book a best seller and may even have been a significant influence in the decision made by so many of its readers to try to implement the book's proposals. Certainly no utopian writer has made better use of the dream episode.

It is dangerous, however, to draw conclusions about any utopian proposal in purely literary terms. The association of utopia with dreams has been a profitable one for the utopian writer, for both dream vehicle and dream episode, properly handled, can increase the effectiveness of the communication. But from the utopian point of view that is not enough. It is relatively unimportant that Blanchard employed the dream vehicle badly and Cowan employed it well. The only fact that counts is that neither caused even a ripple in the sea of social reform. It would be foolish to claim that the difference in handling the dream episodes alone caused Bellamy's work to become a best seller while Fuller's never rose from obscurity. There is no explaining public taste or the peculiarities of the publishing industry. In many ways twentieth-century America is closer to the world portrayed by Fuller than to that of Bellamy, and a whole generation of young people seems to agree with Blanchard. One is tempted to conclude that the bad writers are closer to humanity's aspirations than the good.

As with any literary device, maximum effect requires the careful construction that makes the device an integral part of the work rather than merely a decorative appendage. With utopian writing as with any other kind of writing the better craftsmanship produces the better work. But a successful literary work is not necessarily a successful exposition of the utopian ideal. For the believer in a better tomorrow, communication of principles will always take second place to the task of putting them into effect. The dream as literary device must give way to the dream made real. So far it has not happened.

Notes

1. Title of chapter 1 of Edith Mannin, *Bread and Roses* (London: Macdonald, 1944).
2. Marie Louise Berneri, *Journey through Utopia* (London: Routledge & Kegan Paul, 1950), p. 2.
3. Lewis Mumford, *The Story of Utopias* (New York: The Viking Press, 1962), p. 1.
4. Francois Bloch-Lainé, "Utopias for Reformers," in *Utopias and Utopian Thought*, ed. Frank E. Manual (Boston: Houghton Mifflin, 1966), p. 217.
5. Mary Griffith, *Three Hundred Years Hence* (Philadelphia: Prime Press, 1950), p. 31.
6. Griffith, p. 130.
7. Chauncey Thomas, *The Crystal Button* (New York: R. F. Fenno, 1891), p. 14.
8. Thomas, p. 12.
9. Calvin Blanchard, *The Art of Real Pleasure* (New York: Calvin Blanchard, 1864), p. 7.
10. Blanchard, p. 8.
11. Edward Kent, "A Vision of Bangor, in the Twentieth Century," in *Voices from the Kenduskeag* (Bangor: David Bugbee, 1848), pp. 63–64.
12. W. W. Satterlee, *Looking Backward and What I Saw* (Minneapolis: Harrison & Smith, 1890), p. 1.
13. Satterlee, p. 2.
14. Satterlee, p. 3.
15. James Cowan, *Daybreak: A Romance of an Old World* (New York: George H. Richmond, 1896), pp. 12–13.
16. Cowan, p. 13.
17. See my "Introduction" to the Arno Press reprint, 1971.
18. See my "Introduction" to the Arno Press reprint, 1971.
19. Lt. Alvarado M. Fuller, *A. D. 2000* (Chicago: Laird & Lee, 1890), p. 37.
20. Fuller, p. 244.
21. See my "Introduction" to the Arno Press reprint, 1971.
22. Edward Bellamy, *Looking Backward, 2000–1887* (Cleveland: World Publishing, 1945), p. 282.
23. Edward Bellamy, *Equality* (New York: D. Appleton, 1897), pp. v–vi.
24. *Looking Backward*, p. 316.

Four Fathers for Barbara

Stanley Weintraub

G. B. S. was seldom as specific about the real-life models for characters in his plays as he was for *Major Barbara* (1905). He would title it "Gilbert Murray's Mother-in-Law," he teased Murray, and made it clear that not only was Murray's stuffy mother-in-law, Lady Rosalind Howard, Duchess of Carlisle, the play's dowager Lady Britomart, but that Murray himself—a young Australian-born professor of Greek—was the model for Adolphus Cusins. (To make Cusins' identification obvious, Shaw not only borrowed from Murray's own version of *The Bacchae* the lines Cusins quotes from Euripides but prefaced his indebtedness.) Major Barbara herself, it later became known, was modeled after the vivacious young American actress Elinor Robson. "I want to see if I can make a woman a saint," he had confided to her, and wooed her for the cast of the first production in the epistolary manner with which he usually had such success. "I can't connect Barbara with anyone but you," Shaw wrote; "and am half tempted to take the play right up into the skies at the end because there is a sort of desecration in your marrying even your poet."[1] But Miss Robson chose to continue her American tour with the sentimental and successful *Merely Mary Ann*, and G. B. S. reluctantly found someone else for the role. Later she became the bride of United States Steel magnate August Belmont. It was almost as if she had married Andrew Undershaft.

G. B. S. identified Undershaft, Barbara's father, with no immediate prototype, although he suggested—more seriously, this time—that he thought the character so overshadowed the rest of the cast that the play might well be called *Andrew Undershaft's Profession*. The profession itself was crucial for Shaw, although he used it to symbolize all antisocial sources of wealth, for no profession endorsed by Mammon—not even Mrs. Warren's well-known one—had such potential for negative dramatic impact. Three imposing figures in the armaments industry apparently were in Shaw's mind, as well as at least one more prototype forgotten everywhere but at Ayot St. Lawrence, where one of Shaw's friends and neighbors soon would be Stage Society playwright Charles McEvoy. McEvoy's father had supported the Confederate side in the American Civil War, and by the close of the war had established a factory in the South for the manufacture of torpedoes and high explosives.[2]

The gentle, humane McEvoy, of benign appearance but barbarous occupation, must have appealed to Shaw's sense of dramatic paradox.

There was a different, more sardonic, kind of paradox Shaw then could turn to in Swedish arms maker and inventor of dynamite Alfred Nobel. More a sufferer from *Schuldkomplex* than Undershaft (whose industrial motto, "Unashamed," nevertheless implies a moral dilemma), he elected in his last years to "make war on war" by endowing an international peace prize, first awarded in 1901, five years after his death. A complex man, Nobel had his intellectual and humanitarian side, which resulted in his other annual awards, Shaw himself receiving the one for literature in 1926. Before the posthumous Nobel Prizes however, Alfred Nobel was known for his activities in international finance and for the armaments firm he had inherited from his father and built up to enormous size through his hardheadedness in selling weapons and patents, like Undershaft, to all comers regardless of politics. His own politics belied his business practices. An ardent Social Democrat, he was, to his liberal friends, "the gentle Bolshevik," but he earned millions by selling weapons to nations all over the world, many of which desired nothing more than to suppress any form of social democracy; and his motto, "My home is where my work is, and my work is everywhere," would have pleased the motto-loving Undershaft.[3]

Nobel alone might explain the character of a dealer in death who can quote Plato and espouse humanitarian principles, but there was also another reputation available to Shaw. Munitions entrepreneur Sir Basil Zaharoff, a man of mystery to millions of Europeans, not only sold to all comers and even arranged, for his even vaster profit, the large lines of credit necessary (in both cases like Shaw's unashamed arms dealer), but came, like Undershaft, from origins resembling the most romantic Victorian cheap fiction. Barbara's father is an abandoned East End orphan, of mysterious origins. The goateed Sir Basil (whose eventual name was almost certainly neither that of his mother nor father) was born in 1849, probably in the brothel quarter of Constantinople, but rumor had him originating all over Europe, one version even claiming that he was an orphan from the slums of Whitechapel. By the early 1900s he was notorious as the Prince of Blood and Steel (Undershaft is called the Prince of Darkness, and claims to Barbara that the Salvation Army's motto might be his own—"Blood and Fire"). In the 1890s he had formed a munitions-making partnership with Sir Hiram Maxim of the famous machine gun, and soon merged with Vickers, manufacturers of naval cannon. In the wars of the period—Japan and China, Turkey and Greece, Britain and the Boers, Russia and Japan, Bulgaria and Serbia—Zaharoff and his agents were on the scene selling to both sides and often accused of having provoked the conflicts for the firm's advantage. Regularly, he put his political affiliations to use, via shares he controlled in firms in which many who owned stock were influential in English public life, the Admiralty and the Army. To the end of his life, although he became a Knight Commander of the Bath, he was a public figure of undiminished secretiveness and mystery, having influenced a venal press in his client countries so effectively that it is not surprising that hardly any of his extensive press dossier is even remotely accurate. This underside of his career helps explain Undershaft's outburst to his naive and nearly forgotten son Stephen—*"with a touch of brutality,"* Shaw notes in the preliminary stage directions.

The government of your country! *I* am the government of your country: I, and Lazarus. Do you suppose that you and half a dozen amateurs like you, sitting in a row in that foolish gabble shop, can govern Undershaft and Lazarus? No, my friend, you will do what pays *us.* You will make war when it suits us, and keep peace when it doesn't. You will find out that trade requires certain measures when we have decided on those measures. When I want anything to keep my dividends up, you will discover that my want is a national need. When other people want something to keep my dividends down, you will call out the police and military. And in return you shall have the support and applause of my newspapers, and the delight of imagining that you are a great statesman. Government of your country! Be off with you, my boy, and play with your caucuses and leading articles and historic parties and great leaders and burning questions and the rest of your toys. *I* am going back to my counting-house to pay the piper and call the tune.[4]

And then there was the portly and unprepossessing Fritz Krupp, inheritor of the Krupp munitions dynasty, which he ruled from 1887 to 1902, building the cannonmakers of Essen into a world industrial power that sold arms from Chile to China, under the firm's unofficial motto, *"Wenn Deutschland blüht, blüht Krupp"* (When Germany flourishes, Krupp flourishes).[5] Undershaft, like all of his dynasty, has taken, on the instruction of his predecessor, the name of the firm's founder. As Lady Britomart tells the story,

The Undershafts are descended from a foundling in the parish of St. Andrew Undershaft in the city. That was long ago, in the reign of James the First. Well, this foundling was adopted by an armorer and gun-maker. In the course of time the foundling succeeded to the business; and from some notion of gratitude, or some vow or something, he adopted another foundling, and left the business to him. And that foundling did the same. Ever since that, the cannon business has always been left to an adopted foundling named Andrew Undershaft.[6]

Via this aspect of his play, Shaw, with brilliant, almost miraculous, foreshadowing, prepared the way for life to follow art. Aided by special governmental decrees (even one from Hitler later, in 1943), the Krupps had followed the strictest rules of primogeniture, endowing the whole of family wealth and power upon the eldest son. Siblings, when necessary, were absorbed into the firm, but only as drab underlings. All the world knew in 1905, as Shaw wrote his play, that the Krupp dynasty lacked a male successor. After Fritz Krupp's death in 1902, the succession had fallen awkwardly (as there was no male heir) to his daughter Bertha, with a younger sister, Barbara, disinherited. In 1905 both were approaching marriageable age. Barbara, Shaw could not help having observed, with a fine sense of irony, might have been named for the patron saint of armorers and artillerymen. Shaw, after all, wanted a saint for his play.

Barbara is substituted for Bertha. Deliberately? In the play there is a weak son in addition to the two sturdier sisters, a son who complains, "I have hardly ever opened a newspaper in my life without seeing our name in it. The Undershaft torpedo! The Undershaft quick-firers! The Undershaft ten-inch! The Undershaft disappearing rampart gun! The Undershaft submarine! And now the Undershaft aerial battleship!"[7] So too the headlines about the Krupps and their products, although Shaw can have been nothing less than uncanny in his foreshadowing of several weapons still to be turned out at Krupp arsenals, one the secret U-1, already underway and under wraps at Kiel. Further, the discussion in Act III about the Undershaft nursing home, libraries, schools, insurance and pension funds and building societies, bears a resemblance to Krupp paternalism in Essen. As a foreign visitor to the *Konzern* reported in the days of Fritz Krupp,

Everywhere the name of Krupp appears: now on the picturesque market-place, on the door of a mammoth department store, then on a bronze monument, now on the portals of a church . . . over a library, numerous schoolhouses, butcher shops, a sausage factory, shoemakers' shops and tailoring establishments, over playgrounds and cemeteries. . . . There is a German beer garden close to each park, and over each of them is written plainly, "Owned by Friedrich Krupp."[8]

Far more uncanny, however (for there were more modest English equivalents to this industrial paternalism known to Shaw) is the parallel between what is to happen to Barbara Undershaft—her eventual marriage to the professorial Adolphus Cusins and his thereupon preparing to become, even in name, the next Andrew Undershaft—and what *does* happen in 1906 to Barbara Krupp's sister Bertha.* Hand-picked for her as consort by the Kaiser was a scholarly, obscure diplomat, Gustav von Bohlen und Halbach. And as a dramatic conclusion to the nuptials *Sein Majestät* announced that "To ensure at least an appearance of continuity of the Essen dynasty" (*damit wenigstens eine ausserliche Fortführung der Essener Dynastie ermoglicht ist*), henceforth the bridegroom would take the name of Krupp and the right to pass it and the armaments empire that went along with it to his eldest son. The huge instrument giving legality to the procedure, with royal red wax seal seven inches in diameter, reaffirmed "the special position of the House of Krupp" (*die besondere Stellung des Hauses Krupp*), but, the Kaiser added (as might Andrew Undershaft himself), it was up to the bridegroom to prove himself *"ein wahrer Krupp"*—a real Krupp.[9] Had *Sein Majestät* taken the idea

---

* After whom her husband sentimentally named the big 420 mm. cannon used in France in 1914.

from Shaw? German newspapers (G. B. S. was popular there) had been full of reports of the play. If so, it may be the most amazing case of life utilizing art in our time. But in any case, the possibility that Shaw in the play was among other things, satirizing Krupp dynastic problems, cannot be overlooked.*

That Shaw knew what he was doing when he thought in terms of Krupp became obvious two years after *Major Barbara* was produced, when for a German edition of *The Perfect Wagnerite* G. B. S. added lines about the mythic Alberich of *The Rhinegold*. Each would-be Alberich in real life, Shaw wrote,

> discovers that to be a dull, greedy, narrow-minded money-grubber is not the way to make money on the modern scale; for though greed may suffice to turn tens into hundreds and even hundreds into thousands, to turn thousands into hundreds of thousands requires economic magnanimity and will to power as well as to pelf. And to turn hundreds of thousands into millions, Alberic must make himself an earthly Providence for masses of workmen, creating towns, and governing markets. . . . Consequently, though Alberic in 1850 may have been merely the vulgar Manchester factory-owner portrayed in Friedrich Engels' *Condition of the Working Classes*, in 1876 he was well on the way towards becoming Krupp of Essen, or Cadbury of Bournville, or Lever of Port Sunlight.

As the last line makes clear, even beyond the four dealers in death there were—at a farther remove—other likely "fathers" for Barbara, not dealers in cannon but in chocolate and soap. But there was also a dealer in the stuff of armaments—steel. Shaw's curious statement in 1900 that he thought that "Mammon can be developed into a socialist power, whereas Jehovah makes any such change of mind possible,"[10] sounds like an anticipation of the Undershaft philosophy (as well as the Alberich lines); and it has been suggested that indeed it is, and that Shaw had industrialist Andrew Carnegie in mind.[11] J. P. Morgan had just purchased Carnegie's factories for an estimated hundred million dollars in order to form U. S. Steel, and Carnegie's ventures in philanthropic uses of the staggering sum had led him to the writing of "The Gospel of Wealth," in which he wrote, in Bunyanesque cadences,† that his gospel "but echoes Christ's words. It calls upon the millionaire to sell all he hath and give it in the highest and best form to the poor by administering his estate himself for the good of his fellows, before he is called upon to lie down and rest upon the bosom of Mother Earth." Shaw's response, in a new prefatory note to a reissue of his pamphlet

---

* Shaw was also satirizing, like Wilde in *The Importance of Being Earnest*, the Victorian dramatic cliché of foundlings recovering their identities, fortunes and finances.

† Which Shaw must have recalled when he wrote, in the Preface to *Major Barbara*: "I do not call a Salvationist really saved until he is ready to lie down cheerfully on the scrap heap, having paid scot and lot and something over, and let his eternal life pass on to renew its youth in the battalions of the future."

"Socialism for Millionaires" (1901), was that "a Millionaire Movement" had taken place, "culminating in the recent expression of opinion by Mr. Andrew Carnegie that no man should die rich." Only in this way, Shaw thought, could Mammon develop into a Socialist power, when traditional inheritance formulas were eschewed. English editor and crusader W. T. Stead reported Carnegie's ideas as to how this could be done in a way that seems to foreshadow the Undershaft scheme of disinheriting one's children—the basic plot device of *Major Barbara*:

Carnegie laid it down as a fundamental principle upon which the partnership should be conducted that when a partner dies his estate should be settled up within thirty days, and his interest in the business acquired by the remaining partners, and also that no son or child of any of them should have a share in the concern or a voice in its management. This policy has been rigidly observed down to the present. The consequence is that the partnership from time to time has been refreshed and invigorated by infusions of new blood, and the active managers have been young and energetic men.

Stead also provided a link with the Salvation Army aspect of Shaw's play, suggesting that there were passages in Carnegie's exhortations which might lead one to predict that the industrialist "might even become a strong supporter of the social scheme of the Salvation Army." But it was a hint Shaw did not need, for one of his earlier writings had even sketched out what seems the germ of the West Ham Shelter act (II) of the play, with its salvationists and the grudgingly saved:

The solitary rough is not brave. He is restless and shamefaced until he meets with other roughs to keep him in countenance. He especially dreads that strange social reformer, the Hallelujah lass. At first sight of her quaint bonnet, jersey, and upturned eyes, he rushes to the conclusion that chance has provided him with a rare lark. He hastens to the outskirts of her circle, and after a few inarticulate howls, attempts to disconcert her by profane and often obscene interjections. In vain. He may as easily disconcert a swallow in its flight. He presently hears himself alluded to as "that loving fellow creature," and he is stricken with an uncomfortable feeling akin to that which prompted Paul Pry's protest, "Don't call me a phoenix: I'm not used to it." But the Hallelujah lass is not done with him yet. In another minute she is praying, with infectious emotion, for "his dear, precious soul." This finishes him. He slinks away with a faint affectation of having no more time to waste on such effeminate sentimentality, and thenceforth never ventures within earshot of the Army except when strongly reinforced by evil company or ardent spirits. A battalion of Hallelujah lasses is worth staying a minute to study. . . . As long as they speak strenuously, they consider themselves but little about lack of matter, which forces them to repetitions which, it must be confessed, soon become too tedious for anyone but a habitual Salvationist to endure. . . .[12]

Also a wealthy industrialist, and even less related to armaments than Carnegie, was the Englishman George Cadbury, whose community-planning work Shaw knew well. Perivale St. Andrews, the utopian community built by Undershaft for the workers in his factories, seems based in part upon the model town movement which Cadbury championed and which pioneered the decentralization of industries about planned communities complete to company-sponsored schools and municipal services. Cadbury had been a poor boy and was a self-made man. A Quaker and a humanitarian who believed in providing people with jobs rather than charity, he was the inverse of Undershaft in choosing to enter the chocolate business (in which the company is still eminent) rather than heavy industry. By the turn of the century his community-planning ideas were attracting wide attention, but the Boer War had begun, and he turned his wealth and energies to campaigning for peace.

There was a successor, however, someone Shaw also knew. Ebenezer Howard, a less practical but highminded dreamer, had nevertheless founded the Garden City movement in 1898 and counted Shaw among his earliest supporters. Shaw even gave the movement the benefit of some of his most benevolent satire in *John Bull's Other Island* (1904), the immensely popular comedy about Ireland and Anglo-Irish manners which he wrote just before beginning *Major Barbara*:

BROADBENT. Have you ever heard of Garden City?

TIM [*doubtfully*]. D'ye mane Heavn?

BROADBENT. Heaven! No: it's near Hitchin. If you can spare half an hour I'll go into it with you.

TIM. I tell you what. Gimme a prospectus. Lemmy take it home and reflect on it.

BROADBENT. You're quite right: I will. [*He gives him a copy of Ebenezer Howard's book, and several pamphlets*] You understand that the map of the city—the circular construction—is only a suggestion.

TIM. I'll make a careful note of that [*looking dazedly at the map*].

BROADBENT. What I say is, why not start a Garden City in Ireland?

TIM [*with enthusiasm*]. Thats just what was on the tip of my tongue to ask you. Why not? [*Defiantly*] Tell me why not.

BROADBENT. There are difficulties. I shall overcome them; but there are difficulties. . . .[13]

Town-planners such as Howard, and company-town planners on the order of his predecessor Cadbury, almost certainly were in Shaw's mind when he completed *John Bull* and began his new play, in which Undershaft's pollution-free factory-community of Perivale St. Andrews "*lies between two Middlesex hills, half climbing the northern one. It is an almost smokeless town in white walls, roofs of narrow green slates or red tiles, tall trees, domes, companiles, and slender chimney shafts, beautifully situated and beautiful in itself.*" Surveying the Undershaft domain, Cusins remarks half in elation, half in disappointment, "Not a ray of hope. Everything perfect! wonderful! real! It only needs a cathedral to be a heavenly city instead of a hellish one."[14] But as Cusins quickly learns, Perivale St. Andrews has, in addition to the libraries, schools, building funds, community ballrooms and banqueting facilities, several churches prudently provided by Undershaft, one ironically a

"William Morris Labor Church."* But the most important church of all to Undershaft's Utopia may be one physically not in Perivale St. Andrews at all. In East London is the Church of St. Andrew Undershaft, erected 1520–1532. It is called Undershaft—after an earlier church on the same site—according to the chronicler and antiquary John Stow because in the early days of its existence "an high or long shaft, or May-pole, was set up there, in the midst of the street, before the south side of the said church."[15] As it rose higher than the steeple, the church on the corner of St. Mary Axe, Leadenhall Street, became known as St. Andrew Undershaft, distinguishing it from the numerous other London churches dedicated to the popular St. Andrew.†

On one occasion during the reign of the first Elizabeth, Stow records, a puritanical cleric named Sir Stephen (here one may usefully recall Undershaft's mediocrity of a son, of the same name) preached against the shaft as a profane source of happiness, accusing the inhabitants of the parish of St. Andrew Undershaft of sacrilegiously setting up for themselves an idol, the proof being their addition to the name of the church—"under that shaft." Stow further writes, "I heard his sermon at Paul's cross, and I saw the effect that followed." What followed was that the parishioners, eager to assert their religious orthodoxy, pulled down their beloved Maypole, hacked it into pieces and put it to the pyre.[16] Blood and fire.

Shaw's play has been called his *Divine Comedy*[17]—in brief, because its pervasive religious aspect includes three acts possibly divisible allegorically into Dante's Hell, Purgatory and Paradise.‡ If the genealogy of Major Barbara's father ironically recalls the conflict at the great shaft of Cornhill between bleak, negative orthodoxy and the small-scale but positive juxtaposition of divine and materialistic happiness represented by the paradox of the Maypole and the Mass merging at St. Andrew Undershaft—a literal *Divine Comedy* in itself—it may be that Shaw intended it so. Certainly his christening of Barbara's father suggests,

---

* On which is the motto around the dome, "NO MAN IS GOOD ENOUGH TO BE ANOTHER MAN'S MASTER." (There actually was a Labour Church Union at the turn of the century, founded in 1891 in Manchester by John Trevor, who attempted, as did Christian Socialism, to combine the social and religious rebellions against the Establishment into one movement. By 1895 there were fourteen congregations in the Labour Church Union, but the concept never caught on in London and did not survive the 1914–18 war.)

† Undershaft has clearly meant to suggest particular relevance to his vale-situated company town through the St. Andrews part of its name. The first of Shaw's "Saint Barbara's" many forefathers may thus be a saint himself, the St. Andrew of the lost Gospel (alluded to by tradition) who gave the playwright his excuse to title part of his preface "The Gospel of St. Andrew Undershaft," and who had special significance to Shaw's audience as (with St. George) one of the two patron saints of Britain.

‡ In an irony which very likely escaped G. B. S. it is St. Bernard who, when Dante reaches the heavenly zone, assumes the role of guide and reveals to the poet the final aim of man.

as does the entire density of allusion in the drama, that he had thoroughly done his homework. Yet had Shaw's Undershaft solved the spiritual problem in his armaments-dependent Utopia? "Try your hand on my men," he confidently invites Barbara as they tour his "City of God": "Their souls are hungry because their bodies are full."[18] And Barbara is ensnared by that temptation, as has been her husband-to-be. It is not without reason that Cusins earlier had labeled Undershaft "Mephistopheles-Machiavelli," for ironic Faustian overtones are not merely in the Satanic mills which nourish the heavenly city, but permeate the play.

Four fathers for Barbara? The four armorers are but a beginning, in a play inspired not only by people and events Shaw saw around him but by the *Republic* of Plato, the *Bacchae* of Euripides, the *Pilgrim's Progress* of Bunyan, the *Prince* of Machiavelli. In visualizing so many threads drawn together, not only do we achieve an insight into a remarkable creative process but through that insight a sense of the ramifications of a single dramatic personality. A character with such complex origins cannot be one from whom we can extract simple answers. Although much can be learned about Shaw's intentions within various levels of meaning from Barbara's many forefathers—not only from the four dealers in death—*Major Barbara* resists simplification and remains the most complex of Shaw's plays. Decades after he wrote *Man and Superman*, with its structure of preface, play, mythic play-within-the-play, appendix purportedly written by one of the characters and aphoristic fireworks of an appendix to that appendix, Shaw boasted that he had put all of his intellectual goods in the shop window in that play.[19] He had put even more into *Major Barbara*, but not with such shop-window obtrusiveness. In the paradoxes of Barbara's many fathers is the intellectual center of Shaw's most profound play.

A final, post-play irony brings together Saints Barbara and Andrew, for a Second World War air raid blotted out the buildings on the opposite corner of Leadenhall Street and St. Mary Axe, leaving the Church of St. Andrew Undershaft relatively unscathed. The bomb very possibly was manufactured by Krupp.

Notes

1. Shaw to Elinor Robson, 4 July 1905, in Elinor Robson, *The Fabric of Memory* (New York: Farrar, Straus and Cudahy, 1957), p. 39.
2. Archibald Henderson, *George Bernard Shaw* (Cincinnati: Stewart and Kidd, 1911), p. 380.
3. Louis Crompton, *Shaw the Dramatist* (Lincoln, Nebraska: University of Nebraska Press, 1969), pp. 115–16.
4. *Major Barbara*, Act III.
5. William Manchester, *The Arms of Krupp* (Boston: Little, Brown, 1968), p. 179.

6. *Major Barbara*, Act I.
7. *Major Barbara*, Act I.
8. Manchester, p. 206.
9. Manchester, p. 249.
10. David Bowman, "Shaw, Stead and the Undershaft Tradition," *Shaw Review*, XIV (January, 1971), 29.
11. Bowman, 29–32.
12. Ms. draft of article, probably 1880s (Texas).
13. *John Bull's Other Island*, Act I.
14. *Major Barbara*, Act III.
15. John Stow, *A Survey of London* (1658), ed. Henry Morley (London, 1890), p. 163.
16. Ibid.
17. Joseph Frank, "*Major Barbara*: Shaw's *Divine Comedy*," *PMLA*, LXXI (March, 1956), 61–74.
18. *Major Barbara*, Act III.
19. Preface to *Back to Methuselah*.

James Joyce and the Mythologizing of History

Michael H. Begnal

For Stephen Dedalus in James Joyce's *Ulysses* history is a nightmare from which he is attempting to awake.[1] One of the basic premises of this novel, as well as of *Finnegans Wake*, is that this same kind of bad dream of historical fact enmeshes all the inhabitants of our contemporary society. It is only through a revitalization of myth that men can come to know themselves clearly. Rather than clarifying one's place in the temporal flow of events, the study of history as history serves only to break up man's past into disjunct units which seem to have little relation to each other. Frank Budgen, one of Joyce's closest friends, aptly encapsulates the situation:

> James Watt invented the steam engine, and the steam engine begat the loco-motive, and the locomotive begat the time-table, forcing people to grapple with its complexities and think in minutes where their grandfathers thought in hours. All their yesterdays, that in an earlier age would have been quietly buried in the hope of a glorious resurrection as myth, lie embalmed in files of newspapers and snapshot albums.[2]

History, then, can be understood only in its immediate context, and has no universal application. The history of Ireland itself, for example, is a terrible jumble, since when we begin to pierce the mists of the past it becomes impossible to separate fact from fiction. Were the Tuatha de Danaan real people, were Cuchullain and Finn MacCool once tribal chieftains and warriors, were there two Saint Patricks or only one? To Joyce these are questions which can never be answered, and we incapacitate ourselves if we dwell too much upon them. As he says in *Finnegans Wake*: "In this scherzarade of one's thousand one nightinesses that sword of certainty which would identifide the body never falls" (51.14).

In an essay first published in *The Dial* in 1923, T. S. Eliot perceived that Joyce was doing something different in *Ulysses*, that the form of the novel was changing: "In using the myth, in manipulating a con-tinuous parallel between contemporaneity and antiquity, Mr. Joyce is pursuing a method which others must pursue after him."[3] Eliot goes on to underline what is perhaps the core of Joyce's method: "It is simply a way of controlling, of ordering, of giving a shape and a significance to the immense panorama of futility and anarchy which is contemporary history. . . . Instead of narrative method, we may now use the mythical method. It is, I seriously believe, a step toward making the modern world possible for art."[4] What is implicit here, whether Eliot realizes it or not, is that the novel must be read, as well as written, in a new way. Narration, or mythic history, has come to move on a different level.

It is only if the figures and events of the past are viewed upon an archetypal or mythological level that their true significance can be understood. The past, to Joyce, is something which is important only as it sheds light on the present, as it makes clearer the basic patterns of existence which are common to all men in all ages. The mythic is actually the archetypal. Thus in *Ulysses* Joyce treats several bodies of myth— the wanderings of Odysseus, the theory that the Irish are the lost tribes of Israel, the life of Jesus, the quasi-historical-mythic life of William Shakespeare. These are the building blocks for today's truth. In *Finnegans Wake*, too, Joyce accepts fact and fiction on the same level: Tim Finnegan of the music-hall ballad coexists with Parnell, Finn MacCool with Napoleon, and the Ant and the Grasshopper with Brutus and Cassius. The rhythms of history are a thousand times more immediately discernible in myth. Individual events or dates are unimportant and irrelevant—it is myth which is the true history of any race and, ultimately, of mankind. It is in *Ulysses* that Joyce creates a living myth for his own immediate time.

The greatest and most obvious practitioner of this kind of history is Homer, and the ties between *Ulysses* and *The Odyssey* are well known. For Joyce it would seem that Homer, in choosing to place his narrative on a middle ground which incorporates history and myth, comes closer to an explanation of an epic yet human situation than have chroniclers before or since. Joyce himself let out the news of the superstructure of *Ulysses*, and in the *Wake* he is at pains to acknowledge the same debt. He describes his account of the Earwickers in one place as: "Storiella as she is syung" (267.7)—the Italian word for "history" is *storia*—and later as: "History as her is harped" (486.06). For a contemporary Irish Homer, who lived most of his life in Trieste, Zurich, and Paris, it is the technique or the approach to history which is all. Northrop Frye explains this in biographical terms: "In Joyce's personal life his break with the Catholic Church meant, not that he wanted to believe in something else, but that he wanted to transfer the mythical structure of the Church from faith and doctrine to creative imagination, thereby exchanging dogmatic Catholicism for imaginative catholicity."[5]

In the Telemachiad, the three opening chapters of *Ulysses* which deal most specifically with Dedalus, each of the central characters of the section is either constricted by history or uses it to explain away the problems of the present. The Englishman Haines excuses centuries of British tyranny and oppression in Ireland with the detached statement: "We feel in England that we have treated you rather unfairly. It seems history is to blame" (20), while Mulligan tries to enlist Stephen's aid in Hellenizing Ireland, whatever this may mean. To the schoolmaster Mr. Deasy: "All history moves toward one great goal, the manifestation of God" (34), while to the boys in Stephen's class: "history was a tale like any other too often heard, their land a pawnshop" (25). Dedalus himself sees the record as one of: "Jousts, slush and uproar of battles, the frozen deathspew of the slain, a shout of spear spikes baited with men's bloodied guts" (32). History is chaos or artificially structured confusion, and it is all too easy to read it in whatever way one wishes. Though it poses as being objective, history in fact is highly moral, and each set of events is subject to the personal interpretation of the historian. The moral tags of "good" and "bad" are interchanged rapidly as we move from one account to another. In the *Wake*, the narrator tells us that we have learned nothing: "You ruad that before, soaky, but all the bottles in sodemd history will not soften your bloodathirst" (52.05).

Stephen does have a sense of the oneness of experience: "The cords of all link back, strandentwining cables of all flesh" (38), but he dismisses the idea self-consciously with his humorous umbilical telephone: "Hello. Kinch here. Put me on to Edenville. Aleph, alpha: nought, nought, one" (38). He, like his fellow Irishmen, is so paralyzed by the sterility and pointlessness of his world that thinking has become simply an academic exercise. His thinking is a thinking on thinking, for he has divorced himself from others while piling up dry facts in the dusty corridors of his mind. He has become an intellectual voyeur, peeping at the learning of the past, and the heroic tradition of his native land has been relegated to: "Five lines of text and ten pages of notes about the folk and the fishgods of Dundrum" (12). Ireland herself, in the person of the old milkwoman, is now: "serving her conqueror and her gay betrayer, their common cuckquean" (14). Such is the state of affairs as Joyce introduces us to Leopold Bloom.

The thematic movement or progression of Bloom's odyssey is one from history to myth. Leopold Bloom does not begin as Ulysses; he is rooted in the mundane facts and data of a single historical moment: June 16, 1904. Joyce takes great pains to engulf his reader with specific detail after detail, until finally we come to know Bloom's character and environment almost as well as we know our own. It is only as the day progresses, and his portrait is fully sketched, that Bloom transcends the immediate reality and assumes mythic proportions. He is mythic not as the unique Leopold Bloom, but in the many archetypal guises he assumes as he moves from place to place. He is heroic not in his physical strength or his ability to outwit others, but in his affiliation with and sympathy for those around him. In chronicling Bloom, Joyce mythologizes his history, so that in understanding him we may understand ourselves, or at least our personal places in mythic history, our "family histrionic" (230.29) as Shem says.

In actuality, just as Bloom does not begin as Ulysses, he does not end as Ulysses either. Joyce's purpose is not to compare or contrast a Dubliner to a hero from Greek mythology, nor to fashion a twentieth-century Irish-Jewish-Catholic-Protestant Cuchullain. Rather, he is intent to underline the mythic potentiality inherent in anyone. As father, lover, husband, cuckold, ad man, and in his myriad other roles, Bloom achieves mythic stature in his own right. Joyce's assumption (in contrast to that of Yeats) seems to be that existing mythological systems have lost their relevance because they have been historicized, because they are viewed by contemporary men as past history which can have no bearing on today. It is thus through the mythologizing of present history, the immediate moment, that myth can regain its vitality. The process is both magical and pragmatic, and Joyce is "making mejical history all over the show!" (514.02).

In an early essay entitled "Drama and Life," Joyce had commented: "Every race has made its own myths and it is in these that early drama often finds an outlet. . . . When the mythus passes over the borderline and invades the temple of worship, the possibilities of its drama have lessened considerably."[6] It certainly is true that our present day society continues to fashion its own mythology, but unfortunately these creations have sunk to the level of the romantic ladies' magazine. Thus, on the beach in the Nausicaa chapter, Gerty MacDowell transforms Bloom into the dark and handsome stranger who will carry her away from the squalor and sorrow that her life entails:

Here was that of which she had so often dreamed. It was he who mattered and there was joy on her face because she wanted him because she felt instinctively that he was like no-one else. The very heart of the girlwoman went out to him, her dream-husband, because she knew on the instant it was him. If he had suffered, more sinned against than sinning, or even, even, if he had been himself a sinner, a wicked man, she cared not. Even if he was a protestant or methodist she could convert him easily if he truly loved her. [358]

The problem is, of course, that this pseudo-myth is actually no more than a dream, which has no tie whatsoever to reality. Gerty would certainly have her hands full with Bloom, who would pose more problems than the average "protestant or methodist." But, even more important, the dream can last no longer than a fleeting instant, as Bloom completes his masturbation and realizes that the girl is lame. The shift in style alone can provide the undercutting:

Poor girl! That's why she's left on the shelf and the others did a sprint. Thought something was wrong by the cut of her jib. Jilted beauty. A defect is ten times worse in a woman. But makes them polite. Glad I didn't know it when she was on show. Hot little devil all the same. Wouldn't mind. [367–68]

Illusion is no substitute for myth, and actually such illusion, once it is shattered, makes living in the world only that much more hard.

The damning flaw of twentieth-century man is that he has become myopic. He attempts to describe and define the spiritual in terms of facts and figures. This is why it is a monumental task for Stephen to awaken from his nightmare. In *Finnegans Wake* Joyce takes us beyond or below the conscious, waking mind, so that mythic archetypes can be loosed for our inspection, much the same thing he does in the Circe chapter of *Ulysses*. To embrace history is virtually to embrace science, and events must then be described in a way which robs them of their humanity. As Bloom prepares the cocoa during his early morning conversation with Stephen in the kitchen at 7 Eccles Street, the boiling water in the kettle is described as:

The phenomenon of ebullition. Fanned by a constant updraught of ventilation between the kitchen and the chimney-flue, ignition was communicated from the faggots of pre-combustible fuel to polyhedral masses of bituminous coal, containing in compressed mineral form the foliated fossilised decidua of primeval forests which had in turn derived their vegetative existence from the sun, primal source of heat (radiant), transmitted through omnipresent luminiferous diathermanous ether. [673–74]

The ludicrousness of the description is intentionally self-evident. If man's existence is a cycle or circle, or perhaps more correctly a series of gyres, what is important is the patterns of similarity which emerge as different cycles are superimposed or put up against each other. The dream book should be the history book, or, as the narrator tells us in the *Wake*: "What has gone? How it ends? Begin to forget it. It will remember itself from every sides, with all gestures, in each our word. Today's truth, tomorrow's trend. Forget, remember!" (614.19)

A salient characteristic of Joyce's technique is to deflate conventional myth through parody and satire while affirming and elevating the mythic elements of the present. The Cyclops chapter of *Ulysses* is an obvious example of this, and once again Joyce achieves many of his effects through style. Alternated along with such realistic descriptions of Barney Kiernan's pub as this rendering of the Citizen's love for his dog Garryowen: "And with that he took the bloody old towser by the scruff of the neck and, by Jesus, he near throttled him" (296), is this heraldic picture of bucolic Dublin social life:

Lovely maidens sit in close proximity to the roots of the lovely trees singing the most lovely songs while they play with all kinds of lovely objects as for example golden ingots, silvery fishes, crams of herrings, drafts of eels, codlings, creels of fingerlings, purple seagems and playful insects. [294]

The Citizen himself, an old Fenian who displays virtually every form of prejudice and bigotry known to modern man, is first characterized with the epic catalogue of adjectives usually reserved for Finn MacCool:

The figure seated on a large boulder at the foot of a round tower was that of a broadshouldered deepchested stronglimbed frankeyed redhaired freely freckled shaggybearded widemouthed largenosed longheaded deepvoiced barekneed brawnyhanded hairylegged ruddyfaced sinewyarmed hero. [296]

As Joyce continues to lampoon such pillars of society as medicine, journalism, academia, and politics, Bloom appears on the scene, and a countermotion to the downgrading begins. Politely chatting with the bar loungers, Bloom rises in stature through his very humanity. He is there to meet with Martin Cunningham and to straighten out the insurance policy of the deceased Paddy Dignam, so that Dignam's family can receive the benefits they need to live. Scorned as a Jew, a cheapskate, and even a Freemason, Bloom, when attacked by the Citizen, states most clearly Joyce's solution to the strait jacket of history:

—But it's no use, says he. Force, hatred, history, all that. That's not life for men and women, insult and hatred. And everybody knows that it's the very opposite of that that is really life.
—What? says Alf.
—Love, says Bloom. I mean the opposite of hatred. [333]

While Bloom is compared in this chapter to Ulysses, Christ, and Elijah, among others, it is as himself that he becomes mythologized. It is obvious that he has little to do with these aforementioned figures, and actually the comparison is ridiculous, as Joyce points out when he has Bloom ascend into Heaven "at an angle of fortyfive degrees over Donohoe's in Little Green Street like a shot off a shovel" (345). Yet, at the same time, Bloom's heroism, with all its bumbling, cannot be denied. He is a "new apostle to the gentiles" (333), but with a difference. To explain or to describe him in comparative terms is impossible, so that a new place in a new mythological system must be created to contain him. What makes him unique, paradoxically, is that his heroism is actually only humanness, something we would not ordinarily expect to be so unusual in a human being. The obvious, painful fact, however, is that charity and love are characteristics not often met with in this modern age, so that Bloom must tower above his fellows, a new Ulysses or Finn MacCool. As Joyce's womanly-man, his deeds are acts of compassion rather than strength,[7] so that Bloom, again despite his many flaws, becomes a genuinely authentic mythic figure.

It is in the Circe chapter most directly that Bloom's history is mythologized, since this Walpurgisnacht section describes the stripping away of mental pretense and repression and the ultimate facing of a different reality. It is the nightmare from which Leopold Bloom, and even Stephen Dedalus, will awaken refreshed. Here both characters are forced to assume the roles and positions which their conscious minds had forbidden, and thus they are compelled to deal with the elemental aspects of their beings. To be sure, each has his own personal idiosyncrasies—Stephen's guilt over his mother's death and Bloom's sexual fantasies—but the reader soon comes to see that these are common to every man. It is in the recognition and acceptance of the nightmares of the mind that these two Dubliners free themselves from history and appear as mythic.

Stephen proposes ironically at the outset of the chapter that: "gesture, not music, not odours, would be a universal language, the gift of tongues rendering visible not the lay sense but the first entelechy, the structural rhythm" (432), and this is exactly what occurs in Circe. Bloom is attacked by all of the women of his life, from Martha Clifford to Mrs. Breen, and he is put on trial for his past peccadilloes. All of his sins are personified and march past him accusingly, while in a counter-fantasy he is elected Lord Mayor of Dublin and prophesies the "new Bloomusalem in the Nova Hibernia of the future" (484). It would seem that the cleansing is complete when he gives birth to eight children, is dubbed the "womanly-man," and is humiliated by Bella Cohen. Yet the most revelatory and central of his experiences follows—his voyeuristic participation in the lovemaking of Molly Bloom and Blazes Boylan. His realization of this scene is the one thing he had forced from his consciousness throughout the day:

Boylan
(*To Bloom, over his shoulder.*) You can apply your eye to the keyhole and play with yourself while I just go through her a few times.

Bloom
Thank you, sir, I will, sir. May I bring two men chums to witness the deed and take a snapshot? (*He holds an ointment jar.*) Vaseline, sir? Orange-flower? . . . Lukewarm water? [566]

From this point on, Bloom has accomplished himself, and Joyce has accomplished a mythic figure who stands at the center of the twentieth-century consciousness. In facing up to his innermost fears, and accepting if not exorcising them, Bloom is universalized as an essential entity. A formal account of June 16, 1904, would tell us nothing of this.

What is equally important about the events of this chapter is that they pose as history yet they are actually figments of the innermost imagination, the subconscious. They are more real than the "real" events in Bloom's past history, since they reveal and document the inner life of an individual and tell us (and him) more about the man than any biography or historical account could ever do. In fact, these fantasies are much more Bloom's history than any record of what transpired at some specified point in time. They are mythic in that they represent feelings and predicaments which are common to the race, which configure and explain the history of a people. When Stephen smashes the chandelier with his ashplant: "*Time's livid final flame leaps and, in the following darkness, ruin of all space, shattered glass and toppling masonry*" (583). Joyce has here destroyed history as well, and men's eyes are set right for seeing in the darkness.

In *Finnegans Wake* Joyce continues with this negation of history, but here he goes even farther. By accompanying each character with strings of multiple historical and mythological identifications, he denies the single historical identity of each. Rather than saying that Anna Livia, for example, is *like* Eva, Cleopatra, and Queen Victoria, he insists that she *is* all of these and more. None of the Earwickers can exist finally in his own right, for each is interchangeable with a myriad number of separate entities. None of them can really be dealt with singly, for each needs his many complements in order to be understood. Ultimately we must concern ourselves with the fathoming of woman, man, mother, father, and must discard the futile hope of ever knowing an individual. Beset with a problem such as this, the history book will be of little help.

The intent in the *Wake* is no less serious than that in *Ulysses*, but the problem is complicated by the bantering tone which the narrator often assumes. From the first page of the novel, the reader is swamped with questions, riddles, anagrams which he cannot solve, and the narrator's reaction is usually a snicker or a jibe: "You is feeling like you was lost in the bush, boy? . . . You most shouts out: Bethicket me for a stump of a beech if I have the poultriest notions what the farest he all means" (112.03). We may compile list after list of allusions to Irish folklore or references to skirmishes in the many wars of history, but we cannot even begin to answer Shem's first riddle of the universe: "When is a man not a man?" (170.05). The narrator is attempting to sting us into seeing.

One of the central keys to an understanding of *Finnegans Wake* is the realization on the part of the reader that all these puzzles are false trails. There are literally hundreds of versions offered as to what happened to HCE in Phoenix Park, and each is just as valid and invalid as any of the others. Postulated behind the teasing of the narrative is the idea that a man's existence cannot be defined by the specific events which comprise it. All of the characters are mythic and archetypal—there are no dependable physical descriptions of any of them—and most often they are reduced to such basic oppositions as tree and stone, river and mountain. They have no real or definite histories of their own.

Thus Joyce gives the final speech of the novel (if there can be anything finite in a cyclical work) to the spirit of the river Liffey in Dublin. The voice is timeless and spaceless, as is the act of regeneration which it describes:

And it's old and old it's sad and old it's sad and weary I go back to you, my cold father, my cold mad father, my cold mad feary father, till the near sight of the mere size of him, the moyles and moyles of it, moananoaning, makes me seasilt saltsick and I rush, my only, into your arms. [627.36]

Anna Livia cannot be pinpointed as the wife of a pubkeeper named Humphrey Chimpden Earwicker—the washerwoman tried earlier and failed. She is the basic female principle, as HCE is the male, and she must be apprehended on this mythic level. Joyce leaves us no choice if we are to comprehend his work.

It would be misguided to attempt to see James Joyce as an original thinker. He founds no new philosophic system, nor does he point the way to the accomplishment of a bourgeois utopia. He sees his role as essentially an artistic one, as the shaper or arranger of the basic materials of life into a meaningful form. Especially in his last two novels, *Ulysses* and *Finnegans Wake*, he is mainly concerned with the description of a technique for contemplating reality, and such a perspective necessitates the destruction of a pragmatic, historical point of view. He does not ask that one transcend the commonplaces of the everyday, but only that one remain aware of larger patterns and rhythms which adhere to the movements of a single man or a single nation. His fictions are blatantly fictions—art—and they are believable only in what they have to say about humanity. A Daedalian figure himself, Joyce fashions and clarifies the mythic bedrock upon which contemporary civilization must rest, transforming "all marryvoising moodmoulded cyclewheeling history." (186.01)

Notes

1. References to *Ulysses* (New York: Random House, 1961) and *Finnegans Wake* (New York: Viking Press, 1964) will be drawn from these editions.
2. *James Joyce and the Making of Ulysses* (Bloomington: Indiana University Press, 1967), p. 129.
3. "*Ulysses*, Order, and Myth," *James Joyce: Two Decades of Criticism*, ed., Seon Givens (New York: Vanguard Press, 1948), p. 201.
4. Givens, pp. 201–202.
5. "Quest and Cycle in *Finnegans Wake*," *James Joyce Review*, I (February 1957), 39.
6. *The Critical Writings of James Joyce*, ed., Ellsworth Mason and Richard Ellmann (New York: Viking Press, 1970), p. 43.
7. Richard Ellmann notes that: "The victories of Bloom are mental, in spite of the pervasive physicality of Joyce's book," *James Joyce* (New York: Oxford University Press, 1965), p. 371.

Image and
Imagery
in Joyce's *Portrait*:   *John B. Smith*
A Computer-Assisted
Analysis

The most widely discussed aspect of *A Portrait of the Artist as a Young Man* has been the esthetic theory developed by Stephen Dedalus in Chapter V of the novel. Examinations range from considering Joyce's modifications of his Thomistic sources to assessing the utility of the theory as a basis for writing. Most critics agree that the theory is important for an understanding of Joyce's own art; some think it represents the esthetics he held the rest of his life.[1] But no one has demonstrated fully its applicability to the novel.

The second most widely accepted critical notion about the novel is the irony that accompanies the portrait of Stephen, particularly in the later chapters. It is unnecessary to mention very many specific examples; however, the most extreme irony of all may be that a young "poet" who has written only a handful of bad poems can seriously propose a complex esthetic theory. Perhaps Joyce intended the theory to be as ironic as the theorizer. I don't believe this to be the case, but even the possibility makes debatable the theory's applicability to Joyce and the novel.

My discussion will focus on the most fundamental aspect of the esthetic, the definition of image. From the theory presented in Chapter V, I shall derive a thesis that can then be applied to the whole *Portrait*. If confirmed, it will demonstrate that the theory is, indeed, Joyce's own. Possibly, it will also lead to new insights into the artistic structure and form of the novel itself.

The theory of image developed by Stephen during his conversation with Lynch is based on a sentence from Aquinas which he translates as follows: "Three things are needed for beauty, wholeness, harmony, and radiance."[2] Wholeness he identifies with *integritas*:

An esthetic image is presented to us either in space or in time. What is audible is presented in time, what is visible is presented in space. But, temporal or spatial, the esthetic image is first luminously apprehended as self-bounded and self-contained upon the immeasurable background of space or time which is not it. You apprehend it as *one* thing. You see it as one whole. You apprehend its wholeness. That is *integritas*. [212]

Several important points are implied in this passage. First, the image is related to the act or process of perception itself. Second, the mind which receives the sense impression, by reflex or intent, is an active agent in the process. It *distinguishes* the image from the non-image by separating a portion of the sensory input from the rest. Clearly, then, the image described here is part of the phenomenological level of experience and not the actual physical reality that induces the sensory response.

Phenomenological experience can be regarded as the interface between two components of the mind, the subjective and the objective. Subjective experience consists of the subconscious and part of the conscious mind. Together, these two aspects of the subjective form the continuity of personality. Objective experience, while originating in the sensory mechanisms, represents that aspect of the mind where sensory stimulae accumulate. It is the interface between the subjective and the objective where perception takes place and where the image exists.

The next stage in the process, *consonantia*, Stephen identifies with harmony:

—Then said Stephen, you pass from point to point, led by its formal lines; you apprehend it as balanced part against part within its limits; you feel the rhythm of its structure. In other words the synthesis of immediate perception is followed by the analysis of apprehension. Having first felt that it is *one* thing you feel now that it is a thing. You apprehend it as complex, multiple, divisible, separable, made up of its parts, the result of its parts and their sum, harmonious. That is *consonantia*. [212]

During this analytic stage, the perceiver discovers the relations among the various parts of the image as well as their relations to larger aggregates and to the whole image. These relations Stephen considers harmony, but he does not say where this harmony exists. Is it part of the physical world? is it solely within the mind? or is it part of the perceptual interface between the two? Stephen does, however, hint at an answer: "Having first *felt* that it is one thing you *feel* now that it is a thing." Since the sentence is at the center of the discussion of *consonantia*, the two uses of the verb *feel* suggest that the harmony is part of subjective experience. The danger in this interpretation is that if pushed to its extreme it could lead to misunderstanding. That is, if the stage of harmony takes place after conceptualization and is not subject to verification, that harmony could be illusory.

The relation between harmony and objective experience is suggested in the discussion of *claritas*. After rejecting the notion of a transcendental idealism for art as well as an art that is autonomous, Stephen goes on to define the term:

When you have apprehended that basket as one thing and have then analysed it according to its form and apprehended it as a thing you make the only synthesis which is logically and esthetically permissible. You see that it is that thing which it is and no other thing. The radiance of which he speaks is the scholastic *quidditas*, the *whatness* of a thing. This supreme quality is felt by the artist when the esthetic image is first conceived in his imagination. The mind in that mysterious instant Shelley likened beautifully to a fading coal. The instant wherein that supreme quality of beauty, the clear radiance of the esthetic image, is apprehended luminously by the mind which has been arrested by its wholeness and fascinated by its harmony is the luminous silent stasis of esthetic pleasure, a spiritual state very like to that cardiac condition which the Italian physiologist Luigi Galvani, using a phrase almost as beautiful as Shelley's, called the enchantment of the heart. [213]

On the most basic level the synthesis described above represents recognition. After distinguishing the image from the non-image followed by analyzing the relations among its parts, the perceiver recognizes what it is. Defined in this manner, the image exists in virtually all acts of perception, even the most mundane. But this reading ignores the affective dimension of the passage. In the discussion of harmony, the strongest terms used were *feel* and perhaps *harmonious*; this passage abounds with words and expressions that carry definite emotional overtones: *radiance, mysterious instant, fading coal, supreme quality of beauty, clear radiance, silent stasis of esthetic pleasure, spiritual state, enchantment of the heart.* However, not all images are of this intensity—esthetic images or epiphanies as they were called in the earlier *Stephen Hero*. Experiences vary in their intensity and importance for the individual. What Stephen is rejecting is the idea that art must concern itself only with certain themes or aspects of life. Thus, Stephen later in *Ulysses* can equate God with a shout in the street. Even the most seemingly trivial experience is capable of great, even religious-like, relevance for an individual. This difference in impact of various images can be explained in terms of synthesis and harmony.

Coincident with recognition is the synthesis of the objective experience as it becomes part of the subjective experience of the perceiver and merges into the continuity of personality. Both the individual parts of the image as well as the structural relation among them are synthesized in the perceptual act. An analogy suggested by A. D. Hope is helpful for understanding this process:

If we take the metaphor of the traveller pausing on the hill top and surveying the landscape before him with the help of a map it may be possible to give some idea of the nature of the conception that underlies Joyce's description of *claritas*. If we imagine the map as in the traveller's mind and as the work of his mind, such that instead of the formal signs of roads, houses, fields and hills the mind has constructed a map-picture, we shall have something like the phantasma, or in the case under discussion, the esthetic image. We can further imagine the map-picture to be a transparent one such that when it is held between the intellectual eye and the landscape the traveller not only perceives the landscape endowed with its formal meaning, he is also able to observe the exact correspondence of the details of the map with the details of the landscape before him. He becomes aware of the truth of his mental work.[3]

The harmonious relations among the parts felt or sensed by the perceiver are seen to fit, to be verified in the objective experience. In that instant when expectation is confirmed we might expect a rush of emotion, as if the individual has sensed among the components of experience a harmonious structure that actually exists in the physical world. He may feel a harmonious union between himself and the universe he perceives. That union, of course, is not between physical reality and epidermis, but between the subjective and objective components of experience. Furthermore, the magnitude of that emotional response is likely to be related to the number, variety, and personal importance of the components that are seen to come into conjunction, like the figures in the map that fall into place relative to the landscape; the greater the number of pieces that are seen to fit, the greater the emotional response. Stated another way, the intensity and importance of an image for a particular individual is likely to be directly related to both the number of components of an experience and some measure of their importance for him, personally. It is this thesis or expectation that I wish to evaluate for Stephen Dedalus in the novel. It suggests that the most important moments in the development of his personality should be related to those passages in the text where the heaviest concentrations of important images or image components occur. If substantiated, this argument will demonstrate the applicability of Stephen's esthetic theory toward Joyce's esthetics, at least in *Portrait*.

Before going on I should clarify the terminology that will be used. There have long been major differences of critical opinion concerning the term *image*. Frank Kermode, for example, has adopted Stephen's definition in its most intense form;[4] Caroline Spurgeon, on the other hand, has used the term to refer to any word with sensory or thematic value, like *black*, *hot*, or *bitter*.[5] I shall use the term *image* in the sense that Caroline Spurgeon uses it (earlier this was called an image component); for the more intense experiences, I shall use the term *epiphanal image* or more simply, *epiphany*, as Stephen did in *Stephen Hero*. My thesis asserts a fundamental quantitative relation in *Portrait*, at least, between the two poles of thought within literary criticism concerning the definition of images. If true for *Portrait*, the approach may have interesting applications in other works as well.

In order to apply the thesis uniformly and comprehensively to the novel, I used a high-speed computer. This involved two major steps: the first consisted of a series of rather mechanical operations that began with the complete, printed text and ended with a list of words selected as images and stored in a form that made them readily accessible for the computer; the second step involved translating the thesis, expressed in traditional literary critical terms, into a model that the computer could evaluate. Since my emphasis is on interpretation and not methodology, I shall pass over the first step except to point out that the selection of some thirteen hundred words that have sensory or thematic value represents my own judgment. I have shown my list to several other Joyce scholars whose opinions I respect highly; and we agree that it is a reasonable list, particularly for a study that is concerned with the larger, global patterns in the novel. Logically, then, this set of words selected as images represents an axiom on which the study is based.

The second step, the translation of the thesis into a form that the computer can apply to the novel, is more interesting and crucial to the study. The textual phenomenon of the number of images in a passage and the relative importance among these individual images I termed *richness of imagery*. That is, richness of imagery in a particular scene in the novel is related to both the numbers of images occurring in that scene and the degree or weight of importance of the particular images. From an affective point of view, then, it is possible for two scenes with approximately the same number of images to differ in their impact if the images in one scene carry strong connotations for the character and those in the other represent merely his impressions of the physical locale. For a measure of importance for any single occurrence of an image I used a weight of the total number of times that image occurred in the entire novel. Thus, more frequent images *tend* to have greater impact than less frequent images. I would not argue this assumption for pairs of images or even small groups of images—indeed, there are images that occur only once in the novel that are very important; however, in global terms, when applied to all of the imagery, the assumption seems reasonable.

The model was applied to each 500 word segment of the text (500 words represents slightly more than a page in the standard Viking edition) and a value representing the richness of imagery for that section was computed. As the number and importance of the images in these sections vary, so the value reflecting these factors varies. The results are plotted on the graph (p. 225). To read the graph, assume that the novel runs from left to right (first word, *Once*, occurs at the extreme left side and the last word, *stead*, occurs at the extreme right). The richness of imagery rises and falls as one proceeds through the novel.

An examination of the graph shows that the richest scene in the novel in terms of imagery is the pandybat episode at the end of Chapter I. This should not be surprising since virtually all major themes in the chapter focus at that point in the narrative; similarly, its impact affects Stephen throughout the rest of the novel and into *Ulysses*. If we look closely at the base of that peak, we can see that it tops a long, sustained buildup in intensity of imagery. This pattern suggests why some experiences reach epiphanal intensity while others subside before that point. One criterion for epiphany may be the necessity of sustaining the experience for a period of time. During this particular scene, more and more of Stephen's attention is on what is occurring around him; conse-

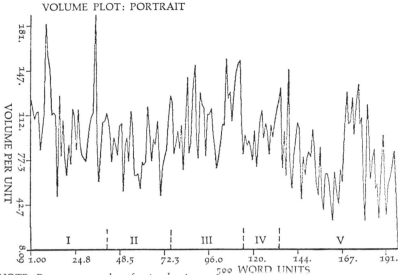

VOLUME PLOT: PORTRAIT

VOLUME PER UNIT

181. 147. 112. 77.3 42.7 8.09

500 WORD UNITS

I II III IV V

1.00 24.8 48.5 72.3 96.0 120. 144. 167. 191.

NOTE: Roman numerals refer to chapters.

quently, he is aware of more factors of experience than usual. This stimulation leads to even greater concentration and awareness until the
experience explodes into epiphany as the pandybat strikes. The interesting aspect of this particular epiphany is that it is highly negative
connotatively; but, as suggested earlier, the basic criterion necessary
for the "esthetic image" or epiphany is its emotional intensity for the
developing personality. The other high point of richness in the chapter
occurs during Stephen's fevered dreams in the infirmary when he confronts empathically for the first time the reality of death.

The general level of richness in Chapter II is low relative to the other
four chapters. The chapter ends, however, with the most intense scene
in it where Stephen has his first sexual experience. That the richness
and intensity of this scene are low relative to the others discussed here
perhaps reflects the lack of sustained buildup in the passage. Thus, some
epiphanal experiences appear to be richer on an affective level than others.

Chapter III has two clusters of peaks. The first deals with the frightening
sermons of the retreat in which the horrors of hell are presented in graphic
and sensuous detail. The emotional impact of these experiences is realized
in the subsequent dream of the goatish figures and Stephen's headlong
flight to confession. The latter marks an epiphanal experience of extreme
religious ideality.

In Chapter IV there is a sequence of three peaks culminating in the epiphany on the beach in which Stephen sensed that the girl's image has merged with his own. Earlier, it was suggested that the sense of dissolution of the gap between subjective and objective experiences would mark moments of epiphanal intensity. This seems to be explicitly the case here: "Her image had passed into his soul for ever and no word had broken the holy silence of his ecstasy." (p. 172) The beach scene is most important since it represents the turning point in Stephen's search for a vocation. At this point, having left the priesthood behind, his dedication of himself to esthetic creativity is consummated.

Chapter V is interesting because it contains, in addition to a scene of sustained richness, the passage with the lowest level in the entire novel. That scene concerns Stephen's walk with Lynch during which he develops his esthetic theory. There the emphasis is on the intellect as opposed to the senses. The scene that follows the conversation and which appears on the graph to be of definite epiphanal intensity shows Stephen waking and composing the villanelle. After dedicating himself to art at the close of Chapter IV, Stephen here realizes the first creative product of that decision.

In summary, the thesis derived from a consideration of the esthetic theory of Chapter V suggested that there would be a close correspondence between the sections of text richest in imagery and the moments of major importance in the development of Stephen's personality. The model, when applied to the text, draws our attention to the pandybat episode, Stephen's first awareness of death, his first experience with sex, a retreat marked by frightening descriptions of Hell, a nightmare and subsequent confession, the esthetic experience on the beach when he decides that his destiny is to become an artist, and, finally, the composition of this first respectable poem. Clearly, these are the experiences that are most influential in the development of his personality. One implication which I will mention only in passing is that the personality of Stephen progresses by stages and remains relatively stable between experiences such as those listed above. It should be possible, therefore, to define the structure of his mind by noting the exact changes in associations among images that take place at these moments.

Secondly, the thesis suggested that there should be differences in intensity among these epiphanal experiences as well as between them and "everyday" acts of perception. A difference among epiphanal experiences is particularly apparent in the pandybat episode and the experience with sex. As we might expect, the former is much more influential in the long run than the latter. Continuity exists among all acts of perception; but because some experiences are sustained and culminate in epiphany while others are interrupted and dissipate to the level of ordinary awareness, a difference in degree may appear a difference in kind. Consequently, even the most trivial event—such as a shout in the street—is capable of extreme, even religious significance for an individual.

Finally, the thesis suggested that the rush of emotion accompanying an experience of epiphanal intensity is related to the perceiver's feeling that he has in some way merged with the physical reality around him. This phenomenon has been shown to exist explicitly in the esthetic experience on the beach at the end of Chapter IV and it could doubtlessly be found in other scenes.

By using the computer, I have sought to demonstrate from a logical basis what is taking place on the affective level both within the fictive world of Stephen and in the phenomenological world of the reader as he progresses through the novel. This reconciliation of logical abstraction with affective response is, ultimately, the function of esthetic theory for the artist and of literary interpretation for the reader.

Notes

1. A. D. Hope, "The Esthetic Theory of James Joyce," *Australasian Journal of Psychology and Philosophy*, XXI (Dec., 1943). Reprinted in Thomas Connolly, *Joyce's Portrait: Criticisms and Critiques* (New York: Appleton-Century-Crofts, 1962), p. 183.
2. James Joyce, *A Portrait of the Artist as a Young Man* (New York: Viking Press, 1965), p. 212. All future references to *Portrait* are from this edition and page numbers will be given in the text.
3. Hope, pp. 200–201.
4. Frank Kermode, *The Romantic Image* (New York: Vintage Books, 1964), p. 1.
5. Caroline Spurgeon, *Shakespeare's Imagery and What It Tells Us* (Boston: Beacon Press, 1961), p. 5.

An Eye-Poem
for the Ear

Kenneth Burke

(With Prose Introduction,
Glosses, and After-Words)

Introduction

The author spent the winter of 1968–69 on Brooklyn Heights, in a hotel apartment overlooking New York Harbor and the skyscrapers of lower Manhattan. It was a fate-laden season. His close companion of many years was still with him, but physically immobilized by an inexorably "progressing" illness. And while the couple could but watch it grow worse, in response to her condition he developed an attitude which he thought of as being "psychically" immobilized.

They were living on the same street where Hart Crane had lived when in Brooklyn. Below them was the river which Whitman had crossed by ferry. Accordingly the relation between Whitman's symbolic crossing on the river and Hart Crane's symbol of crossing on a bridge above the river suggested a third step, a mental state in which a Poetic *I* but *looked* across. Hence the poem's title: "Eye-Crossing—From Brooklyn to Manhattan."*

Marianne Moore had already moved from Brooklyn to Manhattan, but she graciously agreed to let the author honor himself by dedicating the poem to her. However, when it was printed in *The Nation* (June 2, 1969) last-minute editorial exigencies resulted in the omission of all but her name. I take this opportunity to restore the dedication in full:

> To Marianne Moore
> whose exacting yet kindly verses
> give us exceptionally many twists and turns
> to rejoice about
> even in a lean season

In one regard at least, it is especially fitting that I should contribute these particular pages to this particular book. Before the poem was published, Henry Sams had kindly distributed copies of it to a graduate class

---

* The poem itself, without glosses and introductory matter, first appeared in *The Nation,* and the author and editors are indebted to Carey McWilliams, editor of *The Nation,* for permission to reprint it in a slightly different text than its original appearance.

of his at The Pennsylvania State University, and had sent me copies of the students' comments, which they wrote before receiving any information about the work's authorship.

Needless to say, I personally was much engrossed with the comments, which ranged from very friendly ones to some that were quite rough. I had fully intended to send an answer insofar as the various observations and judgments (which, as is usual in cases of this sort, were often at considerable odds with one another) provided opportunities for a general discussion of related critical issues.

The ups and downs reached their extreme when one student, whose paper had been on the gruff side, parenthetically remarked: "If there ever was an *oral* poem, this is it"—and I cannot conceive of a comment I'd be more happy to hear, as the title of this offering bears witness. But not until now could I find the time to write thus belatedly the intended reply, which loses by the delay, though it may profit by some considerations I encountered when reading the poem to audiences in the course of my journeyings on the "Academic Circuit."

But to the poem itself, interlarded with some Glosses.

EYE-CROSSING—FROM BROOKLYN TO MANHATTAN

I

Scheming to pick my way past Charybdýlla
(or do I mean Scyllybdis?)
caught in the midst of being nearly over,
not "midway on the roadway of our life,"
a septuagenarian valetudinarian
thrown into an airy osprey-eyrie
with a view most spacious
(and every bit of it our country's primal gateway even),
although, dear friends, I'd love to see you later,
after the whole thing's done,
comparing notes, us comically telling one another
just what we knew or thought we knew
that others of us didn't,
all told what fools we were, every last one of us—
I'd love the thought, a humane after-life,
more fun than a bbl. of monkeys,
but what with being sick of wooing Slumber,
I'll settle gladly for Oblivion.

Gloss I

The opening distortion of Scylla and Charybdis is mildly an annunciation of some sort, the vague sign of a temperamental inclination. Or it is like pointing with a sweep of the arm rather than with the index finger.

AN EYE-POEM FOR THE EAR   229

Count me among those for whom not the least of their delight in Chaucer is the fact that his vocabulary has somewhat the effect of modern English deliberately distorted, a kind of "proto-Joyceanism."

As regards my allusion to the opening line of *The Divine Comedy*: Since Dante's line is so "summational," my reference to it from the standpoint of a "septuagenarian valetudinarian" is meant to be summation by contrast.

I like to pronounce "bbl." as "b-b-l."

II

Weep, Hypochondriasis (hell, I mean smile):
The bell rang, I laid my text aside,
The day begins in earnest, they have brought the mail.
And now to age and ailments add
a thirteen-page single-spaced typed missile-missive,
to start the New Year right.
On the first of two-faced January,
". . . the injuries you inflict upon me . . . persecution . . .
such legal felonies . . . unremitting efforts . . . malice, raids,
slander, conspiracy . . . your spitefulness . . ."
—just when I talked of getting through the narrows,
now I'm not so sure.
Smile, Hypochondriasis, (hell, I mean wanly weep).

III

So let's begin again:
Crossing by eye from Brooklyn to Manhattan
(Walt's was a ferry-crossing,
Hart's by bridge)—
to those historic primi donni,
now add me, and call me what you will.
From Brooklyn, now deserted
by both Marianne Moore and the Dodgers—
an eye-crossing
with me knocked cross-eyed or cockeyed
by a saddening vexing letter
from a dear friend gone sour.
I think of a Pandora's box uncorked
while I was trying to untie
Laocoön's hydra-headed Gordian knot,
entangled in a maze of Daedalus,

plus modern traffic jam cum blackout.
Let's begin again.

Gloss III

"Primi donni." An invention remotely in the tradition of the classical satiric usage (as with Catullus) whereby, since the male sect of Galli (priests of Cybele) resorted to castration as one of their rites, they were referred to in the feminine form, *Gallae*. But my male plurals for the Italian *prima donna* botch things twice, by being made as though Italian feminine *donna* were matched by a Latin word of masculine gender, *donnus*. My only argument for this solecistic neologism is that there is a crying need for it with regard to artistic psychology, even where matters of sexual persuasion (as with Walt and Hart) are not involved.

IV

The architectural piles, erections, impositions,
monsters of high-powered real estate promotion—
from a room high on Brooklyn Heights
the gaze is across and UP, to those things' peaks,
their arrogance!
When measured by this scale of views from Brooklyn
they are as though deserted.

And the boats worrying the harbor
they too are visibly deserted
smoothly and silent
moving in disparate directions
each as but yielding to a trend that bears it
like sticks without volition
carried on a congeries
of crossing currents.

And void of human habitation,
the cars on Madhatter's Eastern drive-away
formless as stars
speeding slowly
close by the feet of the godam mystic giants—

a restlessness unending, back and forth
(glimpses of a drive, or drivenness,
from somewhere underneath the roots of reason)

me looking West, towards Manhattan, Newark, West
Eye-crossing I have seen the sunrise
gleaming in the splotch and splatter
of Western windows facing East.

V

East? West?
Between USSR and USA,
their Béhemoth and our Behémoth,
a dialogue of sorts?
Two damned ungainly beasts,
threats to the entire human race's race
but for their measured dread of each the other.
How give or get an honest answer?

Forgive me for this boustrophedon mood
going from left to right, then right to left,
pulling the plow thus back and forth alternately
a digging of furrows not in a field to plant,
but on my own disgruntled dumb-ox forehead.

My Gawd! Begin again!

Gloss V

Here the East-West shifting of the previous stanza, moving into the
political dimension, takes advantage of the fact that the word "behemoth"
can be accented on either the first or second syllable.

  Not all readers are likely to know (as the author didn't know during
most of his lifetime) that "boustrophedon" is an adjective or adverb for
a kind of writing that proceeds alternately from right to left and left to
right. Ideally the reader should consider not only the *meaning* of the
word (here applied by analogy to political quandaries), but also its *etymology* should be taken into account: as the ox turns in plowing; from
Greek *bous*, ox, and *strophos*, turning, plus an adverbial suffix.

VI

Turn back. Now just on this side:
By keeping your wits about you,

you can avoid the voidings,
the dog-signs scattered on the streets and sidewalks
(you meet them face to faeces)
and everywhere the signs of people
(you meet them face to face)

The Waltman, with time and tide before him,
he saw things face to face, he said so

then there came a big blow
the pavements got scoured drastically

—exalted, I howled back
into the teeth of the biting wind
me in Klondike zeal
inhaling powdered dog-dung
(here's a new perversion)
now but an essence on the fitful gale

Still turning back.
Surmarket—mock-heroic confrontation at—
(An Interlude)

Gloss VI

"Now just on this side." Although the emphasis in the poem is upon the
view of Manhattan and the harbor (in the attempt to profit by the summational connotations of a panorama) there arises secondarily the need
to build up some sense of the *terminus a quo*, in Brooklyn Heights. To
this end a characteristic "civic issue" is chosen. It is at once trivial and
serious. In keeping with the theme, the adverb "drastically" is to be
recommended for its etymological exactitude.

As regards the substitution of "surmarket" for "supermarket" (after
the analogy of "surrealism" for "super-realism"), I plead poetic license.

VII

CONFRONTATION AT BOHACKS
(an interlude)

Near closing time, we're zeroing in.
Ignatius Panallergicus (that's me)
his cart but moderately filled
(less than five dollars buys the lot)
he picks the likeliest queue and goes line up
then waits, while for one shopper far ahead
the lady at the counter tick-ticks off and tallies
items enough to gorge a regiment.

Then, lo! a possibility not yet disclosed sets in.
While Panallergicus stands waiting
next into line a further cart wheels up,
whereat Ignatius Panallergicus (myself, unknowingly
the very soul of Troublous Helpfullness) suggests:
"It seems to me, my friend, you'd come out best
on that line rather than on one of these."
And so (let's call him "Primus")
Primus shifts.

Development atop development:
Up comes another, obviously "Secundus,"
to take his stand behind Ignatius, sunk in thought.
No sooner had Secundus joined the line
than he addressed Ignatius Panallerge approximately thus:
"Good neighbor, of this temporary junction,
pray, guard my rights in this arrangement
while I race off to get one further item,"
then promptly left, and so things stood.

But no. Precisely now in mankind's pilgrimage
who suddenly decides to change his mind
but Primus who, abandoning his other post,
returns to enroll himself again in line behind Ignatius.
Since, to that end, he acts to shove aside
Secundus' cart and cargo, Crisis looms.

Uneasy, Panallergicus explains:
"A certain . . . I am sorry . . . but you see . . .
I was entrusted . . . towards the preservation of . . ."
but no need protest further—
for here is Secundus back,
and wrathful of his rights
as ever epic hero of an epoch-making war

Both aging champions fall into a flurry
of fishwife fury, even to such emphatical extent
that each begins to jettison the other's cargo.
While the contestants rage, pale Panallerge
grins helplessly at others looking on.
But Primus spots him in this very act and shouts
for all to hear, "It's all *his* fault . . . *he* was the one . . .
he brought this all about . . ."
and Panallergicus now saw himself
as others see him, with a traitor's wiles.

I spare the rest. (There was much more to come)
How An Authority came swinging in,
twisted Secundus' arm behind his back
and rushed him bumbling from the store.
How further consequences flowed in turn,
I leave all that unsaid.
And always now, when edging towards the counter,
his cargo in his cart,
our Ignatz Panallerge Bruxisticus
(gnashing his costly, poorly fitting dentures)
feels all about his head
a glowering anti-glowing counter-halo . . .

Is that a millstone hung about his neck?
No, it is but the pressing-down
of sixty plus eleven annual milestones.

(It was before the damning letter came.
Had those good burghers also known of that!)

Gloss VII

As the reader might suspect, this episode is the account of an incident
that did actually take place.

On the assumption that "bruxism" means an inclination to grind or
gnash the teeth, as the result of his *agon* Panallergicus is endowed with
a transfigured identity appropriately named "Bruxisticus."

About the edges of the line, "and rushed him bumbling from the store,"
the author (perhaps too privately) hears a reference to the "bum's rush."

The word "counter-halo" was intended to draw on two quite different
meanings of "counter": (1) as with the adjective "opposite"; (2) as with
the noun for the check-out desk where the encounter took place.

The inclusion of this episode may present something of a puzzle to
those readers who do not share the author's apprehensive attitude toward
supermarkets. Though he shops at them regularly, he never enters one
without thinking of the whole breed as the flowering of a civilization in
decay. There is the criminal wastage due to sheer tricks of packaging
(and the corresponding amount of trash-disposal involved in such mer-
chandizing). But first of all there is the fantastic amount of poison that
is now looked upon as "normal" to the processing and marketing of foods.
Toss it. On one side up comes the TV commercials for indigestion. On
the other side up comes the TV dinners.

VIII

But no! Turn back from turning back. Begin again:
of a late fall evening
I walked on the Esplanade
looking across at the blaze of Walt's Madhatter
and north to Hart's graceful bridge, all lighted
in a cold, fitful gale I walked
on the Esplanade in Brooklyn now deserted
by both Marianne and the Dodgers.
Things seemed spooky—
eight or ten lone wandering shapes,
and all as afraid of me as I of them?
We kept a wholesome distance from one another.
Had you shrieked for help in that bluster
who'd have heard you?

Me and my alky in that cold fitful bluster
on the Esplanade that night
above the tiers of the mumbling unseen traffic
    It was scary
      it was ecstacatic

Gloss VIII

This section does not do justice to the Esplanade, which is built above highways, yet is like a park that is in turn like the extension of back-yards. And there is the fantastic vista. The Esplanade is an architectural success, well worthy of civic pride. But the words "Me and my alky" explain why our agonist had the courage, or bravado, or sheer fool-hardiness to go there thus late at night.

IX

Some decades earlier, before my Pap
fell on evil days (we then were perched
atop the Palisades, looking East, and down
upon the traffic-heavings of the Hudson)

I still remember Gramma (there from Pittsburgh for a spell)
watching the tiny tugs tug monsters.
Out of her inborn sweetness and memories
of striving, putting all that together,
"Those poor little tugs!" she'd say.
God only knows what all
she might be being sorry for.

And now, fronting on sunset,
repeatedly we watch the tugs, "poor little tugs,"
and hear them—
their signals back and forth as though complaining.
The two tugs help each other, tugging, pushing
(against the current into place)
a sluggish ship to be aligned along a dock,
a bungling, bumbling, bulging, over-laden freighter.

Their task completed,
the two tugs toot good-bye,
go tripping on their way,
leaning as lightly forward
as with a hiker
suddenly divested
of his knapsack.
"Good-bye," rejoicingly, "good-bye"—

whereat I wonder:
Might there also be a viable albeit risky way
to toot
"If you should drive up and ask me,
I think you damn near botched that job"?
"I think you stink."

What might comprise the total range and nature
of tugboat-tooting nomenclature?

Gloss IX

This section happens to have a summational development that is touched
upon in the poem, but that would not be as pointed, or poignant, for the
reader as it is for the author. Nearly half a century before, when first
coming as a boy to New York, he had lived with his family on the Palisades
overlooking the Hudson. Thus, as regards his later "vista vision" that
is the burden of this poem, he was quite conscious of the symbolism implicit in the change from an outlook facing sunup to an outlook facing
sundown. In the apartment on the Palisades the tugs could not be
heard. But their industriousness (the sturdy little fellows' ways of ma-
neuvering monsters) was just as apparent, and as inviting to an on-
looker's "empathy."

X

a plunk-plunk juke-box joint
him hunched on a stool
peering beyond his drink
at bottles lined up, variously pregnant
(*there's* a gleaming for you)

Among the gents
a scattering of trick floozies.

Maybe they know or not
just where they'll end,
come closing time.

He'll be in a room alone
himself and his many-mirrored other.

It was a plunk-plunk juke-box joint
its lights in shadow

Gloss X

This is one of the episodes that, owing to exigencies of space, were
omitted from the previously published version of the poem. Among other

AN EYE-POEM FOR THE EAR   237 things, it was intended to introduce a change of pace. For whereas things had been going along quite briskly, these lines should be subdued, and slow. But there's no sure way of making a reader's eyes behave—and the printing of verse lacks the orthodox resources of a musical score, which would readily allow for such instructions as *adagio, pianissimo*.

This episode is the closest the poem as a whole comes to representing (symbolizing) the essence of the purely *personal* grounds for an "immobilized" crossing-by-eye, as distinct from the various kinds of *public* threats dealt with in my exhibits.

Considering this episode *ab intra*, I can report on first-hand authority that the agonist of the verses corresponded "in real life" to a citizen who, having dropped into that joint, alone after a long night-walk alone, would not actually have gone home alone. Rather, he'd return to a hotel apartment and a physically immobilized companion who, in earlier days, would have shared the walk with him—and they'd have stopped in together, for a drink or two, while touching upon one or another of the many interests they had in common. The lines were somewhat morbidly anticipating, as though it were already upon him, a state of loneliness not yet actual yet (he took it for granted) inexorably on the way towards his Next Phase unless some sudden illness or accident disposed of him first. The details of the episode also drew upon the memory of occasions when, off somewhere lecturing (in a one or two-night stand on the Academic Circuit) he had dropped into such joints, there to commune with his watchful aloneness before going to his room, with the likelihood that, before switching off the lights, he would confront, in several mirrors, passing fragments of himself.

Since this episode, whatever its deflections, does probably come closest to the generating core of the whole enterprise so far as motivations local to the author personally are concerned, my reason for bringing up this fact, from the purely technical point of view, is that it illustrates a major concern of mine as regards speculations about the nature of symbolic action in the literary realm. Within the poetic use of a public medium, I take it, there is a private strand of motives that, while not necessarily at odds with the public realm, is at least not identical. It's as though some of the poet's words had secondary meanings not defined in a dictionary. But in saying so, I am well aware that a dishonorable opponent could use my own statement against me—and honorable opponents have always been a rare species.

XI

But turn against this turning.
I look over the water,
Me-I crossing.

I was but walking home,
sober as a hang-over with a fluttering heart
and homing as a pigeon.
There comes a dolled-up Jog-Jog towards myself and me.
We're just about to pass when   gong!   she calls—
and her police dog (or was he a mountain lion?)
he had been lingering somewhere, sniffing in the shadows
comes bounding loyally forward.

Oh, great Milton, who wrote the basic masque of Chastity Protected,
praise God, once more a lady's what-you-call-it has been saved—
and I am still out of prison, free to wend my way,
though watching where I step.

I frame a social-minded ad:
"Apt. for rent. In ideal residential neighborhood.
City's highest incidence of dog-signs."

XII

Profusion of confusion. What of a tunnel-crossing?
What if by mail, phone, telegraph, or aircraft,
or for that matter, hearse?

You're in a subway car, tired, hanging from a hook,
and you would get relief?
Here's all I have to offer:
Sing out our national anthem, loud and clear,
and when in deference to the tune
the seated passengers arise,
you quickly slip into whatever seat
seems safest. (I figured out this scheme,
but never tried it.)

Problems pile up, like the buildings,
Even as I write, the highest to the left
soars higher day by day.
Now but the skeleton of itself
(these things begin as people end!)
all night its network of naked bulbs keeps flickering
towards us here in Brooklyn . . .
then dying into dawn . . .
or are our . . . are our what?

Gloss XII

I boasted to a colleague about "or are our" on the grounds that, though
the words didn't mean much, they couldn't be pronounced without

growling. He observed that I could have done pretty much the same with "aurora"—and thereby he made me wonder whether, since I was on the subject of dawn, I had been feeling for that very word.

And I have often puzzled about the possible ultimate implications of our structural-steel buildings' reverse way of growth: *first* the skeleton, the stage that we *end on*.

XIII

As with an aging literary man who, knowing
that words see but within
yet finding himself impelled to build a poem
that takes for generating core a startling View,
a novel visual Spaciousness

(he asks himself: "Those who have not witnessed it,
how tell them?—and *why* tell those who have?
Can you do more than say 'remember'?")

and as he learns the ceaseless march of one-time modulatings
unique to this, out of eternity,
this one-time combination
of primal nature (Earth's) and urban, technic second nature,
there gleaming, towering, spreading out and up
there by the many-colored, changing-colored water

(why all that burning, all throughout the night?
some say a good percentage is because
the cleaning women leave the lights lit.
But no—it's the computers
all night long now
they go on getting fed.)

as such a man may ask himself and try,

as such a one, knowing that words see but inside,
noting repeated through the day or night
the flash of ambulance or parked patrol car,
wondering, "Is it a ticket this time, or a wreck?"
or maybe setting up conditions there
that helicopters land with greater safety,

so puzzling I, eye-crossing . . .
and find myself repeating (and hear the words
of a now dead once Olympian leper),
"Intelligence is an accident,
Genius is a catastrophe."

A jumble of towering tombstones
hollowed, not hallowed,
and in the night incandescent
striving ever to outstretch one another
like stalks of weeds dried brittle in the fall.

Or is it a mighty pack of mausoleums?
Or powerhouses of decay and death—
towards the poisoning of our soil, our streams, the air,
roots of unhappy wars abroad,
miraculous medicine, amassing beyond imagination
the means of pestilence,
madly wasteful journeys to the moon (why go at all,
except to show you can get back?)

I recalled the wanly wingéd words of a now dead gracious leper.

(My own words tangle like our entangled ways,
of hoping to stave off destruction
by piling up magic mountains of destructiveness.)

Gloss XIII

The poem comes to a focus in one great line: "Intelligence is an accident, genius is a catastrophe." Since the whole is written in the spirit of that oracle, I feel that, however perversely or roundabout, its dubieties are qualified by a sizeable strand of appreciation. For after all, the poem is talking about the fruits of intelligence and genius, albeit that they are visibly beset by sinister "side effects." When the poem was first published, I was asked, in an anonymous phone call, who the author of the line is, and why I speak of him as an "Olympian leper." I answered, "I call him 'Olympian' because in his writings he seemed so lightly to transcend his misfortune. I call him a leper because he was a leper." He was a writer to whom, only in later years, I have come to understand the depths of my indebtedness: Remy de Gourmont. Regrettably, the English version limps, in comparison with the French original: *L'intelligence est un accident, le génie est une catastrophe.* The comparative limp seems inevitable, since we can't pronounce our four-syllable "catastrophe" like the French three-syllable "catastróhf." Jimmy Durante got the feeling in his comic twist, "catástastróhf."

Since this section unfolds an epic simile that deliberately gets lost along the way, I must again plead poetic licentiousness.

XIV
Do I foresee the day?
Calling his counsellors and medicos,

do I foresee a day, when Unus Plurium
World Ruler Absolute, and yet the august hulk
is wearing out—do I foresee such time?

Calling his counsellors and medicos together,
"That lad who won the race so valiantly,"
he tells them, and His Word is Law,
"I'd like that bright lad's kidneys—
and either honor him by changing his with mine
or find some others for him, as opportunity offers."

No sooner said than done.
Thus once again The State is rescued—
and Unus over all, drags on till next time.

Do I foresee that day, while gazing across, as though that realm was alien
Forfend forfending of my prayer
that if and when and as such things should be
those (from here) silent monsters (over there)
will have by then gone crumbled into rubble,
and nothing all abroad
but ancient Egypt's pyramidal piles of empire-building hierarchal stylized
    dung remains.

Oh, I have haggled nearly sixty years
in all the seventies I've moved along.
My country, as my aimless ending nears,
oh, dear my country, may I be proved wrong!

Gloss XIV

The conceit on which this section is built is not offered as "prophecy."
I include it on the grounds of what I would call its "entelechial" aspect.
For instance, a satire would be "entelechial" insofar as it treated certain
logical conclusions in terms of *reduction to absurdity*. Thus, when con-
fronting problems of pollution due to unwanted residues of highly developed technology, one might *logically* advocate the development of
methods (with corresponding attitudes) designed to reverse this process.
But a satire could treat of the same situation "entelechially" by proposing
a burlesqued rationale that *carried such potentialities to the end of the
line*, rather than proposing to correct it. In the name of "progress" one
might sloganize: "Let us not turn back the clock. Rather, let us find ways
to *accelerate* the technological polluting of the natural conditions we inherited from the days of our primitive, ignorant past. Let us instead move
forward towards a *new* way of life" (as with a realm of inter-planetary
travel that transcended man's earth-bound origins).
   But also, at several places in my *Philosophy of Literary Form*, I discussed

such "end of the line" thinking in other literary modes (James Joyce's later works, for example). I did not until much later decide that I had been groping towards an ironically non-Aristotelian application of the Aristotelian term, "entelechy," used by him to designate a movement towards the *formal fulfillment* of potentialities peculiar to some particular species of being.

Thus the conceit informing this section would be "entelechial" (though grotesquely rather than satirically so) in that it imagines the "perfecting" of certain trends already "imperfectly" present among us, though first of all would be the need for further purely scientific progress in the technique of organ transplants, whereby the healthy parts of human specimens could be obtained either legally or illegally and stored in "body banks," to be used on demand. The most "perfectly" grotesque summarizing of such conditions would prevail if: (a) the world becomes "one world"; (b) as with the step from republic to empire in ancient Rome, rule becomes headed in a central authority whose word is law; (c) the "irreplaceable" ruler needs to replace some of his worn-out parts.

The purely "formal" or "entelechial" justification for this summational conceit is that it would be the "perfecting" of these elements already indigenous to our times: dictatorship, organized police-protected crime, the technical resourcefulness already exemplified in the Nazi doctors' experiments on Jews, and in the purely pragmatic contributions of applied science to the un-Constitutional invasion and ravishment of Indo China.

XV

"Eye-crossing," I had said? The harbor space so sets it up.
In Walt's ferry-crossing, besides the jumble of things seen
(they leave him "disintegrated")
even the sheer *words* "see," "sight," "look," and "watch" add up
to 33, the number of a major mythic cross-ifying.

In the last section of the Waltman's testimony
there is but "gaze," and through a "necessary film" yet . . .
"Gaze" as though *glazed*? It's not unlikely.
"Suspend," he says, "here and everywhere, eternal float of solution."
And the talk is of "Appearances" that "envelop the soul."

Between this culminating ritual translation
and the sheer recordings of the senses
there had been intermediate thoughts
of "looking" forward to later generations "looking" back.
Walt the visionary, prophetically seeing crowds of cronies
crossing and recrossing
on the ferry that itself no longer crosses.

Six is the problematic section.
There he takes it easy, cataloguing all his vices
as though basking on a comfortable beach.
His tricks of ideal democratic promiscuity
include his tricks of ideal man-love.
In section six he does a sliding, it makes him feel good.

Blandly blind to the promotion racket stirring already all about him,
he "bathed in the waters" without reference to their imminent defiling
(Now even a single one
of the many monsters since accumulated
could contaminate the stream for miles.)

He sang as though it were all his—
a continent to give away for kicks.
And such criss-crossing made him feel pretty godam good.

Flow on, filthy river,
ebbing with flood-tide and with ebb-tide flooding.
Stand up, you feelingless Erections,
Fly on, O Flight, be it to fly or flee.

Thrive, cancerous cities.
Load the once lovely streams with the clogged filter of your filth.
"Expand,"
even to the moon and beyond yet.
"There is perfection in you" in the sense
that even empire-plunder can't corrupt entirely.

Gloss XV

As regards this section, built around Whitman's "Crossing Brooklyn
Ferry," I have not dared to check my entries, that add up to 33. If I have
missed the count by a little, please at least let me keep the sum *in principle.*
In any case, implicit in the qualitative difference between those terms
and "gaze" there is indeed a crossing, a transcendence. Something critical,
crucial, has happened *en route.*

XVI

And what of Hart's crossing by the bridge?

"Inviolate curve," he says. Who brought that up?
The tribute gets its maturing in the penultimate stanza,
"Under thy shadow by the piers I waited."
Hart too was looking.

But things have moved on since the days of Walt,
and Hart is tunnel-conscious.

And fittingly the subway stop at Wall Street,
first station on the other side,
gets named in the middle quatrain of the "Proem"
(Wall as fate-laden as Jericho, or now as mad Madison
of magic Madhatter Island.) Ah! I ache!
Hart lets you take your pick:
"Prayer of pariah and the lover's cry."

(If crossing now on Brooklyn Bridge by car,
be sure your tires are sound—
for if one blows out you must keep right on riding
on the rim. That's how it sets up now
with what Hart calls a "curveship"
lent as a "myth to God."
I speak in the light of subsequent developments.)

Elsewhere, "The last bear, shot drinking in the Dakotas,"
Hart's thoughts having gone beneath the river by tunnel, and
"from tunnel into field," whereat "iron strides the dew."
Hart saw the glory, turning to decay,
albeit euphemized in terms of "time's rendings."
And by his rules, sliding from Hudson to the Mississippi,
he could end on a tongued meeting of river there and gulf,
a "Passion" with "hosannas silently below."

Treating of our culture's tendings
as though its present were its own primeval past,
making of sexual oddities a "religious" gunmanship,
striving by a "logic of metaphor"
to span whole decades of division,

"I started walking home across the bridge,"
he writes—
but he couldn't get home that way.

Only what flows *beneath* the bridge
only that was home . . .

All told, though Walt was promissory,
Hart was nostalgic, Hart was future-loving only insofar
as driven by his need to hunt (to hunt the hart).

And as for me, an apprehensive whosis
(cf. Bruxistes Panallerge, *Tractatus de Strabismo*),
I'm still talking of a crossing on a river
when three men have jumped over the moon,
a project we are told computer-wise
involving the social labor of 300,000 specialists
and 20,000 businesses.

Such are the signs one necessarily sees,
gleaming across the water,
the lights cutting clean
all through the crisp winter night.

"O! Ego, the pity of it, Ego!"
"Malice, slander, conspiracy," the letter had said;
"your spitefulness . . ."

Gloss XVI

In this, Hart's section, I couldn't resist the gruff contrast between the idealistically symbolic bridge and the materialistic one with its current exigencies of traffic . . . . The reference to men who had jumped over the moon was written when we had but sent astronauts *around* the moon. . . . I hope I can be forgiven for my most ambitious pun, that puts "Ego" in place of Othello's "Iago." . . . Texts differ as to whether the author of the *Tractatus de Strabismo* is named Bruxistes or Bruxisticus.

XVII

Crossing?
Just as the roads get jammed that lead
each week-day morning from Long Island to Manhattan,
so the roads get jammed that lead that evening
from Manhattan to Long Island.
And many's the driver that crosses cursing.

Meanwhile, lo! the Vista-viewing from our windows at burning nightfall:
To the left, the scattered lights on the water,
hazing into the shore in Jersey, on the horizon.
To the right, the cardboard stage-set of the blazing buildings.
Which is to say:

> To the left,
> me looking West as though looking Up,
> it is with the lights in the harbor
> as with stars in the sky,
> just lights, pure of human filth—
> or is it?

> To the right,
> the towerings of Lower Manhattan
> a-blaze at our windows

> as though the town were a catastrophe

> as doubtless it is . . .

After-Words

In *A Grammar of Motives* (1945) I expended quite some effort trying to show how philosophic schools differ in the priority they assign to one or another of the different but overlapping motivational areas covered by the five terms: act, scene, agent, agency, purpose. There is no point to my restating any of those speculations here. However, the terms may lend themselves to some differently directed remarks with regard to the poem about which I have been prosifying (possibly at my peril, since some readers will resent such comments either because they are needed or because they are not needed).

Applying the terms differently here, first, I'd want to go along with the position in Aristotle's *Poetics*, which features the term *act* with regard to drama (in keeping even with the sheer etymology of the word). The realm of *agent* (or character) seems to me most at home in the novel (of Jane Austen cast).

Some over-all *purpose* serves well to hold together epics like *The Iliad* (where the aim to fight the Trojan war can also readily accommodate episodes of interference, as with Achilles sulking in his tent), or *The Odyssey* (a *nostos* that piles up one deflection after another, an organizational lure that is doubtless also at the roots of a literal report of homecoming such as Xenophon's *Anabasis*). A group of pilgrims with a common destination (as per *The Canterbury Tales*) will supply over-all pretext enough—or even the inertness of a boatride in common (*Ship of Fools*). Steinbeck's *Grapes of Wrath* is interesting in this regard. There was movement enough so long as the migrants were on their way to California, but the plot became a bit aimless as soon as they arrived. One is reminded of that ingenious conceit about how we settled this country by moving West until we got to the coast, then all we could do was jump up and down. Would that it had been so, rather than as with our zeal to make the Pacific *mare nostrum*.

The notion of deriving all narrative from a "monomyth" generically called "the myth of the quest" owes its appeal to the fact that, implicit in the idea of any act, there is the idea of a purpose (even if it be but "unconscious," or like the "built-in purpose" of a homing torpedo, designed to "contact its target"). Even an Oblomov could be fitted in, when *not* getting out of bed.

Scene figures high in historical novels (such as Scott's). Zola works the same field, though in quite a different fashion, and Faulkner's regionalism in another.

Though I have read little science fiction, I'd incline to say that its fantasies (in being a response to the vast clutter of new instruments with which modern technology has surrounded us) endow the realm of *agency* (or means) with an importance that it never had before as the locus of motives.

But all this is preparatory to the discussion of a term that has not been mentioned, but that bears strongly upon some issues now at hand. If I were now to write my *Grammar* over again, I'd turn the pentad into a hexad, the sixth term being *attitude*. As a matter of fact, even in its present form the book does discuss the term, "attitude," and at quite some length. I refer to a chapter entitled " 'Incipient' and 'Delayed' Action." It is included in my section on Act; for an *attitude* is an incipient or inchoate act in the sense that an attitude of sympathy or antipathy might lead to a corresponding act of helpfulness or aggression. But I also had to consider some ambiguities implicit in the term. And to this end I discussed its uses in George Herbert Mead's *Philosophy of the Act*, in contrast with I. A. Richards' treatment of attitudes as "imaginal and incipient activities or tendencies to action" (in his *Principles of Literary Criticism*). I also introduce related observations with regard to Alfred Korzybski's concern with "consciousness of abstracting." And in my essay, "Symbolic Action in a Poem by Keats" (reprinted in an appendix to the *Grammar*) I tell why I find it significant that Keats apostrophizes his Grecian Urn as a "Fair Attitude." But besides impinging upon the realm of "act," attitude also impinges upon the realm of "agent" in the sense that, while inchoately an *act*, it is one with an *agent's* (a character's) mood or feeling.

As applied specifically to literature, I'd say that "attitude" comes most to the fore in the lyric (or in a short story of pronouncedly lyrical cast). In this connection, I'd like to quote a relevant passage from Keats, as pointed up in my autobiographical divulging, "The Anaesthetic Revelation of Herone Liddell" (a piece built around some highly attitudinal experiences in a sick-room):

An *attitude* towards a body of topics has a unifying force. In effect its unitary nature as a response "sums up" the conglomerate of particulars towards which the attitude is directed. See a letter of Keats (March 17, 1817), modifying a passage in Act II, Scene iv, of first part of *Henry IV*: "Banish money—Banish sofas—Banish Wine—Banish Music; but right Jack Health, honest Jack Health, true Jack Health—Banish Health and banish all the world." Here, he is saying in effect: The feeling infuses all things with the unity of the feeling.

The lyric *strikes an attitude.* Though the feeling is not often so absolute as with the health-sickness pair that here exercised poor Keats in letters written while he was hurrying on his way to death, any attitude has something of that summarizing quality.

Along those lines, I once proposed (*The Kenyon Review*, Spring 1951) this definition for the lyric:

A short complete poem, elevated or intense in thought and sentiment, expressing and evoking a unified attitude towards a momentous situation more or less explicitly implied—in diction harmonious and rhythmical, often but not necessarily rhymed—the structure lending itself readily to a musical accompaniment strongly repetitive in quality; the gratification of the whole residing in the nature of the work as an ordered summation of emotional experience otherwise fragmentary, inarticulate, and unsimplified.

In commenting on the various clauses of this definition, with regard to the words, "a unified attitude," I observed:

The "lyric attitude," as vs. the "dramatic act." Attitude as gesture, as posture. . . . Strictly speaking, an attitude is by its very nature "unified." Even an attitude of hesitancy or internal division is "unified" in the formal sense, if the work in its entirety rounds out precisely that.

When making that last remark I had in mind Aristotle's recipe in Chapter XV of the *Poetics* where he says that a character who is represented as inconsistent must be consistently so.

As the attendant discussion of the definition makes clear, when referring to "thought and sentiment" I also had in mind "the contemporary stress upon the purely *sensory* nature of the lyric image," and noted that the whole process would involve "the 'sentiments' implicit in the 'sensations,' and the 'thoughts' implicit in the 'sentiments.' " As regards a situation "more or less explicitly implied," I added:

The lyric attitude implies *some* kind of situation. The situation may be of the vaguest sort: The poet stands alone by the seashore while the waves are rolling in; or, the poet is separated from his beloved; or, the poet is old, remembering his youth—etc. Or the situation may be given in great detail. Indeed, a lyric may be, on its face, but a list of descriptive details specifying a scene—but these *images* are all manifestations of a single *attitude*.

While holding that "the lyric 'tends ideally' to be of such a nature as would adapt it to rondo-like musical forms," with stanzas "built about a recurrent refrain," I proposed that a poem "need not preserve such a structure explicitly, to qualify as a lyric," though it might be studied "as a departure from this 'Urform,' or archetype." (Just think: There was a time in England when music could be authoritatively defined as "inarticulate poetry.")

Where then are we, with regard to the "Eye-Crossing," viewed as a lyric? You ask: "It is, then, to be viewed as striking some kind of over-all attitude?" Me: "Yes, sir." You: "And would you kindly tell me just what attitude your (let's hope) lyrical lines will be taking?" Me: "Please, sir!" You: "Stand up! Why the grovelling?" Me: "There is no name for the attitude, sir." Then in sudden hopefulness, Me adds: "Unless, that is, you will accept the title of the poem itself as a summarizing name for the summarizing attitude." You: "You mean that there is no word in the dictionary, such as 'happy' or 'sad' or 'cynical,' to designate the poem's attitude?" Me: "If there already were such apt words in our dictionaries, I doubt whether there'd be any incentive for the symbol-using animal to write poems." You: "?" Me: "I mean there is a sense in which each poem strikes its own specific attitude"; then hastily, "not through pride, but because it can't do otherwise"; then winsomely, "So it says in effect 'Come attitudinize with me.' " You: "In that case, could you at least give us a first rough approximate, by selecting one word or another that at least points vaguely in the right direction (for instance, like pointing with a sweep of the arm rather than with the index finger)?" Me: "Well, there is a spot where the narrator, or agonist, having referred to Walt as promissory and Hart as nostalgic, calls himself 'apprehensive,' and he fits that notion into his over-all scheme. So, for a first rough approximate, I'd propose that the summarizing lyric attitude be called 'apprehensive.' "

Yet to say as much is to encounter a problem. A state of apprehension can be variously modified. Otherwise put, the adjective admits of many adverbs. For instance, one can be solemnly apprehensive, or sullenly apprehensive, or sportively apprehensive, or experimentally apprehensive, or arbitrarily apprehensive (as when imagining some grotesque possibility that has a kind of formal appeal because it would "carry to the end of the line" certain tendencies already observable though not likely to attain actual dire fulfillment or "perfection," if I may use the word in an ironic sense). Or one can even be deflectively or secondarily apprehensive, as when referring to a time when tendencies that are now found to have turned out badly were, in their incipient stages, viewed in promissory rather than admonitory terms. (Would the Indians, living in what was to become New England, have had the attitude that led them to help the Pilgrims survive a first critically severe winter if those Indians had foreseen how their hospitality was to be repaid?)

To what extent can an attitude seem adjectivally consistent when it is adverbially varied? French neo-classic drama, for instance, could not have found consistency enough in the grotesquely tragic aspect of *Macbeth*, which readily allows for the strong contrast between the Murder scene and the Porter scene (while, if you are so inclined, the knocking at the gate can suggest the knock of conscience, and the Porter's ribaldry can suggest an Aristophanic analogue of bodily incontinence due to fright). Thus, there are varying degrees of tolerance, when adverbial diversity tugs at the outer limits of an attitude's adjectival unity. For some readers more than others the sense of a general apprehensiveness can get lost in a sense of the diversity among the ways of being apprehensive.

Or, the poem may be judged, not as *a* lyric, but as a lyric *sequence*. Also, there is a kind of typical consistency, more easily sensed than defined, in a work's style. And insofar as *le style, c'est l'homme même*, there may arise a sense of the narrator, or agonist, as a character, a *persona* prevailing willy-nilly throughout the work's changes of mood. Such a fiction *within* the conditions of a poem may or may not accurately represent the character of the author, as citizen and taxpayer, *outside* the conditions of the poem. But inasmuch as the realm of *attitude* greatly overlaps upon the realm of *agent*, the attitudinizing nature of a poem might derive assistance from the fact that the poem's style may generate the sense of a single *persona* with whose imputed character all the range of expressions in the poem could seem to conform. Thus the sense of a single figure as the constant attitudinizer may help extend the range of variations which strike the reader as relevant to the problematical nature of the sights which are the objects of the poetic *persona's* contemplation.

But in the last analysis, the same issue arises. Some readers may feel that the whole range of stylizations contributes to the definition of the fictive narrator's character; other readers may not. In the letter he sent me along with copies of the students' comments, Henry Sams succinctly though differently touched upon this point when referring to the "man side" of the poem "as opposed to the city side." Henry knew, as his students could not know, the damnable *personal* situation at the roots of my being in Brooklyn that season when the poem was written. So he could more easily approach the poem in *attitude-agent* terms, whereas his students would be most exercised about the shifts of attitude towards the public *scene.* In keeping with my theories of "symbolic action," these words afterwards are but designed to present the issue.

Of course, I'd love to talk back and forth about every sentence the students said, whether it be for or against. But obviously Time Does Not Permit. Yet before closing, I'd like to mention an article "On Doing & Saying," built around an obviously and admittedly overblunt distinction between one hominid who is planting seeds and another (the "mythman") who "completes" the task by enacting the appropriate ritual of a planting-song (*Salmagundi,* No. 15, Winter 1971).

I was consciously concerned with a range of associations clustered about the term, "cross." But I had to admit that "not until I had finished the poem did I realize how another dimension had crept in without my slightest awareness." I have in mind my recurrent references to the "theme of light," connected with the fact that "at all hours of the night I had watched the fantastic gleam of the lights across the river." Whereupon:

Lo! an archetype had crept up on me: the "city of light," no less! But hold. Here was an archetype with a difference. For many of the connotations surrounding my images and ideas of light were of a sinister sort, involving "formidable things" (thoughts of empire, war, and imminent decay).

However:

Since the "city of light" does not attain its "perfection" as a "magic" vision gleaming through the night until the poem has built up an attitude of apprehension, obviously a "universal" interpretation here as archetype would be but a "first rough approximate."

But at that point I had to add: "Yet, after all, there was 'Lucifer!' "

At this point the author interrupted his writing long enough to go into the next room and wind his eight-day clock which now has to be wound twice a week. The day was dark, with much downpour. No mail came—and though he did get one phone call, it was a wrong number.

He could go on and on—until the last time . . .

On
Competence

Joseph L. Grucci

What shall I say
of this poem you bring me?
All the ingredients are there: diction's fresh,
imagery's precise, rhymes are ingenious,
you alliterate subtly, yet somehow
the poem fails to leave the ground.

Your chagrin suggests I've withheld
something—at least my praise
for competence alone.

I am reminded of a neighbor of ours
who was an unsparing cook,
though she envied my mother's breadmaking.
She would follow the recipe
even to making her loaf
on the same day at the same time
that mother baked,
mixing the dough in our kitchen,
using the same flour (borrowed from mother),
as if to make a game
of her suspicion that something
had been withheld because
her own loaves never rose
to the brown fullness of hers . . . .

The ingredients were all there, she said,
but maybe it was her oven
or the size of her kitchen,

perhaps the difference in humidity
or maybe a draft . . .
whatever, her loaf (like this poem of yours)
came out limp or puffed to hollowness,
with all the signs of exhaustion.

And like our cunning neighbor
(although I can't tell you
without seeming rude or arrogant),
you no doubt employed every device
and all the ingenuity
at your command,
but as Heine said of another poet—
"Uhland's poetry reminds me
of Bayard's horse: it has
every conceivable virtue,
but it is dead."

The Twilight Double-Header: Some Ambivalences of the Reviewer Reviewed

Paul West

It was as a resentful 24-year-old, stationed by the air force on an island in the Irish Sea, that I first began reviewing books for money. Almost a mental island on that geographical and military one, I wanted to keep in touch with what I then fondly generalized as the literary world. I wrote to the literary editor of *The Spectator* and told him so, and, almost by return mail, there came Marcel Brion's life of Schumann, translated from the French, about which I composed 600 approving, clandestine-feeling words. My complimentary copy of the magazine arrived before the copy that sat on the periodicals table in the mess ante-room where white-coated and mutinously deferential Manx waiters fussed over silver racks of toast and giant urns of tea. Came the day: West about Brion on Schumann was there for all to relish, competing with *Punch* and *The New Yorker*, but no one even noticed it. In London, though, and wherever in the civilized world *The Spectator* went, there were surely thousands of readers tapping a finger at the column in admiration: Where would the boy wonder strike next? Never again, as it turned out, in *The Spectator*, although *it* conscientiously reviewed *him* when he began producing books of his own. But a habit I'd begun, and the check for six guineas confirmed it. With not even a book to my name, but only poems and essays in such unfrivolous organs as *World Review* and *The Adelphi*, I set up to be a power in the world of letters while accumulating on the side money for vice. To review was a concise, profitable, educative, and communicative chore, both good writing practice and an effective counter to the doltish regimens of the peacetime military. Looking back, I can now see how some of the reviewers writers rage about get into the action, staying there, maundering and rebuking, until the Great Air-Conditioner in the Sky calls them to higher service.

Anyway, soon after, functioning as an ideational light industry among the ranking goons, I was reviewing French books for *The Times Literary Supplement* (TLS hereafter), thanks to the good offices of its then editor, the cordial and often misrepresented Alan Pryce-Jones, and books in English for *The Sunday Times*. On occasion it seemed as if I'd become the TLS's thauroplasty man (so long as the operation was written about in French) and the other paper's boyhood-memoir man: I envisioned my last assignment as a reviewer being the apocalyptic recollections of a lungless boy-scout translated into French by André Malraux's chauffeur; but, in fact, I advanced to becoming the *New Statesman*'s air force man, specializing in air history and the egregious memoirs of Air Marshals (a solecism I got away with, though I think I could have been court-martialled for it). Sometimes, from all sources, I received three books a week, of which my reviews would bring in about 20 guineas, more than my weekly pay. I soon became so busy there was no time for vice.

To firm up my connections, I would hitch a flight to London in our twin-engined transport Avro Anson and march, with a para-military stride out of T. E. Lawrence by St.-Exupéry, into the baronial halls of *The Sunday Times*, the mahogany cubby-holes of the *TLS* (where the walls warn you in large print This Is A Printing House), and pick my cliff-hanging way up the outside iron staircase of Great Turnstile, where the *New Statesman* was. Such was my *entrée* to the literary commotion of our times, or so I thought, much as I had thought that being in the literary set at Oxford was (with editors arriving to find out who was getting ready to set the literary firmament on fire). I did in the event receive many kindnesses from several writers, among them Walter Allen, V. S. Pritchett, and C. P. Snow, and I knew the excitement of a Friday party at which people who had read one's latest piece were actually discussing it (which is very different, I find, from the United States, where few of one's university colleagues and hardly any of one's students read literary reviews; reviewing or reviewed, you publish and perish in limbo unless you live in New York City). The important thing in those days was that editors and readers took you seriously as a writer and so made appropriate demands, and the people at the *New Statesman* in particular thought of their paper as a literary nursery. And that it was, except that playing with words was not encouraged; you could be savagely dimissory but not impressionistic.

Over the years, and during my transition from essayist to novelist, from England to the United States, my reviewing activity has broadened out, from a year as *Statesman* fiction critic to regular work for the old Herald Tribune's *Book World* (in its successive manifestations) and, later, for the *New York Times Book Review*. Usually, the books I would have read anyway have been the books I've been sent to review, so it has been pleasant to be compensated for doing what came naturally. The deadline I found a useful discipline; and, I used to think, people who read your reviews might go on to read your books (but it is now clear to me that 15 minutes on NBC's *Today* show, even after you have risen at 4:30 A.M., sells more books than any review can). Such excellent editors as Eve Auchincloss and Ted Solotaroff became my friends, took a lively interest in my books, and encouraged me (as an editor should) to write reviews which went beyond themselves and turned into short critical essays, not so much using the book in question as a peg for rehearsed arguments as planting it in contexts both generic and general, regarding it as a piece of the main. Not all reviewers want to do this, or can, but the one who does want to does it, or he quits altogether.

So much, it seems to me, of what passes for literary criticism and is respected as such on principle, while by the same token reviews are denigrated as hack work, begins in reviews, both in those printed and those the mind undertakes for its own satisfaction. True, the judgments in the former are made under pressure of time, but so are many of the judgments made during so-called leisure. An opinion arrived at over three weeks is not inevitably less reliable than one marinated for a year. What we have to do with is a series of instants in which the mind makes up its mind, an act just as arbitrary after a year as after three weeks, an act which sunders the comforts of dubiety. If you do not retreat into an opinionless scholarship, or resolve to luxuriate in a tasteful funk, you have to commit yourself, for this is the tendency of the human mind, which waxes appetitive and evaluative about cars and food and sex, so why not books? The conscientious reviewer trusts in his own taste, wants to form opinion, goes on writing reviews lest someone inferior to him take his place, fastens on to some area of writing (say, experimental fiction, so-called) where the squares and the deadheads do much damage, and, most of all, works to two standards: the genial and the hostile.

The first of these tests the work against authorial intent (all intentional fallacies notwithstanding), and against works fairly similar—say something by Jane Austen against something by Edith Wharton, say *Across the River and into the Trees* against *An American Tragedy* (for the sun also Dreisers). The second rams *Emma* alongside *Moby-Dick*, *The Waste Land* alongside *Faust*, and here the fundamental hard work begins. The genial mode reveals, the hostile one exposes; the one, without taking sides, advances what is good; the other, in which gut-preference and mind-made-up dominate, treats books as commodities you want or don't want to install as commodities in your own life, as if one were to say, there is good in Ivory Soap, Franz Hals, Mahler, and Gide, but I prefer to buy Dial, Bosch, Hindemith, and Shaw. I have in mind something mercantile and idiosyncratic that, while representing the genial mode, goes beyond appreciation into conviction, beyond being fair into being quite bigoted. The irony is that reviewers, who ought to be concerned with the genial, affect the hostile rôle, while time-taking critics, who ought to be hostile rather than genial, end up eschewing major judgments altogether. On the one hand we have commercial histrionics, on the other academic prudence, which I think is why paperback editions of books that have stayed in print bear jackets with reviewers' and not critics' comments. A better argument for having the best critics do reviews, I cannot think of, and that is why we should be grateful when, say, Hugh Kenner or Kenneth Burke actually reviews a book, thus arming us with an on-the-spot sagacity, an instant bit of definitive rumination.

My proposal—the literary anchorite with dirtied hands—reflects a prejudice of my own in favor of the market-place, where the busy have to do their living, which I contrast with what goes on in the universities, where, too often, plenipotentiary Pecksniffs exert themselves toward converting literature into becoming something other than a display case of buyable articles. They turn it, or would like to turn it, into a corpus of strategies, a treasure trove of morals, a stockpile of cases for the therapist, a tidied-up Shield of Achilles for the semi-washed to strengthen their citizenship with, as if, at heart, they distrust the creative person and his vibrant, importunate output, knowing so well what he is *for* (in their terms at any rate) that they hardly know what he *is*. Something rabbinically, jesuitically, and bureaucratically Procrustean thrives in academe and is far from rectified by the presence of writers on campus, while the students —alas for the students—want not to learn the ways of exegesis and codification, taxonomy and *Tendenz*, but (now more than ever) to be overwhelmed by a book, to be wowed, to be given a lead or a charge on an almost messianic level. And that level, I suggest, no I don't suggest it, I damned well know it, is much closer to the creative impetus than the cool propriety of the scholar-prof who, resolutely making a lifetime's living out of Lit, nonetheless respects it so little as to have students read all of Emily Dickinson in a week, ten plays by Shakespeare in ten weeks, and *Bleak House* over the weekend. It's no use protesting that there are just too many books, for that evokes the Oxford degree program dubbed *Literae Humaniores*, in which the hapless candidate, who is no doubt being groomed to be prime minister, in three years reads all of Greek and Roman history, literature, and what have you. The result is a classical supermarket in the head, a far better alternative being ten seminal works read again and again while the student is free to follow what ramifications he fancies. It has seemed to me for a long time that the literary education as we now know it is obsolete, has precious little to do with living, and helps our young people not a jot when they go "out" into a world that has more than enough resources to streamline them into conformity in three years. If we cannot selectively unfit our graduates for society, then we should not, as professors, profess. That students do not regard current books and current reviews as pertinent to them, or to anything they care deeply about, signifies the *malaise*: a dying tradition that still has the ascendancy creaks along beside them, and the gap between is not so much one of credibility as of relevance. They will all outlive us, we cannot win, so we should at least try to lose in a learning manner. A generation that has no sense of the past, whether that is a "good thing" or no, is bound to have an almost traumatically different sense of literature, or, since even literature as such doesn't exist for them, of books—of novels, of memoirs, of poems.

Which brings me back to the market-place, where LP albums and drugs and extravagant costumes are sold; books too, so long as concerned writers are prepared to do their part in hawking them. I speak as that contemporary abortion, the professor-novelist-reviewer, who nonetheless sees his doings as all of a piece and thinks there is a more vital principle to be invoked than gets evinced in the fawning, premature professionalism of the graduate schools. Something alive in us, in our students, who ought to be *our* readers (not Austen's, not Hugo's, not Goethe's, not Dante's), has got to be attended to, and the way to do this is not aloof, clinical, pedagogically tradition-bound, it is combative, immersive, more than a bit undignified. Which brings me back to reviewing, the only kind of lit. crit. the space age is likely to have time for: an activity not so much sordid and opportunistic as (at its best) at-the-world and urgent, about which I now want to be more personal than I have been this far, lest anyone think I am proposing it as a substitute for what Boethius thought the consolation of philosophy.

All things considered—the haste; the readiness of some editors to cut out qualifying phrases or clauses; the wastelands that some reviewers keep unirrigated between frontal lobe and cerebellum—reviewers function more responsibly than they have any right to; the proportion of just comment to twaddle is reassuringly high. Or so I have found, even though I myself have not come unscathed through the last ten years of publishing. For example, several months after it was published in the United States, but only a month or so after it went into its fifth printing and was picked by *Time* magazine as one of the best 10 non-fiction books of 1970, *Words for a Deaf Daughter* received the favor of a malicious, verbally congested pseudo-review, only a fraction short of libellous, in a periodical called *Commentary*, which I had always thought to be the tribal organ of football and baseball commentators, edited by Dizzie Dean out of Spokane and printed on pigskin. Concerned persons wrote in, I gather, protesting what one American poet called the apparent cruelty of the review. . . . So be it: a chorus of praise, such as the book received, always, although belatedly, brings some expectorating yahoo out from under his rock, some hatchet-equipped nonentity up out of the sump of envy. The spit blows away; the hatchet merely exposes the bone in the assailant's own skull; and you go on doing what a hundred reviewers praised you for doing, only you do it even more so. Dylan Thomas, in a rage, nursing his fists on the steps of the Athenaeum Club in London, looking for a reviewer, is one response, with which I am in total sympathy; another is disdain, which is fine by me, and especially suitable for the carrion crows of the Manhattan literary Mafia. The best way, I reckon, is to bide your time but never to pass up the chance, if it offers, of ramming your reviewer's head into a loaded bidet.

No doubt of it, the kitchen is hot from the oven, there will always be the lady spiders who review for the London *Observer* and chide such as me for writing a novel about a character who has "bad habits" or, somewhere in an especially putrid sector of the Philadelphia press, a self-confessed incompetent octogenarian who begins his review by saying he doesn't know how to begin but begins nonetheless, ending only after a half-yard of leprous fustian has obscured from him what he set out to do in the first place: a review like a pair of false teeth embedded in its own pancreas. *Dies irae*? No, plural days of the semi-Olympian laugh, while you get on with your work. There will also always be those literary puff-adders, the paralytics who black out as you walk verbally by; the antique-fanciers who explain that the novel ended with Arnold Bennett; the mid-West pundits who think, say, Michel Butor is the name of an angel caught up on the objective-alternative dilemma; the hairy-daring ones who reckon it's avant-garde to drop Scriabin's name when talking of Shelley; the fatheads who relentlessly attribute to you everything your characters say, thus involving you in paradoxes that would paralyze even Oscar Wilde; the categorical popinjays who begin a review, "Sequels always disappoint" or end one with "The novel is not about words"; the literary puritans whose hatred of style is so cankerously ingrown that they equate paronomasia with Sunday fellatio performed upon a caviare-addicted giraffe; the reviewers whose perpetual tone is that of ulcerous custodians of a school for delinquent Oliver Twists; those who *know* that God intended literature to be gentility enshrined; even the head censor of the London *Financial Times*, who with mild knowingness, opined that I had been spending too much money on—never mind what: the world is full of people who could live your life for you much better than you yourself are doing.

Then, of course, there are the responses to your own reviewing, things that always brighten a winter, snap you out of summer torpor. Shame on you for slurring faith, cried a devout trout from Mississippi. Get thee to a psychiatrist, commanded an overgrown Eagle scout from Ohio. People who write reviews in Pennsylvania are provincials, cried an apoplectic American novelist all the way from Paris, France. I have never heard of you *or* Doris Lessing, huffed and puffed a Missouri mink-rancher. Some people are never satisfied, moaned a professor who specializes in introducing things and clearly likes to have his name on books. What else? The Tolkien Society denounced me at a plenary session, and placards appeared under my door saying FRODO LIVES! An emancipated girl from Chicago wrote and told me she was glabrous *everywhere* and what was I going to do about it. Some busybody from the wilds of Wisconsin or Iowa wrote and claimed I'd attributed Donne's version of "Come, live with me, and be my love," to Donne, whereas Marlowe wrote it, which he did, but not Dr. Donne's version. And there have been excellent, argumentative letters too, some from happy authors; some from agents who wonder if I have an agent, which I have; some from persecuted polar bears who wonder if I can spare a dime for their campaign against the helicopter. . . . But you get many more letters from folk who have read your books than you get from people who have only read your reviews.

And . . . And. . . . It would be disingenuous not to mention the business of anonymous reviewing, for which the TLS is notorious even now. On the one hand, that paper's coverage in English of books published in other languages is unrivalled and makes it a far better buy than *The New York Review of Books*, which one enthusiast told me was going to be "our own TLS, kind of," but which I find more like a pressure-cooker for abstruse metapolitical propaganda than like a review paper. On the other hand (getting back to the TLS), how odd it is, in these Personality-ridden times, to find a weekly review, and a useful one at that, pretending to an almost sibylline infallibility, as if books have only to be fed into its bowels to be identified as pearls or turkeys by one homogeneous omni-competent mind. Even the names of Popes are known, and the TLS team is very various indeed, both in quality and training. I can only think that the anonymity is meant to discourage self-indulgence, whereas all it really does is to half-canonize it. Meanwhile, the lauded or blamed author is left to wonder if he's being lauded by the man who last time blamed him (or lauded him) or if he's being blamed by the man who last time lauded him (or blamed him), a game of musical chairs of suspicion if ever I saw one. Is the reviewer an assistant professor of termitology in Nebraska, or the chief humus sampler at the Golders Green cemetery (where so many dead literati lie moldering), or the constipated ghost of Matthew Arnold still searching for an enema both sweet and light? Shafted or showered with praise, the author hardly ever knows, and he ends up realizing that he is being discouraged from caring *who* thinks well or ill of his work and is being fobbed off with a bourgeois variant of the Royal Command, fortified by homogenized divine right. Or, to change the figure, he is being *informed on*, as if the TLS's editorial-column clock had been put back to the nineteen-thirties in Central Europe.

It's not often we see idiosyncrasy safeguarded in so totalitarian a way, or the conduits of human communication blocked on such ostensibly virtuous premises. Surely the TLS doesn't expect its reviewers to be threatened, as Swinburne was, with a blindfolded castration in a dark alleyway. Most of the reviewers, one gathers, live in the Azores anyway (unless the rumor is true that there is only *one* reviewer, a polypsychic tea-addicted descendant of Friar Tuck inhabiting a mouse-infested time-warp extending from Mortlake to Putney, who does everything except remember his name). As an old TLSer, I count my sins and repent ('twas the loot and the lift that drove me to it, not the lust after fame—for obvious reasons). Indeed, in the old days, the publicity of a byline would have been more valuable than the money, whereas now, with my name on my own novels and nonfiction, it would seem dishonest, *incomplete*, on my part, and ungenerous on the paper's, not to sign what I contributed. Last things the TLS cannot dodge: reviews are by chaps, and the severance of the latter from the former—in the interests of creating an uninvestigable print megalith—is closer to Kremlin technique than affable swearers-by *The Times* admit. Perhaps, in the circumstances, the TLS should suppress not only the names of reviewers but also those of authors, as well as such betraying trivia as titles, publishers, prices, and number of pages, thus opening the game out a bit, multiplying the chances of reciprocal slander-at-random, finally reducing the paper to a weekly swirl of atomized opinions in search of books which, in turn, are in search of authors, in effect reducing all that's paid to a gangrene thought in a pirandellian green shade.

Penitent about some things, impenitent about many, I have come to see the double position of one who, reviewed, also reviews, as that of a twilight double-header, an ambivalent Janus who avoids the light of day only to seek the floodlights of the arena. I respect the writers who jealously guard their purity, their apartness; but I respect them only a bit more than I don't. I still fancy the idea of the man of letters to whom no mode of writing is alien, even though he's better at some modes than others. Has *he* no place in this ultra-specialized society of ours in which the accountant is king? The category-minded public will probably say no, but only because categorical-minded opinion-formers have told it to. In the end, you go your own way: there are no rules, not even for the breaking of rules by those who think that rules exist; I just reckon that a practicing novelist, playwright, or poet owes it to his calling now and then to go beyond the boundary of his artefact and traffic in print with his fellow-practitioners, especially those in other countries, about whom the reading public rarely learns anything accurate. Extra work? Why not? A man's fingernails will keep.

Over the past few months, from reading books to review, I have learned not only about the difficulties of writing fiction in East Germany and Doris Lessing's notion of "inner space" (and have had to think about such things, give an opinion) but also about gypsies, Linnaeus, Terezín the Nazi internment town, and the New Orleans Red Light district *circa* 1912 (things I just might have sought out for myself eventually, though I doubt it). To review or not to review, that is not the question; the question is, Can you do it in such a way that it evinces your mind without getting in your mind's way? As I said, there are times when I too dislike it, as I sometimes dislike talking or sleeping, or (on the receiving end) being barked at by dogs or patronized by oafish patricians; but I come back to it, doing it while it is being done to me, as something natural to do, subordinate to other work, certainly, but hardly avocational. It feeds me in more ways than one, even when I've no appetite at all and my books are conveniently bringing in the money for steaks.

Contributing Critics

DEBORAH AUSTIN, poet and specialist in nineteenth-century English literature, is Professor of English at The Pennsylvania State University.

JOHN BALABAN, poet and expert in Vietnamese literature, recently returned from Vietnam, is teaching at The Pennsylvania State University.

JOHN BARTH, author of *The Sot-Weed Factor, Giles Goat Boy* and other novels, is Professor of English at The Johns Hopkins University.

FREDERICK W. BATESON, editor of *The Cambridge Bibliography of English Literature* and founder of *Essays in Criticism,* is recently retired from his post at Oxford University.

MICHAEL H. BEGNAL, specialist in Irish fiction and author of a monograph on Sheridan Le Fanu, is Associate Professor of English at The Pennsylvania State University.

FRANK BRADY, editor and biographer of Boswell, is director of the Ph.D. program in English at the City University of New York.

KENNETH BURKE, dean of American literary critics, is best known for *The Philosophy of Literary Form* and *A Grammar of Motives.*

RALPH W. CONDEE is Professor of English at The Pennsylvania State University and author of *Structure in Milton's Poetry: from the Foundation to the Pinnacles.*

MAURICE B. CRAMER, expert in Victorian literature, is Professor Emeritus of English at The Pennsylvania State University.

ROBERT W. FRANK, JR., editor of *The Chaucer Review* and author of *Chaucer and the "Legend of Good Women,"* is Professor of English at The Pennsylvania State University.

JOSEPH L. GRUCCI, author of several volumes of poetry and editor of *Pivot,* a magazine of verse, is Associate Professor at The Pennsylvania State University.

JOHN HAAG, author of *The Mirrored Man* and other poems, is Associate Professor at The Pennsylvania State University.

CHADWICK HANSEN, author of *Witchcraft at Salem,* is Professor of American Studies at the University of Minnesota.

LAWRENCE KOHLBERG, Professor of Education and Social Psychology at Harvard, directs the Laboratory of Human Development there.

ARTHUR O. LEWIS, JR., editor of a recent reprint series of classic American Utopias and other books, is Professor of English and an Associate Dean for Resident Instruction at The Pennsylvania State University.

JACK McMANIS, poet and teacher of poetry, is Assistant Professor of English at The Pennsylvania State University.

HARRISON T. MESEROLE, Bibliographer of the Modern Language Association and editor of *Seventeenth Century American Poetry*, is Professor of English at The Pennsylvania State University.

JOSEPH G. PRICE, author of *The Unfortunate Comedy: a Study of "All's Well that Ends Well,"* is Professor of English at The Pennsylvania State University.

BRUCE ROSENBERG, author of *The Art of the American Folk Preacher*, is Associate Professor of English at The Pennsylvania State University.

JOHN B. SMITH, a Joycean, is Assistant Professor of English and Computer Science at The Pennsylvania State University.

STANLEY WEINTRAUB, biographer and editor of Bernard Shaw, is Research Professor of English and Director of the Institute for the Arts and Humanistic Studies at The Pennsylvania State University.

PAUL WEST, critic and author (*Alley Jaggers, Caliban's Filibuster, Words for a Deaf Daughter, Wine of Absurdity*), is Professor of English at The Pennsylvania State University.

PHILIP YOUNG, author of *Ernest Hemingway: a Reconsideration* and *Three Bags Full: Essays in American Fiction*, is Research Professor of English at The Pennsylvania State University.